Angus Mackay

The Australian Agriculturist and Guide for Land Occupation

Angus Mackay

The Australian Agriculturist and Guide for Land Occupation

ISBN/EAN: 9783337073138

Printed in Europe, USA, Canada, Australia, Japan

Cover: Foto ©Lupo / pixelio.de

More available books at **www.hansebooks.com**

HUDSON BROTHERS Ltd. CLYDE WORKS, GRANVILLE.

THE CLYDE STRIPPERS AND WINNOWERS.

From North, South, West, we hear:—

"Could not be more satisfied."

"Something splendid."

"In every way faultless."

"Light Draught."

&c., &c.

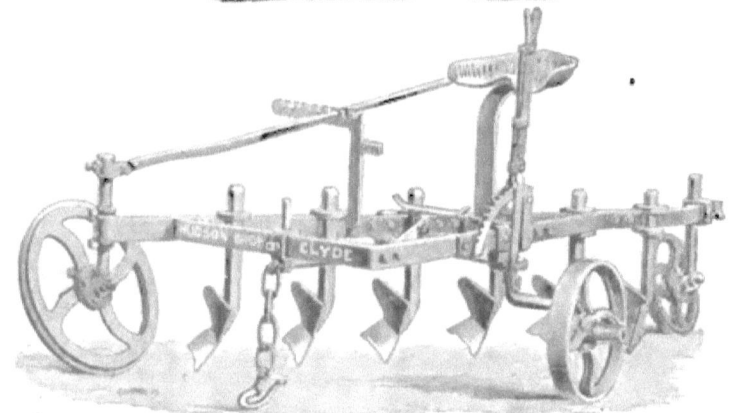

"I have named your PLOUGH the CAN'T-BE-BEAT.'"

"All you say in advertisement MORE THAN borne out in my experience."

"Your Chaffcutter is BETTER and CHEAPER than the IMPORTED article."

Letters open to inspection

Catalogues Post Free.

THE
AUSTRALIAN AGRICULTURIST

AND

GUIDE FOR LAND OCCUPATION

Plain Experiences in Station, Farm, Orchard and Garden Work,
Dairying, Cattle, Sheep, Pigs, Ensilage Making, Poultry
Farming, Fruit Preserving, Pests of the Agriculturist
and how to Check Them, Home Helps, Directions
for Treating Wounds, Snake-bite, Drowning,
&c., &c., with

Directions for Field and Garden Work, from January to December

By ANGUS MACKAY, F.C.S.

INSTRUCTOR IN AGRICULTURE, TECHNICAL COLLEGE, SYDNEY

Author of "The Sugar Cane in Australia," "Elements of Australian Agriculture,"
"Helpful Chemistry for Agriculturists," &c., &c.

NEW ISSUE

GEORGE ROBERTSON & COMPANY

MELBOURNE, SYDNEY, ADELAIDE AND BRISBANE

1897

PREFACE TO FIRST EDITION.

This work is simply an arrangement of every-day Colonial Experiences in Bush Life, Stock Raising, Farming, Gardening, Dairying, Fruit Preserving, and kindred subjects. Throughout, the leading effort is to connect the systems of Agriculture, including Stock Farming and Gardening, as followed in the Old Land, with what is gradually proving to be the best practice in Australia. In arranging the work the author had no beaten track to follow. There were no similar works to help him. The track of the settler in new country, whichever branch of life he may choose, is rugged at best, and the assistance that can be given by those who have travelled in advance and earned experience on the journey, cannot fail to be serviceable.

Although the bulk of the contents of this volume were written with a view to their ultimate publication in book form, there is no desire to supplant any of the valuable works at the disposal of the agricultural reader. The author could wish that such guides as those of Lindley, Loudon, Stephens, Johnston, Burn, Morton, Youatt, Gamgee, Oliver, Wright, Mechi, and the several excellent journals that devote space to agricultural subjects, were more extensively studied by his fellow-workers. The object in view is to furnish a connecting link between the practice of the Mother Country and America, as laid down in the standard works, with the practice found most suitable here. In treating of grain crops, for instance, the desire is merely to connect the seasons and the necessary alterations in detail with the practice followed in older countries. The same system is followed in the articles upon Stock Farming and Fruit Growing. Each chapter, at the same time, being, as a rule, sufficiently full to form a comprehensive guide in itself.

The articles upon Budding, Grafting, and other means of propagation, will, it is trusted, tend in no inconsiderable degree to the cultivation of Fruit throughout the country. With the aid of the illustrations given, and directions as to proper time and condition for operating, with ordinary skill and care, there need be comparatively little difficulty in budding or grafting the better sorts of fruits upon the suitable stocks available.

Machinery, implements, and the various mechanical appliances that do much to simplify labour and reduce the expenses of colonists, have received considerable attention. In the use of machinery, horse, and steam power, the author feels assured, comes the surest way out of the labour difficulties that beset colonists in every pursuit they enter upon.

Throughout there has been an effort to avoid semi-scientific terms, and to make the work acceptable and useful to those engaged in all the departments of agriculture, and to residents in the country districts generally. To what extent he has succeeded, the reception of the work will prove; and with this understanding the author places "The Semi-Tropical Agriculturalist and Colonists' Guide" at the disposal of the public.

Enoggera, Queensland, March, 1875.

PREFACE TO SECOND EDITION.

On returning from a Commission to the United States and the West Indies, the author was asked to prepare a second edition early in 1880; but he had not opportunity for doing so till now. Since the time mentioned the work has been practically out of print, and has become scarce and dear. It is now re-arranged, so as to be suitable for teaching purposes, while still continuing to be the guide for practical work, as designed in the first instance.

Several new chapters are added, bringing us up to what is going on at the present time in Dairying, Ensilage-making, Poultry Farming, &c., and special chapters concerning our Soils, Native Grasses, &c., of which much less was known when the first edition was published.

The thanks of the author are tendered very heartily to the officers of the Education Department, and to their chief (the Hon. J. H. Carruthers, M.P.) for recommending the work as suitable for students in the advanced classes for agricultural instruction in the National Schools. As now arranged, it really contains a series of lessons for an entire course of teaching upon the lines followed with so much success in the Sydney Technical College. The practical part of the work, and those divisions which have so long been followed as affording seasonable useful information concerning the working of Soils and Crops, have been carefully revised and added to with the hope that they may prove even more useful than formerly.

Balmain, N. S. Wales, February, 1890.

PREFACE TO THIRD EDITION.

The second edition having gone out of print, I have been called on for a third, and have tried to bring the experiences up to date. Chapters are added upon the Mechanics of Agriculture, Attractions of Plant Life, Rotations for Cropping, and Irrigation. The chapters on Land Selection, Dairying, Pigs, Poultry Farming, the Home Garden for Vegetables, Fruits, and Flowers, Dairying, Insect Pests and how to check them, and Home Helps have been re-written, extended, and brought up to the experience of the present time. I have again to thank the chief of the Public Instruction Department, the Honourable Jacob Garrard, and his officers, for including the work amongst those considered useful for teaching purposes in Public Schools. It is in very general use in advanced schools throughout Australia for object lessons on Australian agricultural subjects, and is the class-book for Elementary Agriculture in the Technical College and country classes. I can but trust that this third edition may prove as acceptable and useful to agriculturists generally as its predecessors.

The publishers, Messrs. Batson & Co., Ltd., deserve all credit for the expense and trouble they have devoted towards illustrating the work.

Balmain, N. S. Wales, January, 1895.

CONTENTS.

PREFACE to First edition; to Second; to Third - - - - 4-5

CHAP. I.—INTRODUCTORY: The Land—Agricultural Soil; The Best is the Cheapest; But what is Richness of Soil? Process of Soil Formation; What Growing Vegetation Tells of the Soil; The Seasons, Climatic Influences, Rainfall, Semi-Tropical Seasons - - - 9-18

CHAP. II.—SELECTING AND CLASSIFYING LAND: Chemical Contents of Soils; What Chemistry Tells Us; Some Representative Australian Soils - - - - - - - - - - - 18-28

CHAP. III.—CLEARING LAND, FENCING, BUILDING, ETC.: Seasons for Clearing; Timber and Materials Used - - - - - 28-41

CHAP. IV.—AGRICULTURAL DRAINING: What It Means; Distances Apart and Cost of Drains; Tools and Materials for Draining; Open Ditches and Covered Drains; Cropping Healthy and Unhealthy Soil 41-47

CHAP. V.—MECHANICS OF AGRICULTURE,—The Principles brought into Use; Science in the Plough; Hand and Horse Tools for Different Kinds of Work; Good Tools the Cheapest Labor - - - - - 47-56

CHAP. VI.—CULTIVATION OF CROPS: The Objects in View; The Means Employed; Hand Tools; Horse Implements; Methods of Cultivation; Surface Stirring; Subsoil Ploughing; Harrowing, Rolling; Commencing with Horse Labor- - - - - - - - - 56-70

CHAP. VII.—GRAIN CROPS: Quantities of Seed per Acre; Maize, Wheat, Barley, Oats, Rye, &c. - - - - - 70-83

CHAP. VIII.—ROOT CROPS. Potatoes: To Make Sure of a Crop; Sweet Potatoes, Yams, Beets, Mangolds, etc. - - - 83-88

CHAP. IX.—SEMI-TROPICAL CROPS: Sugar Cane, Tobacco, Arrowroot, Millet, Sorghum, Planter's Friend, &c. - - - - 88-101

CHAP. X.—PRODUCTS WE MIGHT GROW: Silk, Cotton, Tea, Coffee, Ginger, Chicory, Rice, Hops, Cocoa, Chocolate - - - 101-116

CHAP. XI.—ROTATION OR CHANGE OF CROPS: Results and Advantages of Rotation; Oil and Fibre Yielders; The Olive, Peanuts, Flax or Linseed, Broom Corn, Castor Oil; Getting Out the Oils; Banana Fibres - - - - - - - - - 116-127

CHAP. XII.—MAKING AND USING MANURES.—How Crops are Made; What Plants Take Out of the Soil; Vegetables, Field Crops. Fruit; The Australian Compost Heap; Materials Available; Artificial Manures; The Time for Manuring; Waste of Manures. - 127-135

CHAP. XIII.—IRRIGATION AND WATER STORAGE: Relation of Plants to Water; Crops by Artificial Watering; Methods; Scarcity of Water; Sources of Supply; Irrigating Hill Sides, For Grass, Crops, Orchards, Vegetables; When Water is Scarce; Water Storage; Pumping; Temperature of Water - - - - - - - 135 149

CHAP. XIV.—LIVE STOCK IN AUSTRALIA: Grazing-Farming; The Stock Available; Physiology of Life; Shorthorns, Herefords, Devons, Polleys, Crosses; Live and Dead Weight; Connection between Live Stock and the Soil - - - - - - - - 149-157

CHAP. XV.—SHEEP AND WOOL: Small and Large Flocks; The Merino; Country for Fine Wool; Mutton Sheep; Leicesters. Lincolns South Downs, Romney Marsh, Crosses; Classifying Wool; Weight of Fleeces 157-166

CHAP. XVI.—THE HORSE IN AUSTRALIA.—Buying a Horse; Judging Age; Good Mothers Good Stock; Breeding Horses, Training 166-175

CHAP. XVII.—THE DAIRYING INTERESTS: Materials Available for Profitable Dairying; A Business-like Cow; Breeds for the Dairy; Points of a Real Milk Maker; Milking; Testing the Qualities; How Much Feed? Treatment of Milk; BUTTER MAKING; The Factory System; Creameries; CHEESE MAKING - - - - 175 201

CHAP. XVIII.—THE PIG: The Kind that Pays; Breeds; What Pig Points Mean; Pen and Paddock Pig Keeping; Killing and Curing; Lard versus Meat - - - - - - - - 201 213

CHAP. XIX.—POULTRY: Requirements for Success; Fences, Buildings, Roosts; Feeding; Water; Peculiarities of Breeds; The Egg Layers; Table Breeds; Crosses; Breeding; Incubation; Incubators; Testing Eggs; Ducks, Geese, Turkeys; Diseases of Fowls - - 213-236

CHAP. XX.—CROPS FOR FEED, SILOING, HAY, ETC.: Requirements for Feeding; The Crops Available; The Silo, and Ensilage Making; Feeding with Ensilage; Chemistry of the Operations; Haymaking 236-241

CHAP. XXI.—GARDEN AND ORCHARD: Vegetables, Fruits, Flowers; The Home Garden; Arranging the Land; Starting with Vegetables; Warm and Cold Weather Crops; Sowing Seeds; Bush House Experiences; How to make Big Crops; Market Gardening on a Big Scale; ORCHARD WORK: Selecting Trees; Sorts Available; Planting; Budding; Grafting; Propagating; Pruning; Cultivating; Marketing. GRAPES AND WINES: Working a Vineyard. FLOWERS AND SHRUBS: Plants Available; Annuals; Roses, Climbers; Bulbs, &c., &c. 244-280

CHAP. XXII.—FRUIT AND VEGETABLE PRESERVING: Requirements for Success; Factory Processes; Bottling; Canning; Drying; Candying, &c. 280-295

CHAP. XXIII.—ATTRACTIONS OF PLANT LIFE: Rudimentary Botany 296-305

CHAP. XXIV.—FUNGUS AND INSECT PESTS: Their Methods of Life; How to Check and Destroy Them - - - - - 305-315

CHAP.—XXV.—HOME HELPS: Good Bread and How to Make It; Maize as Food; Puddings, Cakes, etc.; Soap and Candle Making; Rough Paint for Rough Work. TREATMENT OF ACCIDENTS: Burns, Scalds; Drowning; Lost in the Bush - - - - 315-333

CHAP. XXVI.—Seasonable Field and Garden Work for the Whole Year—Spring, Summer, Autumn, Winter- - - - 335-351

WORKS ON AUSTRALIAN AND OTHER AGRICULTURE - - 352

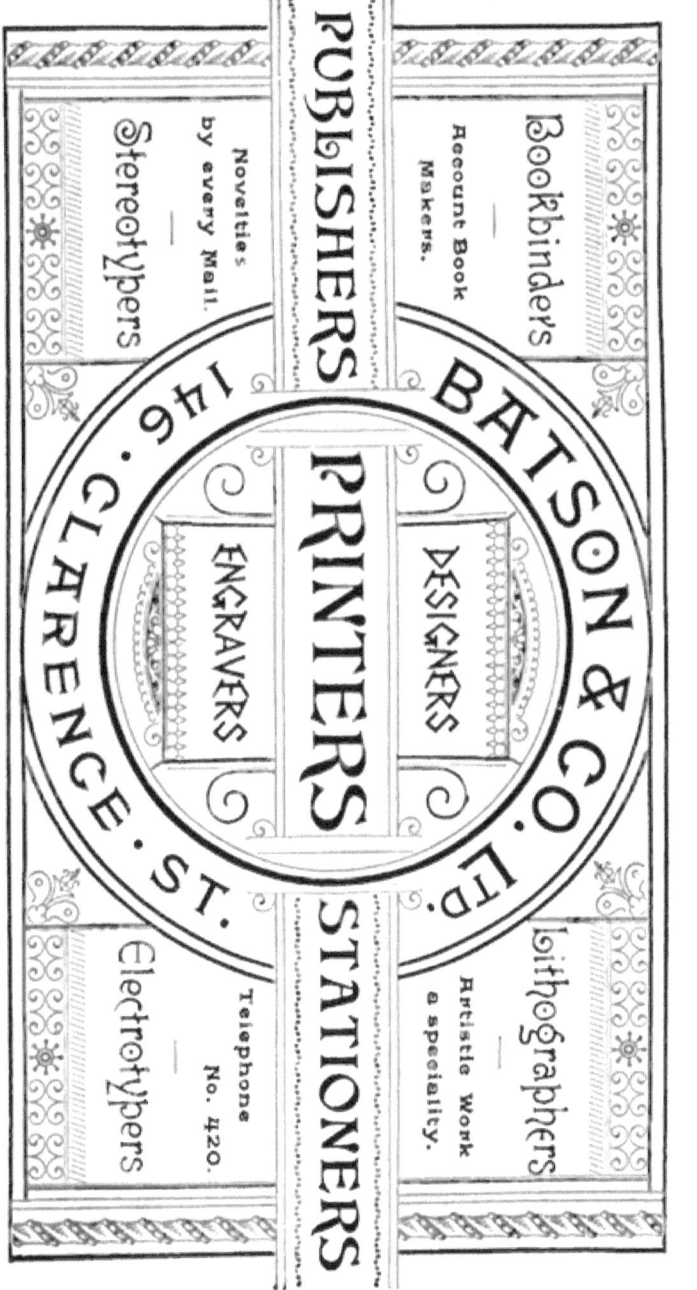

AUSTRALIAN AGRICULTURE.

I.—INTRODUCTORY.

THE LAND—AGRICULTURAL SOIL.

Possibilities from Rich Soil.

"THE best is the cheapest." In no walk of life does this truth carry more force than in that pertaining to land—to the operations of the agriculturist. Comparatively, it matters little which department we enter into: whether that of the farmer pure and simple, the grazier or squatter, the gardener, or a combination of two or more of those somewhat divided pursuits, we find that the prospects favor the men who have the best land. This matter, consequently, of close examination of the nature and quality of the soil, is most important. And as we come more closely to examine the matter, it is found that good agricultural land is good for whatever branch we may take it up, always providing the mechanical and chemical conditions of the soil, its formation, situation, surroundings, and extent are suitable for the object in view.

"But, What Is Richness of Soil?"—There is an agricultural answer to this query, when we come to look into

"Selecting and Classifying Land," Chapter II. But, as an introduction to the nature and qualities of soils, it may be desirable to make—before proceeding to soil selection—a commencement here. The time is not so far past, and there may be the idea still, that soil is just a mass of dead, inert, mineral matter, in which, by some means or other, plants grow somehow, and when they are good enough, animals can live by eating the plants, and crops can be got from such soil by merely turning it over. As an advance in knowledge concerning the real practical nature of soils, we may see that decayed and dead vegetation, insects, and animals, with the mineral matter, all go to aid the formation of rich soils. The vegetable contents make up the loamy or humus matter of the agriculturist, the organic matter of scientific agriculture. We may next, and in perfect safety, go another step forward, and treat soil as a mass of living material, having more or less life and richness in proportion to its contents of mineral substances and healthy humus, or vegetable, or organic matter.

It is at this stage that first acquaintance may be made with the wonders and the extreme usefulness of that microscopic life which connects the dead past with the living present. The purpose of those minute organisms—so small that myriads of them in a body would scarcely be visible to the human eye—is to break down what has been in growth—both vegetable and animal—into the elements, the plant food, which we use again for building up flowers, fruit, vegetables, grains, grasses, for nourishing animal life. This is one of the visible purposes of the micro-organisms, the microbes, the bacterial life upon which the very existence of all other progressive life is dependent.

Next we may find that these minute things have another purpose; that they are the means by which that most valuable aid to agriculture, nitrogen, which we may know more intimately as ammonia, is absorbed from the air, becomes part of the soil, an essential part of the nourishing food of both plants and animals. Such, in brief, is an outline of the process by which soils have been formed; their richness being dependent upon the proportions of mineral and organic matter in such state that plants can use this food, and live upon it, develop into healthful flowers, fruit, and yield crops for the benefit and sustenance of man and animal life generally.

The Process of Soil Formation.—The changes, the growth, the evolution in soil, from the first breaking down of rocks, upon the dust of which woody lichens may grow, until it becomes rich enough to produce the heaviest vegetation, say 100 bushels of maize, or 60 tons of sugar cane per acre, offer a wonderful lesson—the forethought and industry of the great Creator—a lesson, valuable, curious, and interesting. The process is visible all through the stages of development in our new country. The rocks, broken down, as we see, by the agency of the weather—" weathering down " is a very suitable term applied to the process—and the fine dust thus produced is the first stage of soil formation. Coarse, woody plants manage to live upon it. They decay, helped by bacterial action, and go to the formation of richer soil, upon which richer plants live. Then animal life comes in, living upon the vegetation, and decaying in due course, help to make still richer soil; and so the process goes on until the land is rich enough to support the wants of man—and the more exacting requirements of woman, upon whom man himself is dependent!

The combined contents of various rocks give us the minerals lime, magnesia, potash, soda, sulphur, iron, silica. From air and water come nitrogen, oxygen, carbon, and hydrogen. All of these must be in agricultural soil and the air around it. They all enter into plant life and animal life; and the work of the agriculturist is to use, maintain, and increase this plant food, and by supplying what becomes necessary, and by the admission of air and rain into the soil—by "cultivation," in short—secure the conditions necessary for making crops.

Sources of Soil.—The rocks are the sources of all soils, but, as explained in the chapter on soil selecting, where analyses are given representing several of the leading formations of New South Wales, they differ very much in the proportions of material they hold for the use of plants. In Australia the disintegration, or breaking up of the rocks, is going on very rapidly, the agents being rain, air, &c. The very excellent geological works published by Mr. Wilkinson (geological surveyor), Professor Liversidge, and Messrs. Cox and Ratte, afford much and very interesting information on that subject. The soils referred to have been analysed mechanically, in the farming sense, and chemically, in order to get at the proportions of plant food available and stored up, awaiting the skill and labour of the agriculturist.

Then, Vegetation Speaks of the Soil.—The native grasses, herbs, shrubs, and trees offer a capital index to the quality of the soils in which they grow. It is simply impossible to find a heavy growth of rich herbs and grass upon poor land. The timbers also form a guide. As a rule, the softer woods are on richer soil, the harder on poorer soil. Taking, then, the land in its native state, there is less difference in the best soils suited for the purposes of the grazier, the farmer, or the gardener, than might at first appear. They all require land rich in the elements that produce rich grass, and with the exception of the scrub, brush, and other lands, so heavily timbered that there is no grass whatever, the best naturally-grassed lands are the best, as a rule. In taking up land that has been in use, the plants or crops growing upon it aid very much in coming to a decision regarding its present state, and the kind of treatment it has received. When the country is open, and used for grazing only, the grass and herbs offer as good an indication of its capabilities as the animals feeding upon the land. The dense thick growth of annual grasses, or herbage, closely matted together and fresh looking, tells an unmistakable tale of the natural wealth of the soil. The symptoms of decay are undue preponderance of long, coarse grasses, which during the winter months become dry, brittle, and of a dark brown colour. There is but little nourishment in them. Weeds, coarse thistles of various kinds, sorrel, shrubby and weedy plants generally, tell their own tale of poor cultivation, overstocking, and of poverty that nothing short of skill in treatment, heavy manuring, or long and absolute rest can bring back into fertility. In the sections of country longest settled, but too much land in this state can be seen. It is neither profitable to the farmer, grazier, nor gardener. Worn-out land is a millstone round the neck of the man who owns it; and neglected land is but a stage better. We can only bring it into fertility by clean cultivation and manuring.

Under the most favorable circumstances, land improvement is costly, and still favours him who has the best to operate on. This we find to be true all over the country, in the grain-growing as well as the sugar-producing districts. Drainage is amongst the valuable of land improvements; but it is costly, and we would give the preference to the land that requires least artificial drainage. As a rule, soil that is liberally mixed with sand is less costly in working than more stiff or clayey soils. We would also give the preference to land that will allow most horse labor, and has no more fall than is necessary to carry off water readily. The less it is cut up with gullies or water-courses, the more profitably it can be worked.

To Make Agriculture Pay.—So to get to the first requirements for comfort and success, we see that agriculture, look at what branch of the occupation we may, to make it pay, must be followed as a business: that skill, capital, and perseverance are all necessary. It is one of the serious mistakes in connection with colonial life that men enter upon grazing and farming without any special training or knowledge of what they undertake. Agriculture is the only business into which men enter largely upon such terms, and it is no matter of surprise, therefore, that many fail, and that others complain about the want of success. When a man has plenty of money he may be able to buy experience, but it is very expensive. In other cases men commence without either capital or skill, but with strength, courage, and perseverance, and above all with tact to take advantage of every circumstance in their favor that presents itself. They gradually make headway. The colonies are dotted with successful men who have commenced in that way. They are certainly more numerous than the successful men who have purchased their experience. But at a glance it will be seen that the talents thus brought to bear would have gone far to carry a man successfully through any pursuit. And such is the fact: There are few occupations that call for more skilful perseverance than agriculture. On the other hand, with these requisites, there are few that offer safer prospects of making an independent livelihood.

The Seasons—The Climate.

Australia, to those who know little or nothing of the country, is a land of perpetual summer, subject to terrific floods and excessive droughts—the latter, as a whole, prevailing. This belief is not confined to persons in other countries, whose knowledge of Australia has been acquired from books of the kind which state that flowers have no odors in Australia, that birds do not sing here, and other absurd things. Colonists, old colonists among them, have opinions of the country and the climate that differ but slightly from the foregoing. One reason for this belief is the extraordinary similarity of the climate of the seaboard towns, considering the distance they are apart. Take Adelaide, Melbourne, Sydney, Brisbane, the whole year round, and the climate is wonderfully alike; nor does it change to anything like the degree the geographical situation of these places might warrant us believing. As we travel northwards to Newcastle, Grafton, Brisbane, Mackay, Townsville, or southwards to Melbourne, Adelaide, Perth, the change is just a little more decided. There is a little more winter in the southern sections; a little more summer in the northern. The cultivation of sugar-cane has shown, to an extent unthought of before, that in Australia the frosts of the winter season are felt for hundreds of miles within the tropics.

But leaving the coast and travelling inland, the common notion that perpetual summer prevails is soon upset, and very often in a manner that is telling. A hundred miles inland from the coast, unless in low-lying situations sheltered by mountain ranges from the west, the winter season is very decided. Frosts prevail in these inland districts all over the country, even to the centre of Australia. In the south, and as far north as the Queensland border, snow is common during the months of July and August. Even in the north, the climate inland more than 100 miles from the sea can only be considered semi-tropical in so far as the summer months are concerned. The cold of winter is very decided, and the summer vegetation dies off. It is well to understand this fact. It is the key to the serious misunderstandings that exist regarding the nature of the country, and the but too prevalent impression that the climate is very dry and uniformly hot.

Seasons; the Rainfall.—For practical purposes, the seasons may be divided as follows:—Spring: August, September, October. Summer: November, December, January; in wet seasons, February is added to the summer, and in the northern sections of the country is often the most decidedly hot month of the whole. March and April are autumn months, in so far as the bulk of the indigenous grasses ripen and go to seed during that time. May, June, and July are the winter months. The seasons vary to some extent according to latitude, but climatic influences are due in a still greater degree to local causes, to the existence of ranges of mountains running parallel with the sea, to the direction of the prevailing winds, and the quarter from which the rains come, that modify the force of high winds. It is no mere figure of speech to say that within six hours' ride by rail from any of the large cities, we reach places that differ as much from the semi-tropical summer of the coast as the Highlands of Scotland differ from the Midland Counties of England, as Denmark does from Spain, or Western New York from South Carolina. Travel where we will, much the same peculiarities are found. The seasons, the rainfall, and the local productions are modified by the formation of the country to a much greater degree than is observable in other climates.

Dry and Wet Seasons.—Droughts have been experienced in this country. 1828, 1838, 1849, 1862, 1878, 1895, were seasons of that kind. The average rainfall of the coast country may be taken as between 40 and 50 inches; and here again the fall is found to be due more to local surroundings than otherwise. Inland the rainfall is less, but the same rule holds good with sufficient certainty to justify great care on the part of any one who desires to choose a location for any particular description of agriculture. Thus, for instance, sections of the hill districts, on the slopes of the Dividing Ranges, are found suitable for all kinds of European fruits and grain. The average rainfall there is about 30 inches; while other places, at nearly the same distance from the sea, have scarcely one half the rainfall. And so it is all over the country. Local knowledge is of great value; for places are found at no great distance apart where the seasons, the cold, heat, and rainfall are essentially different. Still, these peculiarities are merged in the leading seasons of the country which mark the time of spring, summer, autumn, and winter with a degree of accuracy which does not seem to be generally understood. In so far as the grass vegetation is concerned, the seasons are unmistakable, and in neglecting what they teach we are but shutting our eyes to facts, and complaining against conditions of climate over which we have no control, but concerning the effects of which we can do much. The great bulk of the grasses die off during the winter months. In sheltered places this is scarcely noticed. Here the grass merely goes to seed, stands like so much hay, and makes tolerable food for stock—it keeps life in them at least. So the case stands during the winter. In such places the soil heat seldom goes lower than 50 deg., and as soon as rain falls in the spring months, young grass displaces the old, and so the seasons run into each other. But where frosts occur, the case is different. Its first effect is to reduce the indigenous grasses to dust, or dry woody particles; its next is to lower the point at which indigenous vegetation grows vigorously. When the rain falls at this stage—while the soil is cold—the evil is aggravated. The soil takes longer to rise in heat when wet, and the land continues bare of grass until the temperature is sufficiently high to cause a spring, so that the growing season is shorter. It is in noting this peculiarity that we see the adaptability of the climate for cultivating European grasses and forage plants. During the cooler, damp season of the winter, that destroys the indigenous grasses, wheat, oats, barley, rye, potatoes, turnips, and the annual grasses of Europe generally, thrive freely in good soil, and form a sufficient basis for feeding purposes. During a moist spring, the growth of the cultivated grasses is very strong, while the same weather that makes them grow keeps down the heat that is necessary for the vigorous growth of the indigenous grasses; but by combining the two, that is, by having cultivated pasture with the indigenous, the seasons are very rare indeed in which continuous growth cannot be maintained all the year round.

Semi-Tropical Seasons.—In the true semi-tropical sections of the country, including the seaboard northwards from Sydney, the whole of the settled portions of Queensland, and the Northern Territory of South Australia, the seasons may be still further divided. In these warmer sections there are in reality two growing seasons in the year. One commences as the temperature moderates in March, and continues through the winter months. It is during this time that European grains and vegetables are grown, and in sheltered situations where the soil is rich, they come to extraordinary perfection during this short season. In sheltered places, the time of growth for grains and vegetables is extended through September and October. In other places in the north, rain falls in April and May, and semi-tropical vegetation, such as cotton, corn, &c., does very well when planted at that time. The true tropical spring of the country commences in September and October, and summer continues until March. In very warm, moist localities, such as the Tweed in New South Wales, and Mackay, Mooroochie, and other places on the northern coast of Queensland, the season of growth runs right through the year; the best time for sowing and harvest being selected in accordance with the usual rainfall of the locality.

There is but one planting season for fruit culture—April-May to August—according to locality. Fruits come into leaf in the true spring of the country, and mature during the summer.

Grasses indicate the Seasons.—As the peculiarity of our grasses as indicators of the soil, the seasons, and the climate are better understood, there are fewer complaints regarding the unsuitability of portions of the country for cultivation purposes. Large numbers of the grasses speak so plainly in this respect, that they offer conclusive proof that without irrigation to develop the vegetation of spring at the time of seed sowing, it were folly to attempt growing crops where perennial grasses only are found. But though thus indicative of irregularity of seasons, and of a capacity to grow and mature during whole seasons without a shower of rain, those very grasses, and the climate in which they grow, have proven unexceptionally favourable for sheep and the production of the very best quality of wool; and with skill, wheat with sheep comes in as a desirable branch of Australian agriculture, as explained in the chapters which deal with sheep, cattle, horses, as part of the live stock of Australian agriculture.

II.—SELECTING AND CLASSIFYING LAND.

They Usually Camp near Water, and on Good Land.

In the introductory chapter and those upon cultivation, native vegetation, and what it indicates, we may see how useful and valuable is the knowledge offered by the indigenous and other plants. Meantime, we have available the means which science with practice places at our disposal for judging the qualities of soils. Chemical analysis is an immense help in this direction, but it must be something more than a mere laboratory analysis. Inspection of the mechanical condition is necessary, and the geological formation. When a knowledge of the peculiarities of the indigenous vegetation is also brought to bear, there is a closer approach to certainty in our work. By analysis of soil, we get at its various parts by separating them, in the mechanical or practical, and the chemical sense, and can come to very definite conclusions regarding the suitability of any soil for grazing or cultivation purposes. Plants live like other things, and the soil must supply the basis of the means of life—that is, the plant food—otherwise there must be poor grass or short crops, or no crops at all, and the attendant risks of disease and bitter disappointment.

Earth Substances for Making Grass and Crops.—For grazing and for cultivation one of the most important substances—indeed, the most important part of the soil—is the vegetable or organic matter. This contains the available nitrogen, which plays such an important part in building up plant life. When with this the mineral substances are sufficiently abundant, the best grasses and the most plentiful crops can be got. In this climate the vegetable matter contains most of the plant food in such condition that the roots of plants can take it up at once, and enables them further to reach all the mineral food they can find in the soil and the subsoil. But this matter is not very abundant, and the agriculturist acts wisely who saves all he can. By cultivation, by rotation of crops, by manuring, and by resting or fallowing the land, the process of making plant food is quickened. The soils having the most vegetable matter take in rain-water most readily, and hold it longest for the use of crops or grass. This, in dealing with Australian soils, the analyses going on prove, is a rule almost without an exception, and it proves conclusively how destructive is the custom of burning grass, or stubble, or indeed any vegetable matter on the land. We have none to spare for the purpose.

Judging Soils by Analysis.—The soils here described have been separated, or analysed mechanically (in the farming sense) and chemically to prove their contents; also tested for their capacity to absorb and hold water, in the manner suitable for vegetable life. The figures represent each soil divided into 100. parts of the whole, which affords an easily understood basis for calculation and comparison :—

Contents of Soils.*	Rich Loam (Manning River).	Rich "Clay" (Gunnedah).	Sandy Loam (Hawkesbury).	Poor Sandy (Pine Scrub).
Organic (vegetable) matter	20·40	12·96	3·70	2·00
Nitrogen – ammonia	·10	·07	·01	Traces
Clay matter (alumina) and iron	19·60	18·95	1·00	4·00
Lime	1·40	1·22	Traces	·02
Magnesia	Traces	·18	Traces	—
Sulphuric acid	·01	·04	Traces	·01
Potash	·90	·09	·05	Traces
Sodium chloride (salt)	·20	·07	·06	·02
Phosphoric acid	·08	·03	Traces	Traces
Sandy matter and loss	56·50	66·05	94·10	93·75
	99·19	99·66	98·92	99·80
Capacity for absorbing water	5	4	4	4
Capacity for retaining water	5	3	2	0
	10†	7	6	4

The Clay and Iron.—Clay in soil, though not a plant food, is useful to a certain degree, as giving closer texture and capacity for retaining moisture. Iron may be healthy for plant growth, or it may be injurious. Tests to get at the state of the iron are very useful.

Lime is present in all useful soils. It exerts marked effects in preparing the food of plants. When it is almost absent, or the proportion is low, say less than is represented in the analysis as ·2, that soil is very slow in yielding crops, and the indigenous vegetation is poor. The applica-

* Soil analyses, and the analyses of water, plants, milk, and substances generally of use in agricultural practices, including manures, are dealt with fully in the author's work on "Helpful Chemistry for Agriculturists," 4s., Batson and Co., Clarence-street, Sydney, and all booksellers.

† The standard 10 is a perfect soil for absorbing and retaining moisture.

tion of lime, in some of its many forms, in sufficient quantity for grass and crops, is one of the least costly of soil improvements, and one of the most effective. Lime is abundant in Australia.

Magnesia is an alkaline earth in much the same sense as lime. It is not a scarce ingredient in New South Wales soils.

Phosphorus as *Phosphates*, in combination with other substances, is fairly plentiful in our soils, but, as a rule, additions of this mineral are desirable in the form of bone material. In conjunction with lime, &c., the phosphates form bone, and not a few of the defects in grazing and dairying country can be traced to scarcity of these materials. Wheat is very heavy on phosphates, an ordinary crop of 30 bushels absorbing some 25lb., a demand which but few soils in a state of nature can supply for many successive crops. But, like lime, the phosphates can be easily made good by manuring.

Sulphur, or *Sulphuric Acid*, is an essential to plant life. It is fairly plentiful, though additions are advantageous for some crops, such as peas, onions, &c.

Carbon, as carbonic acid, is gathered by plants from the air.

Potash is not plentiful in our soils. It is a most essential part of plant life. Where it is scarce the indigenous vegetation, both grass and timber, is poor and coarse. Fruit trees, as a rule, search greedily after potash ; the success of potato crops, tobacco, and grape vines is dependent upon it. Wool also absorbs much potash, and a deficiency in sheep feed is quickly seen in less and less yolk in the wool. Potash, as a mineral, may be present in the subsoil more plentifully than in the surface soil.

Soda has, to some extent, the same characteristics as potash in plant life ; but, unlike potash, soda is not uniformly present in the ash of healthy crops. Potash also acts as a substitute for soda in manurial operations, but soda is not found to act for potash in ordinary crops.

Chloride of Sodium (common salt) is abundant in our soils as a rule, and supplies the soda that is necessary.

Sandy Matter (silica).—It is a plant food to some extent. The greater or lesser proportion of silica in a soil indicates whether it can be worked easily.

What Chemistry Tells Us.—The foregoing, with water sufficient to maintain the food in a fluid state, are, practically, all the materials with which the agriculturist need make himself acquainted, as plant foods that he must have present in the desired proportions or he cannot get the quality of grass, crops, or fruit trees he aims at. Plants absorb them in varying proportions, but all require some of each. When in the accompanying analysis the presence of ammonia, potash, phosphates, sulphuric acid are indicated by "Traces," there is, for the time, likely to be a sufficiency of these substances for grasses and fruits, but not for grain or root crops, and they should be supplied with other manures. Mere "Traces" of lime are not sufficient for grass or any other purpose. It can be supplied direct in the form of newly slacked lime or as bone manure. The latter is the better form for sandy or thin soils.

Some Representative Soils of New South Wales.—A few of the analyses made for the little work, "Grazing, Farm and Garden Soils of New South Wales," which can be had for 1s. from Batson and Co., Ltd., Sydney, are here appended. The first soil dealt with was taken from the excellently worked garden of Mr. H. Heard, some three miles from the pretty town of Ryde, on the Parramatta River. It is typical of a very large area of the metropolitan shale series of the Ryde, Lane Cove, Seven Hills, and Parramatta districts. The red colour is due to iron. It is a good sound loam, and seems more clayey in composition than analysis shows the state to be in reality. The native timbers in the district include the eucalyptus generally, the gum and box trees being of great size. Oak, cherry, hickory, and black butt are still seen. Until cleared of the native timber, which costs from £7 to £10 per acre, there is very little pasture land, but the leading grasses present indicate the character of the soil very clearly, and that draining and liming are the first requirements.

Organic matter	13·560
Clay or alumina, and iron	5·305
Lime	0·023
Magnesia	0·012
Potash	0·672
Soda	0·020
Salt (chloride sodium)	0·047
Phosphoric acid	0·042
Sulphuric oxide	0·024
Moisture	1·160
Sandy matter and loss	78·647

Nitrogen (in the organic matter), 0·163.
Capacity for absorbing and retaining moisture, 7.

Goulburn Soil.—From a paddock of Mr. Grunsell, and adjoining his fine garden. The soil is alluvial, and is of excellent quality for both cultivation and grass, being a mixture of silurian with trap-rock soil, granite and limestone, brought down by the Mulwarrie River. Analysis shows:—

Organic matter	6.00
Alumina and iron	5.00
Lime	0.90
Magnesia	Traces
Potash	0.05
Chloride sodium	0.06
Phosphates	0.06
Silica and Loss	87.00

Nitrogen = ammonia, ·16.
Capacity for absorbing and retaining moisture, 8.

This land, for fruit-growing purposes, has sufficient alkalies, and should be excellent for grass. Nitrogenous manure of any kind would be advantageous, and for potatoes, potash would be helpful.

Lucerne Soils of the Hunter Valley.—From undisturbed alluvial deposits below the line of cultivation, and near the bridge, West Maitland:—

Organic matter	15.60
Alumina and iron	16.00
Carbonic acid	0.02
Lime	1.11
Magnesia	0.20
Potash	0.65
Chloride sodium	0.50

Phosphoric acid	0.08
Sulphuric acid	0.02
Silica and loss	65.00

Nitrogen = ammonia, 0.44.
Capacity for absorbing and retaining moisture, 10.

This soil, taken as a whole, is very rich, and being naturally well drained, with its heavy vegetable and lime supplies, it has all the advantages of very first-class soil for bearing extra heavy crops. The fertility can be easily maintained, and at no great outlay for fertilizers or labor. Should the proportion of organic matter be allowed to wear down, the soil will become heavier to work and less productive.

New England Soil.—From near Exhibition Paddock, Armidale. Fair for fruit; grasses very excellent for dairying, for butter especially :—

Organic matter and moisture	10.00
Alumina and iron	12.80
Lime	0.05
Potash	Trace
Chloride sodium	0.02
Sulphuric acid	Trace
Phosphates	Trace
Magnesia	0.08
Silica and loss	77.00

Nitrogen = ammonia, 1.5.
Capacity for absorbing and retaining moisture, 9.

Suitable for Irrigation.—From cultivation land of Mr. Fuss, some two miles from Narrabri. Soil alluvial, and of great depth. Quality apparently uniform to river level, about 30 feet below soil surface. A very quick soil during rainy weather, or under irrigation. The Namoi is a muddy river, bringing down debris of claystone, shale, and slate, rotten basalt, &c., which deposits rich material by floods or irrigation. The capillary attraction of the soil near the river banks is equal to raising water in the wells from five to seven feet above level of the river. There can be no layers of clay in the soil under such circumstance. It is an exceptionally capable soil for irrigation, for gardening, or for grass, provided there is ample water available for dry spells. In the mechanical sense this soil is perfect :—

Organic matter	5.510
Alumina and iron	4.000
Lime	0.630
Magnesia	0.012
Potash	0.020
Chloride sodium	0.063
Phosphoric acid	0.014
Sulphuric acid	0.031
Moisture	1.870
Silica and loss	87.730

Nitrogen = ammonia, 0.112.
Capacity for absorbing and retaining moisture, 9.

A Soil Capable of Immense Improvement.—From portion of the Government lands at Rookwood, some 10 miles from Sydney, the formation is of the Wianamatta shales series. Until cleared, there was very little grass upon the land:

Organic matter	14.70
Alumina and iron	9.10
Lime	0.01
Magnesia	Faint traces
Phosphates	Traces
Potash	Traces
Chloride sodium	0.02
Sulphuric acid	None
Silica and loss	76.00

Nitrogen = ammonia, 0.15.
Capacity for absorbing and retaining moisture, 5.

The subsoil is stiff clay, the first six inches red, and bearing oxidised iron; under that, white clay in a bad state, from the presence of unoxidised iron; but analysis shows considerable traces of alkalies, magnesian earth, &c. Draining should improve this soil very much; without drainage, but little can be expected from it. As an experiment, a portion of the land under grass, is drained to a depth of 3 feet, with 2-inch and 1½-inch pipes.

Peculiarities of Our Soils.—There is now opportunity for seeing what is the real character of some hundreds of our soils—fairly representative soils from all parts of the country. Main features of our soil are wonderfully alike in many respects, soils taken from locations hundreds of miles apart. There is also, and it is said with decided regret, marked uniformity in a deficiency of necessary materials characteristic of even rich grazing and cultivation soils. The ingredients are not numerous, fortunately; but as the absence of even one is quickly felt, poverty of grass and crops must result, unless the deficiency is made good. The marked deficiencies are in the alkalies, alkaline earths, and nitrates, all of which can be made good in such quantity as warrants their use for profitable agriculture. Their absence, in not a few cases, accounts, in unmistakable manner, for the falling-off in both grass and crops—and not them only, but for deterioration of live stock on the land, which suffer very soon from absence of bone-forming material. The dairying districts also suffer from this cause.

Poverty of Soil v. "Blights."—From several of the soils of which analyses were made, heavy crops of corn, wheat, barley, tobacco, roots, &c., were got in years gone by. Thirty to forty bushels of wheat, eight tons potatoes, eighty bushels of corn, and up to 1500 lbs. tobacco were got per acre while the land was in full vigour. This went on from three to ten years, then the crops began to be lighter and lighter; and then—and this is heard in many of the older settlements—"The blight fell upon the land: and since that happened, it is no use cropping. We may get a bit of corn, and the grass, but nothing else." "Blights" are attributed to numbers of causes—to long-continued dry weather; to grasshoppers and caterpillars; to insects, westerly winds, and various other causes, all of which are annoyances, and the cause of loss here as they are in all other agricultural countries. But soil impoverishment accounts for no small portion of such pests, and there is ground for confidence that, as more attention is given to the state of the soil, and the conditions of fungus and insect life, we will be the better able to ward off the enemies always on the watch to ravage suffering vegetation.

What Skill Has Done.—There are exceptions to the long list of complaints, and men amongst us who have been sufficiently successful all along to give confidence that as the better system becomes more general, agriculture must make the advance so very earnestly desired all over the country. These men have treated their land, usually from the outset, with consideration and judgment. The effects of skill are very clearly defined in many quarters. There is grazing land to-day which is as good, possibly better, than it was fifty years ago; and farms, orchards, and vineyards which have improved in quality and condition of soil by the system of treatment and cropping followed. We can hope that the better system is to extend from this time forward.

The entire agriculture experience of the country goes to prove that very much the same processes of soil treatment, selection of seeds and plants, and their feeding and cultivation, according to the best methods, yield results here on much the same terms as in other countries.

Fire and Water Tests for Soils.*—Two diagram sketches are given illustrative of how soils can be tested. In the first, a weighed portion of *dry soil*, usually 1000 grains, is being tested by fire. The operation is best performed in a calcining dish (cost 1s. 6d.), which withstands the heat of a Bunsen burner, or a spirit lamp, until all the vegetable matter is incinerated or burnt out. Or the operation can be carried out on a strip of iron, as shown. When complete, the soil is reweighed. The difference shows the quantity of organic matter, with moisture (even from air-dried soil) which was in it. Anything over eight parts of the 100, expelled by heat, shows such proportion of vegetable matter as indicates a soil of good quality in that respect. By reference to the various analyses and the accompanying notes, the value of this test will be still more apparent.

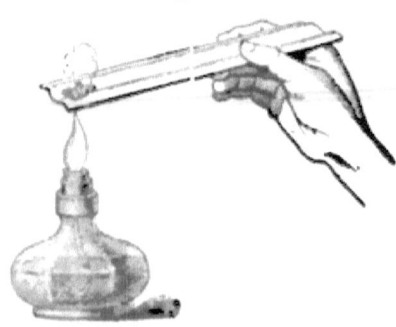

Fire Test For Soil, &c.

* From "Helpful Chemistry for Agriculturists," &c., from the publishers of this work, and all booksellers. Methods of testing soils, manures, water, milk, &c., &c. are given in detail in "Helpful Chemistry."

Testing for Water Capacity.—Glass vessels answer best for this test, so that we may see what is going on; but other vessels of the same form may be made to do duty. 10 ounces of air-dried soil answer very well. A glass funnel, or filler, with an ordinary paper filter, is placed in the cylinder, as shown. Then the soil to be tested is put in the funnel, the paper preventing it from passing through. For the test, gently pour water upon the soil. A fairly good loam, with say 10 per cent. of vegetable matter, will be found to absorb the water freely, and may take up and hold, by capillary attraction, over one-half its own weight, or, say the 10 oz. of soil may take in and hold in suspension 6 ozs. of water. A rich, loamy soil, having over 18 per cent. of vegetable matter in its composition, may absorb 8 ozs. of water. In practice it is found that the soils which take in water most readily by this test give it off most slowly by evaporation. Hence their value in a climate where so much of the success of agriculture of all kinds is dependent upon the capacity of the soil to absorb rain and to resist dry spells.

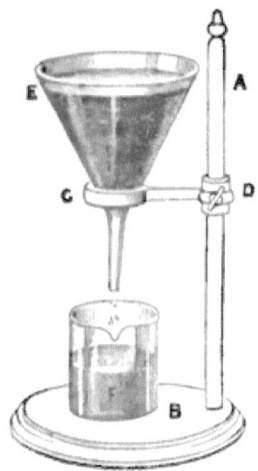

Testing Soil for Water Capacity.

III.—CLEARING LAND, BUILDING, FENCING.

Clearing off Timber, &c.—The help of an experienced hand, or the advice of a neighbour is of great value in falling heavy trees, scrub or any dense growth of timber that has of necessity to be burnt off. The winter season— June, July and August—is the time for this work. The blacks in the less populous parts of the country are expert at it. They cut down vines and light timber first, then tumble the heavy stuff on top, lopping off the branches to get the whole mass packed as close as possible. Bushmen follow the same plan. The stuff is allowed to lie until it is perfectly dry. This brings us into November, at which time the weather is usually dry; when in that state, the mass is fired, and when the packing has been sufficiently close the fire clears off all except the trunks of the big trees. These are then rolled together and burnt, and garden stuff, for home use, corn, potatoes, or sugar-cane, or other crops can be planted at once, right in the ashes. As much as 110 bushels of corn per acre have been got in this way.

Ringing, or Ring-barking Trees.—Trees are killed without falling them, by cutting a deep ring through the bark into the solid wood all round. The operation has proved beneficial in cases. If grass is the only object in view, and the land is at all liable to visitations of frost, then some of the timber, say from twenty to thirty trees to the acre, should be left alive for shade and shelter to stock. All the undergrowth, including ferns and young saplings, should be grubbed out, for they do more to prevent grass from growing than the larger and deeper rooting trees. One of the annoyance of ringing is the danger from and the getting rid of bark, branches, and timber as they fall. On moderately timbered land that has been ring-barked, eight, ten, or more years elapse ere all this dead stuff is got rid of, and in every case it is desirable to calculate whether it would not be cheaper to cut down and burn the timber at once, rather than ringbark.

Ringbarked.

Falling Timber.—The autumn is the best time to fell timber for building, or for posts, rails, vine stakes or other purposes. At that season the wood is at maturity, and there is less free sap and soft matter in it than there is at any other season of the year. In timber fallen and split up in autumn, the seasoning process is much more gradual and perfect, because the weather is cooler, and the grain of the timber contracts more equally and uniformly. Fencing stuff made from almost any of the hardwood trees, felled and split in autumn, outlasts stuff from the same timber cut at other times.

FENCING.—It is of importance to the agriculturist, whether he be squatter, farmer or gardener, to have such fences as enable him to protect growing crops, and to get the benefit of all his grass; to have grass eaten down even and clean; to enrich any desired piece of land; and to work his place at the lowest cost. The kind of fence best for each locality depends upon the nature of the timber, or other material, and the labor available.

Wire and Netting Fences.—A thoroughly colonial garden fence is made of wire netting, fixed to split posts. The posts are set in the ground 8 feet apart, and two feet deep; then three barbed wires are stretched and fixed to the posts by staples, and wire-netting is fastened to the wire and the posts. To prevent rabbits, &c., getting under the netting, it is set in a trench 3 inches or so under the surface. This fence then presents 5½ feet of wire-netting. The cost is from 7s. 6d. to 10s. per rod.

Wire Fences.—Six wires of No. 6, with the posts a rod apart, make a good farm, cattle or sheep fence, spaced thus:—Lower wire 10 inches from the ground; first space 4½ inches; second, 4½ inches; third, 5½ inches; fourth, 10 inches; and the top space 12 inches. Two wire ties, at equal distances should connect all the wires in each panel, by being passed round each, and then staked to the ground. The above distance is better than having posts set closer together. Fasten the wire to the posts with staples. A good "bush" strainer is a round piece of wood, three or four inches in diameter and three feet long. This is turned by a pin, worked in a hole, near each end. The wire is thus made to coil round the centre, and the power is quite sufficient. The posts ought to be two feet in the ground, and the straining-posts four feet, a foot in diameter and twenty rods apart

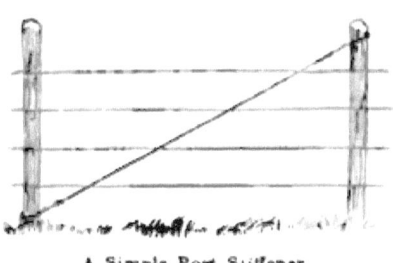

A Simple Post Stiffener.

A man can sink twenty-five holes a day in ordinary soils. The straining post may be secured by a stay resting in a notch, and on a block sunk in the ground; the stay can be moved forward as the work proceeds, two being used alternately. The wire should be so tough as to coil closely round itself without giving way. Such a fence, under ordinary circumstances, costs from £80 a mile. Neither the ground auger for making post-holes nor the driving of posts by hand has been found to work particularly well.

Wire is sold by the hundredweight and ton. Prices vary according to the guages. Nos. 6, 7, 8 and 9 are favourite sizes for sheep fences, and answer very well, with a top rail or two barbed wires, for cattle and horses.

Stretching and Tying Wire.—Wire strainers of various forms are sold by the ironmongers for a few pence each. The strainer shown consists of a mowing machine finger bolted to a stout stick; a stick curved as shown in the engraving is preferable to a straight one, as it does not turn in the hand. When using it, the wire is held firmly in the slot of the finger, and may be easily stretched by applying the stick as a lever.

A Home-made Strainer.

Post and Rail Fences.—Ironbark, bloodwood, blue and red gum, or other hardwood are in favour for fences They are very durable. Three-rail fences cost from 3s. 6d. to 7s. per rod, according to location. Two-rail fences are about 1s. per rod less.

Paling Fences.—An effective close-paling fence is made by sinking posts nine feet apart, one top rail on top with an open trench about six inches deep between the posts. Set the bottom ends of the palings in the trench, letting the tops rest against the rail. In stiff soil, well rammed against the palings, this fence answers well, and costs from 10s. to 16s. per chain.

Double Post and Rail, with Saplings.—This style of fence is more frequently used for sheep yards than for paddocks. It is formed by sinking two posts in the ground about six inches apart, at intervals of from twelve to fifteen feet. Saplings of any diameter not exceeding eight inches are then dropped between the posts, and when built up to the height of about four feet the posts are secured together at the top by wire, hoop, green hide or, in some instances, stringy bark.

Virginian Snake or Zigzag Fence.—When constructed of heavy timber this is a substantial fence. It is made by embedding the butt end of one tree in a notch cut for the purpose in the top end of another, laying them along the ground in zigzag form, so that each log intersects the line at an angle of forty-five degrees. When the logs have been piled up to the desired height, cross-legs and a heavy top-rail are then put on so as to bind the whole.

"Basket Fence" is found serviceable for those residing in scrubby or brigalow country. It is made by driving five feet six inch stakes in the ground with mauls to a depth of nine to twelve inches, and four feet six inches apart; saplings from about two inches in diameter are then closely entwined with the stakes to the height of four feet six inches. It can be strengthened by staying firmly at intervals with strong forks, or, if erected in scrub, stumps of saplings can be made available where practicable instead of driven stakes. This fence can be run up rapidly at a cost of about £20 per mile.

"Brush Fence" is that most commonly erected on sheep runs. Two descriptions are in use; the first being formed by cutting down trees along the line of fence, laying down the butts, as well as any dead timber that may be lying about, as a foundation, and making it up to the height of four or five feet with the branches obtained from the trees, just cut down. This is the same as the ordinary brush fence used in the construction of sheep yards, and may be erected at as low a rate as £7 in thickly timbered country and £15 in ordinary bush land. The other description of bush fence is formed by cutting down a tree, drawing it by means of a strong team of bullocks on to the line, and chopping off only such branches as come to a height of over seven feet. The next tree is then drawn on and placed so that its branches commence to form part of the fence immediately where the branches of the first tree left off, and so on throughout. This fence costs from £15 to £20 per mile. Division boundary fences are frequently erected of this description of material in Victoria, and can be made perfectly cattle proof. But, like all timber fences, there are the risks from fire.

Contracts for Fencing.—A written agreement between the parties concerned is in all cases desirable. In timbered country the contract should specify by whom the line is to be cleared and the width of the clearing; dead timber should never be allowed to remain within five feet of a fence. Also the height of the posts out of the ground; their depth in the ground (usually two feet); the size of the rails; whether posts are to be barked (always desirable); arrange for slip rails and gates; whether any of the stuff is to be hauled upon the line by the owner; and, if possible, the timber to be used should be specified. Towards the erection of boundary fences it is usual for all parties concerned to pay equal shares. The law provides that this shall be done, but a written understanding between the parties is more satisfactory. Where fences have Government land for boundary the occupier has to erect fences at his own cost.

Settling on the Land.

Having selected the land suitable for his purpose, the handy resourceful man finds ways and means for making wife, family and himself comfortable, which others may fail to see. And the wife and little ones help all along the line. There is not much prospect of a home unless help is given by all interested. A temporary shelter of bark may be set up by stripping black butt, turpentine, stringybark, or other trees. The sheets may be six feet long, and as wide as can be got. Lay them out to flatten with logs or other weights on top; then set the bark upon a sapling

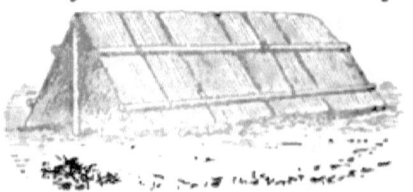

A Primitive Humpy—Bark held by Saplings.

framework (as shown). There has been and is much happiness in such shelters. A great deal can be done, by selecting the location in a suitable spot, for shelter from prevailing winds and the afternoon sun. Convenience for water is another consideration; and it may be possible to set upon a spot where a bit of a garden, if only for pumpkins, melons, beans, potatoes, &c., can be commenced at once. Always avoid land subject to floods. Where corrugated iron can be availed of, a humpy of this kind can be set up in an hour or two. When erected in a shady place—for iron takes fierce heat from the sun—a very tolerable shelter can be made. Trees showing straight bark in the grain from which sheets can be got two feet wide or wider are the best. With a small axe or tomahawk cut into the bark, saw tooth fashion, as shown in the illustration, along the top and bottom. Then make an upward cut to join the two, and gently prize off the bark from the tree, and spread it out for use.

Taking off Bark in Strips.

Tents.—When well set up, and of strong material, a comfortable temporary home can be made in a tent. The erection shown in the illustration is of a good type. The "fly"—an extra sheet stretched over the tent proper, having about a foot of air space between them—is an advantage. It shades the tent from the sun heat, and throws off rain. A coil of good stout rope is amongst the handy things in bush life. All the parts of the tent require to be thoroughly fastened, either to stout forked stakes or to pegs driven

Well-arranged Tent with Fly.

into the ground firmly. A tent loosely set up and without a fly suffers badly in stormy weather.

A More Permanent Erection.—Split stuff is the more solid and durable for permanent buildings. But saplings answer. They should

Badly Arranged—Without Fly.

be as straight as possible, not less than three inches through

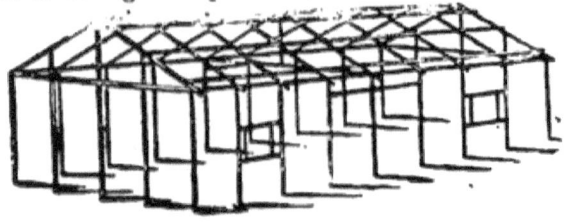
Framework of Saplings.

when the bark is knocked off, or as much thicker as can be managed. The whole framework of the building may be set up

with window and door openings arranged before the covering of bark, iron, shingles, or other material is put on. Saplings of ironbark or red gum are durable, and are not so likely to shrink or warp as other timbers.

Cutting Down and Falling Trees.—The illustration shows how this is done. Close examination should be always made to make sure of the direction in which the tree leans, for in that direction it can be made to fall. Cut the side first upon which it is to fall, then the other.

Cutting Down a Tree. Corner Posts and Window Sills.—It is well to square the timber for the corners (A) and

Corner Post

notch in the sills (B) if possible, as shown in the illustration. The corners are all the better for being of heavy timber, and set well in the ground, say two feet deep, and well rammed. Each corner of the building, whatever size it may be, should be stayed firmly by cross pieces, and every care exercised to have the posts straight; otherwise there will be trouble when the covering is put on.

The Finished Building.—The covering of that shown in the illustration is of bark. The accommodation is five rooms — one large general room and two bedrooms in front, and two rooms in the lean-to behind. The floor is of earth raised six inches above the level of the ground, and rammed solid. But boards are better for flooring.

Cottage of Saplings and Bark.

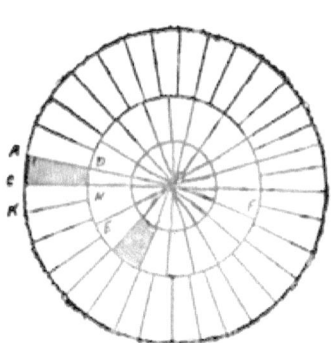

Section of Log for Splitting.

Splitting Timber.—A tree in which the grain of the timber runs straight can be split into thin shingles, palings, posts, rails, or other materials. The illustration shows how this is done by first bursting the log into two or more "flitches" or slabs, and then selecting the parts for the purposes to which they are best suited.

Bursting the Log.—This is the first operation after barking the fallen tree, and sawing it into the lengths required. Wedges (*a* and *b*) are driven into the log along the lines we require.

Bursting a Log.

SETTLING ON THE LAND.

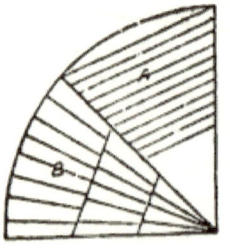

Shingles, Palings, Rails, &c.

Slabs, Shingles, Palings, Rails.—The illustration shows how the different parts of the log from the outside to the inside are brought into use by splitting for the different purposes required for fencing, building, and the many requirements of a home for a bush home.

Getting out Shingles.—The stump of the fallen tree (*a*) may make an excellent block for splitting shingles. A heavy forked stick (*b*) is arranged to lie across the stump, and into this fork the shingle block (*c*) is wedged.

Arranged for Shingle Splitting.

The Knife.

Shingle Knife.—This is a heavy wedge-shaped blade of steel (*a*) set into a handle of wood (*b*). The piece cut out for shingles is laid upon the block, as shown in preceding illustration, between a forked piece of heavy timber. The block being thus in position the edge of the knife is laid where required upon the block and a shingle is severed with one blow.

The Maul.—The splitting is helped by making a maul of wood, generally heavy solid hardwood, formed so that it can be worked with comfort and effect.

Maul for Splitting.

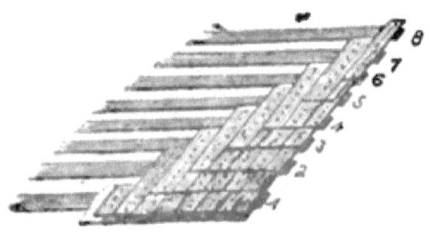

Shingling a Roof.

Laying Shingles.—This operation requires skill and attention to what will result from the manner in which the work is commenced. Battens are nailed down firmly upon the rafters, and to the battens the shingles are nailed. A row of short shingles, say 10 in number, is laid down and upon them a second row (1) usually three inches longer, is laid, so that the joints between the first row are covered right up to the edges. Then a second, third, fourth, and other rows are laid until the ridge or top of the roof is reached. Each row being so laid as to cross the joints of the row under them.

Bed of Bags and Saplings.

Sleeping Places.—There is neither comfort, happiness, nor inclination for work in the bush or anywhere else unless there is comfortable sleeping accommodation. Much sound, healthful sleep has been got with the makeshift arrangement shown. It is simply a couple of flour or other stout bags through which saplings are inserted. The ends of the sapling supports rest on logs, and the sleeper is thus off the ground. The short sapling (a) may answer for a pillow.

A More Elevated Bed. — The couch shown is raised upon forked stakes, which are all the stronger when strips are nailed across at the head and foot to prevent the bed buckling under a

Bags on Forked Stakes.

SETTLING ON THE LAND.

heavy sleeper, and shutting him up like an oyster. Where it can be managed by any available contrivance, sleeping upon the bare ground should be avoided. Strong men may think it all right for a time; but rheumatics and other complaints are contracted in that way.

Home-made Box Chair.

A Box Chair.—This design in furniture explains itself. It is a style brought to scientific development in mining camps. It is said that no end of gold has been planted under such chairs, and that in addition to being comfortable as seats, they offer more difficulty to thievishly inclined visitors than the ordinary burglar-proof safes.

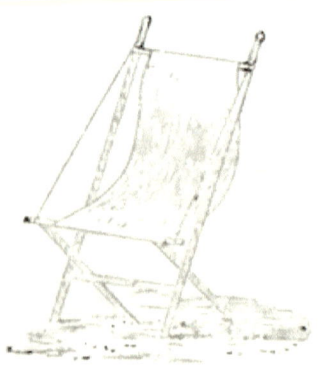

Home-made Verandah Chair.

Verandah Chair.—This is a really comfortable rest for a tired housewife, or the man after his day's work is done, and rest is helpful in preparing for another day. The timbers may be 1¼ by 2½ inches, which is strong enough for any tired mortal under 14 stone. The box seat, a stump, log, or the floor might be safer under heavier weights. Or the design shown, by making the timbers 2 x 3, would be strong enough for ¼ of a ton. Strong canvas, well sewn, is necessary for these chairs. A man with sailor experience is the one to manipulate such canvas.

Tables can be made of boxes, or from slabs, and bark has been made to do duty where nothing more suitable could be got.

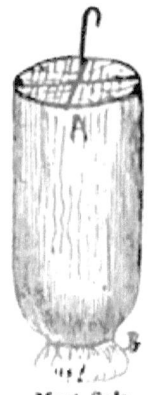

Meat Safe.

Safes for Provisions.—We must have something to keep ants, flies, and other bush visitors from investigating our provisions. Until some more permanent conveniences can be arranged, the makeshift shown in the illustration answers the purpose. At *(a)* and *(b)* are rings of wire, the upper ring being strengthened by two cross pieces, in the centre of which a hook is attached, for hanging the "safe." Mosquito netting or calico answers for covering. Fine wire netting is best of all. The opening below is so arranged that it can be closed by a piece of netting. The arrangement answers for hanging meat.

To Keep Ants from the Sugar.

The next "safe" is more substantial, and when covered with wire netting, is good and effective for a long time. The framework is stiff wire. The entrance *(a)* of mosquito netting, to be drawn or tied when closed.

The Home in Prospective. - Verandah and Fixings to follow.

And all the time, while we are making such materials as can be got, canvas, saplings, bark, iron, answer what is necessary to make temporary shelter, we are looking forward to the house in prospective, which can be made a home in the best sense of the term.

IV.—AGRICULTURAL DRAINING.

To see that the drainage of his land is right is amongst the most important matters the agriculturist has to deal with. It is all important in warm, semi-tropical countries, subject to excessive falls of rain, and to spells of parching drought. In a sentence it might be said that soil to be of its true value to the cultivator should be porous to the depth of from two to four feet, to admit water to filter through it, and with free egress for any surplus rain, so that no water can rest or accumulate in the surface soil, or the subsoil reached by the roots of cultivated crops. When water saturates a soil, its first effect is to expel the air which it contains and the gases which may have been generated in it. But as the water moves along in the soil, as from D to C to A, and into the drain, it is followed by fresh atmospheric air, the oxygen in which at once stimulates into activity important chemical changes, furnishing a fresh supply of food for plants. There are some subsoils naturally porous, and which admit the water to pass downwards and drain off; but the majority of subsoils are tenacious; and in land which abounds in iron, hard cement-like layers are formed. These layers prevent water and the roots of plants from penetrating, although there may be rich material below. When rain falls, the shallow surface is soon saturated, and is either washed into ruts or

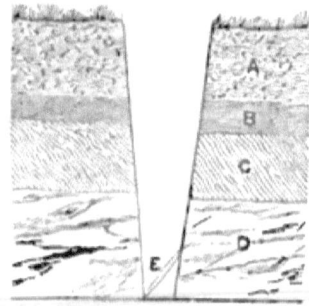

Barren until Drained.

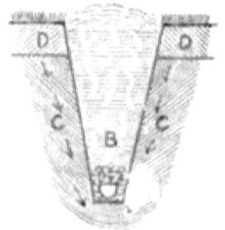

How Soil is Deepened.

it remains wet until evaporation has dried it up, and it becomes hard like brick earth. The effect is destructive to vegetation. Evaporation from the surface is unhealthy for vegetable and animal life. It produces cold, and the land is chilled below the vegetating point. Putrefaction in such a soil takes the place of that more perfect oxidation which brings about the healthy change so needful for healthy cultivation.

The case shown in the first illustration in this chapter is that of a section of what is now a prosperous plantation in the Richmond River district, which was barren until drained. There was a good coating of loam (a), but under it was a layer of clay (b), through which rain water could not pass. Consequently the land suffered badly from frost and during wet and dry spells. Several crops of cane were lost. The surface soil was in a state of mud during wet weather, it baked hard as soon as the water on the surface was evaporated. But the trouble was cured by putting in drains of slabs (e) in 4ft. lengths. They are 3½ft. below the surface. The cost was 6s. 4d. per chain, and the draining converted what was a deceptive, dangerous flat into rich loamy soil.

Draining has developed an immense variety of tools of the spade, or wedge and lever type, to every one of which the features apply of quality and weight and material dealt with in the treatment of spades and digging tools generally. Draining itself has opened out other developments in the science of agriculture. Prior to 1750 it seems to have been scarcely known that water in the soil is only beneficial to agriculture while it is in a state of movement. Stagnant water is known to be injurious to vegetation, to crops, to grasses, and the animals upon or near where the water stagnates. When this fact became evident to the advanced British agriculturist of 100 years ago—and there were some advanced men in those times—open ditches were made to carry off the stagnating water, and during some twenty years open drains and ditches were supposed to answer all the purpose. Then another advance was made by laying stones, wood, &c., in the lower part of the drains, filling in the soil, and cultivating the surface. The effect was surprising. The land about the drains was found to be easier to work, it became warmer in winter, and cooler in summer, and gave much better returns. 1836 saw the first tile drains laid. Pipe drains followed soon after. Now it is known that not only does draining carry off stagnating and undesirable water, but important chemical changes follow, the soil is deepened, and the drained land withstands drought, while undrained land becomes parched and bakes hard as bricks.

Cost of Drains.—In places where considerable quantities of this work are done, drains three feet deep and formed of a single slab covering the lowest six inches (made narrower on purpose) have been put down at a total cost of 5s. per chain; that is 66 feet of drain. The price, then, varies according to the material used and the nature of the land, from 5s. to 12s. per chain. In a big job of 2-inch pipe draining, the cost (men working at 5s. per day and rations) proved to be 9s. 8d per chain. One and 2-inch pipe drains, laid 3ft. deep in stiff, shaley soil at Rookwood, cost 10s. per chain.

Distances and Depth.—As it is in other countries, so it is here, various distances and depths are in favor. Perhaps the most general depth for field crops is three feet. Drains at this depth, and 20 feet apart, make an improvement upon land that becomes more and more marked year after year. But distance and depth in this matter must be regulated by the nature of the soil. Fifteen feet apart is found quite far enough in draining stiff clay soil, while 40 feet apart is found effective in sandy loams. To facilitate the getting together of material for draining, the following calculations may be useful. The pipes referred to are each one foot in length. In slab draining the slabs are commonly four feet long, so that one slab would represent four pipes.

NUMBER OF DRAIN-PIPES REQUIRED PER ACRE.

10 feet apart.	12 feet apart.	15 feet apart.	17 feet apart.	18 feet apart.	20 feet apart.
4356	3630	2904	2562	2420	2178

The cost and weight of pipes vary so much that it would not be safe to quote them. But at present 1½-inch pipes cost from 30s. to 40s. per 1000; pipes of that size weigh about 2lbs. per foot, other sizes of pipes, ordinarily made, are 2-inch, 3-inch, 5 and 6-inch, the cost of which is in proportion to the size. Pipes from 3 inches and larger are used for taking the drainage from the smaller or feeding drains.

Levels for Draining.—Steep hillsides may be as much in need of effective drainage as more level land; even more so, as soil is most likely to be washed from the steeper land. Where possible, levels of the whole place should be taken; but the ordinary spirit level and a length of straight-edged batten may do duty for ordinary draining, and so well is the work done that capable drainers can open a pipe track 6ft. deep, 4in. at bottom, and 22in. at top, and lay in the pipes without a speck of loose earth about them, until the work is ready for filling in. Drainage can be done at any time of the year, but as a rule the quickest effects are noticed in summer.

Materials for Draining.—Porous drain pipes, stones, slabs of hardwood, or saplings, and various other materials are used for draining. It is a good plan to look about before commencing such work, and see what can be used for the purpose. Stone, or rubble, drains are very effective and durable, and in some places land could be improved immensely by gathering stones, which are a nuisance on the surface, and make them do valuable work as draining material. Slabs of hardwood make excellent drains, and tee-tree saplings, laid so that a passage under them is secured, are effective. Short lengths of tee-tree, so laid that the butt of each may rest on the end of the piece above, answer very well for "weeping drains." In our stiff, clay soils, when once a drain is opened, the opening seldom closes up. Drain pipes require less soil moving than other material, and may be the least costly of all. The leading principle of all drains is alike,

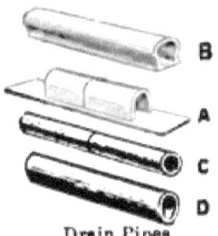
Drain Pipes.

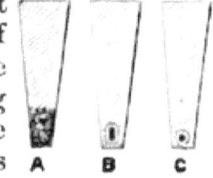
Agricultural Drains Filled In.

AGRICULTURAL DRAINING. 45

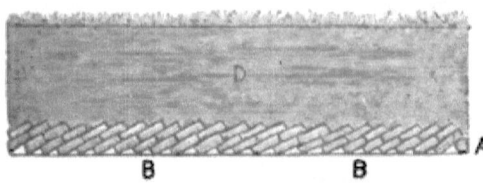

Branch or "Weeping Drain" of Tee-tree.

that is, they should be so arranged, and the material into and from which the water is to pass should be so laid that water can enter from below and from both sides freely. The depth at which drains can act most effectively depends upon the nature of the soil and the character of the cultivation. Two and a-half feet is the most shallow limit for field crops; three and a-half for orchards.

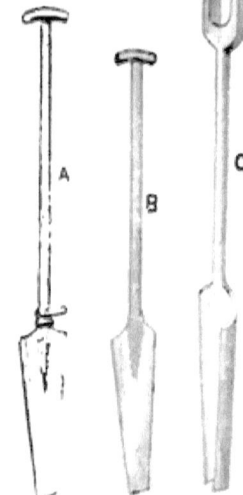

Deepening Spades for Draining.

Draining Tools.—If but a small area is to be drained, suitable tools make the work less expensive. For big jobs the best kind of tools soon pay for themselves. They are not costly. The requirements are a steel spade and mattock, deepening and clearing spades (A. B. C.), a scoop, and a hook for layin pipes when they are used.

Where much work has to be done, a draining plough may be an advantage. The revolving coulters cut the edges, 5 or more inches deep, the soil being raised by the mould board and deposited at the side, thus making the first opening. Draining tools are then used for getting to the required depth. Not an inch more soil need be moved

Draining or Ditching Plough.

than is absolutely necessary at either top or bottom, and in filling up, the poorer soil should be nearest the drain material, and tramped firmly on top, so as to make the effects of drainage as deep as possible, by the water entering from under.

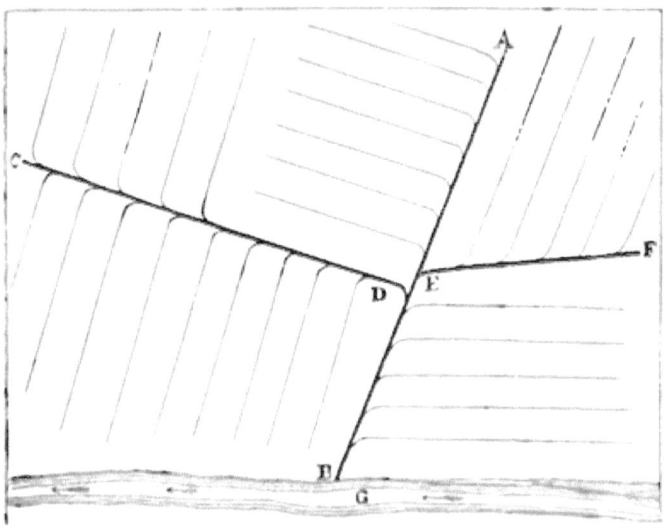

Draining Hill and Valley Land.

The case illustrated shows how leader drains (*a*) (*c*) (*d*) (*e*) (*f*) are laid down in the lowest parts, to get an outlet at (*b*), into a gully or natural water course. Between (*b*) and (*d*) the pipes are 3 inch inside measurement, and from this leader drain from (*c*) to (*d*), (*e*) to (*f*), (*e*) to (*a*), 2-inch pipes. The feeder pipes are 1½ inch bore. As soon as the pipes are down, commencing at the lower side through all the work, the soil is filled in, the drainers treading the soil over the pipes as they fill in, and are careful that no soil gets into the last pipe laid.

Open Ditches and Covered-in Drains.—The effects of cutting even a ditch through a piece of such land as described are very great. Reeds and coarse grasses give place to finer qualities, and what may have been a source of danger from sickness, or a useless swamp in wet weather becomes healthy, valuable cultivation land in all weathers, and especially valuable in dry spells. When underground draining is adopted, the improvement is very marked. On cultivated land and grass land also in warm climates we see satisfactory results follow this kind of improvement. It not only tends to make the soil workable and capable of bearing crops and sweet grass during wet seasons, but in dry seasons the drained land holds out better than undrained land of the same character, a change due to the powers of drained land to absorb moisture from the damper subsoil below, by the force of capillary attraction. Experience has proved that soils gorged with water cannot perfect crops; that excess of water is a hindrance to the due mechanical action of the soil; that it diminishes or checks the power of all kinds of manures; that it lowers the temperature of the mass of the soil; that it precludes the free entrance and exchange of air, without which plants cannot live or their life processes go on; that it prevents the free descent of rain through the soil. These amongst other truisms concerning drainage are even more effective in warm than in colder climates.

Cropping Unhealthy Soil.—When gardening is attempted in soil which is not sufficiently open to allow the roots to penetrate freely, the orchard dies off; no pruning or dressing can keep the trees alive. The systematic analyses carried out in the Technical College, Sydney, show plainly how the unoxidised iron in the soil has done very serious injury. In hot and dry seasons the water evaporates from the surface, baking yet harder the subsoil and chilling the land. Oxidation is but imperfectly carried out, and, despite the application of manure, vegetation languishes. Draining suddenly changes all this, and brings the soil into a condition to render a grateful return for the care of the agriculturist. The reason for the change brought about by draining becomes very evident in a warm climate, and especially where iron is abundant in the soil. During moderately moist seasons trees and crops may do fairly well. Both develop in the soil, gathering what may be available for them in it, to a depth of three feet, possibly deeper under favourable conditions. Then a wet spell follows. The roots become surrounded by stagnating water, are gorged by the unhealthy material about them. They sicken and die, the first direct indication to the owner being the unhealthy look of his trees or crops. This state of things occurs on hill sides as surely as on more level lands. Indeed the case of hill sides is the worst. For, in addition to the drowning of roots and development of unhealthy stuff in the subsoil, the best of the surface matter may be washed away and lost.

CHAPTER V.—MECHANICS OF AGRICULTURE.

Before entering upon the work of crop making, it may be well for us to look still more closely into the nature of the mechanical appliances available for our operations. Agriculture has advanced in two very distinct lines during the hundred and fifty years since the science emerged from the long dark period during which the cultivator of the soil was the drudge of the time, whose main efforts were dependent upon his own manual strength. Those two lines are chemistry and mechanics. The former has

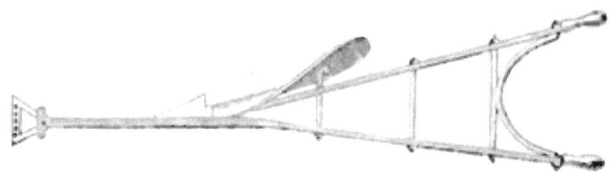

The Plough—Wedge, Screw, and Lever.

done much for agriculture, tending as it has, directly and in the most effectively practical manner, to make clear and plain what, prior to the days of agricultural chemistry, were dark, doubtful, or mysterious. This branch of chemistry, fortunately for agriculture, has been fostered and encouraged by public as well as by the individual efforts of the many grand and noble men who employed their talents in that direction during late years. And in the various schools opened for agricultural instruction, chemistry has been recognised as a leading principle, and due attention has been paid to it.

But mechanics, as applied to agriculture, have not fared so well. With the exception of the American agricultural schools, and notably those of New York, California and Illinois, comparatively little has been done for educating the farmer in agricultural mechanics. And the impression has gone abroad that while mechanics and engineering have done so much for the industries generally, agriculture is far behind in that respect. The supposition is not correct. As we shall see while investigating and illustrating this department of agriculture, the aid afforded by mechanical engineering is nothing short of wonderful. And it will be seen further that the skilled agriculturist of the present day has to be, of necessity, an efficient mechanic. The tendency of all agriculture is in that direction very decidedly, and towards further advancement. And there is still ample scope for improvement.

So far, the developments of agricultural mechanics are due very largely to private effort, and to the pushing business tact of the many individuals and firms who have made specialties of the agricultural tools and machines manufactured and brought into notice by them. Progress of that kind is not without its advantages; hence, every credit is due to those who have been the direct means of many of the immense advances made in the form and quality of farming tools and machines generally. But the process has its disadvantages. It has led to the palming off upon the classes who cultivate the soil of immense numbers of machines and contrivances which actual work prove to be absolutely unsuitable for the purposes for which they were recommended and pushed into notice. Worry, loss of time and money, and disappointment follow the purchase of bad and unsuitable tools and machines. But, in spite of all drawbacks, the agriculturist has now the choice of tools and machines equal to the best seen in other countries. The author's object then in drawing attention to the foregoing facts is twofold: First, in order to show the effective services already extended to agriculture by mechanical developments in the form and quality of the tools and machines in use. Secondly, to show further that mechanical skill is absolutely necessary to the agriculturist of every degree, that he may be able, from his own knowledge, to decide whether an implement offered him is suitable in a practical way for the work to be done; that he may be able to use his implements to the best advantage, and to make such repairs, alterations, or improvements upon them as may become necessary. It has been a boon to agriculture that implement makers and others have done so much; it is still better when the agriculturist himself is a skilled mechanic—the two divisions are combined in the one man with great advantage.

The Royal Agricultural Society of England and the Highland Society of Scotland have done much for the development of agricultural mechanics and engineering. Those societies offered prizes not only for such machines as were coming into use, but gave special prizes for doing special work, and by this means many very desirable improvements have been introduced. Other societies, in Australia as well as in other places, have followed in the wake of the great institutions of the mother land; but the latter have always been prominent, a circumstance due largely to the exceptional ability of the men the Royal and Highland Societies were able to secure as experts and judges. The most notable case of this kind in Australia, as yet, was the very handsome offer of the Government of South Australia for the invention of a harvesting machine that would reap the grain, thresh, winnow, and bag it, all in the field. The author had the privilege of seeing that trial, and, although none of the machines submitted came up to the requirements of the case, he was much taken with the very great skill and enterprise made manifest by the competition. South Australia is peculiarly adapted for wheat farming on an immense scale, and upon a system in which mechanical engineering is all important. The only parallel to South Australia is seen in parts of California and in Colorado. The South Australian wheat soils, with but rare exceptions, are very light. The soil is loose in nature, and very rich in lime. It overlies immense beds of limestone. By the aid of gang ploughs—a series of two or more light plough bodies in a frame—the soil is turned over four or five inches deep, each furrow being from 8in.

to 10in. wide, a team, with two men and four to six horses, going over from four to ten or more acres daily. Seed is at once sown by centrifugal seed sowing machines—the first of which were brought to Australia by the author—doing from 50 to 100 acres daily, and in very excellent style. The crops grown are light in quantity, from six to ten bushels per acre being about the average. The harvesting is done by stripping machines, reaping 200 to 400 bushels daily. The grain is threshed winnowed, and bagged in the field by different machines. Altogether the system is peculiar, and would not be rated as high-class farming in either Europe or America. But it is adapted to the light, open treeless lands of South Australia and sections of Victoria and New South Wales, and the skilled agriculturist is careful in securing the tools best adapted for the work he has to do. The results per man, that is, the number of bushels produced per man and horse engaged, are not low by any means. The whole process offers excellent illustration of what mechanical aids are doing for wheat farming. It is very safe to say that, without their peculiar ploughs, their seed sowers, and their harvesting appliances, it could not pay, possibly, to reap 10 bushels of wheat per acre. But by the South Australian system six bushels pay. The author has not a doubt that, with further mechanical aids for ploughing deeper, and as manuring or pasturing enters into their system, much larger returns will be got for the same outlay.

The principles of agricultural mechanics are identical with the science of mechanics. The lever, wedge and screw have all their outlets in agricultural engineering, in the same manner precisely as in the other branches of mechanics. In the plough, in seed-sowing machines, in mowers, reapers, hay-cutters, baling presses, and the other machines used in agriculture, the knowledge, the practice, and theory of mechanics is as useful in agriculture as in shipbuilding, railroad engineering, or other branches of the art. In the spade, mattock, pick, trenching, draining, and other tools of that type we have the very first principles of the lever and the wedge. To be effective, to move soil with the least exertion to the worker, and to enable him to get the best results, the tools should not weigh an ounce more than is necessary for the strain put upon them. Quality of material, steel, iron, and wood, and substance where required only, rather than weight and bulk, should guide in the choice of tools of that kind, even more than in those used for horse, steam, or other mechanical power.

Science in the Plough.—The history of improvement in ploughs and ploughing is amongst the curious in agricultural advancement. The implement, as we have it nowadays, is the direct outcome of scientific skill in the mechanics of agriculture. The implement is a lever of the first order. It also acts as a wedge, and when well and proportionately made, is a most effective and scientifically arranged implement. At *a* the draught of horse or bullocks is brought to bear; *b b* are the handles for the hold of the driver; *c* the points of the share and the coulter. When leverage is required at *c* or higher up on the mould board, power applied at *b* is very effective. In good ploughing the implement should run perfectly true in the furrow from the draught at *a* without extra application of force from the ploughman at *b*.

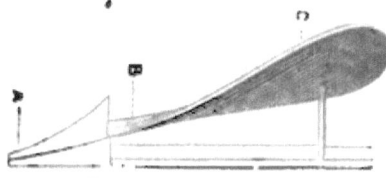

As Wedge and Section of Screw.

The share (*a*) acting as a wedge raises the soil or furrow slice. When *b* is reached the slice of soil is still further raised, and the top is tilted gradually outwards from the surface. When at *c*, the soil is turned over.

Here we see how the soil is turned over, and the principle upon which the share and mouldboard

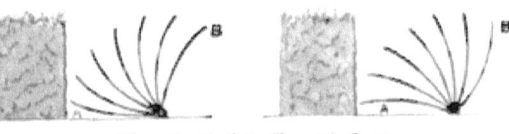

How the Soil is Turned Over.

of the plough do their work. At *a* the soil has reached the mouldboard, and as the implement moves forward the furrow slice is raised and turned gradually, until finally laid against the preceding furrow from the end of the mould-board at b.

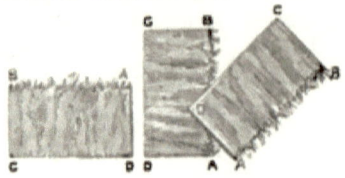

Moving the Soil.

b represents the surface, and the course of movement of the soil until it is turned over is seen in the following sections of the diagram. Next we have the furrows laid up in regular order for the reception of seed or for harrowing down for other crops. When grain is sown it falls into the angles between the furrows and is covered by passing harrows over the land, which smooth down the tops of the furrows. The movement of horses and men over the surface

Section of Regularly Laid Furrow.

tend also to break down the furrows and close up the spaces under them. The covered surface growth is thus converted into manure for nourishing the young roots of the crop. The process shows further how green manuring (the growth of green crops for manure) enriches the land.

By ploughing, we make the soil ready for seed and for plants, and by after ploughing, shallow or deep as may be required, the surface of the soil is kept loose and clean, and in the best state for the growth of crops. The cultivator, scarifier, grubber, and other implements drawn by animals or by steam, are used for cultivating the land by pulverising it, killing weeds, &c.

The plough, then, is a combination of the wedge, screw, and lever, and just in proportion to the skill of the maker in developing those principles in mechanics in the plough, each in the right proportion, and of the right material in the right place for the work to be done, those features go to make the most suitable plough. But different soils require differently arranged implements, whether the work be breaking up new land, ploughing where stumps and roots cannot be got rid of for a time—then the stump-jumping plough of South Australia is a boon—ploughing for ordinary crops, subsoiling, draining, ditching, tank-making, and other operations, for each class of work special adaption of the implement is necessary. And in these days, it is better and cheaper to provide suitable tools than to worry men and horses, and waste time and money trying to get on with tools that are not suitable.

In stump-extracting and tree-falling machines, sometimes termed "forest devils," we have most excellent results from the application of lever power. By a combination of levers and chains, or by the use of the screw, trees and stumps are taken down, or raised out of the ground by one or two men—or horses may be used—these contrivances are able to tear out of the ground stumps, roots, stones, etc., that could not be moved by a 10-horse power engine without the aid of the lever or screw, or hydraulic force.

Seed sowers combine the screw, lever, and centrifugal force in such a manner as to sow, with mathematical regularity, from 50 to 100 acres of wheat daily, one man and a horse doing the work.

Mowing, reaping, binding, stripping, threshing, winnowing, and other machines of that type, are all built upon the recognised mechanical principles followed in other classes of engineering. The rules for quality and suitability of the materials in the machine apply in these with even greater force than in ploughs. Every pound of unnecessary weight, every unnecessary combination or increase of parts all tell against complicated machines of this kind. Steel and iron, now-a-days capable of endless applications in mechanics, are decidedly better than wood in all machines in which jolting, dust, and risks of wear from friction of the parts are combined with very rapid speed. Machines of this kind have been improved immensely since their first introduction in Australia, nineteen years ago, and improvements still go on steadily. The results already are that the white man, with their aid, is able, even in these depressed times for grain, to hold his own in the market in competition with grain from Russia, India, and other cheap labour countries. Draining has developed an immense variety of tools of the spade, or wedge and lever type, to every one of which the features apply of quality and weight of material dealt with in the treatment of spades and digging tools generally. Irrigation is not possible without effective drainage, allowing the water to soak into the soil.

The sugar business is much indebted to engineering. The improvement made, both in the speed of doing the work and the cost of production, is nothing short of wonderful. The quality of the product is also vastly improved. Yet there are many openings for farther advances. The author will mention one only on this occasion—the want of a machine to cut down cane in the field. There is a fortune for the man who perfects a contrivance of that kind. The difficulties in the way are all of the mechanical kind, and they are to be overcome by the man who studies the subject carefully, but it must be in the field, and while the crop is being harvested.

Good Tools the Cheapest Labour.—What mechanical skill, worked out upon scientific lines, is doing for agriculture is very clearly demonstrated in the value of agricultural labour in various parts of the world. Taken as a whole, the American agriculturist and the labour he employs, produces and makes most out of his produce. Possibly, Australia comes next, and the condition is assisted materially by the fact that Australian agriculturists use American machines and implements more generally than is usual in Europe, which comes next in the earnings from agriculture. India, which is amongst the oldest agricultural nations, offers telling illustration that cheap labour is not able to compete with the skilful use of modern machinery. The average labour wages of India is barely 2½d. per day. In America and Australia the average is between 3s. and 6s. per day. The Indian farmer uses the implements of his ancestors, and the product of his labour is worth about 6d. per day, or ½d. per hour, for his working days are long. The American farmer's labour brings in an average of 6½d. per hour. He produces enough wheat to supply the requirements of three hundred people. The actual estimate is that four men, working with modern appliances in the field and the mill, produce enough flour for 1000 people! European farming is away behind in the average per hand produced. In Britain it is but little more than one half of the American average per man, and France is far behind Britain, while Germany, Italy, Scandinavia, Spain, Russia, Egypt, Bulgaria, and Turkey, drop lower and lower in the products won per man from the earth. Turkey and Egypt come almost as low as India. All these nations compete in the great markets of the world, and America and Australia come out on top for the amount of products per man engaged, and the wages paid for agricultural labour. That is, in grain and wool production. But, in dairying, Denmark and Sweden have made rapid steps to the front of late years, and our best efforts are called out in this other special branch of agriculture.

VI.—CULTIVATION OF CROPS.

The Objects in View.—Whatever branch of agriculture we follow, the soil has to be so treated that it may yield the best results from the crops sown or planted. These results are got by maintaining the food materials necessary for building the crop in view; by keeping the soil loose and clean, in the mechanical sense, so that air and rain may do their work in the chemical sense. That means cultivation.

Fruits of Cultivation.

The Means Employed.—Tools and implements suitable for the work to be done are necessary. Suitable and effective tools, of good quality, give us the most efficient and the cheapest kind of labour. No one can do the best without effective tools, and the very best are available for Australian agriculturists.

Hand Tools, Horse Implements.—Hand tools are necessary in all branches; spades, forks, hoes, mattocks, rakes, shovels, barrows, &c. But horse labour is so easily obtained and is so effective, that, so far as practicable, it should be brought into use as speedily and as generally as possible. The chapter on Mechanics of Agriculture, treat this subject more fully.

To Keep up Fertility.—This is dealt with in the chapters on manuring, and the "Reminders" for work in season in the garden, farm and orchard, at all periods of the year. For crops must be fed.

Ploughs and Ploughing.—Many implements have been tried, and many efforts made to do the work of the plough by other means. The times were when the spade was considered a formidable rival, and in the description of work for which the plough was considered best suited. Enthusiastic admirers wrote essays upon "spade culture," and the vast improvement it would confer on mankind. But that time has gone, and for ever, from all but the inner recesses of barbarism, where men are considered of no more value than to compete with horses in turning over the soil. Not that we would speak slightingly of the spade. It is a good implement in good hands; but in many kinds of work the same hands might do much more with a well-made plough, and do it as well—better, as market gardeners near the great city of Europe and America believe. And they have about the best opportunities for judging. In the colonies, the plough is the main implement of culture, and, to the credit of the colonists be it added, not only are the best imported implements of this class popular, but a degree of skill has been brought to bear upon the plough by colonial makers that is highly to their credit. Their efforts have been mainly directed to making ploughs suitable for the nature of the work to be done. We see the result in the heavy colonial plough. This breaking up machine is made for new land, in which it has to cut through roots, &c., to a depth of eight or ten inches. This it does in a way that calls out the admiration of those even who at first look upon the implement as ponderous and unwieldly. The form adopted is similar to that of the ordinary Scotch swing plough. The breast is higher, and runs out in a more cutting edge than ordinary. The coulter is very heavy

D

and sharp, and there is a strong draught bar. The dimensions of the plough as made by M'Lean, Brisbane, are—length of beam from draught-bar, four feet; handles, from end of mould board, seven feet; body, two feet; total length, thirteen feet; from point of share to end of mould board, five feet; the coulter is made of four by one inch iron. Altogether it is a most suitable implement for breaking purposes. Ten bullocks or six horses are used for breaking up land. Four acres per week is fair work. The disc coulter is an improvement for cutting through grass land. In each of the ploughs mentioned, and indeed in cultivating tools generally, modifications are made and introduced for special kinds of work and different conditions of soil. Thus friction wheels (see pp. 61 and 62) are found to lessen the draught in free loamy soil. The double mould-board is used for ridging up potatoes, opening furrows for sugarcane, corn fodder, &c., and is a decided labour-saving implement. Hudson Brothers, of Clyde; Ritchie, of Auburn, and others are notable makers of ploughs, and at the warehouses of Lassetter & Co., James Martin, Martin & Martin, Friend, Wm. Fleming, M'Lean Bros. & Rigg, Gandon, and many others, implements of the best kind can be got for all sorts of soils and the different crops.

Double-furrow, three, four, and six-furrow ploughs are coming into favour, and deservedly so, in the grain-growing districts. With a team of three horses for a double-furrow plough, nine or ten acres weekly can be got through comfortably, and the work is nearly as well done as by the single plough. There is less tramping of horses and a decided saving of labour.

Stump-jumping Ploughs are made for getting through land where there are mallie and other roots, and grass is not an active enemy amongst the cultivation.

The steam plough is found suitable for both old land and for breaking up, and promises to become a powerful aid to semi-tropical farming where large areas are under crop.

CULTIVATION OF CROPS.

Various Styles of Ploughing.—First-class ploughing is seen at times; but, as a rule, the roughest kind of work, passes muster. The regularly laid up furrow, laid on edge, (p. 53) seen in our illustration as prepared for grain sowing, is the style of work most in favour with trained ploughmen. It is the system adopted for their prize matches by the Royal and Highland Agricultural Societies, and by colonial societies generally. The test of merit is—"That the plough cut the sole of the furrow perfectly flat, leave the land side clear and true, lay the furrow slices with uniformity, with perpendicular cut on land side, and leave a roomy horse walk." A usual width of furrow is nine inches in width by six in depth. The slice is laid up at an angle of about 45deg.; this exposes a large surface to the action of the air, and is found suitable in old cultivated land, and for soils of uniform richness to the depth stated. On the whole, it is the system best adapted for grain crops where the seed is broadcasted.

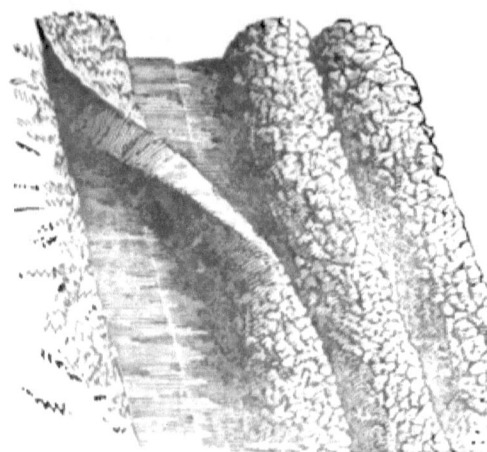

Inverted Furrow, Australian Ploughing.

The crested or peaked furrow is much in use in Scotland, and also in the grain-growing sections of the colonies where stiff soils, or those with more than the average proportion of strong vegetable matter prevails. The peak of the furrow exposes still more soil to the action of the air, and by dipping the share downwards at the land side a depth of seven or eight inches is made at that point.

The inverted furrow is a favorite colonial style of ploughing, and answers very well where the land is not too dirty. On thin open soils the extra wide furrow is, perhaps, the best for general purposes. The rich mould is retained on the surface, and depth can be obtained by running a subsoil plough or grubber in the furrow immediately after the plough. Enormous crops of potatoes are grown in rich sod-land by adopting this plan. The furrows may be drawn 10 x 3, 11 x 4, or 14 x 6 inches. The mould-board must be wide and short for this work, and the ground is gone over very rapidly; one and a-half acre per day being nothing unusual for a good man with team. The furrow is turned completely bottom up, and the thick growth of weeds common on rich semi-tropical soils, are buried and soon rot. Nothing short of inversion will serve them, as their vitality is strong, and they will live again if anything like a chance is allowed them.

A Day's Work Ploughing.—While cutting a furrow 9in. wide the ploughman walks about 11 miles while he is turning over an acre—a fair day's work. That is, without reckoning the journey from the stable to the field and back again. It is one of the advantages of long furrows that the time occupied in turning at the ends is so much less than on shorter stretches. This is worth keeping in view when laying out land for cultivation. In ploughing an acre 352yd. long, cutting a 9in. furrow, the plough goes 27½ times round, and turns on the headland 55 times. If we allow 1 min. for turning, the time thus occupied is equal to 55 min, or say an hour's work—the hardest of the day, too. This would be in a paddock or field of average length, some 16 chains long. The plough pace, to do good steady work varies from 1½ to 2 miles per hour. Applying these figures to the 11 miles walked in ploughing an acre at the rate of 1½ miles an hour, takes 7¼ hours. With a 10in. furrow there is one mile less of walking, which may be reckoned as half an hour to three quarters, according to the estimate of travelling pace. With a 10in. furrow on light land, where the furrows are 352yd. long, from six to seven hours are occupied per acre, at the ordinary pace of two miles per hour. Thus, in making short furrows, with plough, cultivator, or other implement, a great amount of extra work becomes necessary, and time is lost in turning.

CULTIVATION OF CROPS.

So an acre may require eight or nine hours. Ploughs cutting a double furrow, or three, four, or more furrows at the same time may be estimated on the same lines.

Points in Ploughing.—Ploughs with one or two wheels are the easiest for the inexperienced, and practice, with the advantages of a good steady team, and an implement suitable for the soil, with the further advantages of being acquainted with the principles upon which the machine does its work, are all effective in training for this kind of labor. The plough body and beam should be upright in the furrow while at work. The wheels are for regulating the width and depth, and for turning the plough round at each end of the furrow.

Wheel Plough—British Style.

The small, or land wheel, runs on the surface of the ground, and the higher it is drawn up, the deeper the plough will work. The large or furrow wheel runs in the preceding furrow, level with the bottom of the plough, and regulates the width of the furrow slice. The plough should come out of each furrow easily at the end, by a little pressure on the handles whilst the horses are moving forwards. The plough should not be lifted or carried round at the end of the work, but must follow the horses or draught power, and should be turned on the large, not on the small wheel. A little practice soon enables this to be done easily. The draught chain at the head should be set so that the plough will run straight forward in work, and the best point will soon be found by trying it in the different positions from the centre either to the right or left. It can also be raised or lowered for hard or soft land. Two horses or six bullocks are found sufficient for ordinary work. Yoke them in pairs. In dry soil the animals should be further from the plough than in loose or soft soil. Steel breasts or mould-boards are better than iron for stiff soil. The share should have more or less inclination downwards at the point in proportion to the hardness or softness of the soil. Stiff soils require sharp keen shares; half-worn shares may be kept for softer soil. Strong sharp coulters are necessary to cut through the strong, matted grasses of warm climates. In heavy grass land the coulter should have a decided slope forwards

American Style of Plough.

at the point; in clean land it may be almost straight down from the beam. The point of the coulter should just clear the share, and always cut in a straight line with the sole.

American Ploughs.—They are shorter than those described, and do good work. The coulter is not common in America. A gain of draught by dispensing with the coulter of 15·6 per cent., American makers say, is got by ploughs designed with sharp cutting edge on the body.

Chilled Shares.—On stony and sandy soils the share of the plough wears away very quickly, and time is lost in taking it off for relaying, sharpening, &c. The chilled share is an advantage in modern implements. The share being chilled, or made harder on the under side than it is on the upper, the metal wears sharp until the share is worn out.

Chilled Share.

Subsoil Ploughing.—The value of subsoiling by means of the plough—of giving as great a depth as possible to land under cultivation without bringing the poorer, raw soil to the surface—cannot be overrated in a warm climate. The work is effectively done with the subsoil plough, many forms of which are made, for one, two, three, and four horses. We prefer the single horse implement. It is light, handy, and breaks the soil from 4 to 7 inches deep. (*a*) is the sole of the subsoiler, (*b*) the standard for cutting; (*d*) is a nut for holding the standard. When run in the furrow after a plough turning out a slice

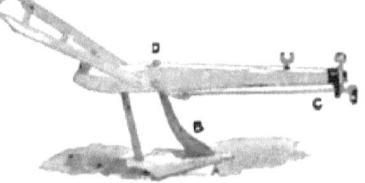
Subsoil Plough.

6 inches deep (see p. 59), a total depth of from 10 to 12 inches is obtained at the lowest cost of labor. Subsoiling may follow draining. Water allowed to lodge under in a shallow furrow converts the subsoil into a sour mud that is destructive to every root that comes into contact with it. With combined drainage and subsoiling, we have the means of growing crops at all seasons, whether they be very dry or very wet, or the happy medium between the two.

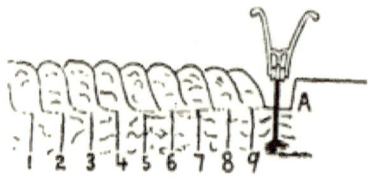

Subsoiler at Work.

Implements for Surface Cultivation.—The plough may do wonders in the hands of a man who knows how to use it. There are those among us who do all the labour of cultivation with the plough and harrow, and do it well. But these are exceptional cases, and even in them it is questionable whether there would not be saving of time and labour, and money as a consequence, by the use of other implements. It is in this direction that the colonial farmer has to look for a solution of the labour difficulty that cramps his energies. In dry weather, while it is desirable to keep all the moisture possible in the soil, the grubber is of peculiar value. With it the soil can be loosened to the required depth, and prepared for seed without turning it over, and consequent exposure to the air. This is becoming common practice in preparing land for wheat in the Riverina district, and in other parts where the soil is sandy and inclined to be dry.

Plough Cultivator.

Surface-stirring.—This is a most important branch of the cultivator's art—especially important in hot countries. In warm, moist weather grasses and weeds spring into shape, and flourish with a degree of vigour that surprises European farmers, and they are no novices in the warfare with weeds. This growth has to be checked promptly for two reasons: First, weeds cannot exist without injuring the crop; second unless they are destroyed at once they become too powerful for ordinary treatment, and often cost more than the crop is worth. It is exhausting work for hand labor, this necessary destruction of weeds. We are free to confess to a feeling of pain whenever we see a man trying to cultivate with a hoe or a hand-tool where a horse implement would answer as well; it is neither healthful nor profitable in this climate. The man who attempts to farm by such means works with heavy odds against his health and his success. It is very up-hill work to attempt anything in the way of cultivation more extensive than home gardening without the aid of horse labor.

Expanding Cultivator.

Cultivators are made for one or two horses, and are in high favour for stirring the surface soil between cane, corn and other crops in rows, and for garden and orchard cultivation.

Harrows and Harrowing.—Of late years, and in warm climates especially, much attention has been bestowed upon the harrow as an effective and a labor-saving implement. The work of the harrow is almost identical with that expected from the gardener's rake: it breaks or smooths down the rough places, prepares soil for seed, and rakes in

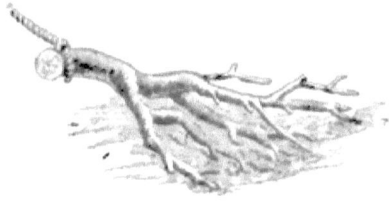
Make-shift Harrow.

and covers the seed. For fining the surface of the soil, the harrow is one of the very best implements we have, and with the large number of different kinds for choice, we can select an implement adapted to almost any kind of soil. Amongst the more generally used are the zig-zag, disc, and pulveriser. The back-tooth harrow is a good implement. In it the teeth have a slope backwards, and do not clog with grass, &c.

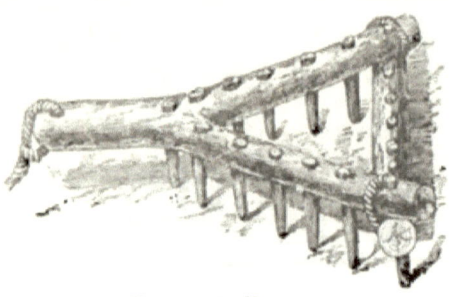

Home-made Harrow.

Bury the Weeds, or Rot Them in the Manure Heap.—Numberless analyses of Australian soils, made with the special object of tracing the changes going on, afford evidence of the need of saving all the vegetable matter we can. *In all the analyses made not a single soil has been found which has, or ever appears to have had, any vegetable matter in it that could be burned with advantage to the soil.* Grass-burning in pastoral districts has been a fearful cause of destruction on the grazing lands; and stubble-burning has been only the less destructive on farming land by reason of the smaller quantity burned. If exception could be made to these terribly suggestive facts it might be found in the extraordinarily rich grazing soil from near Coopernook, Manning River, heavy soil from near Gunnedah, Namoi River, and rich volcanic and limestone loam from Tumut Plains. Each of these is rich in vegetable matter; upon that the fertility of the soil is dependent; and after testing them closely for their capacity to absorb rain-water, and to hold

The Acme Pulveriser.

moisture in suspension during dry weather—for each of which qualities they stand in the very first rank—it is seen that even they have no vegetable matter that could be spared for burning without injury to the fertility of the soil. The conclusion, then, is inevitable, that where burning can be avoided it should be by every possible means.

Skill in Harrowing.—When going over land for the first time, we may harrow the same way as the land was ploughed, after which it does good work to proceed as follows: Start at corner No. 1 and go *straight* to corner No. 2 diagonally across the field, going back to No. 3, from 3 to 4, 4 to 5, and 5 to 6. Keep right on, and when the field is done it will be harrowed over twice, and every mark will be diagonal across the field, which is just as it should be, whether we mark for corn, use the check-row planter, or drill in seed. We will thus finish at (*a*) (*a*). A stiff piece of sod cannot be harrowed properly without going diagonally across the furrows, and we have only to turn half round at the corners. The team need hardly be stopped at all. In a field of fifteen acres possibly one-third more can be done in a day than by taking one-half of the field, harrowing it diagonally, and then the other half. The work is made easier for the horses also. They first travel on ground that has been gone over once; after a short

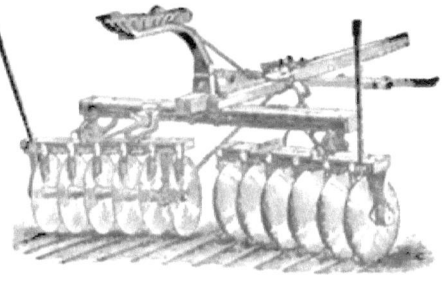

Disc Cultivating Harrow.

time they will be on where it has been harrowed twice, which makes it easier.

The Essence of Cultivation.—It is to keep the soil clean and loose, that the roots, whether grass, field, or garden crops, may grow amongst it and feed in all directions. With practice and skill the best results are got with the least labor, and the soil is maintained in perfect cultivation. To get this result, the soil must be prepared in thoroughly fine condition before sowing or planting. Then to keep the soil in good, loose tilth until the crop is past all danger from weeds, which are much more easily destroyed when young than when they get a start to grow. The soil prepared before planting the seed is in a majority of cases in that condition that the harrow is found the cheapest and best implement for doing the necessary work.

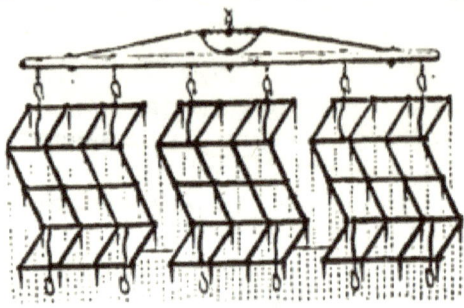
Perfect Cultivation.

For Rolling Land.—The roller is an effective cultivating help. It may be of iron, hollow, and filled with water, where weight is necessary. But a well-rounded log of hard wood, cut in two or more sections, with a spindle passing through, makes a good roller.

The Roller for Cultivation

Mechanical Condition of the Soil.—In all the operations of cultivation, we must see to the mechanical state of the soil—whether it is stiff, or what is called clayey; or loose, or sandy, or gravely or stony; whether it is rich in vegetable or organic matter; or whether there is but a small proportion of this substance in it. All these conditions, as we have seen, are influenced by the mechanical state, not of the surface only, but of the subsoil as well, to as great depth as roots penetrate, or even to still greater depth. A leading object of soil cultivation is to maintain it in such condition that rain and air can penetrate freely; that as small quantity as possible of rain water may run over the surface. It is, in reality, as necessary to have the soil in a workable mechanical state as to have sufficient and the right sort of plant food for the crops we are endeavouring to make. To understand these conditions, and to help in bringing the soil into the state that roots can develop and feed most effectively. is amongst the most valuable experiences of agricultural knowledge. For instance, we may have a soil containing such a proportion of clay matter or clayey substances that during wet weather it becomes plastic or sticky like clay, and which, in dry weather, may become hard, like brick material, and quite unfit for working. Or, going to the other extreme, we may have such a heavy proportion of sand in a soil that, during dry weather, it becomes a loose heap of sand grains which will throw off rain, and yet absorbs the sun heat so freely that the roots of plants, and even the plants above ground are scorched and burned. Both these conditions are mechanical, and the skill of agriculture comes into action in making the best use of the conditions which have to be dealt with. The stiff soil, though the most likely, by far, to be rich in plant food, is the more difficult for treatment in this climate. Where heavy frost would swell and break up the clayey mass, we would plough up such soil rough in autumn, possibly while the land was soggy wet, and allow the frost of winter to "cure and sweeten" it. But where there is no frost, the treatment is different. Heavy liming would, unless it were already fully supplied (not a likely condition in Australia) come into the first course of treatment. Then surface, rooting crops, like maize, sorghum, etc., or such fruit as apples or pears would be suitable. Our object being in all the methods of treatment followed, to keep the soil open- that air and rain may penetrate, and that the roots of crops may spread and find what they require. Unless this latter condition exists, neither rich grass, nor trees, nor field crops, nor vegetables can prosper, and the good qualities of manure are lost. With sandy soil, after breaking it loose by plough, fork, hoe, or other implements to the depth required, our object is to retain as much moisture as possible in it. This is done in the most effective manner, as the case is in all soils, by seeing that the drainage is effective to the depth required. That being right, we keep the immediate surface loose, but the soil below in a more compact state than the others. And to prevent overheating of the surface, well rotted vegetable matter, bush scrapings, leaf mould, etc., make very helpful manure dressings. All soils are influenced by the conditions stated, and are aided further, both in the mechanical and chemical sense, by using manures in comparatively fresh state in the stiffer soils, and well rotted in the more sandy. In the latter, lime is best supplied as bone dust, over one half of which is lime. Capillary action, sending up moisture from the subsoils—which seldom dry up entirely under well cultivated land—is quickened by the foregoing conditions of soil and cultivation.

Commencing with Horse Labour.—Numbers of horses are spoiled by being put to harder work than they are fit for at first. Putting horses to stiff ploughing as a commencement for what is expected from them is a common cause of trouble. Rather let them do lighter work for the first few days. See that the collars fit well, that they do not gall. Loose collars are frequent cause of sore shoulders. Sponge the shoulders night and morning with a strong tea made from wattle or iron bark until they get hardened. It repays the trouble in added comfort to plough horses to change the team or rest them at midday, in the shade if possible. It is like taking off your hat when you come in tired and heated by work. When a gall does arise, bathe it at least three times a day with cold water, and then kerosene. If possible let the animal rest until the spot is healed, but by all means try to relieve the sore place by winding cloth around the collar to ease off the pressure. Do not hurry too much. Let the horses take their own natural pace as nearly as good work will allow, and they will not need to rest so often, and will leave the field fresher than if hurried along. For many kinds of work it is better to use two light than one heavy horse. In marking out ground for corn or potatoes, one horse is not so easy to drive in a straight line as two. But when a single horse is used he goes straighter and better when going slowly. A horse that is jerked and yelled at becomes nervous and does not know what is required. Give a horse a loose rein when he is at work. He cannot use his full strength if his head is drawn up with a tight rein.

VII.—GRAIN CROPS.

SEED PER ACRE.—Calculated for average good land in a fair state for the reception of seed. But prepare land and sow early. A sown crop is safest. Rain stops sowing, but makes crops grow. Poor land requires most seed. Thin sowing gives best crops to good farming.

	Bushels.
Corn for grain	1
Corn for fodder or ensilage	2 to 3
Wheat, broadcast	1½ to 2
Wheat, in drills	½ to 1
Barley, broadcast	2 to 3
Barley, in drills	1¾ to 2
Oats	2 to 3
Buckwheat	1 to 1¼
Sorghums and Millets, broadcast	½ to ¾
Grass, lawn	2 to 3
Grass, orchard	2 to 3
Rye, broadcast	1½ to 2
Rye grass	2
Vetches	2 to 3
	Pounds.
Beets and Mangel Wurzel	4 to 6
Cabbage (to be transplanted)	1 to 1½
Carrot	2 to 3
Cucumber, in hills	1 to 2
Clover, red, broadcast	15 to 20
Clover, white, broadcast	12 to 16
Lucerne, broadcast	14 to 20
Lucerne, drilled	8 to 12
Onion, in drills	4 to 5
Parsnip, in drills	4 to 5
Rape, in drills	5 to 8
Radish, in drills	5 to 8
Turnip and Ruta Baga, broadcast	3 to 5
Turnip and Ruta Baga, in drills	2 to 3
	Ozs.
Tobacco	1 to 3

		Quarts.
Beans, pole, in hills, 3½ x 4	... ...	8 to 12
Broom, corn, in hills	... ...	6 to 8
Sorghum, or Chinese sugar cane	... ...	2 to 3
		Cwt
Potatoes, in drills or hills, cut tubers	...	4 to 6
Potatoes, cut in single eyes	... ...	2 to 4

The Grain Crops Available.—All the finer grains—wheat, maize, oats, and barley—are grown extensively, and over a large area of country; and in their production the conditions of good farming that rule in other parts of the world tell equally here. The coarser grains—rye, bere, buckwheat, millet, &c.—are also grown but more as articles of curiosity associated with recollections of other lands, than for food. Rice is a grain differing essentially in the requirements of climate and rainfall from those mentioned. It is a beautiful grain and grows freely in the semi-tropical sections of the coastal country. In cultivating the richer grains, as wheat, maize, and oats, heavy soil, with a proportion of clay, answers best. Deep, clean farming also tells its own unmistakable tale upon each crop; for, although vagaries do occur, it is seldom indeed that slovenly or thoughtless farming secures heavier crops than the sound system and practice which European agriculturists find necessary to secure uniform, good results.

MAIZE, or Indian Corn.—The leading position is given to corn, or maize, as the most valuable grain in semi-tropical countries—the safest as a yielder, and the most certain of grain crops. It is an American product. Columbus found the "Indians" growing maize there; but the quality was much inferior to the "corn" of these times. Unless something very unusual happens during the season, the farmer who sets his mind and his energies to the production of a big crop of maize seldom fails in his object. But there are various ways of making the crop. We must have suitable seed and suitable land; plant at the right time; cultivate as clean and with as little hand labor as possible; protect the grain from vermin out of doors and in; and use or sell it to the best advantage. (See chapter on bread-making, for how to use maize as human food.) The extent of land in Australia suitable for growing maize is very great. Victoria has considerable tracts where good returns are gathered, and the whole of the seaboard country of New South Wales, Queensland, and the Northern Territory, in so far as climate is concerned, is a vast corn area, sufficient to produce grain for millions. The season for planting extends from August to January. In warm, sheltered localities in the Northern districts, corn is planted all the year round, and three distinct crops are gathered, but not from the same land, of course. The usual practice is to sow in August, September, or October, some of the large varieties for a summer crop, which is gathered in January or February; and some of the smaller sorts in December or January for a winter crop, gathered in April. In the cooler districts, but one crop is grown between October and February. Maize changes in character and appearance in different localities; and favorite kinds are found in each district. In reality there are but four or five varieties of maize; and botanists reduce these again to two. We will mention five distinct sorts, in so far as the farmer is concerned, and then proceed to see how they are grown to the best advantage.

Maize.

1. The large, yellow, or whitish corn, with stalks from 9 to 14 feet; cobs from 10 to 15 inches in length. There are many sub-varieties in this family, all of which require from four to five months of tropical weather, with sun heat from 90deg. to 120deg. and rich soil to come to maturity. Under such conditions the yield is from 60 to 120 bushels of shelled corn per acre. (Two bushels in the cob, as a rule make one bushel shelled.)

2. Small yellow or flint corn—very hard grain. Stalks from 5 to 7 feet high; cobs from 6 to 9 inches long. Comes

to maturity, in four months and in cooler locations than the former. Yield about one-third less than No. 1.

3. White corn (Tuscarora). Stalks about 6 feet high; cobs from 5 to 8 inches in length; matures in three months in moderately rich soil. Yield from 30 to 40 bushels per acre.

4. White glazed corn. In habit and size of cob like No. 3. Grain hard, tough, and shrivelled; matures in from 100 to 120 days in temperature ranging between 90deg. and 120deg.

5. Variegated corn—received here with great promise from South America—has not done well.

It can be said with safety that land cannot be too rich nor too "active" for maize. We see the truth of this in the enormous crops grown upon newly cleared scrub land in which, from the density of timber and undergrowth burnt upon the land, the quantity of potash and other active salts is excessive. In such places, by merely scratching in the seed with a hoe—often among half-burnt logs and several inches deep of ashes—crops of from 80 to 120 bushels per acre are gathered. That is cultivation on new land, however, and for but a season or two, while the corn has no weeds to contend with, and is but the first approach to farming. Next to new land, closely cropped sod, freshly turned in, gives the heaviest crops of corn. Then comes regular farming in conjunction with manuring and other crops for rotation, and the yields come in accordance with the richness of the soil and the skill employed.

Preparing Land for Corn.—As much vegetable matter as possible should be retained near the surface; and to effect this, shallow ploughing from three to five inches deep answers very well, and particularly so when a subsoil plough, plough body, or grubber, is run four or five inches deeper in the furrow, immediately after the plough, that merely loosening the under or subsoil.

The Seed.—Much care should be exercised in the selection and care of maize seed. A practice highly recommended is to plant each year a few acres of the most productive land with the most choice seed, and from this select seed for the following year. Selections should be made with reference to both stalk and ear. Good stalks should be from 8ft. to 10ft. in height, with short joints and abundant foliage, bearing the ears at a height of about 4 feet. Good ears should be from 8in. to 10in. in length, and have an uniform diameter to near the tip of about 2½in.; they should be well filled to both ends with from 16 to 20 rows, little space between the rows, and with shanks large enough to support their weight. The kernels should be thick rather than thin, somewhat wedge-shaped, and in length equal to or greater than one-half the diameter of the internal core.

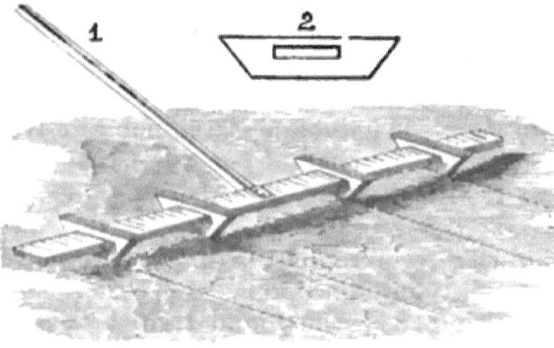

Marker for Corn, Potatoes, &c.

Planting.—There are two established systems of planting corn—in hills, made by taking out a lift of soil with the hoe from 3 to 4½ feet apart each way; in each hole thus made half-a-dozen or more seeds are dropped; from three to six of the plants that come up are allowed to grow, and all the stronger when the hills are well manured. In cultivating by this system the soil is drawn up towards the corn as it advances in growth, thus forming the hills. The plan is the best where the land is new, and encumbered with burnt logs, roots, &c. Hill planting is also managed by running out furrows with the marker or plough from four to five feet apart, then crossing them with furrows about three feet apart. In the checks or corners thus made, where the furrows cross, the corn is planted, and answers very well when a little rich manure meets the roots. The other system is to drill in the seed by machine or hand, and where horse-labor is available, this is the system that enables men to do the most work. Where the land is thoroughly ploughed and smoothed down with the harrow, six acres per day, in rows from 4 to 5½ feet apart can be put in by a man with a one-horse machine, without exposing the soil to a dry atmosphere. In other cases drills are marked and opened with plough or hoe, seed scattered in by hand, and covered with the harrow or hoe, and the crop worked to maturity as in he preceding plan.

Cultivation.—To allow the crop a fair start, it is customary in good farming to harrow just before sowing, "that corn and weeds may have an equal chance," as the saying is." Some farmers go a step further than this, and harrow again after the corn is up above ground. It seems to be rough practice with the ordinary vertical-toothed harrow, as a glance at the form of the teeth will explain; the crop is torn of necessity before the weeds could be got out; but still it is considered better practice than allowing the two to struggle for mastery, and hand-hoeing for corn is out of the question—the crop would not stand the expense. In America the same difficulty was experienced, and to overcome it the smoothing or weeding harrow, with teeth sloping backwards, came into use. As the crop advances the plants are thinned or pulled until they stand 6 to 12 inches apart, according to the strength of the soil, and the cultivation is then carried on to maturity with the harrow, single-horse ploughs, cultivators, or hoes.

Harvesting.—Farmers in the damp, tropical sections where heavy crops are grown, know that it is more difficult to preserve than to grow the grain during the summer season. Whether one, two, or three crops are gathered it the course of the year, the main yield is ripe during the hot months, in January or February, when the weevil, the pest of pests to the grain farmer in warm countries, is very active. But before investigating the proclivities of the weevil, it will be well to follow the cobs from the pulling in the field to the barn. They are shot upon the floor, the grain being thoroughly protected by the wrappers around the cobs. These wrappers are stripped or husked by hand. Any one who has the use of both hands can husk corn, which is merely tearing the wrappers from the cobs; but some operators get wonderfully expert at it. An average day's work of a good hand (and amongst the best hands are active young women) may be taken at about thirty bushels of ears, although over one hundred bushels have been got through at husking matches. The fingers and finger-nails suffer severely while husking; and it is usually done in spells, in the evenings, during the heat of the day, &c. To aid in the work, a glove is made with small hooks at the points of the fingers and at the palm of the hand. This glove helps the worker very much.

Shelling Corn—Maize Fevers.—Very excellent shellers are made in the colonies. Hand, horse, and steam power are employed for operating; and power is very helpful, for the work is hard when done by the hand. The corn should be winnowed or cleaned as effectively as possible, in order to look well when sent to market. While shelling, the fine dust (fungus dust amongst it) from the sheaths of the cobs, is apt to get into the throats of the operators. It is disagreeable, and has caused fevers, by irritation. The most effective preventive is to arrange the work and the shellers so as to blow the dust away from the operator.

Shelling Corn.

WHEAT.—The land available for wheat farming in Australia is enormous. Where the rainfall ranges between 20 and 30 inches, the location is likely to be suitable. South Australia exports this grain largely; Victoria is also a heavy producer; New South Wales grows nearly enough for her own use : and Queensland grows a considerable area. It is a winter crop, the seed being sown during the months of March, April, May; the harvest is in September, October, November. Location and the state of the wea-

Wheat, Oats, Barley.

ther—whether it be dry and unfavorable for ploughing, or dropping and suitable—have much more to do with the getting in of this crop than in Europe. But each district has its favorite time for sowing—say the first or second half of April, or a little earlier or later, as the case may be. There are also favorite varieties in each district, prominent amongst which, for suitability to the climate, are the Tuscans (for quickness and heavy crops in favorable seasons); Talavera and purple straw (favorite with the millers); Lammas (heavy plump grain, but disposed to make too much straw); Fenton (velvet or woolly ear); Bearded wheats from India and Egypt, are also in favor. The Egyptian is specially hardy, and, perhaps, the safest wheat for home use on new land. Much depends upon the climate as to which variety is most suitable, and the safest way to avoid mistakes is to sow the favorite of the neighbourhood until a better is found. Regarding hardiness and freedom from rust (*see chapter on fungus enemies*), the red and bearded varieties are most in favor; but the millers prefer the plumper and whiter grains. All wheats give the heaviest crops from rich, heavy land, and the rule found best with corn—to keep the vegetable matter as near the surface as possible—applies equally well with wheat. It is becoming a customary practice to skim or merely surface plough land that has been under this crop previously, or under grass, at such time as will allow the surface coating to rot before sowing the seed; to harrow roughly twice or thrice, and then sow broadcast at the rate of $1\frac{1}{2}$ to 2 bushels per acre. Thin seeding is much in favor where the land is rich and quick. The smoothing harrow covers this grain especially well. Wheat does not demand a moist seed-bed; but it must be well packed in with the harrow or roller. Drilling has been tried, and with marked success, and, as the land is brought into better tilth, and skilled labor can be easily obtained, drilling promises to take the lead of all other methods of sowing.

Steeping the Seed.—To prevent fungi, it is usual to dress or steep the seed in liquids made up of bluestone, salt and water, lime and salt, manure-water, hot water to 155 degrees, F., &c. The object of all steeps is to destroy the seed of rust, smut, or other fungus that may be clinging to the grain. All the steeps mentioned are useful, and without entering into their respective merits, it may be added that some of them should be used. The grain can either be set into the steep in baskets, or the liquid can be sprinkled over the seed, which is all the better of a dusting with lime or ashes before sowing.

Hand Seed-Sower for Grain, Grass, &c.

A fair steep is made by dissolving in hot water ½lb. bluestone per bag of seed, which takes up about two gallons of water.

Sheep and Wheat.—To bring land into heart that has become too poor for this grain, the Australian farmer has two powerful aids in his sheep and cattle. Grass land eaten down closely (as it generally is in small paddocks about the beginning of the year), when well worked, offers

Broadcast Seed-Sower.

a fine seed-bed, and by feeding lucerne to the stock the land soon regains the strength it has lost. When the yield falls below 10 bushels per acre the land is too poor for wheat.

Science in Wheat Farming.—In a recent lecture to the Liverpool Plains Agricultural Association, the author gave the following particulars of how wheat is built up in the field:—The nature of wheat—of its component parts—had received very close attention at the Technical College, and searching analyses had been made of the different substances it obtains from the soil, and what from the atmosphere. An impression existed that if we had rain there would sure to be good crops of wheat. Such an idea was erroneous. But of course the supply of rain affects the crop in a great measure. Wheat contained water, as hydrogen and oxygen, 45.86 parts in each 100. These are two of the gases that form water, it might be rain or irrigation water. Thus wheat is made up of some 46 parts of moisture. It was necessary to have at least five inches of water, and seven inches would be better, before crops of wheat, of about 35 bushels to the acre, could be raised. Then, from the air, the grain absorbed carbon to the extent of 44·43 parts in each 100. So that altogether from the atmosphere and rain, wheat obtained some 90 parts of its whole bulk. Thus, it was seen how bountiful was nature. Of lime, soda, chlorine, sulphuric acid, magnesia, iron and silica (or sand), other ingredients essential to the growing of wheat, 4 per cent. were absorbed, and there was an abundance of them in the soils of this country. But the other six parts had, after a crop or two was reaped, to be supplied by man unless in very exceptional cases, for the crop exhausted the substances that composed these six parts more quickly than nature provides, as a rule. Nitrogen, or ammonia, must be supplied. Wheat required it in the proportion of 2·6 in the 100. The Gas Company of Sydney were sending away immense quantities of this substance in the form of sulphate of ammonia, which could be purchased in the colony cheaper than in Britain, where thousands of pounds worth were purchased yearly. Wheat got some nitrogen from the atmosphere, but not sufficient to make a paying crop. Then the wheat required of phosphoric acid 1·28 parts, of potash 1·3, of lime ·79. If it were to rain 100 inches each year, not one part of these ingredients would be supplied. And yet, without phosphoric acid and lime, it was an impossibility to get wheat. But bone manures supplied them. He had noticed that some new land of the Namoi Pastoral Company had given a yield of 45 bushels to the acre, and the old land had only yielded 22 bushels. The cause of this was that there were phosphoric acid and lime in the new land, whereas it was reduced considerably in the old. Unless the wheat found these substances in the soil, a large crop was not possible, and the constitution of the grain deteriorated. Deficiencies of plant food in the soil might not be the cause of rust, but there was no doubt that by weakening the plant it became more susceptible to the attacks of the insidious parasite. Wheat was the main food for the white man, because it contained a large amount of bone and muscle making substances; phosphoric acid and lime help materially to make bone. The recommendations made were to use every care in the selection and treatment of seed, and earlier sowing and quicker maturing of the crop, in order to avoid the dangerous time for rust—October and November.

BARLEY.—In Australia, this is both a summer and a winter crop. In the wheat districts it is sown a month or so after that grain—say in June or July. In other places, August is a favorite month for sowing. Many varieties of barley have been tried. The sorts in general cultivation are Early English or common; long-eared or Nottingham; Cape, German, or Pomeranian; Chevalier, the best for malting; Bere, or four-rowed barley. Any good corn land will answer for barley; and soil too poor for the former can, with careful treatment, be made to yield fair crops of barley. It is a deeper rooter, seldom liable to attacks of fungus, and will stand direct manuring; while, for wheat, manure is best applied to a preceding crop or by grazing. Barley will not do with wet at the roots, and is a slow grower and shy bearer upon clay. For malting barley, magnesia is a requirement in the soil, and a heavier rainfall than for wheat is necessary. The land should be drained. Plough as deep as possible, and harrow clean before sowing. Barley, as a crop, follows well after lucerne; it has also done well when sown after sugar-cane, and is a useful rotation crop for either cutting green or for grain where horse feed is grown. It is also a quick, useful catch crop for wild, porous land, intended for ensilage, cane or other summer crops.

BERE.—A variety of barley, and the same treatment answers. It can be sown from April to July. It is an almost certain crop on moderately good, well-drained land.

OATS.—One of our most useful crops. Any soil answers, and rough treatment; oats require more rain than wheat or barley, the yield being in proportion to the richness of the soil and rainfall. When grown for grain, it is a winter crop, sown in April or May, according to location; for hay or green feed, it can be sown as a catch crop from March to August. The varieties in favor are Tartarian, Grey or Angus, Potato, and Indian—the two former for cool districts, the latter for the coast and warmer localities. For hay, as much as four bushels per acre are sown. From a quarter to a half bushel of tares or vetches per acre make an excellent mixture; to the presence of vetches the extra superiority of oaten hay from certain localities is traceable. It has been said that the oat does well with rough treatment. This is owing to the extraordinary strength and searching powers of the roots; but good farming, draining, and manuring, all tell when the crop is harvested. There is a great deal in sowing also, and in acquaintance with the rainfall of the locality. The danger of sowing too thick, and the attendant risk of the crop falling or lodging in wet ground, are especially to be guarded against.

RYE.—This grain is a favorite with the German colonists. Otherwise, rye as a crop is neglected. It makes capital bread, of dark colour; it is also used for poultry and cattle. In the green state it is amongst the best food for sheep, and is worthy of attention where sheep are kept on the farm. Rye is grown under several names—Broad leaf, Midsummer, and Tyrolese; but the varieties run into each other so much that one description will answer. Wheat land answers for rye; as a rule, the cultivation for wheat is suitable. The effects of drilling and after treatment with the harrow are very marked upon this crop, and where it is sown late, say after June, and comes into contact with the summer grasses, after-harrowing should not be neglected. Rye is a good hay crop in wet seasons, when it may be sown as thickly as may be desired (say five bushels per acre). The stiffness of the straw prevents it from lodging, and when half a bushel of tares or vetches are sown with the rye, the mixture is excellent for stock feed, or making ensilage. For grain the same quantity of seed used for oats answers for rye. Drilled in, one and a-half bushel per acre is sufficient. Ergot, a kind of rust to which rye is subject in Europe, has not been noticed here.

BUCKWHEAT.—This, like rye, is one of the neglected crops. Properly speaking, it is not a wheat, but a soft herbacious plant of the botanical order *polygonaceæ*, of which sorrel is a representative. But buckwheat is a heavy seed-bearer (from 30 to 60 bushels per acre with fair culture), and the meal of the seed is of good color, fine, and very wholesome. In various parts of Germany, and in America, it is in high favor for making bread and cakes, which, like rye bread, has the reputation of being easier of digestion than bread made of wheat flour. It contains but little sugar, and is in high repute for the food of sufferers from diabetes disease. Buckwheat is one of the quickest of grain crops, and one of the easiest cultivated, but the soil, to give quick full crops, must be rich in nitrogen and potash. In our climate it is sown, grown, and reaped in ninety days. It can be sown any time from June to December; in warm localities the cooler season is best; in colder locations it may be either grown as a spring crop, sown in July or August, or as an autumn crop, sown at the end of February. The treatment of the soil is similar to that for oats, buckwheat being even better than that crop for fining down rough land. The seed is sown in drills from 14 to 18 inches apart. The author has grown buckwheat on new and not over-rich forest land only once ploughed, and while the grass was green between the furrow laps. One bushel of seed was sown per acre; the returns were nearly thirty bushels of seed and seven loads of straw. In harvesting, the grain is very apt to shell out, and it is well, therefore, to get it into the barn before the seed cases are quite dry. It ripens freely after being cut. This crop is used extensively for green manuring, and is amongst the best for that purpose. It grows on average soils except those that are wet. It is also shy of great sun heat, and perishes from frost.

VIII.—ROOT CROPS, CLEAN CROPS.

THE BASIS OF AGRICULTURE.—Potatoes, turnips, mangolds, beets, and other root croops, in European agriculture, are estimated as the very foundation of perfect farming. We cannot get crops of this kind from either poor land or slovenly work—that is crops that pay. They must be fed, and they must be kept clean; hence the high repute of root crops in skilful agriculture.

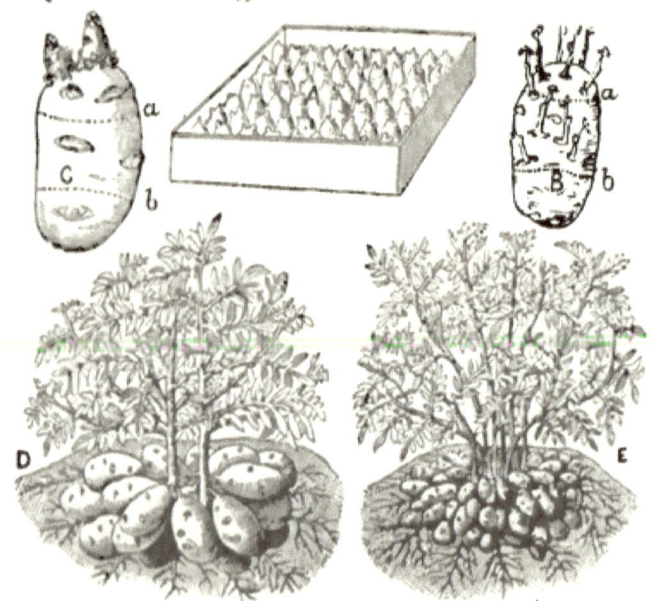

Potatoes—Treating the Seed to Make a Big Crop.

Potatoes.—In this family we recognise the potato proper —the "English potato," as it is misnamed; the Americans call it the "Irish potato," and have much better reason for their choice, although the potato proper is an American product. Then there are sweet potatoes and the large family of yams. The common potato holds the first place in the colonies, as it does in the mother country and America. In the cooler districts of Tasmania and Victoria, and in New South Wales, very fair crops of potatoes are grown, which seem to have found a proper location near such places as Port Fairy and Warrnambool. Crops of from

12 to 15 tons per acre are not uncommon in favourite localities. The quality is very superior. The varieties grown are pink eyes, Brown's River, fluke kidneys, Warrnambools, regents, cups, ash-leaf kidneys, Circular Heads, &c., &c. Many other sorts are described, possibly too many. Care is necessary in experimenting with them. In the warmer districts, the potato is also a favourite, but it is a much more uncertain crop; the weight per acre seldom exceeds six tons, and it is found necessary to change the seed every other season, in some places every season, drawing the supplies of seed from Tasmania and the other southern colonies. Several new varieties—Early Rose, Brownell's Beauty, Snowflake, Ash-leaf, Manhattan, Webster's best, Smith's early, Somner's hundredfold, and others have been tried; but with the exception of Brownell's Beauty and Early Rose, growers have had to fall back upon seed from the cooler latitudes.

Planting Seasons.—There are two decided planting seasons for the potato in Australia; in the cooler districts, June and July are chosen for the first crop, August and September for the latter crop. In the warmer districts, February and March are chosen for a winter crop, July, August, and September for a summer crop. In close, moist situations, a crop is grown during summer, by planting at Christmas time. In other places wet weather is chosen for planting at any season. In other respects, the cultivation suitable to the potato in other countries answers here.

Preparing the Seed.—Either whole potatoes, uncut, or cut, may be used for seed. The illustration (*B*) shows how three cuts, or more, may be made from a well-matured potato of medium size. Large tubers are not so reliable for seed. After being cut, the seed can be started into growth by placing them in layers in a box (*A*), surrounded by dry wood ashes. Two or more layers may be arranged in this way in each box, while the land is being prepared and manured. The seed takes from ten to twenty days before growth starts. They can then be set out in rows from twenty-four to thirty inches apart, and the seed from eight to twelve inches apart in the rows. The advantages of thus preparing the seed are that only those that show signs of growth need be planted, and misses are fewer—an important point in sections or country where potato culture is less certain.

Chemical Soaking of Potato Seed.—A method of soaking seed potatoes in a solution of nitrate of potash and sulphate of ammonia—¼lb. of each in two gallons of water —for 12 to 18 hours, is followed by some growers. The seed, after soaking, is dried with wood ashes and planted. Extra returns are said to follow this treatment; but it is risky.

To Make Sure of a Potato Crop.—The requirements are, loose soil, sufficient rain or irrigation, and the necessary cultivation. The soil must be rich in vegetable matter and potash material. Exhaustion of the latter is the most common cause of the crop falling off, and possibly of disease, but it can be supplied now, from potash manures. Then to help the crop, all the vegetable matter obtainable, all the leaf mould, all the wood ashes, seaweed, &c., should be added to the manure heap prepared specially for potatoes. They well deserve such attention. The case of Ireland may be instanced, where, as well as in other parts of the old land, the potato had become such a victim to fungus disease in years gone past that it was said over and over again that the crop was done. But science and skill came to the aid of the potato growers; and now, heavier and better crops of potatoes than ever are produced—crops up to 15 and 20 tons per acre. We certainly can learn much from the grand old land, and from the splendid men who devote such care and skill to agriculture over there. When studying the careful plodding, with which such magnificent work as the Woburn experiments were carried on, to test the quality of crops for feeding and the manures got by stock under varying conditions, it might well kill the conceit that we have nothing to learn from the old land.

The Sweet Potato.—This is the root crop of the semi-tropical farmer. With care, and certainly at less expense for seed, it yields from 10 to 20 tons of roots per acre, and fully as much green feed. Every part of this crop is available for use; the vines or tops being very valuable feed for dairy stock, for working cattle, pigs, sheep, and horses. Four named varieties are grown—the white, a long almost cylindrical root that grows in bunches from the main plant only (this sort is mealy and rich, and not very sweet); the large red, a globular-shaped sort, with long trailing vines, a rather watery potato; the small red, which forms bunches of small potatoes wherever the vines touch a spot of unoccupied ground (an excellent variety for stock-feeding purposes; it is an enormous bearer); and the "Maltese," with a serated leaf, the vines springing in bunches instead of singly from the main root, as in other varieties (the roots of this sort are mealy, firm, and very rich). All the varieties are planted and cultivated alike. Two methods are followed for raising plants: the first is by planting potatoes in rich, loamy soil over a hotbed, and is peculiarly suitable for colder locations and where it is necessary to carry the seed long distances. Put in the seed potatoes as soon as the cold weather is over—say in August. The vines come up in bunches, which, when about six inches long, can with ease be drawn out from the parent potato and set out. The other method of obtaining plants, and the best for warm districts, for it gives by far the hardiest vines, is to leave a few rows of the old potatoes, vines and all, in and on the ground. These, when covered up from cold and risk of injury, commence to shoot as soon as the weather gets warm. A sprinkle of weak, liquid manure helps them on. As the vines run out and show white points, or "root pens" at the joints, they are cut off in eight or ten inch lengths, and planted out at once. Plants of this kind very seldom fail; but if they or the drawn plants are to be sent to a distance, they ought to be packed in small bundles, wrapped up snugly in paper. The soil for sweet potatoes need not be very rich, but it should be worked as deep and fine as possible, and then laid up in ridges about three feet apart. Flatten off the tops of the ridges, and insert the cuttings or sets about a foot apart. Make holes about three inches deep with the hand, a piece of wood, or garden trowel. Lay in the sets nearly flat, leaving about one-third of each out of the ground. If the soil is dry, pour in about a pint of water to each; then cover with soil, but do not press hard. When the soil is clean and well worked, the plants are not liable to fail. They catch at once, or fail altogether. When right, they commence to throw out side shoots from the trailing vine or hulm. The soil should then be ridged up around them, the ridges being similar to those for common potatoes, but in this case broader and higher. Keep working the soil loose and clean as long as the vines will permit of it, to help the roots travelling in search of food and the tubers to swell. On very light soil there is a danger of the potatoes forming too far down, and being long and thin. To prevent this, pass a scuffle-hoe, or the broad share of a plough under the ridges before finishing the cultivation, the object being to cut the deep roots and force them into forming thick, chunky potatoes. As this crop advances it covers ridge and furrow with a mass of vines from six inches to a foot in thickness. As the crop ripens, the potatoes crack and burst the ridges, and the crowns are often seen in bunches coming up to the surface. At this stage the big ones can be fossicked out with a stick for immediate use, without injuring the growth of their fellows, and the vines can be thinned out or cut off close to the crowns of the potatoes, and used for green feed.

Harvesting Sweet Potatoes.—The crop is dug, forked or ploughed out in the same way as common potatoes. The roots must be handled carefully; they are easily injured. In dry soil they are often left in the ground during winter, and dug as required. They keep well in barrels packed amongst sand or ashes, but they must be kept dry. Without exception this is one of the most valuable crops at the disposal of the semi-tropical farmer, and one that offers a good field for enterprise in preserving this very valuable and always acceptable variety of potato.

Yams.—Various sorts of this tuber are grown; the best are those obtained from the South Sea Islands and from China. They are rough-coated, potato-like tubers, that in favourable soil reach the weight of five to twelve pounds. They are propagated from the crowns of the tubers, and also from seed, not unlike small rough potatoes that grow freely on the vines above ground. All the varieties are climbers; some have beautifully coloured and spiral vines. Plant as soon as the soil heat reaches 60deg. in September or October, in rows about three feet apart each way. Cover the plants with soil, and place a stake from four to six feet high with each. The plants are hardy, shoots appear above ground in 12 to 30 days, and immediately twist around the stakes. The crop is ripe when the vines die back. Yams generally grow deep in the soil. To dig them out two-pronged forks are used. To facilitate the digging attempts have been made to grow yams upon ridges, but the heavy yields are got from flat planting.

Other Root Crops.—Beets and mangolds, or mangel-wurzel, of various sorts, answer well for cropping in the colder districts. They must have the very richest soil, or manure equal to 30 loads or more per acre. Sow in September, 4 to 6 lbs. of seed per acre. Turnips and field carrots also do well, swedes especially; great crops of them are grown as rotation in the Hunter River district. Sow in September, February, March about 3lb. of seed per acre. Other turnips are grown as garden crops. Beets, for sugar, answer in the colder districts. Cultivation much the same as mangolds and swedes.

IX.—SEMI-TROPICAL CROPS.

Maize.—Indian corn is the leading of all semi-tropical products; but in Australia this crop is so general over the the country, that here the making of maize crops is ranked with grains.

Sugar Cane.—In the warmer coastal districts the extent of country suitable for sugar cane, in so far as the climate is concerned, is enormous. It extends from Sydney northwards, along the coast of Queensland, Gulf of Carpentaria, the Northern Territory of South Australia, and probably the north-western coast will also be found

SEMI-TROPICAL CROPS.

to have many places adapted for cane cultivation. The range to which it succeeds inland is not great—seldom further than 30 miles from the sea; the nearer the sea, as a rule, the better the crop, providing always that the land is suitable. Experience has shown that cane likes a moderately, but not too rich, soil; both stiff land and sandy loams answer; it requires perfect drainage, a humid atmosphere, and rainfall of 50 inches or more. Many varieties of cane are grown, and they differ much in hardiness; a few withstand a moderate attack of frost, say a visit of temperature ranging between 30° and 35° during the night for a week or so. The author has grown cane for years in the Sydney district—the hardy Creole variety, brought by him from Louisiana, U.S.A. But even the hardiest canes do best as sugar-yielders when the thermometer keeps above 40° during the winter season. Convenience of communication by water and land is essential towards working cane successfully. It is a heavy crop (ranging between 25 and 60 tons to the acre), and carriage is a serious item.

Sugar Cane.

The Land for Cane.—Soil with over 10 per cent. of vegetable matter is necessary. The land should not be flat, nor very broken. Around the former frosts gather, water lodges about the roots, and artificial drainage is difficult. In the latter, the cost of working is increased in proportion to the difficulty of employing horse-labor, and the soil is washed into ruts by heavy rains. The mode of preparing land for corn is suitable for cane. The ploughing should be deep, 10 inches at least; to reach which heavy colonial ploughs of iron are used, with teams of 10 or 12 bullocks, or 6 horses. Bullocks are best for new land, where roots have to be encountered in the first deep ploughing. After harrowing, rolling, cross-ploughing, &c., until the soil is made fine (absolutely necessary for cane), furrows are run out with ridging or double ploughs. The furrows should be wide—12 inches if possible—and deepened by passing a subsoiler or a grubber through after the plough. These cane furrows are from 5½ to 7ft. apart, according to the strength of the soil (the stronger, the greater distance necessary), and the description of cane to be planted. In new rooty land that cannot be ploughed conveniently, holes are made with pronged hoes, the spade, crowbar, &c. The distance apart of the holes depends upon the strength of the land and the cane to be planted, in the same way as in furrow-planting.

Varieties of Cane.—Some scores of named sorts of cane are known in Australia, but in their nature and qualities they may be reduced to four, viz., those that are stripped, or ribbon canes; Bourbon and yellow canes generally; purple and black canes, which include the Creole; and Scott's cane or Otaheite. The ribbons are the strongest growers, require the richest soil, and come to maturity in from 16 to 20 months from time of planting. They require space varying from 2½ft. by 6ft. to 4ft. by 7ft. for each stole of plants. Yellow and green canes come to maturity earlier than the ribbons, or between 12 and 15 months. They are planted from 1ft. by 5½ft. to 1½ft. by 6ft., according to the soil. The black canes are still earlier than the green varieties, and are planted at about the same distance apart.

Planting.—Cane planting commences with the true hot weather in September, October. Plants are usually made from the top parts of the canes, consisting of four or six of the top joints, the buds or eyes of which are fully developed or perfect. But any part of the cane (with four to six perfect buds) answers for plants. It is all important that the buds are perfect, and that fermentation has not destroyed the sap. To secure both, the cuttings have to be handled carefully, and planted as soon as possible; although they can be carried long distances by excluding the air. In planting the sets, the furrows should be laid carefully from four to six inches below the surface, and covered with from two to four inches of soil. The shoots come up in from 12 to 20 days. If longer, the plants should be examined and replaced, if sour or withered.

The after cultivation is to keep the surface soil loose and clean until the crop shades the land, in say from three to five months. As they arrive at maturity the lower leaves droop and die, and the canes become hard and very sweet.

Harvesting.—When arrived at a fit stage, "trashing," or stripping off the dead leaves, is proceeded with. The plants are then as thick in the rows as they well can be. The top leaves of the tall-growing varieties meet overhead, and at the sides the canes form a wall through which an opening can scarcely be found. Between the rows a man can barely force a passage, while the trash which has collected during the season is piled up in the centre of the rows, and forms a soft mass from 12 to 20 inches deep. Ripe canes should have, at least, four feet (after cutting off the green sappy top) fit for the mill.

Weight of Crop.—Thirty tons of ripe cane to the acre is considered a fair average. With the best machinery, 80 per cent. of juice is obtained from the canes in their best condition; but 70 per cent. is a high return. At that, 25 tons of cane, the juice of which may mark 10° upon Baumé's saccharometer, gives, with the superior manufacture of the present day, nearly $2\frac{1}{2}$ tons of dry sugar from an acre of land.

Tobacco.—This is an old Australian product. Its cultivation is well understood and followed extensively in a few localities. Tobacco, to yield a creditable crop, must have rich soil, close attention, and steady, clean farming. Varieties grown are Havanah, Yarra, Virginia, Florida, Connecticut, Maryland, German or Cabbage Leaf, Turkish, Bird's-eye, &c. A fair average yield is 12cwt. per acre. Sowing is done from early in August until the end of the year, and planting out during September and October for summer crops, and again in January and February for later crops, in accordance with the seasons found to answer best in various localities. The varieties are liable to mix when grown together, by bees and insects hybridising the flowers. Care has, therefore, to be used when a choice and suitable sort is being grown that it is kept well apart from other sorts.

Sowing.—Seed, at the rate of an ounce to the acre, is sown in beds, a good size for which is 3½ feet wide and any desired length. Three and a half feet by twelve feet gives sufficient plants for an acre. For a seed-bed, select a piece of the richest soil, level it and dig it a good spade deep. Then spread over it a layer about six inches thick of dry sticks or brushwood, and burn the mass well down to ashes. By doing this we destroy seeds of weeds and eggs of insects, as well as eggs of ground grubs that destroy young plants. Frames with bush or calico covering are useful as protection against frosts at night or during cold winds or heavy rains. The bed is raked very fine; then an ounce of seed mixed well with some two quarts of fine sand or ashes, is sown evenly over the surface. After sowing, with the back of a rake smooth the bed lightly, packing in the seed with the teeth of the rake, then sprinkle short stable or cow pen manure or ashes over it—just sufficient to cover the seed. Water as may be required to keep the soil moist and the plants growing. Thin out to harden them, and when about five inches high and the under leaves begin to turn yellow and the top ones a dark blue, they are ready for transplanting. The dangers to young seed plants are fungus growth and grubs. Hence the need of care in preparing the seed bed.

Planting Out.—Let the ground be well worked and harrowed fine. In planting out Virginia, Yarra, Havanah, Cuba and Turkish, the plants are allowed five feet by two on rich soil and closer on poorer soil; Kentucky, German, and Connecticut sorts require four feet by three. Choose cloudy weather or the afternoon for planting out. Before raising the plants, soak the seed bed. Be careful to prevent breakage of the roots, which are very large; take up as much earth with them as possible. In planting, make the holes roomy and deep, and spread the roots as much as possible, pressing the soil gently with the point of a dibble or the fingers against the roots. Should the sun be very hot, the plants may need shelter from a shingle, pieces of bark, &c.

Cultivation.—When the plants are established commence to use the hoe, cutting out weeds and loosening the soil. When about a foot high pull off the under leaves to about six inches from the ground, which strengthens the main leaves and gives room to draw the earth up to the stem in a round, flat-topped hill; this serves to keep the roots moist. As soon as blossom buds appear pinch out the tops, so as to leave not more than nine or ten leaves on each plant; pinch out all shoots that spring from the base of the leaves, and all that may be starting from the roots; this is done with a view to throw the whole strength of the plant into about a dozen leaves on each plant.

Signs of Fitness.—When ripe, brown or yellow spots appear, and the leaf gets a brown or yellow tint; it again changes to a dark blue, the leaf becomes thicker, rougher, and more elastic than at any other time, and on handling we find it to be quite sticky. It is then charged with the true tobacco gum, and cannot be too quickly cut. The gum rises best in close sultry weather, but if, when it is just coming on, the weather changes to wet, the gum may go down again, but it returns with fine weather.

Harvesting.—When the plant is fit to harvest, take a sharp-pointed knife, and split the stem down the middle from about one-third from the top to within about two inches of the bottom; then cut it off below the split. Lay the plants on the ground in rows, and unless the weather is very dry let them have the sun on one side for an hour or two, then turn them over, and give them the sun on the other side. If the nights are dewy, so much the better, as the sun and dew together help to mature the leaf. In very dry weather the crop is cut and brought under cover at once. If rain should fall, pile the tobacco in heaps under cover of some sort, but the heaps must be spread out should signs of heating or mildew arise.

Sheds and Appliances for Drying.—These are absolutely necessary. The shed may be a mere cover for drying in the field, but a building, in addition, is necessary for curing, enclosed all round and with windows or loopholes to admit air when required. Beams are placed across at about three feet apart—say one, two or three tiers—according to the room required, only so far above each that the tobacco hung upon one will not touch the next.

Prepare drying sticks long enough to rest upon two beams, run them through the slits in the stalks and hang each plant up to dry, the thick end upwards. They must be placed on the sticks so as not to touch each other. Before hanging the tobacco, take each stalk by the butt end and shake it well to shake the leaves well asunder. In wet weather the windows are closed, and smouldering wood fires are made on the floor of the shed. The object is to prevent the tobacco turning mouldy, and at the same time giving it a good colour, and also the peculiar flavour prized by the manufacturers. In dry weather no fires are wanted, and the windows may be kept open to admit a free current of air. In very dry weather the curing is helped by sprinkling the floors. Tobacco requires hanging in this manner for three or four weeks. The way to tell when it is dried enough is to "try" one of the stalks, and if it breaks off short it is sufficiently done. Wait for a damp day to take the crop down, when the leaves will be limp and will not break in handling; or damp for this purpose also may be got in well enclosed sheds by sprinkling the floors.

Curing or Sweating the Leaf.—When properly dried, the leaf is put up in bundles or "hands," containing ten or more each, weighing about half a pound. These are then arranged for "sweating"—the size of the heap according to the quantity of tobacco; the larger the bulk the better it sweats. Pack it closely and straight, the butts or tied ends of the "hands" on the outsides, and, if necessary to develope heat in the mass, keep it pressed as close as possible by means of slabs of wood, bags, &c. Watch the bulk well by removing some of the stuff on the top, and feeling into the centre, and when it is so hot that we can scarcely bear the hand in it the time is come for shifting; put the tobacco from the top of the heap by itself, and that from the centre by itself (that being the most sweated), then take the sides and bottoms and place them together. It is then stacked again, putting that which was before in the centre at the bottom and sides, and that from the bottom and sides in the middle; the stalks that are greenest should be kept in the middle. It should be done quickly, so as not to let the mass get cold, or it may not sweat so well the second time. Cover over as before. If done well the tobacco acquires the well-known flavour, and becomes a beautiful brown colour, and is fit for the next operation.

Stripping and Sorting.—In arranging the quality of the leaf, it is classified as near as possible as follows:—The first three leaves from the bottom of the stalk are No. 1, or best quality; the next three No. 2; and the rest No. 3. The sorts are selected because they vary in quality and appearance. Ten or twelve leaves are made a bunch or "hand," by twisting a leaf round the thick end, commencing with the thin end of the leaf and tucking the stalk end between the leaves of the "hand" to keep it fast. The tobacco is then fit for the manufacturer, and the sooner it goes to him the better; but if kept on hand for a time it must be in a dry place, at least three feet above the ground, and not bulked thickly, lest it become partially heated and turn mouldy.

Late Crops.—A second crop is sometimes gathered. For this, break off all the shoots that spring from the stool but the strongest one, and this shoot is treated precisely as the first crop, with the exception that the leaves are considered all of one quality, and are rated as of less value than the first. After the second crop is cut the roots are collected and burnt, thus manuring the ground with the ashes. There is another mode of obtaining a late crop which is useful when the season proves too dry for transplanting. Sow the seed in drills, or put in a pinch of seed where each plant is wanted to stand, and thin them out to the proper distance as soon as large enough. This plan may come to be extensively adopted in the case of the late crops, on account of the difficulty of transplanting during the heat of summer.

Curing in Damp Weather.—One who knows the difficulties attendant upon curing tobacco in damp weather, and who feels for those who are so situated, says: I advise all who can to have something like a stove and flue in their tobacco-curing places. There will be less danger of scorching than when fires are used, the leaf will be free from the smell of smoke, &c., and the colour more uniform. But those who cannot have this should make their barns tight from the ground up for nine or ten feet, and then have frequent openings all around to allow the air to pass freely through while the process of curing is going on, and thus prevent "house burn," or curling up with sudden heat. The number of plants on a stick and distance between the sticks may vary according to the size of the leaf, say, upon sticks four and a half feet long ten plants of small or eight of large size, and about seven inches between the sticks for the small and ten for the large. As the leaf becomes cured, the sticks containing the plants may be crowded closer together to make room for the later cuttings. Then make small fires of chips or bark, with as little blaze as possible. There should be a sufficient amount of heat to bring the tobacco into a wilted state, and when the tails become a little dry and curl up, the heat may be gradually increased until the leaf is sufficiently cured to be out of danger of moulding or souring. The leaf of tobacco should be dried slowly, and the fires kept going regularly day and night. The length of time for drying or curing will vary, according as the weather, from 4 to 20 days. Much labour and risk may be saved by spreading the leaf on scaffolding out in the sun in fair weather, but care must be exercised that it is not caught in rain.

Enemies. — Tobacco, whilst growing, has several enemies—a brown grub commonly known as "the cabbage or ground grub," which attacks the plants when quite young. Its habits are as follows:—During the day it is not seen on the plants, but by scraping or stirring the soil for six or eight inches around the stem it may be found within half an inch of the surface. At night it pursues its mischievous depredations by climbing the stalks and eating holes in the leaves and occasionally the stems. This grub generally disappears when the plant is about a foot high. The best way to prevent it is, when the land is prepared for planting, to spread about a ton of quicklime to the acre. Another enemy is a green caterpillar, which generally makes its appearance with the hot weather. There is sometimes also a small white grub that eats its way from the root and ascends through the centre of the stalk. Its presence is shown by the bulging or swelling of the stalk, in which a sort of knot is formed. On seeing this, open the part with a knife, and pick out the grub; when this is removed the plant thrives again. Grasshoppers are, perhaps, the greatest pests of any, for though cleared off one day, a fresh lot may come on the next. Paris green and copper sulphate sprays are the remedies for the insects that eat. Magpies or seagulls are useful, and turkeys, ducks and fowls generally prevent insects from increasing. Young fowls or turkeys do the best services when let in just before roosting time, and turned out again as soon as they fill up with the grubs they love.

ARROWROOT.—This is amongst the safest of semi-tropical crops, and one which, with the machinery that the white man brings to his aid, enables him to compete successfully with Malays, Indians, negroes, and others, who until late years had the monopoly of arrowroot culture. The article of commerce so extensively used in preparing food for the sick, and for the finer kinds of cookery, is a pure white flour or starch. This flour is obtained from two bulbous plants, the Maranta arundinaceæ and Cana edulis. To growers they are known as white and purple arrowroot respectively. In habit there is but little difference in the plants, and the flour obtained from them is almost identical; but there is a vast difference in the yield, which is fully one-half heavier in the purple sort, which is grown over an area of country stretching from Sydney northwards. For this crop, the preparation of land recommended for corn and sugar cane is about right. It does best in rich soil, but not where freshly manured. It comes in as a very good rotation after a heavy crop of corn, and being light upon the soil (although yielding from 10 to 15 tons of bulbs per acre), it can be grown several seasons in succession. The bulbs vary in size from six inches to twelve inches in circumference, and may, for all practical purposes, be likened to large potatoes in appearance.

Cultivation.—The smaller bulbs are used for plants. Wide furrows, about six inches deep, are run out about four feet apart; into the furrows the seed bulbs are dropped, and covered by the plough or hoe. The soil must be warm (say, from 65deg. to 70deg.), which brings the planting into September and October in the cooler sections of the country. In about 14 days, strong spiral shoots appear above ground, and the soil has to be kept clean as for corn. The plants grow rapidly. The eaves are broad at the tops, and borne upon stalks not unlike those of maize. In three months the tops spread over the whole of the field, and are from three to five feet in height. The bulbs at the same time are growing in a cluster around the base of the stems to which they are firmly attached. As the cultivation proceeds, the soil is worked up around the stems. From six to eight months bring the crop to maturity, some of the bulbs peeping above ground ; a touch of frost aids ripening by shrivelling up the tops and concentrating the sap in the bulbs. In other cases when the tops wilt and dry up, the crop is ripe. Forks and pronged hoes are used for digging, the work being similar in many respects to potato digging, but with the arrowroot the tops and tubers come out in a mass. The latter are trimmed in the field, the tops, and as much of the adhering soil as possible being trimmed off with heavy knives.

Manufacture.—The bulbs are washed until they are absolutely clean, and then grated into pulp in a very simple sort of mill, to make which a sheet of galvanised iron, into which holes have been punched, is nailed upon a round piece or frame of wood, with the rough or grating surface outwards. This grater is fixed under a hopper box, and is turned with a handle. The bulbs must be pressed against the grater, and there must also be a steady stream of water flowing in upon the bulbs. They are thus quickly reduced to a dark brown mass of fibry-looking pulp, which is run into long troughs, boxes, or tubs, in which it is stirred and beaten about briskly in the clean water, the object being to free the starch that is held in the cells and fibres. The starch, being the heavier substance, falls to the bottom, and the fibre and other lighter substances are gathered or drifted off from the surface. The water has to be changed several times, or better still when the settling of starch is in long troughs, a current of water flows over it, until the pure white starch only remains in a mass at the bottom. This starch while wet is liable to ferment, and the fibry matter separated from it is still more liable to fermentation. Cool weather (not hotter than 70deg. in the shade during the day) is desirable at the time of manufacturing. Weather of the requisite description is usual during May, June, and July, during which season the arrowroot is at its best stage for manufacturing. After being stirred until perfectly clean—a simple process, owing to the weight of the starch always bringing it quickly to the bottom of the vessel—the starch is spread out in the sun or in dry rooms upon cloth, and freed from the last trace of moisture as rapidly as possible. When perfectly dry, it keeps in bags, boxes, &c., for years, and is esteemed as a valuable food material for the sick and healthy.

The Australian Process.—Machinery of very ingenious construction has been brought to bear upon the manufacture of this article, the cost of production being reduced in proportion, while the quality is improved, as it is scarcely handled from the time of leaving the field. The Messrs. Grimes (Queensland) are famous for this article, their arrowroot being extensively used in the colonies, in England, and other countries. Instead of the laborious and doubtful process of hand washing and grinding, which is still the ordinary way of manufacturing this article in the Indies, Cape, and other places, Australian arrowroot is barely handled from first to last. The roots are shovelled into long troughs, through which run continuous streams of water. There is a screw in each trough with flanges, which turn, roll and push the roots about, and keeps gradually working them towards the upper end all the time. They are perfectly clean by the time they arrive there, and are pitched (by the flanges on the screws) in ones, twos, and threes upon an endless chain which lifts them some fourteen or fifteen feet and discharges them into the hopper of a grinding machine. Here they are reduced to pulp, which pulp by means of a stream of water is discharged into perforated revolving drums, where it is knocked about, beaten, and washed, all to separate the starch from the coarser particles. The starch, as driven through fine perforations on the outside of the drums, is then carried in suspension by the water to a long series of troughs, where it is gradually deposited in a solid mass, and the water flows off. The arrowroot, now a creamy-coloured starch, is then washed in vats, and becomes almost white. It is then put into centrifugal machines and freed from the water. To complete the drying process, the arrowroot (now beautifully white and sparkling) is laid out in trays in the sun. When perfectly dry it is put up in the bags and packets familiar all over the country, and is ready for use—a delightful, light, nourishing warmth giving food for the invalid and healthy. The yield of bulbs of the purple varieties varies between ten and fifteen tons per acre. A ton of bulbs gives rather more than one cwt of manufactured arrowroot. The white variety is grown and manufactured in the same way as the purple, but the yield is much less.

MILLETS.—Broom Corn, Sorghum, &c.—Under the name of millet, sorghum, farmer's friend, &c., a great variety of grain-bearing plants are cultivated, but mostly for cutting green for feed. They all require hot weather, and are annual summer crops, sown in the cooler districts in August to October, and in the hot districts from April to January. As grain, none of the millets are used to the extent they deserve. In Italy, parts of Germany, in India, China, and many other countries, millet seed, ground into meal, is an important portion of the food of the people. It is inferior to oats or wheat for that purpose, but being an easily produced crop on ordinarily good soil, it is worth growing, first as green feed (it stands cutting four or five times during the season) and secondly as grain for poultry and pig-feeding, &c. Some of the varieties also yield sugar (crushed out of the cane and manufactured in the same way as cane-sugar), but it is an inferior article for that purpose, and will not stand competition with the cane. The soil may be either strong or medium for the millets. Plough as for a grain crop; when wanted for cutting green, drill in the seed in rows of 29 inches apart, and cultivate between the rows until the ground is shaded by the plants. For seed, or cane for sugar, make drills 3 to 4 feet apart; scatter in the seed so that plants may be obtained about three inches apart when thinned out. When well cultivated, this crop grows very rapidly, and in the course of four months from planting, assumes the form of canes from one to two inches in diameter, and from 6 to 12 feet in height. The canes become brownish as they ripen, and a heavy mass of seed is borne on the top of each. If seed is the object, it is allowed to become dry and hard on the plant. If for sugar, the sap is at its best (from 7° to 9° in density) while the seed is forming.

Broom corn is a variety of this family, grown much the same as the others, and cut while the seed is young, and before the branching head that supports it becomes brown. This head makes capital brooms, whisks, &c. The crop is dealt with in Chapter XI., with fibre yielders.

X.—PRODUCTS WE MIGHT GROW.

SILK—COTTON—TEA—COFFEE—GINGER—CHICORY—RICE.

OIL AND FIBRE YIELDERS.—They might come within the list of crops for which the climate and soil are suitable. And, as explained in the chapter on rotations, they have the additional merit of taking but little from the soil.

SILK.—During many years the production of silk has been an attraction in the colonies one after another. Victoria, Queensland, New South Wales, South Australia, have each made efforts to include silk in their products upon a large scale. New South Wales is making efforts in that direction by private and public effort, and Queensland has been exporting cocoons in quantity sufficient to test their real value in the great silk markets of the world. In the production of silk the first consideration should be the cultivation of proper food for the insect from which it is obtained. Next, that there is sufficient and suitable help available. The silk-worm is a caterpillar which grows

102   AUSTRALIAN AGRICULTURE.

from the size of about one-eighth of an inch—that at which it emerges from the egg—to from two and a-half to nearly three inches long. All the best silk-producing

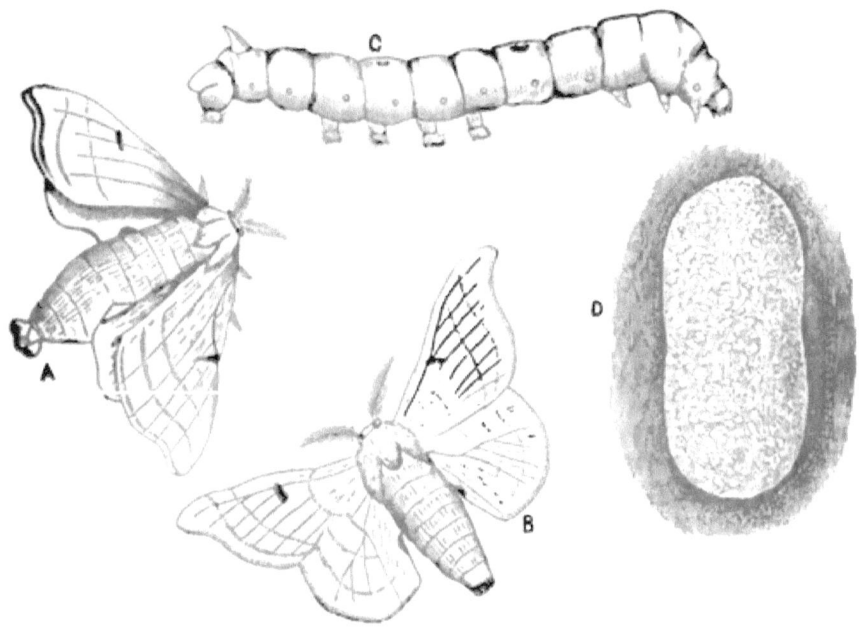

Silkworm, Moths, and Cocoon.

varieties feed upon the leaves of the mulberry; and the primary step to take is to ascertain the best kinds for feeding, regard being made to the rapid growth of the worm, and the quantity and kind of silk to be got from it. That being arranged, the next thing is to cultivate the trees in the best form. In Italy and in China pruned hedge or dwarf growth is preferred, the trees being trained as shrubs. In others, larger growth is encouraged, and the trees are planted at distances of 10 to 20 feet from each other. The difference may account for different methods in feeding, which in one place is by the summary process of throwing branches of trees, with the leaves on, to be stripped by the worms; and in another by leaves picked from the trees, and given, either whole or chopped, to the worms on trays prepared for the purpose. In this climate the wholesale lopping off of branches, even from a shrub tree, would soon result in its destruction; while small-leaved trees would call for an amount of labor in picking the leaves that would increase the cost of production to a perhaps almost prohibitory extent; so that a modified process seems most likely to succeed.

Varieties of Mulberry for Silk.—Of the great numbers of mulberry trees imported into Australia, five or six seem most suitable. The first is that known as the morus multicaulis or large-leaved, or, as some call it, the Chinese mulberry. Its first value is that the worm seems to prefer the young leaves to those of any other kind; its second is economy in picking, since from the great size of the leaves a few will feed more than a considerable quantity of the other sorts. This, however, only holds good of the first crop—the second growth is harder and poorer feed; but by that time other varieties, the morus alba and morus nigra, come into use, and the silk produced by feeding upon their leaves is said to be A1. These two kinds again present each two varieties—the rose-leaved and the oak-leaved—the fruit-bearing morus alba and morus nigra being oak-leaved mulberries. In rich, loose soils, leaves of considerable size and great richness of texture are produced. Generally, the multicaulis begins to break into leaf early in August, the alba and nigra a fortnight to a month later. We may add to these trees the ordinary Cape mulberry, originally a Chinese sort, for the later stages of the worm; and the Indian mulberry for all stages, so far as experience has yet gone. The English mulberry seems well adapted for food as the insect matures, but it has not yet been sufficiently tested. Beyond this, experience tends to prove that it is not necessary or profitable to go. The other varieties here are rather objects of curiosity than usefulness.

Soil for Mulberry Trees.—Good orchard land is necessary, with sufficient depth of soil and drainage, such as orchard trees require. Distances apart may be 10 x 10 feet to 20 x 20 feet, according to variety and method of working.

Treatment of Silk Worms.—All the varieties, Japanese, Italian, Bivoltines, and others are produced from eggs laid by the moth the previous season. The conventional or trade method of dealing with the eggs is to treat a card or cloth of the surface of 80 square inches as containing an ounce of what is technically called "grain," and an ounce should produce from 30,000 to 32,000 worms, or about 100lbs. cocoons. In Australia, the eggs commence to hatch out in August, just as the mulberry begins to break into leaf. The worms generally commence emerging early in the morning, and continue until afternoon. About 2 o'clock it is advisable to take a smooth, soft feather or camel-hair brush, and gently but rapidly sweep the worms from the card or cloth into a tray. This done, some finely cut leaves should be scattered, to which the worms will instantly crawl, and the first operation is so far complete, care being taken to mark the date on each tray. Trays of convenient size are made 18 by 14 inches, and are simply frames of $1\frac{1}{2}$ inch x $\frac{1}{2}$ inch timber, the bottom being calico or Victoria lawn. Eight such trays will be required for the product of an ounce of "grain." The worms should be fed three or four times a day with finely cut leaves, until they have reached their first stage, which will be from four to five days after hatching. The quantity of leaves for an ounce will be at first from $2\frac{1}{2}$ lbs. to 3 lbs. per day to 20-30 lbs. as they grow to maturity. Thirty pounds leaves make about one pound cocoons.

From Worm to Silk.—The time at which the spinning stage is reached is subject to much difference, arising from feeding, from the weather, and from the kind of worm itself. We have known worms to mature in thirty-four days; others were sixty before they began to spin. The average of a good Japanese, however, may be taken, in an ordinary season, at from forty to fifty-five days. The "bivoltines" grow more rapidly than the annual sorts. When the worms show a desire to crawl to the sides of the trays, and assume a transparent tinge, the time for their removal has come. A good method of dealing with them then is to have a table on a strong frame, the top being formed of strong mosquito net. Cardboard cells have to be prepared, each cell about one inch square, and an inch and a-half deep are made of stout paper. Lay a few of these cell-cases on the mosquito-net table, and as you gather the spinning worms from the trays, drop one in each cell. When the worms are all got in, cover the upper side with a piece of mosquito-net fastened down by weights at the sides, or by placing another cell-set on top, and then leave the worms to spin their cocoons. In about four days we may take the cocoons out; in two, if necessary, we may remove the cell-set and hang it up. The object of using cells is to keep the worms separate, and avoid double cocoons. After the fourth day, they are ready for the winder.

The Cocoons.—In the cocoon is the embryo of another moth, which in twelve to fourteen days will eat its way out, and in that interval there is time to determine on one of three processes; to wind the silk off at once; to dry the cocoons (killing the grubs) for exportation; to allow the moths to come out, thus reducing the value of the cocoons for silk production, but to secure eggs for sale as "grain." As to the first, there is no demand for raw silk. As to the second, the method of drying cocoons here is by adaptation of the common iron oven, heated by gas or fire, taking care that there is thorough ventilation by a hole or grating at the bottom of the door, and another at the top. In such an oven, and with three-inch intervals, there may be racks or small bars strong enough to hold trays of cocoons. The cocoons are placed not more than two deep, on cardboard or chip on the racks, covering the topmost layer with paper. When the oven is hot enough just to tinge white paper to a light straw colour, it will do. Twenty minutes kills and dries the grubs. When the cocoons are taken out, they should be spread in the sun to evaporate any moisture left in them. When thoroughly dry—and that can be told by cutting one open, when the grub should fall to powder—they can be pressed and packed in bales of 100lbs. each, for exportation. The price, in Europe, for good clean cocoons is variously quoted at from 3s. 6d. up to 6s. per lb.

Silkworms' Eggs.—The production of "grain," as it is called, has led to more disappointment than can well be imagined. The grain market in Italy is very variable. A great deal depends, experience shows, not upon the actual quality of what is sent, but upon its accredited reputation; and again, the time when sent is an essential element in success. To sell grain profitably, it should leave here to reach Italy by December, so that it may have the benefit of the cold. Arriving later, it will run a chance of being crowded out. In past seasons, good Japanese grain, coming late into the market, could not be sold at more than eighteen-pence an ounce, and hardly at that. From a variety of sources of information concerning the silk market, it would seem that really good grain may be expected to fetch, as a permanent price, from 14s. to 15s. per ounce. As to the reports of 24s., £2 (and we have even read of £6), they are very doubtful. Exceptional seasons will, of course, yield exceptional prices, and 20s. per ounce has been paid for Queensland grain as a sample; but it would be folly to reckon on a higher general rate than that quoted above.

Cotton.—Large tracts of country have been found suitable for this crop in Australia, and when the prices are such as pay, enormous quantities can be produced. The land available is still more extensive than that for sugar, for cotton answers in cooler locations. Good corn land suits it. Cotton is grown from seed, and the usual planting time is August. The crop matures in from six to nine months, and is either re-sown, or in districts where frost does not prevail the plants are pruned close to the ground, and are thus made to yield two, three, or more crops in succession. Two leading varieties are grown, viz., uplands or woolly-seed, and sea island. The latter seed is almost free from wool, is of a dark brown colour, and runs into but few varieties; the longest and silkiest fibre is obtained from it, but the variety is delicate. The woolly-seed has many varieties; it runs into sorts of greater or less strength, length, and beauty of fibre wherever grown, and is capable of indefinite improvement by selections from the best plants in the field. The average yield of cotton gives twice the weight of seed to the weight of fibre. Seed, therefore, soon becomes plentiful.

BEETS for Sugar, Feed, &c.—Beet culture has been carried on in the cooler parts of the country at various times, and with such results as proved that beets might be made profitable. They are summer croppers. Seed, from 10 to 15lbs. per acre, is drilled in in August or September. Plants come up quickly, and are thinned out from six to twelve inches apart, according to soil, season and sort. For sugar making, small beets are best, from $1\frac{1}{2}$ to $3\frac{1}{2}$ lbs. Cultivation much the same as swedes and mangels. Sugar beets should harvest from twelve to eighteen tons per acre at a total cost of £5 to £7.

HOPS.—Hops of colonial growth are earning a high reputation, and their cultivation is extending in New Zealand, Tasmania, Victoria, and South Australia. The soils most favourable are strong, deep loams, with an open or well drained subsoil—good grain land, broken up by the common plough, followed by the subsoil plough. The "breaking up" in the first instance may be accompanied by a dressing of lime or manure. The hop is a greedy plant to excess, and requires good and generous treatment from the very start.

Sowing and Planting.—Hops are grown from seed to get plants or sets, which are put out in the open ground. Planting six feet by six feet, triangular method, is handy and sufficient between the sets. It is advisable to have wide twelve-feet openings through the plantation, for a better supply of air during the stronger growth of the plants.

Cultivation.—The hop grows much faster in the colonies than in England, and frequently produces a light crop from the "set" the first season. Surface cultivation to secure loose, clean ground, is necessary. Early cropping is considered more a disadvantage than otherwise, as it exhausts the young plants too much. In England a common practice is to simply twist the first year's growth into a bundle and place a clod upon it, so as to encourage growth in the roots as much as possible; but occasionally a short pole of six or seven feet is made use of where the growth is rank. The reason for planting in triangle position is because the poles are "pitched" or sloped at an angle of about ten degrees from the vertical; and if the "sets" are allowed to come with their crowns towards each other the bines would soon meet, grow twined together, and so, from the first "tying up," be an endless source of trouble and breakage, in separating them. When the plants are poled, which ought to be as soon as the shoots or "bines" appear in the yearling plants, the space at level with the tops of the poles ought to be equally divided. Each plant, if growing strongly, will have a spread of two feet all the way up, and require as much sun and air as can possibly be provided for it.

Harvesting.—Hops begin to flower, or "bell," in the colonies about Christmas. In a week or two the seeds may be felt between finger and thumb, and in a month after, when the weather is favourable, the clusters of flowers will at first become a pale yellowish or straw colour, and then a lightish brown. At this stage they can easily be broken up in the palm of the hand, emit the familiar fragrance of the mercantile hop, and the sooner they are harvested and dried the better. Gathering hops, or "picking" as it is called, is usually done by women and children by contract; for this reason it is advisable to form plantations in localities where such labour is obtainable, for delay in this operation is ruinous. A grower must have everything in readiness for his harvest; his cribs must be made, and an "oast" or kiln prepared.

Drying.—Kilns are used for this purpose. Hops ought to be dried, if possible, within twelve hours after being picked. This is an important point, as the aroma of the flower is very volatile, and in it lies the "strength" and flavour of the hop. They must not be put in large heaps prior to drying, for although of a brownish colour and apparently ripe, they are full of sap, and will "heat" readily if thus placed, and materially decrease in value. The drying must be carried on day and night until all are finished. The fires (of charcoal) must not be very fierce at first, but the "floorings" will need constant stirrings. A great deal depends upon the weather. When dried sufficiently, they are allowed to lie for a day or two in order to acquire a certain degree of toughness, when they can be pressed, " or pocketed," without going into dust.

Chemistry, Manuring, &c.—Hops contain and require a large amount of potash. It is calculated that seventeen pounds are taken off an acre of ground in the season's growth. Besides the potash, which is principally found in the bine and leaf, the plant also requires ammonia, phosphates, sulphates, lime, magnesia, &c.

Irrigation is helpful, though not actually essential, to hops. When the land is well and deeply broken up, the roots soon find safe quarters from the danger of our summer heat; and when the poles are well covered with bines, they are self-protecting; the evaporation in a hop ground is not nearly so great as in a vineyard.

TEA.—Although the tea plant—the shrub or bush which yields tea in China, Japan, India, Ceylon, the South Sea Islands, and other places—has been well known in Australia for many years it has never come into general cultivation. It is another instance, and a striking one, of the manner in which we go on year after year, buying what we can grow. The tea shrub is quite hardy from the Clarence River northwards. It may be seen growing in gardens in all sorts of soils; but with the exception of a few "old folks," nobody tries to make their own tea, from a most erroneous idea that there is something very mysterious about it.

Cultivation.—The tea bush is handsome in form, with dark green leaves like those of the rose; the flowers are pinkish white, and have a pleasant odor. When full grown, the bush is about three feet high, nicely rounded in form, and altogether pretty. A pound or two of leaves can be picked from a three-year old plant, and the yield goes on increasing for thirty or more years. Seed may be sown or young plants set out in the open ground during August or September. All seeds of this kind require rich soil.

Harvesting.—No doubt tea manufacturers have a certain way of manufacturing, but a very good and wholesome tea is made by putting the young green leaves into a shallow preserving pan over a slow wood fire. When they begin to curl, throw them upon a table and rub them with the hand into the form of ordinary tea. Let them stand in a current of air for a few hours, or swing them about in a basket; then put the leaves in the pan again, heat, and roll them as before. Do this four or five times, and the result is a greenish black tea, of a far better quality than the average post-and-rail compound.

COFFEE.—This plant has been more extensively grown in Australia than tea. It has proved delicate in exposed situations; but in rich soils, on the sides of hills protected from westerly gales, and on well sheltered flats, it is a hardy, handsome tree, and bears great quantities of cherry-like fruit which, in its preserved state, we call coffee.

Cultivation.—The plants are raised from seed sown in August, in rows about a foot apart. If they are to be removed, the seeds are sown in pots or boxes. By the following April the plants are about ten inches in height, and can be set out from eight to twelve feet apart. Choosing wet, sultry, still weather. Coffee does not bear transplanting well. To overcome this difficulty, the seed may be planted three or four at each place where a tree is wanted. In moist weather, during August, September, and October, they come above ground in twelve to fourteen days. By this plan, growing without transplanting, stronger trees are obtained. Unless the soil is very rich and porous—as in the case of what is known as mountain scrub—the soil for coffee should be trenched by hand or plough.

Harvesting.—The trees come into bearing in the third or fourth year, by which time they are five or six feet in height, and pretty, nicely-balanced bushes, with very handsome foliage. To force them into fruit, the tops of the leading branches are pinched or pruned off. This is also done to keep the trees at a convenient height for picking off the fruit. The first crop of berries is usually straggling. The fruit is in the form of dark purple berries along the limbs. These berries are ripe when the two beans in the interior of each move about freely on being pressed with the fingers. Between the outside covering of the fruit and the berries is a gummy-like sweetish substance. To get rid of this, the fruit is allowed to lie in masses until a slight fermentation sets in. The mass is then washed to get rid of the gum, and the fruit spread out in the sun or shade, as occasion may require. Around each is a dry, parchment-like wrapper, and when this is dry the fruit is passed between rollers that separate the beans from the skins. In dry weather the berries dry up when exposed freely to the air, and the tough outside covering can then be removed by rubbing the berries. The flavour of Australian coffee (roasted in the usual way) thus prepared is very fine.

Cocoa—Cacao or Chocolate.—Cocoa, from which the chocolate of commerce is made, is obtained, in the form of seed-pods, from a handsome tree. In its nature this plant is even more tropical than coffee, but it fruits in the northern sections of Australia. The seeds are sown as soon as possible after they are gathered, as they soon spoil for germinating upon becoming dry, as do the seeds of most pines and some other plants. The growth of seedlings and transplanting is much the same as coffee. Cocoa trees in the plantation should stand apart ten to fifteen feet, according to the richness of the soil, twelve feet being a good average distance. In the fourth year a fair crop may be expected. The fruit must be quite ripe before it is gathered. When ripe it has a pale yellowish colour. After being picked, it is allowed to lie in heaps for about twenty-four hours. Then the pods are cut open, and the pulpy mass of seeds taken out and put into baskets to drain. As soon as this drainage of what becomes an acid pulp has ceased, the mass is emptied into boxes, in which "terrage" (a property of sweating) continues for thirty-six or forty-eight hours. After removal from the sweating places, the seeds are freed from any adhering matter, and spread out loosely to dry in the sun, being turned over very frequently. This process of drying occupies about three weeks and when complete the seeds should be of a fine dark red colour. The produce of a tree, when prepared, ranges from five to eight pounds. The crop has the advantage of being easily cultivated, and prepared for export by a few hands.

Manufacture.—The manufacture of chocolate from the seed is an extensive business in England, France, and Germany. The seeds are first roasted similar to those of coffee, and with the same object—to draw out the rich aromatic flavour. The mass is then crushed by a single roller of stone or iron working in a bed of similar material; the bed is heated slightly as the process goes on. The paste thus obtained is mixed with honey, sugar, and other sweet substances in England. In France, Italy, and Germany, pimento, vanilla, cinnamon, &c., are added, in accordance with the taste of consumers. It is then made up into little packets familiar to those who use cocoa, and which furnish an invigorating and healthy beverage: and into tablets, and other forms of chocolate confectionery. In cheap preparations, arrowroot, sago, and similar ingredients are added.

Rice.—This grain is grown somewhat extensively in the northern river districts. It changes considerably according to the soil, location, &c., and the treatment given. The rice of commerce is usually grown in swampy land. Another variety, named Mountain Rice, does tolerably well on dry land; but it does better when water is applied, and still better when the surface of the soil is flooded for a few days. The grains also become similar as they are subjected to similar treatment; so that if they are different varieties, the difference is but very slight. Both the common and mountain varieties are annual grain plants, something like wheat.

Cultivation.—The seed of rice, or "paddy," is the undressed grain. It is sown in drills about fifteen inches apart, and comes through the soil like so much grass, and at first it is not easy to say which is the rice and which weeds; but in wet weather the crop shoots ahead. When five or six inches high, it is an advantage to be able to flood the drills with water, and keep the water on for three or four days. The water kills weeds, and helps the rice wonderfully. It also affords opportunities for filling up blanks, by lifting knots of plants (with soil attached) from where they come up too thick, and filling up blanks and thin spaces. After being thinned out to an average distance of about an inch apart, two or three hoeings bring the crop to maturity. By dry cultivation, rice is found to ripen sooner than when it is flooded, but the latter is unmistakably the heavy crop, and experts say the grain is finer. In America the rice-fields are flooded at planting time, and to a depth of four or five inches around the plants as soon as they are high enough to stand it, and this is repeated at intervals until the crop comes into ear. In favourable seasons and on strong land the roots, in Australia, are found capable of bearing two crops. The first ripens in February and March. When ripe, the grain and straw become yellowish, like wheat, and the tokens of ripeness in that grain apply to rice. The heads of the first crop are then cut off—the wheat-stripper should answer for this work, as the grain stands well up. The second crop (at this stage looking like half-grown wheat) then springs up, and ripens in from five to eight weeks. In ordinary farming, the rice is cut down with reaping-hook, scythe, or machine, bound up in sheaves, stacked, and thrashed out. The husks stick very closely to the grain, and are removed by millstones, set at such distance apart as to split off the chaff without injuring the grain. In America, "hullers" are used for this purpose; they cost from £15 to £40. The rice is then dressed or polished in machinery less or more expensive. The grain is best preserved in the husk or "paddy" state, and is usually sold in that form by the growers. The crop ranges from twenty to forty bushels per acre. It is one of the best-paying and least-exhausting grain crops grown, and in Australia would be harvested at a time when there is little doing on the cane plantations.

CHICORY.—This plant has been cultivated here, as a forage crop principally, for many years. Our German and French fellow-colonists are especially partial to it, and in a few cases have extended chicory culture to over an acre. As a rule, however, a few perches only are grown, mostly used for feeding cattle. Ten tons of roots per acre is a fair average crop of chicory in Victoria, where it is grown somewhat extensively, and sold to wholesale coffee dealers at from £3 to £5 per ton.

Cultivation.—The seed may be sown in either February or March for a winter crop, or in September for a summer crop. It vegetates slowly, and the soil should be perfectly clean to prevent weeds from choking the young plants. 1lb. of seed gives plants for about a quarter of an acre. When fit to handle they are set out in rows two feet by about eighteen inches; or the seed can be drilled into rows two feet apart, and thinned out, like turnips or beets, with the cultivation of which chicory corresponds, when grown for roots. When for forage, the seed can be sown broadcast at the rate of 6lbs. to the acre, and the tops can be either picked off or bladed, or cattle may be turned in to graze them down.

As a Feed Crop.—Chicory is of more value to mow, and consume in a stable or byre, than to graze. It might also be used for ensilage. A small extent of chicory ground fattens a large number of sheep. The best way is to let the plant reach its full growth, the full succulence being retained until the flower-buds appear, in which state (not being permitted to flower) it has attained its greatest perfection; it may be then cut off near the ground, and is eaten by all kinds of stock.

The Chicory for Coffee.—To prepare the chicory-root, it is sliced, and dried in driers much the same as fruit. For use, the dried chicory is heated in iron cylinders, which are kept revolving as in the roasting of coffee. In England, about two pounds of lard are added per cwt. of chicory during the roasting process; in France butter is used; by this a lustre resembling that of coffee is imparted to it. When roasted, the chicory is ground to powder and mixed with coffee. The analysis of chicory gives 25 parts watery extractive, and three parts resin, besides sugar, salammoniac, and woody fibre.

GINGER.—This is another of the roots found admirably adapted to the warmer sections of Australia. Three varieties are grown.

Cultivation.—The white and yellow are much alike in habits; the roots of both grow in clumps close to the surface of the soil, and in dry seasons become tough and fibry, and therefore are not so well adapted for making preserves as the third, which roots deeper, and is more fleshy and tender. All the varieties are propagated from knobs or pieces from the roots. They require very rich, free soil, moist but not wet. Plant from August to November, putting the sets about one foot apart each way; if a quantity is grown, the white varieties answer in rows about twenty inches apart; the plants being put in about eight inches apart in rows. The yellow variety requires a little more space. Merely cover the sets with soil—old cow manure answers well for the purpose. The leaves or shoots come above ground in twelve or fourteen days; they are at first pointed and reed-like, but soon spread out into long thickish leaves, not unlike those of arrowroot. The cultivation necessary is to keep the surface soil loose and clean, and this should be done with a pointed stick or the hand, and not more than an inch of soil should be stirred. During the process the plants are all the better of a few shovelfuls of rich old compost added to the surface, the yield is in proportion to the richness of the soil.

Harvesting.—The roots are ripe in about seven months from the time of planting. Any difference that exists in ginger is due more to its quality than to any peculiarity in habit or growth. The white sorts are richest in flavour; the smaller or narrow-leaved is that used for the dry ginger of commerce; for this purpose the roots are allowed to lie in the ground until the leaf-stalks have withered; they are then dug up and washed; the outside skin is brushed or scraped off and the roots are dried in the sun.

Preserved Ginger.—To make preserves, the roots are dug as soon as they are fully grown, while the root is soft, and before the leaves begin to wither; they are then washed, scraped if necessary, cut into slices or "chunks" of any desired shape, and put into jars with salt and water for a few hours, or just sufficiently long to take away any earthy flavor; then rinse the slices in clean water, and put them back in the jar with a first syrup made from white sugar; change the syrup in three or four days, or as soon as it shows signs of fermenting; re-boil it, for a second syrup, adding more sugar, and pour it upon the ginger again. This strengthening of syrups has to be done three or four times, until the ginger has lost all wild flavor, and is perfectly sweet and aromatic. It can then be put up for use, as one of the richest and most pleasant preserves known. To make it in the highest perfection, and with the delicious flavour peculiar to Jamaica preserved ginger, the roots are allowed to remain in the soil through the winter; they start into fresh growth next season, and in November or December following, the young offshoots from the old roots are dug and preserved as described.

XI.—ROTATION OR CHANGE OF CROPS.

THE OIL AND FIBRE YIELDERS.

The results and advantages of rotation or change of crops are many. They include such treatment of the soil as secures the heaviest returns from the crop in the land at the time; and to give the soil renewed strength for the crops to follow. Some system to secure rotation has been followed from the earliest times. The rule now is that no two crops of the same order of plants should follow in succession. The soil contents—the plant food in the soil—are thus distributed and induced to do duty in the most effective manner, by supplying to one crop what had not been used up by the preceding product. In the process of nature, richer plants take the place of poorer, as the latter decay and furnish the

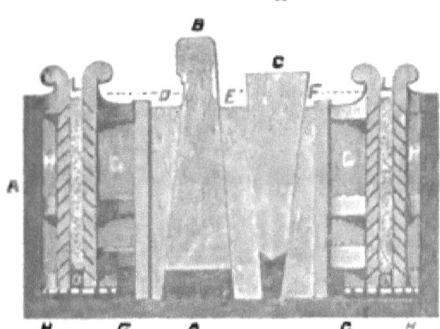

Wedge Press for Extracting Oils from Seeds.

necessary material. The process is the very basis of evolution. In advanced farming practice, by rotation, the land is cleaned from weeds, and many enemies of one crop are starved out of the soil, not finding what they require in the next put in as a succession, belonging as it does to a different family. The process also allows of such heavy manuring as is necessary for potatoes, corn, &c., and which are all the better of such treatment, to be followed by others which do not require manure supplied to them direct. Labor and outlay are saved in this way, and heavier and healthy crops secured. But comparatively little has been done in the warmer sections of the country in the way of rotation. In the wheat districts the aim of the farmer may be to have a fifth of his cultivation land under wheat; another fifth under maize, potatoes, beans, &c., or under lucerne, prairie, or rye grasses, which do exceedingly well, the remainder in indigenous pasture. Yet knowledge of the different crops which may succeed each other profitably on the same land is of as great importance to the skilled colonial as the European farmer, who always works on some system of rotation. All aim at a judicious change, so as to obtain the most valuable produce from any given soil in as quick succession as possible. Thus wheat, potatoes, grass, and maize, might be alternating crops in suitable districts. In other parts, maize might take the place of wheat; and again, wheat, sheep, and grass form a rotation. A usual course is to plough one of the cultivated grass sections for wheat, and the wheat-ground is either allowed to go to grass, under sheep for one or two seasons, or it is ploughed up as soon as the crop is off, and worked for the next crop of beans, potatoes, &c. Lucerne is seldom profitable after seven or eight years; it may then be broken up and the piece sown with wheat. It would not be advisable to re-sow the same paddock with lucerne during a full course of rotation, say seven years. It is found advisable to dress the lucerne land with quick-lime before ploughing for wheat; the same with the prairie grass. Beans (kidney or haricot) are great bearers, and do well planted with maize in alternate hills. They can be put in with the corn-planter, are convenient for cultivation and harvesting with corn, and makes good feed for horses, pigs, &c. Crops with fibrous roots that throw up seed stems with few leaves thrive best after crops with fleshy roots and soft, broad leaves, on a branching stem. Thus wheat thrives after beans, vetches, clover, or grass; barley and oats after turnips, carrots, or potatoes.

Why Oil and Fibre Yielders are Good for Rotation.

They Take so Little from the Soil.—They are built up from carbon mostly, and plants get that from the air. Where suitable, they may be brought in as very desirable rotation crops with wheat, or any of the other grains, as neither oil nor fibre impoverish the soil to any extent, the bulk of their contents being carbon.

Percentage of Oil from Seeds.—The following gives a fair average of oils obtained from seeds, fruits, &c., and may be found useful :—

Castor-oil seeds	about 62 per cent.
Poppy seeds	56 to 63 ,,
Rape, colwort, and Swedish turnip	33 ,,
Colza seed	36 to 40 ,,
Wild mustard, gourd, lemon	30 ,,
Hemp-seed	14 to 25 ,,
Linseed, flax, or lintseed	11 to 22 ,,
Sunflower seeds	15 to 30 ,,
Grape stones	14 to 22 ,,
Cotton seed	18 to 33*,,
Olive-oil, about 2 gals. per tree.	

Fibre Crops.—Australia is peculiarly rich in fibre-yielding plants. The aboriginal natives make very strong lines, nets, &c., from the curriejohng, fig, and many other plants that grow in or on the boarders of creeks and scrubs. Bananas, pine-apples, sida retusa, and others are fibre-yielders. As they are of the order of plants that take very little from the soil, fibre-yielders are excellent for rotation with wheat, &c. New Zealand flax (phormium tenax) grows freely all over the colonies, and produces a fibre of acknowledged value. It does best in rich and rather sandy soil, in this respect being similar to fibre-yielders

* The heavy percentage of husks in cotton-seed accounts for the apparently low percentage of oil.

generally. Seed of New Zealand flax vegetates at any time of the year, and as it seeds freely, even in the warmer latitudes of Queensland, its cultivation could be extended rapidly.

Flax, Lintseed or Linseed.—There are many reasons why linseed might be a general Australian product. I mean as a seed crop. It does well where it has a fair test, and that is somewhat extensively in the southern parts of New South Wales, and to a limited extent in the north and in Queensland. The yield is from 20 bushels upwards. Marketable seed should be as heavy as wheat, or say 60lbs. per bushel. When ground into meal and scalded, it makes excellent feed material for calves and stock, and is decidedly beneficial in dairying. But the main requirement is to make linseed oil, the basis of good paint. The value of the seed in Victoria and in New Zealand, in both of which are oil mills, is from 6s. to 8s. per bushel. And as the crop is much less exhausting on land than either wheat or corn, the value to the farmer becomes evident.

Cultivation.—There is no special requirement in the farming of linseed. It is a summer crop, sown as for wheat, and cultivated much the same. Good corn land answers. Linseed, for dairy feed, is extending in the southern districts, but is just as suitable for the central and northern districts, or in other parts where the rainfall is sufficient to bring on fair crops of maize.

Broom Corn.—The fibre from which "American brooms" are made is got from a variety of millet, or sorghum. It has been grown in various parts of Australia, and does as well as the millets usually do here, and that is as well as in any part of the world. But, hitherto, as a crop, this variety has not made headway. The prospects ought to be better now, because several broom factories are at work in the colonies, and no doubt they would purchase from Australian growers, could they get the material as good as that brought from America.

Cultivation.—Fairly good maize land does for the cultivation of broom corn. The season for sowing is the same as for maize. It does all the better in rich land, and takes kindly to manuring as a means of increasing the yield. The seed is much the same as sorghum seed, and where a quantity has to be planted a seed-dropper does the work rapidly and well. From 15 to 20 lbs. of seed per acre are sown, in drills, 3½ to 4 feet apart. The plants are thinned in the rows to from 3 to 6 inches apart, and ordinary good corn cultivation is followed, in order to get the plants to grow up straight and clean. The "broom" fibre is at the top of the plant, and the object is to have it straight and tough. It would be well for those who may try this crop to examine the fibres of a good "American broom," to see what is required.

Harvesting.—In order to toughen the fibre and hasten maturity, the heads of the "corn" are bent over just as the blossoms appear. The bend is made about a foot below the seed head or "brush." The plants of two rows may be bent over and made to hold each other in that position. The blossoms come out while the "corn" is in this bent position, and when they begin to fall the crop is fit for cutting. At this stage a good deal of the seed has formed, and it has all to be got out, a common hackle being used for the purpose. The heads are laid on the ground as cut, when the soil is dry and clean. The fibre would be injured by dirt of any sort. The drying or curing is done in barns or sheds. All the moisture has to be dried out, which takes from a month to six weeks. The heads are then sorted into bundles of uniform length and color, and are ready for sale. From 500 to 600 lbs. is the yield in Indiana, where broom corn is a general crop. The value ranges according to the length and color, at from 30s. to £2 per 100 lbs.

SIDA RETUSA, or Queensland Hemp.—This, the "paddy's lucerne" of colonial farming populations, is one of the best known fibre-yielders. In the coast districts of New South Wales it grows like a weed, and becomes a serious nuisance where neglected. It is an enormous seed-bearer, and being perfectly hardy, when it gets possession of a piece of good land its eradication is a difficult matter. Nothing appears to injure the plants; on good land, they grow up a dense mass of straight, supple twigs, about half an inch in diameter at the base, and tapering away to a point as the tops reach three or four feet in height. When grown singly, sida retusa is a stocky, branching plant; when in masses, it is straight, handsome, single stem, and a literal mass of fibre. Quantities of this fibre have been manufactured in much the same manner as flax fibre in Ireland, and the yield estimated to be fully up to one-and-a-half ton per acre. The fibre is valued in England at from £30 to £40 per ton. When young and tender, sida has qualities for feed purposes, but it is tough on the teeth.

BANANA FIBRES.—Manilla is got from banana musa textilis. This variety grows freely on the seaboard and on the banks of the rivers and creeks in the coast country. On an average a full-grown plant is found to produce 5 lbs. of clean fibre, and in their own country the best exertions of an experienced workman (Indian or Chinese) produce about 12 lbs. of fibre per day. Their wages are necessarily very low—less than would keep a white man in beef and flour. We fear, therefore, that until machinery is brought to their aid, Australians will have to leave Manilla fibre culture to those who work for 5d. per day and think it good wages. It is not agreeable to give up the matter in this way; but business is business; if it won't pay, our people can have nothing to do with it.

PINE-APPLE FIBRE.—Fibre is obtained from the leaves of the pine-apple, and is amongst the finest; and pine-apple cultivation being capable of extension to any extent, the production of the fibre is a question that depends upon the introduction of machinery.

RAMIE, Chinese-Cloth Plant.—Better things are expected from this, as the fibre has a value with comparative little labor on the part of the grower. The plant has been grown for years in public and private gardens. It is healthy, grows freely from cuttings planted during the spring season, in rows two feet apart.

Extracting Fibres.—Various methods of separating the fibres of flax, hemp, &c., from the glutinous matter with which they are surrounded, have been adopted in various countries. In Ireland, Belgium, Holland, and in France the plants, after being pulled, are dried in the sun, being set up on the root-end in two thin rows, the top interlacing in the form of the letter **A** inverted. Then sun and air soon thoroughly dry the stems, and they are bulked and made into sheaves, and the seed afterwards threshed off. The stems are steeped subsequently. Another mode in general use in Ireland and in part of Flanders, is to steep the green stems immediately after they are pulled. In Flanders the seed is invariably separated from the stems before the latter are immersed in water. In Ireland, although this has been practised to some extent, yet the great bulk of the flax-crop is put in the water at once, with the seed capsules attached. In Belgium and Germany, dew-retting is practised. That is, in place of immersing the stems in water, they are spread thinly on short grass, and the action of the dews and rains in time effect what immersion in a running stream or pool accomplishes in a much shorter time, namely, the decomposition of the gum which binds the fibres to the stem and to each other. But fibre obtained by this method is considered of inferior quality and color. If the fibre of flax be separated from the stem without the decomposition of this matter, it is found to be loaded with impurities, which are got rid of afterwards in the wet-spinning, the boiling of the yarn, the subjection of the woven fragment to the action of alkaline lye and the action of the atmosphere, of rains, and of alternate dippings in water, treated with sulphuric acid and a solution of chloride of lime, to perfect the bleaching. The great object is to obtain the fibre as nearly free from foreign substances as possible. At various periods attempts have been made to prepare flax fibre without steeping or retting. Weak acids, solutions of caustic potash, and soda, soap, lye, and lime, have all been tried, but have all been found objectionable.

COTTON.—What a rotation cotton would make with grain or root crops, were it a paying crop! Three sorts are grown in Queensland: woolly seed, Egyptian, and sea island. All belong to the natural order Malvaceæ, and are heavy oil as well as fibre-yielders; there is a large amount of that order of plants in these colonies, fibre-bearing; they do not impoverish the soil to any great extent. For a rotation on light lands, maize or barley may be sown the first year, cotton the second, grass the third and fourth years. The two-year old grass ploughed up and sown with maize or other corn crop, or planted with potatoes or other roots, would be a rotation.

OIL CROPS—*The Pea and Ground Nut.*—This valuable edible and oil-yielder grows luxuriantly in Northern Australia. It is a lowly soft plant, not unlike well-grown clover. The fruit is found just under the surface of the soil all round the stem. The pea-nut likes a free, rich sandy loam, without stones, and from its nature it is absolutely necessary that the soil be kept quite free from weeds. The fruit is in thin-shelled vessels, each containing two seeds, of greyish white color, about the size of almonds, and of rich nutty flavor. This seed is planted either singly or in pairs as dug, and as soon as the soil is sufficiently warm for semi-tropical vegetation, say in September or October in the cooler, and two months earlier in warmer localities. Prepare the land as for corn; harrow very fine; run out shallow furrows from three to four feet apart. Drop in the seed about ten inches apart, and cover. Harrow or rake the surface soil three or four days after planting; in eight or ten days the plants commence to break through. They come in strong shoots not unlike common potatoes, and rapidly develope clover-like leaves which shade the ground. Cultivate as clean as possible. Flowers come out at the ends of the shoots, and as they fall the shoots bend down and send out stout feelers, or roots, that enter the ground. The fruit is borne in bunches on these feelers, and all round the stem. As the nuts ripen the leaves decay. In all, the crop occupies the ground from eight to ten months. The nuts must be gathered during dry weather, otherwise the color is injured—not a matter of much moment when it is grown for oil, or for feeding stock; but this is a crop that ought to find favor for domestic use, and to that end should be gathered as clean as possible.

SUNFLOWERS.—All the order are heavy bearers of seed that yields a good oil. Sunflowers grow in summer in much the same way as maize; the seed being borne upon large circular heads—some of them twelve inches in diameter. The seed is easily rasped off, and is treated for oil in the same way as other seeds.

THE OLIVE.—Coming to oil-yielders in the tree form, we find the olive a favourite. There are several varieties, some suitable for strong and others for lighter land. Cuttings or truncheons are used for plants; from eight to twelve inches in length is considered a good size; and they may be either from the branches or roots. The olive is also grown from seed by planting in September. Plants thus obtained are fit for setting out in the following September. The tree in all its stages suffers from frost; it is well, therefore, to select warm and sheltered places for it. The olive grafts freely; the sorts found to answer best can be increased in this way upon the less desirable varieties. The trees are planted from sixteen to twenty feet apart, according to variety and strength of the soil. They require ordinary good cultivation, and manure where the soil is not strong enough. Pruning is recommended as a means of inducing fruitfulness. The trees commence to bear in their fifth or sixth year, and are long lived when justice is done them. The fruit is of the plum kind, and usually egg-shaped; when ripe, it is of a reddish color, and is borne in enormous quantities upon the full-bearing trees. It is gathered by hand and by shaking the trees; the product in view being a valuable oil, it is obvious that the cleaner and less bruised the fruit is the better. The test of ripeness is to press the fruit; when oil comes away freely, it is fit for the press.

Olive Oil.—To get the oil, the fruit is ground into pulp; the pulp is put into bags of horsehair or other strong stuff; these bags are put under a screw press, and the oil forced out. The oil is allowed to run into vessels containing water, and is skimmed off as soon as the impurities pressed out with it have separated. A second pressing, perhaps a third, is obtained by heating the pulp, and sprinkling it with warm water. Oil of first quality is of greenish color and of nutty flavor. The coarser sorts are darker in color. To purify it, olive oil is allowed to stand for three or four months in jars or tanks, that all impurities may be deposited. The oil is then put up in bottles for use. The yield of oil varies very much. One to two gallons per tree is considered a fair average, but as high as one cwt. of oil is mentioned as the product of famous trees. The pressed pulp, etc., is used as feed stuff.

Home made Olive Oil.—To those who have a few olive trees the following for getting the oil may be of use. Those who have once tasted the pure article will not be willing to use any other. Crush the olives in a common corn-crusher; put the pulp thus obtained into bags, and press with lever or screw into a vessel containing water. The pure oil swims on the top of what is thus expressed, and is after skimming, clarified by filtering through blotting paper, which answers the purpose; the oil, after thus being filtered, is ready for use or market. A lever for crushing may be made from a stout piece of timber, about 20 feet long, fixed at one end by a bolt to a stump or post, with a heavy weight at the other. The bags containing the crushed olives are put under the lever a few feet from the fixed end and the oil pressed out.

Pickled Olives.—For this purpose the fruit is gathered before quite ripe, and soaked for half a day in lye made from one part quicklime to six parts wood ashes, with sufficient water to extract the alkali. The object of this alkaline steep is to extract a portion of the bitter principle peculiar to the fruit. After steeping, the olives are washed in fresh water and then put up in bottles, with a brine of salt and water, in which aromatic herbs may also be placed. Ripe olives are also used for preserving.

Castor-Oil.—The plant from which the castor-oil of commerce is made has long claimed a home for itself in the coast country of Northern Australia. On the banks of rivers the trees grow in dense masses, and as a dozen trees throw off about a bushel of seed annually, and each seed may make a plant that bears within a year, the rate of extension while they meet suitable soil is prodigious. To succeed as an oil-yielding crop, the plants require good rich corn-land, prepared as for a crop of maize. Plant the seed about five feet apart, in rows; the rows, for the convenience of cultivation, may be from 10 to 12 feet apart. The seed is hardy, and the young plants appear above ground in from 10 to 14 days. No other crop can be grown between the rows, as the castor oil is a decided surface rooter and rapid grower. The smoothing or back-toothed harrow, the horse hoe, or a shallow cultivator is run between the rows to keep down grass, weeds, &c. With moderately fair treatment, in six months after planting we have trees from 8 to 12 feet in height. The fruit is borne in clumps of small rough seed-vessels. As the seed ripens, the covering cases commence to split open. Then is the time to gather. Some varieties "pop," or fly open, and the seed is scattered out on the ground. Others have to be forced open. It is the task of each grower to select such seed as will give him a crop that will neither "pop" too soon, nor be too stiff to separate from the seed-vessels. The crop is gathered by hand, and also by stretching a cloth around the tree, and "yanking," or jerking off the seed with a stick. As gathered, the seed is placed in a heap either under shelter in the field, on a verandah, or in a barn. In any case it must be surrounded with boards one foot or more in height, that the seeds may not pop over. To make the stiffer ones fly open, they may be beaten with anything soft. There is great difference in the yield of different beans; those that are solid, and from which the oil oozes freely on being pressed with the fingers, are the best. They also vary in size and colour; some are beautifully striped and mottled; but colour is no guide to quality in the castor bean. When very large, they are frequently hollow in the centre. Those about the size of common coffee beans are usually the best.

Getting the Oil.—The oil is obtained by bruising or grinding the seed (we have seen an ordinary large-sized coffee mill used for the purpose). The pulp is then put into horsehair or other bags, and the oil extracted by pressure as olive oil. This is the cold-drawn article of commerce. It is also extracted by simmering in vessels heated by steam or fire, as described in article on vegetable oils.

Caution.—The residue of castor oil seeds, after the oil is pressed out, is poisonous. The seeds also are injurious except as medicine. The oil is used largely for lubricating purposes.

XII.—MAKING AND USING MANURES.*

THIS is amongst the most important subjects the Australian farmer has to consider; and it is encouraging to note the growing attention given to it. Let the natural

Manure Makes the Crop.

richness of his land be what it may, the man acts wisely who prepares to feed his crops on manure from the start. For rich land, the quantity required to keep up the soil in its best condition is but small—when the right material is supplied. The poorer the land the more feed has to be supplied in the form of manure, and skill is called out more and more to get what the soil stands most in need of. Skilful manuring, with good cultivation, is the safe road to success, and the only one that enables the agriculturist to prosper in dry as well as in wet seasons. There are many sources of manure available. The best and most effective of all, additional to the compost heap, is to combine grazing with farming, and either to feed stock on land intended for cultivation, or to lay the land down in grass and graze and top dress it until the piece has received a thorough coating. This process is followed with absolute success as a portion of a course of rotation. In the grain districts where sheep are kept this system of manuring is very effective, especially

* Artificial manure making, superphosphate making, and the science aspect of manure making and manuring generally, are dealt with in the author's work, "Helpful Chemistry for Agriculturists," 4s., Batson & Co., Ltd., Sydney, and book-sellers generally.

so where, in addition to the natural grasses, the stock get additions of cultivated feed.

Making Manure.—The dryness of the atmosphere, and the occurrence of very heavy rains, are against the making of manure in open yards or in pits, as followed in Europe. But when cattle are put under the sheds at night, this plan becomes successful here. While working upon this system, and to overcome excessive evaporation, the liberal application of dry, loamy soil to the surface where stock camp is decidedly beneficial. This dry soil absorbs the ammonia and other gases that are otherwise blown away, and after lying for four or five months becomes as rich as the very best portions of the heap upon which the soil is scattered. The free application of dry earth in covered stockyards and upon manure heaps has this additional advantage: the manure can be hauled out on the field with less loss from evaporation than when the compost has been made in the ordinary way. Where cane megass and refuse, corn stalks, coarse grass, &c., are available, enormous quantities of manure can be made in this way in the pig pen, or with the aid of a small lot of working cattle that are yarded at night.

The Australian Compost Heap.—Of dry soil we have already spoken. It is one of the valuable aids in favor of manure-making in Australia, as will be more clearly understood after study of this chapter, and especially of page 133 referring to waste in ordinary farm-yard stuff. Few things will be found to pay better than a shed under which a dray can travel, and in which soil can be stored in dry weather, so that it may be kept fit for use whenever required. Loamy soil is the best for the purpose. The richer it is in vegetable matter, the better and more effective

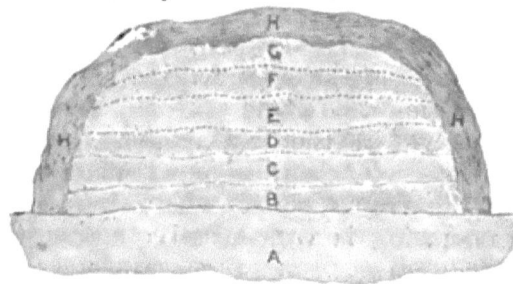

The Australian Compost Heap.

it is. With this agent, nothing need be lost; it absorbs

matter of all sorts. A load or two of it packed around the carcass of a dead beast prevents all smell, and affords a compost equal to the richest for many purposes. It is also the best agent for absorbing night-soil and making it available for use, and many other purposes that will readily suggest themselves. The compost heap should be under cover, if at all practicable, and to prepare for it as much loamy earth—dried stuff from swamps does splendidly, being rich in vegetable matter—should be carted up in readiness. As a foundation for the compost, put down a thick layer of earth (a); and on top of that (b) any weeds, grass, &c., that can be got together, in order to rot them down, and destroy seeds of weeds, &c. Then, any night-soil or refuse stuff can be added, as at (c). Then more earth (d), and so on, adding layer upon layer, cow-pen, stable, or other stuff, and making a heap as large as may be required. If ammonia, in the form of sulphate of ammonia, now made by the gas companies, is required, or potash, or bone manure, or any other rich fertilizing material, it can be mixed up in the compost heap, care being taken all through the process to keep a covering of earth ($h\ h\ h$) all round, to prevent loss. Such a heap as this does not heat; the earth prevents that, and it can be hauled out as required for the immediate use of the crops.

What Crops Take Out of the Soil.—As has been seen in the chapters dealing with soils, what makes soils rich and what causes poverty, the main ingredients taken away by crops are ammonia, potash, phosphates, lime, sulphates, &c. With the exception of the three first named, ammonia, potash, and phosphates, the other substances that build up plant and animal life are sufficiently plentiful in Australian soils, and it is mainly to supply the scarce substances that manuring or feeding of crops has to be attended to by agriculturists in all branches. The accompanying tables show that field and garden crops require the same substances, but in very different proportions, some requiring more ammonia, some more potash, others more phosphates, lime, sulphur, and so on. But all require some, and the skill of the agriculturist tells upon his crops when he supplies their requirements in the right proportions and at the right time.

HOW CROPS ARE BUILT UP.—WHAT THEY TAKE AWAY PER ACRE.

Crop.	Yield.	Nitrogen Ammonia.	Potash.	Phosphates.	Lime.	Magnesia.	Sulphates.
		lbs.	lbs.	lbs.	lbs.	lbs.	lbs.
Wheat	30 bushels (with straw)	46	28	22	11	4	5
Maize	50 bushels	48	12	11	6	3	1
Barley	28 bushels	45	20	16	19	12	4
Oats	33 bushels	50	43	29	15	11	7
Rye	26½ bushels	35	30	13	16	5	4
Lucerne	20 tons green or 4 tons hay	115	87	53	105	16	30
Clover	12 tons green or 2½ tons hay	85	16	40	72	21	13
Native Grasses	10 tons green or 2 tons hay	31	27	19	26	6	11
Tobacco	15wt. cured leaf	54	69	14	23	5	4
Potatoes	5 tons	70	100	12	7	3	8
Sweet Do.	10 tons and 5 tons tops	55	40	10	5	3	9
Turnips	6 tons	78	52	14	9	5	16
Buckwheat	24 bushels (1,200lb.)	42	89	18	12	4	13

Similar substances are absorbed by fruits, and the accompanying table is arranged to show, comparatively, what the proportions are, so that manures may be composted to suit the crop we are making:—

FRUIT AND VEGETABLES ABSORB PER ACRE.

Crops	Nitrogen Ammonia.	Potash.	Phosphates.	Lime.	Magnesia.	Sulphates.	Chlorides Salt.	Silica.
	lbs.	lbs.	lbs.	lbs.	lbs.	lbs.	lbs.	lbs.
Apples	18	10	4	9	2	1	1	4
Pears	19	10	5	7	2	1	1	4
Peaches	14	27	3	12	3	1	1	3
Apricots	14	22	3	11	3	1	1	3
Plums	10	18	2	9	2	1	1	2
Oranges	66	24	11	21	4	4	3	2
Lemons	40	20	9	17	4	4	3	2
Grapes	25	96	14	29	7	8	2	3
Cabbage	118	15	40	11	16	6	2	
Cauliflowers	134	17	28	45	13	18	6	3
Lettuce	80	14	13	27	8	6	4	1
Onions	45	18	14	28	13	20	7	4
Peas	10	22	50	41	17	32	6	5

Natural manures of the organic kind that have been in the growth of vegetable or animal life, such as rich soil from swamps, &c., leaf mould, bush scrapings, stable, stockyard, pig pen, and poultry yard stuff, offal, sawdust, &c., &c., supply some of the ingredients that plants live on, but in still more varying quantities than crops take them. Hence the use of composting, so as to supply in the heap such other materials as may be necessary, and in such form as may mix thoroughly with the others in less or greater quantity in the proportions required. It is a further advantage in using natural manures that as they are broken up and decay in the soil they make room for the development or spread of root growth, and add enormously to the good results got from purchased manures.

The sources of manures available for Australian agricultural purposes include :—

Bone in Various Forms.—By breaking and grinding, bones are made more readily soluable for the use of plants. Bones supply phosphates and lime, and small quantities of the other food materials of crops. Raw bone is most valuable, next cooked bone. Bone ash and burnt bone are least valuable as manure.

Boiling Down Stuff.—This is the refuse material from boiling-down works, and contains all the substance of sheep, cattle, &c., except the tallow, which is of no value for manure.

Offal from Slaughter-houses.—When this contains blood material, it is rich in ammonia in addition to the other substances of animal life. It is valuable in proportion to the less quantity of moisture in it.

Stable, Cow-pen, Piggery Stuff.—The value is proportionate to the feed of the animals, and whether it has been wasted by exposure to he weather.

Fowl Yard Stuff.—This is very valuable, rich in ammonia and phosphates, and other substances in proportion.

Ashes.—Wood ashes contain potash, lime, and various other substances of plant life, the value being dependent on the quantity of potash.

Sea Weeds and Ferns.—Potash, soda, lime, and sulphates are got in sea weeds; also in ferns, both of which make desirable additions to the compost heap.

Sawdust.—Does best when mixed with a small proportion of lime, say a bucketful to a load of sawdust.

Mineral Manures.—These include superphosphate, or bone reduced by sulphuric acid, sulphate of ammonia, a product of gas-making. Potash is imported in the form of sulphate of potash and kanit, or salt of potash, the value of each being dependent upon the potash contents. Manures of the mineral kind give best results when composted with the more bulky natural manures.

Lime.—Very plentiful in Australia, and of excellent quality. It should be applied to the land separately from other manures, and freshly slacked with water, that is, in the form of quick lime, as a rule, where the land contains much clay, or more than 10 per cent. of vegetable matter. On thinner soils, air-slacked lime or bone dust answer better. It is best to apply lime frequently and in small quantities, to keep it near the surface and always active. From one to three tons of lime to the acre may be considered an average application. More may be applied on very strong soil, and less on light land. Excellent results often follow a first application of lime, but future dressings may seem to fail to have the same effects. In these cases, green crops might be ploughed in, and other manures used, when, after a season, lime may again be applied with profit, and to bring the fresh material into active service by breaking them up for the use of crops.

Green manuring—the ploughing into the soil of growing crops—is one of the most certain, as it is one of the always available means of enriching any moderately good land. Amongst the plants specially available for this purpose are peas, corn, buckwheat, oats, cotton, sorghum, and the summer grasses. The effect of this treatment is to supply vegetable matter in heavy quantity and in a form most acceptable to the soil and the crop. It has the effect of keeping the surface soil cool during our hot summers, when crops rooting near the surface suffer badly from the heated surface earth, and especially in sandy soils. The following is a fair estimate of the quantity of vegetable matter from various crops ploughed in. Their nitrogen-ammonia contents are gathered mostly from the air:—

Plant	Tons per acre	Nitrogen lbs. per acre	Value of Nitrogen s. d.	Other substances s. d.
Cow Pea	9.7	151.0	87 7	50 6
Maize	25.5	72.0	41 9	47 6
Sunflower	18.0	100.0	60 11	40 0
Sorghum	15.8	54.1	31 5	36 6
Oats	4.8	54.4	31 7	28 2
Mustard	5 5	39.9	23 2	5 0
Turnips	2.4	34.0	19 9	28 8

Artificial Manures.—Very excellent compounded manures are supplied by Australian manufacturers. Their value is mostly in the ammonia, potash, and phosphate contents, all of which are obtainable now by Australian agriculturists, at rates which put us on an equality for feeding crops with any part of the world. Sulphate of ammonia, got from what was formerly a waste product of gas works, is excellent in quality and low in price. Sulphate of potash and kainit, or salt of potash, supply this essential of plant life. Bones supply phosphates in their very best form. The tables of what crops take from the soil supply the needful information of the proportions required for various crops. When mixed in the compost heap with one or more of the coarser manures described, we get the best result from artificial manures.

Waste in Ordinary Farm Manure.—It has long been a matter of concern in countries where farm-yard manures form the foundation of the general manuring, that there is such a loss of labor in bringing it into use. Thus, an ordinary average ton (2240 lbs.) of farm-yard manure, as made after the careful manner followed in Scottish farming, is composed as follows : solid matter, say, 640 lbs., which contains about 50 lbs of soluble matter; some 1600 lbs. of water make up the ton. The water is of very little value to the farmer in that country, and he has not the dry soil that is available here for our manure-making.

The 50 lbs. mentioned are made up of ammonia, phosphates, potash, lime, soda, salt, sulphuric acid, &c., and the value of the whole ton of stuff is dependent upon the proportions in which the first three—ammonia, phosphates, and potash—are in it. We thus see how the value of the manures are reduced to very small quantities when the right materials are present.

The Time for Manuring.—When we have a choice, in order to apply manure with the best effect for nourishing what is planted, whether orchard trees or field or garden crops, then just before they start into active growth is the time which gives the most effective results. New feeding roots are being formed then, and the sap for building up the plant for the season is coming forward, and necessary material is being stowed away for the growth of the following season, or for maturing the buds, grain or seed. Next to the time for applying manure, is the selection of the right kind chemically, and its nature in the mechanical sense. The effect of manure substances on soils is very various. Long manure made from the straw and litter of stables is not so suitable for sandy soils, unless it can be used on the surface as a mulch. When dug or ploughed into thin soils, it tends to make the land still more dry, and hence should only be applied to this kind of soil after being thoroughly rotted, or better as part of a compost. What sandy soils require, as a rule, is vegetable matter compost, or thoroughly rotted manure in right condition to supply food to the crop without heating the soil. Leaf mould, bush scrapings, etc., help this compost greatly. Crops on sandy soils, when the right manure is there for them, use it up very fast, and hence the apparent disappearance of manure in such soils is accounted for. It goes quickly into the crop, if in a soluble state, and the best results are got when the crop can take it up at once. But loamy soils and clays, on the contrary, store up and digest manure, and are able to hold it until it is given up to the roots. The reason why manure is more quickly eaten out from sandy soils is that they contain less food material for the roots. They are more porous and eat more than the clayey soils. Root action is more rapid in them. That is, provided the sandy soil is sufficiently moist. So when soils are stiff, or clayey, long, undigested manure may be useful. It tends to render such soils more open, light and porous. But for sandy soils, we must aim to render them as compact as possible, while the naturally firm clay soils require breaking up and working to make them most productive.

XIII.—IRRIGATION AND WATER STORAGE.

Admitting Water from River or Creek.

Relation of Plants to Water.—All plants are composed largely of water. Grasses contain 40 per cent., many of the herbage plants, and some of the most valuable, much more. Fruits, vegetables and flowers are made up of water to the extent of two-thirds of their weight. Some of them over 90 per cent. This water has been absorbed through the roots mostly, and is but a portion only of the total moisture absorbed. For water is the medium through which the earthy substances of plant life are carried up.

So that all plants must have water in some proportion; most of them in large proportion. They perish unless it is supplied.

"Irrigation?"—In the agricultural sense, this term applies to watering by artificial means. It has, ever since the time of white settlement, been a subject of interest in Australia, and irrigation has been carried out sufficiently for pastoral, general farming, and gardening purposes, to supply sufficient data to work on. Then Southern Europe, California, Utah, Colorado, Mexico, India, Syria, Egypt, even the South Sea Islands afford further details of use to the progressive agriculturist. From the time of the Romans onwards, works have been constructed for water storage for irrigation purposes—a very different arrangement from water storage for cities, both as to cost, and the quality of the water.

Methods of Irrigation.—They are very various. From the earliest times, water has been applied to plants when the rainfall was not sufficient for the purposes of the agriculturist. The defined methods of applying water are by sprinkling all over the plants; by saturating or soaking the soil without sprinkling, and by a combination of both processes. The basin system is suitable for sandy and gravelly soils, and is followed extensively in California.

Advantages and Disadvantages.—Sprinkling seems the more natural method. It is most like rain. The disadvantages of sprinkling are that sediment and mineral substances in the water dry upon or crystalize on growing plants, and may destroy them by closing the breathing pores. When water is used on the soil only, this risk is avoided, and water may be used in that way with excellent effect, which would be destructive if used the other way. There is also an immense difference in the cost of the methods of applying water.

Irrigation and Drainage.—The chapters no draining and cultivation explain how necessary and beneficial it is to have rain water sink into the soil to the full depth to which the roots penetrate. The same rule applies in irrigation. The water, put it on in which way we may, must sink into the soil, and do its work through the agency of drainage, natural or artificial, or irrigation is worse than wasted labor. The most effective irrigation is where the soil is saturated from the surface to the subsoil, and is on the move all through. Any layers of dry earth under the wetted surfaces would be ruinous to the crop, whether it were grass, corn, potatoes, fruit, or flowers. We must soak the soil right through.

Quantity of Water for Grass, Crops, Fruits, &c.—The nature of the soil and the crops will regulate the quantity of water necessary. Grass may be effectively irrigated by the application of 5 inches of water during a dry season in which no rain falls. Sugar cane, to make a full crop of 40 to 60 tons per acre, requires 30 inches; maize, 14 inches; potatoes, 12 inches; orchards, 10 inches. The Chinese use about 10 inches, and they water all the year round. Heavy yields of wheat are got from 7 inches of irrigation water. When rain falls during the irrigation time, half an inch of rain has wonderfully brightening effects upon the irrigated crops, and does more good than double the quantity of water by irrigation.

"But, an Inch of Water?"—For ordinary purposes, 25,000 gallons is reckoned as an inch, and is estimated to cover an acre, 1 inch deep. Whether we get the water by pumping, or by other means, we have to allow for 10 lbs. per gallon as being the weight, and the calculation is useful in working out systems of pumping, or carrying water over tressels, &c. An inch of water saturates soil from 3 to 6 inches, according to its condition.

Sources of Supply.—There are districts in Australia where snow water supplies may be made available during dry spells. But the rainfall has to be depended on in most cases. Hence, water storage by damming rivers, creeks, and water courses has to be seen to. Artesian supplies are available where the geological formation is suitable, and very valuable experiences are being gained through the wells sunk in the western districts. Wells may supply vast quantities where springs exist. Tanks are used in other places. Rivers, creeks, and lagoons, as storage places, supply the best irrigation water. Wells may contain doubtful mineral substances

All Water should be Analysed.—This is an absolutely necessary precaution before laying out land for irrigation, or applying water to land for agriculture, and is especially necessary before using well or sewerage water.

Irrigation from Wells—At a huge strawberry farm in Santa Clara, California, the author saw the effects of irrigation from artesian wells, and the necessity that exists for exposing water to the air before using it on crops. In the case under notice an immense tank of concrete had been raised some 10 feet above the level of the cultivated land, which is level plain of great extent. In this tank the well water was aerated, and mineral substances were got rid of before the water was used. The elevation was sufficient to give water pressure all over the cultivation land.

Irrigation by Soakage.—This process is followed usually where capital and skill are brought to bear, and is in general favor. Very efficient work of that kind is in operation at the sewerage farm, at Botany, connected with the Sydney water supply. The land is laid out in levelled paddocks, fields, or beds. Crops, such as lucerne, are sown

Irrigating for Vegetables by Gravitation and Soakage

either upon this levelled land or the land is laid up in ridges by the plough, and the crops are planted or sown upon the ridges. The water is brought upon the land at a

IRRIGATION AND WATER STORAGE.

sufficiently high level—7 feet or higher—to be run upon the cultivation by gravitation. The soil is very porous, originally it was barren sand, and the water sinks into it rapidly, feeding the roots in its passage when the water is suitable. At Mildura, and other settlements on the Darling, soakage is the system followed.

Irrigation for Grass.—Where water can be brought upon pasture land at a sufficient elevation, it may be allowed to trickle over the surface and sink into the land. Comparatively steep land may be treated in this way.

Crop Irrigation.—Where water is run upon cultivated land, whether under field crops, orchard, or vegetables, we have to be careful that the soil is not washed away. In laying out the land, the channels through which the water is to pass, opened by plough or hoe, as A B in illustration, should not be steeper than 1 foot

Furrows for Irrigating Field or Orchard.

in 10; 1 in 100 is better. Water runs effectively with a fall of 6 feet per mile; in all steeper gradients there are risks of washing away the soil.

Irrigation Land with Gradual Fall.—In the plan shown,

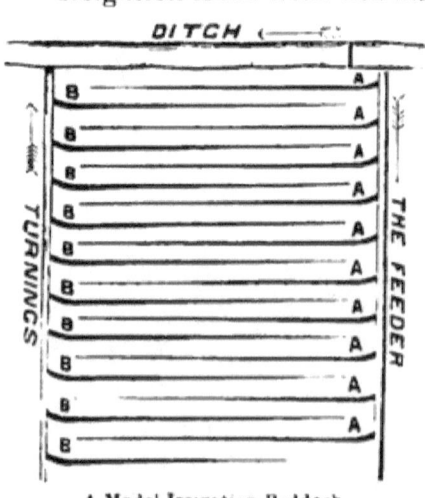

A Model Irrigation Paddock.

at upper end is the ditch, flume, pipe, or other source of water supply. The arrow shows the course of the water-flow. Near the butt of the arrow, in the water course, by a gate or other means, the water is stopped and the flow directed into the feeder, from which it is led upon the ground in furrows (A A A). At the lower end of these furrows it may be turned (B B B) into the channels between, or allowed to flow into the lower channel (shown by arrow), and so returned to the ditch again. The most effective irrigation is where all the water allowed to pass into the feeder is absorbed or soaked into the soil, without allowing a

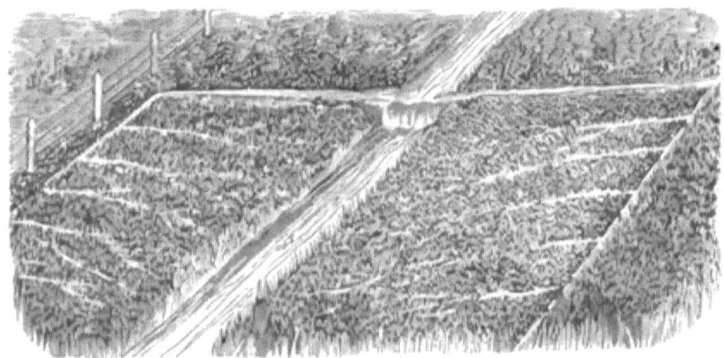

Irrigating by "Stepping" Process.

run of water at any point. Hilly, broken ground is not so suitable for irrigation. The cost and labor of working places of that kind increase rapidly as soon as we get a greater fall than 1 foot in 25. The illustration shows how a very awkward place has been treated. The water is

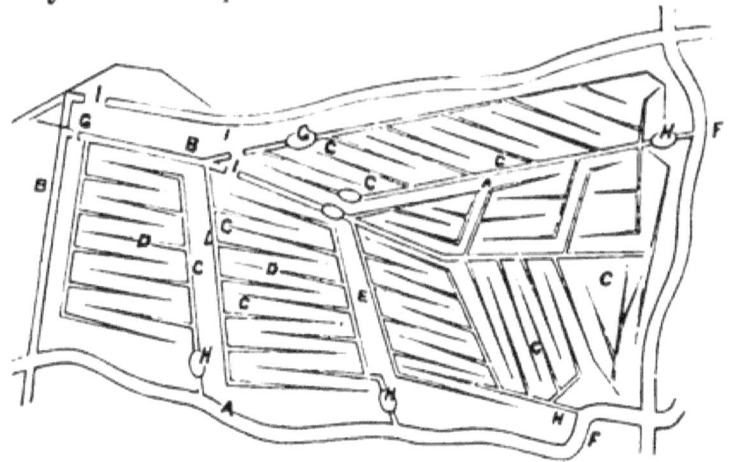

Irrigating Hilly, Broken Ground.

brought in at I, which must be the highest part of the land. B B are feeders from the main supply, and the water is then carried along in still smaller channels (C C), follow-

IRRIGATION AND WATER STORAGE.

ing the formation of the land, so as to allow it to soak in without running, which would be more dangerous than in the first instance cited. In cases where the water must be let down to lower levels, in order to do what is necessary—that is, saturate the soil—catchments or shallow wells (H H) are made, and the overflow water from them used in the still lower parts of the ground. At (C D E F G), while the water is flowing, it is stopped and directed in small streams as required upon the field.

Irrigating Hill Sides—In order to irrigate land thoroughly, channels or furrows with very little fall for the flow of water have to be laid out by levelling instruments, and by this means ridges and inequalities are saturated by carrying the water round their sides, by contouring. Water gates and sluices, for admitting water from a ditch or other channel upon the land to be irrigated, are of various forms. In the gate shown, the flow is regulated by lifting one or more of the pieces of wood which slide between grooves in the side posts, and so

Water Gate.

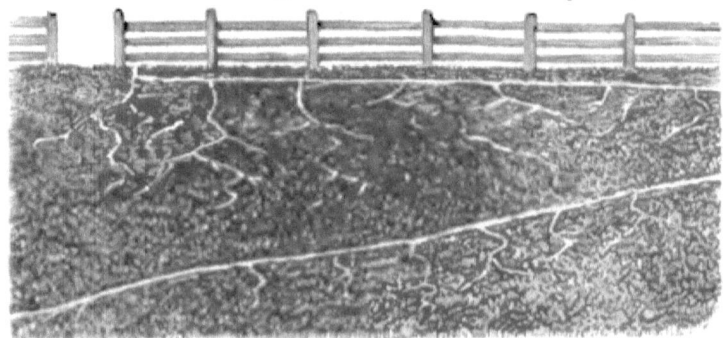

Irrigating by Contouring.

allow the water to flow in, or be stopped, as may be required.

Where Water is Scarce.—Where but small quantities of water are available, for soakage, the always abundant supply of old fruit and jam tins may be brought into use for home garden irrigation pretty much upon the plan by which Mexicans and Egyptians supply water to plants by means of chatties. The arrangement answers best when the crop is grown to some extent, and is then in danger from dry weather. The tins, each having two or three small holes punched in the bottom, are set out

Helpful When Water is Scarce.

amongst the growing vegetables. At nightfall, and again during the day, the tins are filled, and the water enters the earth slowly. The rate of distribution can be regulated by settling the tins deep or shallow into the soil. But, simple and crude though the arrangement may look, it has been the means of keeping up supplies of vegetables where, without this help, there could have been none. Self-help is the lever of success in agriculture.

Sub-Irrigation.—Some acres of drain pipes have been laid down on the Government ground at Rookwood, for combined drainage and sub-irrigation. For the latter purpose the pipes can be filled from the highest level, so that by closing up the outlet, the water may rise to the roots of grass, field, garden, or orchard crops. There is also another plan available for making the most of waste water, or where small quantities only are available. A box is fitted in a convenient place, and from the box pipes are put down so that garden stuff can be grown over them, the roots being supplied in this way.

What Experience Says.—Irrigation for crops can be successful only where the soil is thoroughly drained, either naturally, by having an open sub-soil, or artificially by means of drains. California, Colorado, Utah, and other

States of the Union, with climate very much like that of Australia, have advanced rapidly with irrigation. Victoria, our neighbour, is also moving ahead, as are a few enterprising men both in New South Wales and Queensland. Irrigation is applied successfully for grain crops, grass, orcharding, &c. The mechanical engineering principles involved are not difficult to work out. The papers and reports from officers in the Water Department are helpful in that direction. From lake, river, or dam, water is led in open ditches with a batter of about 45 degrees, where the fall does not exceed 6 feet per mile. Where the fall is greater, or gullies, &c., have to be crossed, flumes made V shape, and of timber, or close pipes of wrought iron or steel (made up to 40 inches diameter) are used. Ploughs and scoops are employed with good effect in opening out the ditches. When the water is got to the place where it is to be used, it is brought upon the land with as little run or fall as possible, otherwise it would quickly cut the land into gullies, wash away the soil, and be worse than a dry spell. What is termed stepping is used where steep land has to be crossed. The steps are made by putting logs or boards across the ditch so as to raise the water a foot or so. The water from each terrace flows out from a bevelled notch in the centre of the log, which is really a dam. Efficient levelling, when the water can be run upon land, may be regulated by the water itself, always being careful not to allow it to run too fast, nor cut away the soil. In practice, it is found the best course to saturate the soil say two, three, or more times during a season, rather than to wet the surface oftener. For wheat and other grains, two saturations are found ample to secure crops; once after the seed is in, and again when the crop is in flower. But much depends upon the soil and the season. There is no hard and fast rule for guidance.

Water Storage—In Australia, river and creek beds offer inducements for storing water. Where the fall of the land is 1 foot in 50, or less, immense bodies of water may be impounded by laying logs across, or by "stepping." Heavier works are formed by earth, having an inside wall of clay—a "puddle wall." Stone, concrete, and timber are all in use for the same purpose.

Wells.—In the sedimentary and other geological formations which hold water so that it can be got by sinking or boring wells, heavy supplies are got. Then boring augers, diamond drills, and other contrivances are used for reaching the water-bearing strata or vein.

Water Boring Gear.

Tubes of metal are in places set in as lining to the wells, and pumping is employed, unless the flow reaches the surface, as the case is in the western districts, in Gippsland and other parts. The cost varies from 15s. per foot to £3.

Tube and Pumping Wells.—Tube wells have been driven with success in various parts, where the formation is suitable, and are found to answer admirably where a limited supply of water is sufficient. When sunk and in contact with a water giving stratum or spring, pumping has to be resorted to. The pointed tube goes with comparative ease through sand, loam, gravel or clay; but when rock is met the tube may be withdrawn—it will bend if forced too much. A likely place for water being selected, the tubes—lengths of ordinary iron-piping—are arranged for driving. Into one of the lengths is screwed a piece of solid iron, pointed, about eight inches long, and the shoulder next the pipe is made of a greater diameter than the pipe.

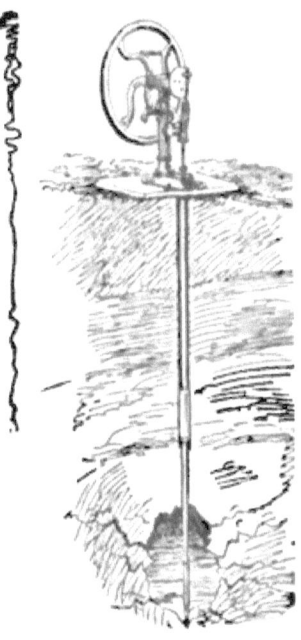

Tube or Driven Well.

This is for driving into the ground, and this pointed part being greater than the pipe, it clears the way. Just above where this solid point is screwed, holes are drilled in the pipe along sixteen or eighteen inches of its length. The number of these holes must of course be in proportion to the size of the pump, so as to admit as much water as the pump is capable of taking up. A No. 6 Douglas pump is as large as can be reasonably worked by manual labour. In order to protect the top of the pipe as well as the driving block from injury by the blows in driving, a cap which screws on to the ends of any of the pipes is fitted, and upon it the forcing power is applied, care being exercised in seeing that the blows are struck fair by a maul or driving monkey, and that the pipe is not bent.

When Water is Reached.—When the tube well pipe is driven to a depth where water may be expected, it is useful to let down a plummet to try for water. When the plummet comes up wet, it may be well to screw on the pump and try whether merely soakage water is reached, or whether it comes from a spring. In a well put down in this way, at a depth of 20 feet, 3 feet of water was got. The pipe was then driven to 26 feet, and the water rose 20 feet in the tube. At first it came up but slowly, mixed with sand, and there was great pressure on the handle. It required several hours' work before the water became clear and came with a free flow. But the success of the pump may be judged from the fact that two tanks, containing each 400 gallons, were filled in an hour and a quarter, the pump throwing out the water as fully at the end as in the beginning, showing that the water found was fully equal to a pipe of 2 inch bore. There is not much difficulty in lifting these pipes, when that is necessary. Get a sapling or piece of timber for a lever, say 15 feet long; put a bullock-chain round the pipe, with the hook to run on the chain; roll the other end round the lever. When the end of the lever is lifted, the chain tightens on the tube so thoroughly that it does not slip, and the tube can be drawn with a strong lift of the lever. When the end of the lever is lowered after the first lift of the pipe, the chain round the pipe slips down, and when the lever is again lifted it tightens round the pipe, so that it takes the pipe up gradually, without any readjusting or re-fixing of the chain.

Helpful in Driving Pipes or Stakes.—The usual method of driving pipes, stakes, &c., is to strike them on the upper end with a maul or other heavy hammer. When driving long poles or the pipes of a tube-well this mode is impracticable. But the driving, if in sandy or soft ground, may be done quickly, and without a high step or platform, by using the device shown in the illustration. This consists of a block of tough wood 1 foot in length, 4 or 5 inches square at the top, made tapering as shown, with the part next the pipe slightly hollowed out. Take a common trace-chain, wind closely about the pipe or pole, and hook it in position. With maul, axe or sledge, strike upon the block. Each blow serves only to tighten the grip of the chain. To keep the chain from falling to the ground when unfastened from the pole it should pass through a hole bored through the block, as shown at B, one end of the chain being fixed on staple, E.

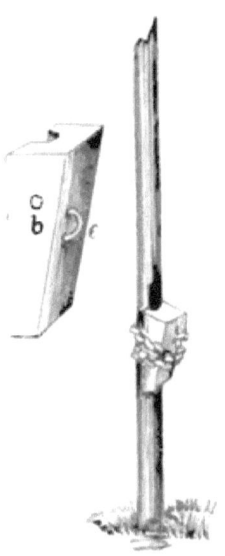

Pumping.—Centrifugal and various others pumps are used for raising water; the quantity, height for delivery, sizes of pipes, flumes, &c., being matters of calculation and engineering skill, which are dealt with fully in many works on that subject.

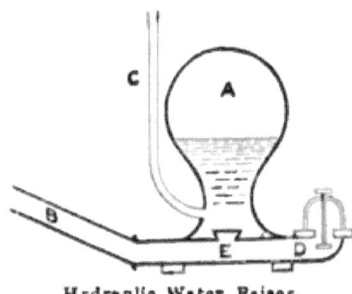

Hydraulic Water Raiser.

Water as a Pumping Power.—In places where there is plenty of water, or where from 8 to 12 parts of what passes through a water raising machine can be used that one part might be raised, then hydraulic, turbine and other machines may be used with good effect. The water in these contrivances is the force used for lifting. In the case of the ram or lifter illustrated, the water is admitted at *b*, and enters an air chamber *a* through valve *e* until there is pressure enough to lift the valve *d*, when the flow escapes until the valve again drops. Meanwhile the water confined under great air pressure in *a* is forced into the pipe *c*, where it finds outlet into tanks or other storage places.

Windmill for Pumping.

Windmills.—In many parts of the country these wind engines do excellent work. The requirements to make them effective are a well fixed mill of sufficient size, set on a well braced tower, an effective lift and force pump, and tank space to hold a body of water sufficient for irrigation purposes. Much experience has been gained in this country concerning the capacity of wind engines of different sizes, for raising water to any exent, where the supply is available, and also concerning the sizes of pipes that are suitable.

Self-acting Syphons.—By so arranging a syphon, set in a tank, that when full the water will overflow, the syphon thus started will flow until the supply is exhausted. Thus windmill and tanks can be made self acting, and supply irrigation water with very little labor and outlay.

Watering Plants in a Dry Spell.—Each plant has its requirements. Some do with very little; others want all they can get. But none can live without water, not even the rock lily or flannel flower, which seem to exist upon dry, barren stones or gravel; yet, even the greatest absorbers of water, as sugar cane, maize, potatoes, water cress, or soft annuals may get too much. Much disappointment arises from mistaken ideas concerning the watering and the way in which water is applied. Pot plants suffer seriously from too much watering, as do plants in the bush-house and conservatory. The general principle with which we have to deal in using water by artificial means applies to field crops equally with pot plants. In the early days of irrigation, in California, large areas of young wheat were destroyed by over-watering, and for a time it was thought that irrigation for wheat would not answer there; watering, it was said, brought on rust, but skill overcame that mistake—the watering had been overdone. The capacity of all plants to take up water is dependent very largely upon the extent of their roots; so that, in watering, say a bush-house, we may be starving some and drowning others, while we continue to serve all alike, by using the sprinkling pot or hose upon them. Thus, a young begonia may be gorged with water, while its full grown sister alongside is starving; or it may be that a plant has not been shifted and that its ball has been over-crowded with roots, and after being repotted, all the water may pass through the new soil while the interior of the hardened ball is dry, and in that state it is so much slower in absorbing water. In this way, shade-tree plants newly set out, may be starved for want of water. As a rule, the larger the leaf surface of plants or the quicker they grow, the more water is required. Plants with narrow leaves, or that grow slowly, do not require water to the same extent. The quantity of water required also depends to a great extent on the situation in which they are growing; thus, in the moist atmosphere of a conservatory, evaporation from the leaves is much less than in an airy bush-house. So with wheat in comparison with maize, less water requires to be pumped up by the wheat from the soil, and it is, therefore, not necessary to give water so often. Among active water absorbers are the ferns that naturally belong to moist, mossy situations; most of the orchids, when in baskets or pots, require to have their roots kept constantly moist while in a state of growth, though they endure almost complete dryness when dormant. Various of our indigenous plants, as rock lilies, staghorns, &c., although able to resist an almost absolute condition of drought, yet to bring them to perfection a regular supply of water must be given when they are in a state of growth; for, though they do not lose much moisture by evaporation or breathing, a large supply is needed to fill the tissues of the growing shoots or leaves.

When Plants are at Rest.—Mistakes in the watering may be made during the resting as well as the growing period. Nearly all tropical and most of our Australian native plants rest during seasons of drought, and start into growth with the advent of rain; the contrary being the case with plants of temperate and cold regions, where the soil contains the greatest amount of moisture during the winter or resting season, and they are thus well provided for on the advent of spring, which is the time when irrigation would be most useful in Australia.

Temperature of Water.—The temperature of water is very important. It is best when the same as the air for the time being, and may frequently be higher with advantage, but water that is much colder than the air temperature is injurious to plants.

XIV.—LIVE STOCK IN AUSTRALIA.

Grazing-Farming.—Agriculture as practised, and as believed to be best for the warmer sections of Australia, differs considerable from that followed in other parts of the world similarly situated with regard to climate. In many parts of the country it would be considered folly to attempt cultivation without sheep; and cattle help in much the same way. It is only the larger grazier or squatter who depends upon the native grasses for his herds or flocks; and cultivation is receiving more attention from graziers every year, for no branch of agriculture is at the mercy of the seasons to an equal degree with that of the squatter who depends solely upon indigenous vegetation. The agriculturist who combines cattle or sheep with his tillage operations is not only secured in the benefits incidental to live stock, but the manure made by them lessens the effects of bad seasons by increasing the fertility of his fields and the capacity of his land to withstand a dry spell.

The Better Prospect.—It is a source of much hopefulness regarding the future of the warmer sections of Australia that farming is already carried on with more full knowledge of the relations between highly-cultivated fields and success. Draining, subsoiling, and manuring are receiving more attention. Consequently horses, cattle, and sheep are in much favour among the farming classes. The practice most in favour is to use the native grasses largely during summer, to cultivate for winter feed, and to have the common run of cattle or sheep as the basis of the herd or flock, resorting to thoroughbred male animals for improving or keeping up the quality. When feeding is attended to from the start, and shelter is provided against the changes of climate felt in warm as well as in colder climates, the groundwork of success is secured. The making of manure is a primary object with the grazing-farmer, and he sells when his stock brings a fair profit. Those who follow this system may get no hundreds for a single animal, nor do the animals sold "cost more than they come to." There are, and will, we trust always be, numbers of gentlemen who have the time, the means, and the taste for breeding fine stock, cattle, sheep, horses, pigs, &c., and to warrant them in maintaining the herds and studs needed for the supply of the active demand always existing; and in case it should cost some of them a few thousands for the gratification of a worthy desire in this direction, nobody is much hurt. But with the ordinary grazier or farmer who practises mixed husbandry as a business rather than specialities, the condition is different. The experimenting has been done for him; on a large scale it is always risky.

The Stock Available.—In this branch of agriculture Australia has followed very close upon the lines of the mother land. The noble cattle of England and Scotland, the massive stately, handsome breeds are all here—the Shorthorns, the Herefords, the Devons, the red-polled cattle of Norfolk and Suffolk, Longhorns from the early importations, South Devons, "South Hammers," an offshoot of the Devons, North Devons, "cobs," plump, lively, enduring, active and decidedly pretty. Then we have the larger Welsh breeds, the polled breeds of Scotland and the handsome, shaggy rugged West Highlanders, so suggestive of mountains and forests and heather-clad moors. The notable dairy breeds of Europe—dealt with in the chapters on dairying—the Ayrshires, Jerseys, Kerrys, Holsteins, have all found favour. The breeders here are not stinted in the material they have to operate on.

Points in Breeding.—That from the male parent is mainly derived the physical strength and structure and outward characteristics, and the locomotive system. From the female parent, the internal structure, the vital organs, and in a much greater proportion than from the male, the constitution, temper, and habit, in which endurance and " bottom " are included. That the purer the race of the parent the more certainty there is of its transmitting its qualities to the offspring. Say, two animals are mated, and where one is of purer descent than the other, then, he or she will exercise the most influence in stamping the character of the progeny, particularly when the greater purity is on the side of the male. That apart from disturbing influences or causes, the male, if of pure race and descended from a stock of uniform colour, stamps the colour of the offspring. That the influence of the first male is not unfrequently protracted beyond the birth of the offspring of which he is parent, and his mark is left upon subsequent progeny. That the transmission of disease of the vital organs is most likely if on the side of the female, and diseases of the joints if on the side of the male parent.

The physiology of life in relation to domesticated animals and birds, the question of the distinctive influences of the sexes, is of essential importance to the stock-breeder in all branches, from horses to poultry and pigeons. That each sex has an allotted part in stamping the offspring with hereditary properties becomes obvious in every stage, but how and to what extent the distinctive attributes are made dominant is not so clear. Experiments in breeding for the purpose of elucidating this mystery must be conducted with due regard to the relative qualities of the sexes. When one of a long-fixed type is mated with another of mixed breeding, it follows almost for a certainty that the influence of the former will overbalance that of the latter. So that in experimentalising it is requisite to select those only which may be said to start equal, when a fixed result is aimed at.

A striking instance in support of this observation was presented in the poultry yard, where very close tests of this nature can be made. The case was with a well-bred brown Leghorn male, mated with two good light Brahma hens. Twenty-six chickens resulted, fourteen of them cockerels, twelve pullets. The hen chicks were small-boned brown birds, as much alike as possible, with little or no feathers on their legs, everyone without exception a presentable reproduction of their grandmother, the pure brown Leghorn hen. The fourteen cockerels developed into fine birds, very similar in appearance to each other, big-boned, stalking, muff-legged, of decided Brahma type, and excepting for a few dark feathers on the backs and spotted beaks of a few of them, they might be taken for the lineal descendants of their maternal grandfather, the light Brahma, none showing more than a trace of Leghorn blood. They all follow almost closely the lines found correct in so many cases as to the reproductive influences of the sexes. The study of the science of reproduction is at once important and interesting. Perhaps the foregoing may induce younger breeders when selecting their stock to make careful enquiries as to the properties of the parents, as upon these in a great measure will the qualities of their stock depend.

Shorthorns.—"The Durhams, as they were originally termed, and by which name they are still generally known in the bush districts of Australia, were originally confined to the counties of Durham and York, in England. They were large, loose, short-horned cattle, in the early times celebrated as milkers. Although the shorthorns of the present day bear very little resemblance to the original Durhams, there can be no question but that they are the same breed of cattle. The breeders on the banks of the river Tees, favored by their rich soil, by practising careful selection, soon moulded them into a different and almost distinct type, and they then became celebrated throughout Great Britain as the Teeswater cattle. It is claimed for the shorthorns that they mature earlier, fatten more kindly, and produce a greater amount of superior meat, with less proportionate amount of bone and offal than any other variety of cattle. As milkers they stand unrivalled by all except the Ayrshire and Jersey or Alderney. The prevailing colours are red, red and white, white and roan. The light roan body and dark roan neck, with red or brown-tipped ears, is the favorite colour with Australian cattle owners. The latter is perhaps the prevailing colour of the Booths, whilst the dark red, characteristic of the Duchess family, is preferred by many in the Bates' strain.

Herefords.—Next to the shorthorns, the Herefords, or "white faces," are considered the most valuable of modern beef cattle. They are proving amongst the best for export shipping. Unlike the shorthorns, however, which have at times been denominated an "artificial" breed, the Herefords may be considered an aboriginal race, having been bred up to their present state of perfection quite within their own blood. Originally, the Herefords were brown or red-brown, without any white, but for nearly a century the white face has been a characteristic of the breed. The improved Herefords, until late years, were of a light, almost yellowish, red; but the fashionable colour of the present time is a dark red, white face and crops, and in most instances white dewlaps. The Hereford of the present day is a magnificent animal for the butcher, possessing in a marked degree the propensity to lay on flesh, particularly on the hind quarters. So much is this the case that to the symmetrical eye they appear gross, and lack the beautiful appearance so much a characteristic of the shorthorns. They are poor and inferior milkers, and it has been observed that their calves do not withstand rough usage so well as the Durhams. But it is claimed for the Herefords that they are better adapted for our coast lands than the shorthorns; and that they mature earlier on our natural pasturage, being as a rule fit for the butcher at four years. It is also claimed for them by their admirers that they travel better to market than the shorthorns; but this is stoutly denied by the shorthorn men. It cannot, however, be denied, that if we take the market prices as a guide, they are held in even greater esteem by the butchers in these colonies than the shorthorns; although this is not the case at Smithfield. For purposes of improving other breeds, the Herefords are in no respect equal to the shorthorns.

Devons.—Like the Herefords, the Devons, "The Reds," have been preserved pure from the aboriginal cattle inhabiting North and South Devon. They are also proving hardy for shipping purposes. The breed were formerly known as the "Middle Horns." They are considerably smaller than either of the previously described breeds, and were, until recently, comparatively little known in Australia. They are now, however, fast rising into notice. It has been said that the grand secret of breeding is *to suit the breed to the soil and climate,* and where the fattening of cattle is limited solely to natural herbage, the Devons would appear eminently suited to thrive where larger and less hardy breeds cannot hold their own so well. The Devons are better milkers than the Herefords, and next to the Sussex they make the best and most effective workers. In color the Devons are dark-red, without a spot of white. Their skin is somewhat thin, but not delicately so, and they feel and handle like a glove. They are more what a breeder would call "pretty" with fine bone; but without the squareness of outline so justly appreciated in the shorthorns and Herefords.

Hornless or Polley Cattle.—The development of the cattle export trade is attracting more attention to the polleys. They have long been in favour in New Zealand, and to a lesser extent in Australia. They are gentle and thrive well under the conditions that develop high-class shorthorns. So far dehorning—the cutting off of horns, or the dissolving of young horn material by acids—has not been practised here to any extent as yet. The true polleys are the favourites for hornless cattle.

As Beef Yielders.—The relative merits of the beef stock may be gathered from the following details of a recent Smithfield Show:—The top weights were—Shorthorns, 23cwt. 1qr. 7lb.; Hereford, 23cwt. 20lbs.; Sussex, 23cwt. 3qrs. 12lbs.; Highland, 21cwt. 3qrs. 16lbs.; polled, 21cwt.

3qrs. 16lbs.; Devon, 18cwt. 2qrs. 27lbs.; cross (shorthorn and polled), 27cwt. It will thus be seen that this shorthorn polley cross topped the shorthorns and Herefords by nearly 4cwt. and the Devons by nearly 8½cwt.

Crosses.—By this term is not meant the indiscriminate use of two or more varieties of cattle in the same herd, with the hope of ultimately establishing a fixed breed midway between the two. Any attempt in that direction will result, as it has always done, in disappointment. Between certain breeds, however, a first cross produces a better animal for the butcher than even the very best pure varieties, but it does not follow that a cross between two of the largest varieties will result in the production of the best and heaviest ox. On the contrary, experience has shown that a cross between the shorthorn and Hereford, although these are individually the two most valued breeds, does not equal the cross between the shorthorn and Devon, and is far inferior as a butcher's ox to a first-class cross with the shorthorn and Highland cattle. But unquestionably the most valuable cross, both for the butcher and breeder, is that between a shorthorn bull and the Aberdeen black-polled cow. A reference to the reports of the Smithfield Club experiences show that this cross has reigned supreme for many years, not only as regards weight and the small proportion of bone and offal; but the flesh which is beautifully marbled, is superior to any other known class of cattle, and they are therefore held in the highest esteem in the London market.

To Succeed with Cattle.—They all require rich feed and plenty of it. This means good country, helped by cultivation, which in turn means quiet cattle which can be handled without wasting.

Live and Dead Weights.—An average of dead to live weight of cattle is 57 per cent. in an ordinary fat beast. This percentage is frequently largely exceeded in stall-fed cattle some having given as much as 71 per cent. of dead to live weight; but for ordinary bush fattened Australian cattle, 57 per cent. is fair. In very fat cattle, an odd one of which may be found in most mobs, the percentage may reach 60; occasionally, 61-62.

Connection Between Live Stock and Soil.—That a knowledge of geology is desirable in laying out land for stock-rearing, we have only to note some of the effects evidently produced by soils. Whether speaking of horses, cattle, or sheep, in either species we find a great many really different varieties designated by the common term of breeds. These have originated partly through selection and cultivation, but chiefly by the influence of soil and climate. Breeds owe their origin to these two conditions to no inconsiderable extent. Sheep of the same breed placed on different soils in Australia, in a few years, become so much altered in appearance and in condition as to be almost unrecognisable as belonging to the same family. Much the same effects become apparent in cattle and horses. All modern breeds correspond in size and weight with the nature of the soil and the climatic conditions where they were developed. All the established breeds tell the tale of climate and feed. They may alter somewhat in color, according to the tastes of the breeders; but the animals are in reality what the soil and the feed grown on that soil has made them. No amount of artificial feeding or breeding has the same result. Nature has certain laws, and none more strict than in the matter of breeding live stock. Were it not for that limit which soil and climate put upon races of animals, new breeds might be evolved indefinitely. Animal life essentially owes its originality to the geological and chemical contents of the surroundings in which "they live, and move, and have their being." No breeder of live stock should overlook this great fact when settling in a new locality, with the intention of breeding. In cases where climate and soil are similar, stock can be removed with safety and success from one district to another, not otherwise, or failure is sure to follow.

Soil, Health, Diseases.—And while soil influences are proverbial in regulating the formation of breeds, they have important influences upon the health. It has been ascertained, for example, that in carboniferous country certain diseases are prevalent, which are markedly absent in other parts. This is in cases attributed to the presence of lime, iron, &c., or their absence in other cases, which give different results. Again, the sandstone and other formations which are notably deficient in lime, are subject to many diseases peculiar to them. When pleuro-pneumonia was rife in America some years ago, it was then stated that on farms where the cattle had access to water coming from the limestone formation, there was the least infection of animals from the disease, and the fewest deaths. Nearly every district has its own individual experience with diseases, which are affected largely, there is every reason to believe, by the prevailing geographical surroundings. Chemical analysis has revealed that the framework of animal life is composed largely of minerals found in the soil. Enough has been ascertained on these points to encourage further investigation; and it is hoped that science may yet be able to map the area and region of diseases as accurately as the different characters of the surface soils.

XV.—SHEEP AND WOOL.—SMALL AND LARGE FLOCKS.

There has been enough done to prove that sheep can be made to pay in flocks of hundreds as well as thousands, and that the idea of the country being suitable only for squatting, and dependence on the native grasses only is amongst the notions of the past. Victoria and our own southern districts offer striking examples of successful changes from the old style of squatting to a system of grazing-farming. The bulk of the cattle and sheep raised there are on sections of less than 2,000 acres. Some of the most successful men carry on operations on less than 500 acres; though for years we were assured that in the hands of farmers the staple product of export—wool—was to disappear or become so worthless as not to pay for carriage to the European market! Beyond this, the carcase was thoroughly to deteriorate. Of course, no one with any exercised sense believed such extreme views, and none without an overpowering or interested motive ever sought to make converts to them. Time has gone on, and we read in a report of one of the largest wool sales catalogued in Australia that "the wool interest has changed its character. A new set of producers has come into the field." The catalogue consists of 1444 lots, representing 12,274 bales, nearly the whole of it the produce of farms in Riverina, Pentland Hills, Bacchus Marsh, the Werribee, Kyneton, &c.

SHEEP FOR WOOL—THE MERINO. This celebrated family, from the time that they first attracted attention

under their present family name, may be considered as indigenous to Spain. The Spanish merinos were divided into two grand families—the *Transhumantes*, or migratory sheep, which were driven from the southern provinces in April or May to the mountains in the north, some 400 miles, and driven back again in the autumn; and the *Estantes*, escurials, or stationary sheep, which remained on the estates.

Introduction into Australia.—This national event was in 1797, and afforded an illustration of the hackneyed saying, "It's an ill wind that blows no one good;" for to the circumstance of a Colonel Gordon at the Cape of Good Hope having shot himself, Australia was indebted for her first shipment of merino sheep. They had been presented by the King of Spain to the Dutch Government, had passed into the possession of Colonel Gordon at the Cape, and at his death were sold by his widow, and shipped in the war ships "Reliance" and "Supply" for Sydney. They were of the escurial breed, and were considered very superior. On their arrival, Captain Macarthur purchased three rams and five ewes, and these formed the basis of his celebrated Camden flock. In 1805, Captain Macarthur, when in England, purchased some of the Kew flock, which had been presented to George III. by the Spanish

Government. Although inferior to Colonel Gordon's, these were added to the Camden flock, and from these two lots Australia has gradually risen to the first rank of the great wool trade of the world. Mr. Cox, of Mulgoa, also purchased some of Colonel Gordon's sheep, but he does not seem to have been so successful with them as Captain Macarthur. At a subsequent period, however, having purchased the flock of Mr. Riley, of Raby, he added some Rambouillet ewes from the French flocks, and removed them to Mudgee, and from this dates the origin of the now celebrated Mudgee flocks.

The Australian Merino.—The flocks have been spreading over the land ever since the Macarthur days. The merinos being now, as then, the sheep for wool. The experience of years has proven that merinos, when well cared for, are as suitable for small flocks as large. With the cessation of importations, the European names Saxon, Negritti, Rambouillet, &c., have almost dropped, and the great family name of Australian merino adopted.

Country for Wool.—The wool of the Australian merino varies in quality with the influence of climate and pasturage, but it may be divided into two classes, combing and clothing. Clothing wool is the class principally grown, but of late years it has been found that a large portion of the country lying on the western slopes of the main dividing ranges favours the growth of a staple considerably longer than that recognised by the manufacturer as clothing, hence many breeders so situated have adopted, and with great success, the growth of the longer combing wools. In the far inland and saltbush districts, a medium combing has been found profitable. The coast lands have been found unsuitable for the merino, and are being gradually brought under cattle. But here, as in other lands, quality of soil has its decided effect on wool.

Sheep for Mutton.—These are the coarser wool producers, with heavier frames, and giving a carcase more suitable than the merinos for European consumers. The development of chilling and freezing and export of live stock have given an impetus to the breeding of mutton sheep which was quite unforeseen a few years since.

Leicesters.—Of all the long-woolled, or—as the Americans term them, the mutton-producing varieties—the Leicester ranks first. As the Booth tribe of shorthorn cattle have always been famous for the great improvement their blood makes in a herd, so there are few varieties of long-wools of the present day that have not been indebted to the blood of the Dishley Leicesters for improvement in shape and aptitude to fatten; in fact, as has been quaintly remarked, they have almost completely eaten up every other long-woolled breed. To such extreme perfection has the frame of this animal being carried, that one is lost in admiration at the skill and good fortune of those who worked out such an alteration. It would seem as if they had chalked out upon a wall a form perfect in itself, and then had given it existence. For a number of years Leicesters have at various times been imported into Australia and have been successfully bred in New South Wales, Victoria, Tasmania, and New Zealand; but it was not until 1868 that the breed was finally established, and their value in crossing with the merino thoroughly demonstrated.

Lincolns.—Next to the Leicester, the Lincoln is the most valuable of the long-wools. Although at one time a distinct variety, the Lincolns have of late years been so modified and intermixed with the Leicesters that they may now be dominated a sub-variety of the latter. The Lincoln of the present day is a larger sheep than the improved Leicester, with a heavier fleece of very lustrous wool; so much so that in some instances samples of Lincoln wool have been mistaken for those of fine Angora mohair. The Lincoln, however, has not the fine bone and head, nor the same extreme white and beautiful silkiness of hair on the face and legs as the Leicester. For purposes of crossing, however, it is considered superior to the Leicester, inasmuch as whilst giving an equally large carcase, the fleece of the Lincoln-*cum*-merinos are heavier and much more lustrous. They are, therefore, held in great esteem by the breeders on rich volcanic and limestone country.

The Cotswolds rank next to the Lincolns; but

although the largest of any known variety of sheep, they are not on that account considered the most suitable for these colonies. It may interest some to know that the name of this family originated from the circumstance of their having been housed in *cots* or sheds in winter, and from being grazed over *wolds* or hilly grounds in summer. The Cotswolds can be traced back as a pure and distinct variety to an earlier date than any other breed of British sheep; but within the last quarter of a century they have greatly modified, and lost many of their original characteristics by repeated infusions of the Leicester blood. The wool is coarse and open, and it has been found, in the southern colonies, that they do not amalgamate well with the merino. It is a peculiarity of the three last described varieties that, when fattened, the ewes are heavier than the wethers, by amounts varying from 10lb. to 40lb.

South Downs.—They are also handsome sheep, with close fleece of comparatively fine wool, speckled face and legs dark, in some instances almost black. To one whose eye has long been accustomed to the merinos, the South Down would probably be more fancied at first than any other of the longwool breeds. Unlike those previously described, South Downs have been handed down pure, any attempt at crossing with larger varieties having resulted in failure. It was thought that the South Downs would be well suited to the higher lands in Australia, and consequently were at one time extensively used in New England and Monaro; but they were superseded by the merino.

Kentish or Romney Marsh.—This breed possesses additional interest to us from the fact that it has been found that they have the power to resist fluke and foot rot better than other sheep, and on this account are considered the best class for the coast lands of Australia, which may be said to be subject to these diseases all along the south and eastern seaboard. The Romney Marsh is a large sheep, carrying a heavy fleece of long staple, but it lacks the deep round chest of the Leicester, and cannot compare either with the latter or with the Lincoln for symmetry.

The Cheviot.—The fact of this race of sheep inhabiting and thriving well on the precarious and mountain pasturage of Scotland must stamp them as a very hardy race. The Cheviot of the present day is a handsome animal weighing from 130lb. to 150lb., capable of enduring great privations, thriving equally well under the same conditions with the hardy black-faced mountain sheep. On this account, those who have had practical experience in their management in Scotland, are of opinion that they would be eminently suited to our broken, hilly country and coast lands. The wool of the Cheviot is coarser than that of the South Down, but when crossed with the merino the progeny has been found little inferior to that of the Leicester, except that the fleece presents an appearance of wanting yolk when on poor country or the feed is not sufficient for their best development.

Crosses.—It is found that a first cross between the merino and a long-woolled variety produces an excellent crossbred wool and a valuable sheep for the butcher or for export, a sheep that matures much earlier than the merino. The Leicester crosses are superior in carcase to those of the Lincoln, while the latter excel the former in length and lustre of wool. Both crosses are fit for the butcher at from 16 to 18 months. When these crosses were confined to a few breeders, very little demand existed for cross-wools; since, however, large numbers have embarked in its production in the different Australian colonies, sound crossbred wool has been adapted by the manufacturers to special purposes. It should, however, be clearly understood that only the first cross are safe while the sire and dam on both sides are pure of their respective families. Beyond this, results will be disappointing. If ewes of a first or subsequent grade are bred from, it should be to pure males, so as to breed back to the pure stock on either side; and if to Leicester or Lincoln rams, the fourth or fifth generation will be tolerably pure for general purposes. It has been said that "an attempt to unite the fleece of the merino and the carcase of a Leicester, for instance, is an unqualified absurdity." No crossbred males should, therefore, be used for stud purposes.

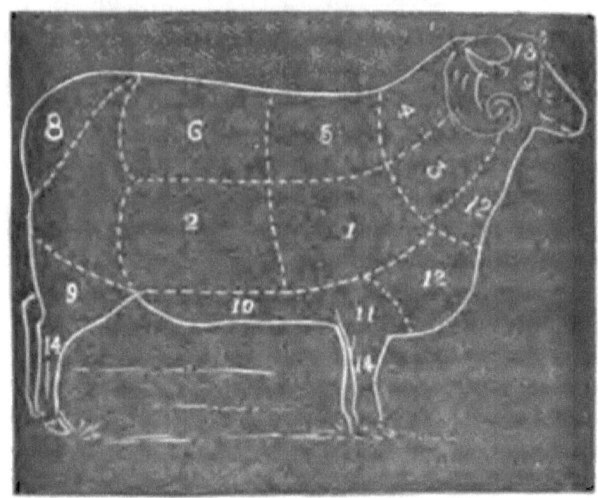

CLASSIFYING WOOL.—The illustration shows the different parts or sections of a fleece. Sections 1 and 2 have the finest, longest, and strongest wools; sections 3 and 12 short but close; 4, somewhat longer, but a shade lower than 3; 5 and 6, good; 8, lower still, and called the britch or breech; 7, good length, but rather lower in quality than 1 and 2; 9, shorter, and loses vitality as compared with better parts; 10, short, and generally frowsey; 11, shorter than 12; 13, the cap, dry and harsh; 14, fribby and of little value; 9, 10, 11, 13, and 14 constitute the skirt.

Combing and Other Wools.—The difference between combing, clothing, and other wools is comparatively in the length of staple. A combing wool is seldom less than 1½ inch. A desirable arrangement or classification may be made as follows:—1st. Super-combing from fleeces that have a soft, silky appearance, strong and dense in the staple, a considerable length and very bright. 2nd. First combing from fleeces not so silky and dense in the staple, but strong and bright. 3rd. Second combing, coarse long wool, handling rather harshly. 4th. First clothing 5th. Second clothing. 6th. Dingy: that is, sandy, stained and cotty fleeces.

Shearing and Sorting.—It is necessary that the wool be cut as nearly as possible to the same length all over. When the shearer makes a cut which is not quite so near the skin as the others, he should not be allowed to take it off with a second cut, for that piece of wool is of no use in the fleece, and if found there reduces its value; but if left on the sheep could be shorn off the following year to better advantage. After the fleece is shorn, it should be spread fleshside down, on a table made of battens placed an inch apart, that all the small pieces of wool may fall below, and leave the fleece perfectly free from locks. It then should be carefully skirted, the stained parts taken off and put by themselves; then the hind legs and britch, which also should be kept separate, and called second pieces; next the fore legs and neck, and any other wool which is not of the same quality as the fleece. These should also be kept by themselves and classed as first pieces. The pieces may be divided into five classes, viz.: First pieces; second pieces; third, stained pieces; fourth, belly pieces; fifth, locks. After the fleece has been properly skirted, it should be rolled up, taking care to have the shoulder part on the outside, as the best wool is on that part.

Sheep in Small Flocks.—The merino continues, and is likely to continue the leading breed in Australian sheep farming. It is as suitable for small flocks as for flocks of tens of thousands. But crossbreeds for farmers and export purposes have many recommendations where the feed is good enough, to bring on early lambs and carcases fit for exporting. Such sheep first of all fill the requirements for butcher meat in the owner's family. They clean up stubble and land that will become foul from weeds developed during cultivation, as no other stock do. And they enrich the land for further cropping for grain, potatoes, grass, &c. Of the many heavier framed sheep available for crossing with the merinos, the improved Leicester is held in high esteem by men in the wheat and dairy districts inland, who farm heavy land. The Merino-Lincoln cross gives very good returns. The wool of these crossbreds is dense, of good fair average quality, and the sheep mature rapidly on rich soil. The crossbred wethers at two years old weigh from 60lb. to 80lb., and yield from 6lb. to 10lb. of wool.

Butcher Lambs.—They sell well when ready for the butcher by August or September. That is, where they have the feed, for lambs will not fatten on poor stuff.

The South Down Merino is very useful where lambs only are required. They take on flesh rapidly, are well shaped, deep and full in flesh. Possibly, the very best sheep to breed butcher's lambs from is the first cross from the Lincoln-Merino, again crossed by the South Down. The progeny arrive at a good size, and weigh well very quickly. But then, wool with the South Down cross in it sells badly; being shorter and harsher, and when once in a flock, it will take a lifetime to breed it out. After the first cross, we have to decide whether to breed for mutton or wool. If for mutton, we must use coarse-woolled sires; if for wool, merino sires. But in either case pure bred sires must be used.

Buying Sheep.—We may work on store sheep all the time, and never breed any. To one who does this, sheep which fatten quickly are of first importance, for any wild wethers accustomed to wide grazing, and which travel long distances do not settle down comfortably in small paddocks. Quiet sheep fit the case in preference to wild station sheep. Small sheep are not desirable, not only for their size—for which the usual difference in price partly compensates—but because they seldom fatten well; their condition being weak, most likely they may have disease.

Risks from Poor Feed.—Sometimes the beginner gets a lot that puzzles him from their never getting "tip top." On killing one of the poorest, we probably find the stomach filled with felted balls of irregular size, caused by taking indigestible feed, especially old fibry grass or leaves, during long journeys in dry seasons. If the sheep are young and the season early with plenty of sound feed, they may partially recover, but if old or the grass is drying up, there is no cure except the butcher's knife.

Points of Sheep.—The most profitable sheep is the most perfect the country will produce. This can only be obtained by close attention and culling; and to do this it is necessary to know the "points" of a sheep thoroughly. The points of a carcase—and they apply equally to merinos, Leicesters, Lincolns, and others—are depth, girth, a roundness of barrel, with ribs well sprung, thickness behind the shoulders, breadth of forehead, and width between the eyes, shortness of neck and legs, and general squareness of frame. The sheep to avoid, are thin-necked, leggy, flat-sided narrow made, small-footed, ill-shaped animals, with prominent, staring eyes, and narrow, hard faces. The carcase of a first-class Lincoln should be covered with a long, bright, lustrous fleece, in length from eight to ten inches, free from fuzziness, which denotes a bad merino cross; so does anything like wool on the face, which should be covered with a soft, white hair. Horns also denote a cross of some sort. Want of attention may quite spoil a flock by breeding from mongrels. Possibly we cannot do better than buy as many ewes as required full-mouthed (as few men will sell their best maiden ewes), from some well-known station breeder. But do not let us have any broken-mouthed or sheep with defective teeth. The rams should be put in five months before the lambs are wanted.

Weight of Australian Fleeces.—Awards for fleeces were made as follows at a recent exhibition at Wagga:—First, total weight 3 ewes' fleeces in grease, 35lb. 7oz.; scoured, 21lb. 14oz. Second, weight in grease, 30lb. 11oz.; scoured, 20lb. 3½oz. Third, in grease, 36lb. 4oz.; scoured, 20lb. 11½oz. Fourth, in grease, 33lb. 9oz.; scoured, 20lb, 15½oz. Fifth, in grease, 32lb. 13oz.; scoured, 21lb. 13½oz.

XVI.—THE HORSE IN AUSTRALIA.

He lives much more in the open air than in Europe or America. The climate allows of his being put upon grass at all periods of the year. Consequently he is a much sounder animal than where he is continuously stable fed. The horses of Australia are noted for sound limbs and rough ungroomed appearance, both due to the freedom of life of the animals, and the excellent native pasturage.

Heads Show Character and Temper.

Buying a Horse.—It may be said without egotism that Australians know a good, serviceable horse when they see him, as well as any people upon earth. And notwithstanding all that is said about the deterioration of horses, in comparison with 20 years ago, there are a few places where a good serviceable horse can be picked up more easily than in Australia. Good horses, both in look and action, abound in the country—compact, hardy animals, which, if light, are light all over; and if heavy, then heavy all over. The head, body, and limbs look as though they belonged to one animal—and in forming an estimate of the appearance of any horse, we should pay attention to this relative position of his body and limbs. The body should give a distinct impression of being placed *on* the limbs, not suspended *between* them. Where the body is placed on the limbs, the horse will have the power of

doing his work within himself, as it is termed, and will not be easily fatigued; while the horse whose body is swinging, as it were between his limbs, will have a very slack, uncomfortable gait, and will be very easily fatigued. He may have a showy action, which might lead the casual observer to imagine that he was going at a tremendous pace; but a few miles of heavy work makes him drag his legs heavily, and, in a long journey, he gives up with downright exhaustion.

Horses are as different as men. In buying, look first to his head and eyes, for signs of intelligence, temper, courage and honesty. The eye should be well developed; hazel is a good colour. Unless a horse has brains, you can't teach him more than a half-witted child. See that tall bay there, a fine-looking animal too, fifteen hands high. You can't teach that horse anything. Why? Well, I'll show you, but have a care of his heels. Look at the brute's head, that rounding nose, that tapering forehead, that broad full face below the eyes. You can't trust him. "That's an awful good mare!" may be said of another. True as the sun. You can see breadth and fulness between her eyes. You couldn't hire that mare to act mean or hurt anybody. I like a small, thin ear, and want a horse to hold his ears well foward. Look out for the brute that seems to listen to all the conversation going on behind him. The horse that turns back his ears till they almost meet at the points is sure to be up to tricks. A horse with a dishing face is cowardly, and a sulking brute is always vicious. I like a square muzzle, with large nostrils, to let in plenty of air to the lungs. So much for the head. Next the build of the animal. Never buy a long-legged stilty horse. A short, straight back and a straight rump, are indications of a reliable type. The withers high and the shoulders well set back and broad. The foreleg short. A pretty straight, hind leg, with the hock low down, short pastern joints and a rounded foot. There are all kinds of horses, but the animal that has these points is pretty sure to be sightly, graceful, and, most likely is good-natured and serviceable for the work that nature intended him for.

The Head Shows Character.—Aye! very much as a man's does. Vice is shown in the eye and mouth; intelligence in the eye and in the breadth between the ears and between the eyes; spirit in the eye and in the nose, in the mobile nostril and active ear. The size of the eye, the thinness of the skin, making the face bony; the large, open, thin-edged nostril; the fine ear, and the thin, fine mane and foretop are indications of high breeding, and the development of a high-strung nervous organisation, which, with good limbs and muscular power, ensures a considerable degree of speed in the animal. The first of the two shown in page 167 is high-strung and mettlesome, with an untrustworthy eye and a vicious mouth—a powerful animal of great endurance, but, being wilful, is hard to control. The other is equally high-bred, with great breadth of forehead, a large, full, friendly eye, not lacking in spirit. The bony face indicates blood, the ear and thin-edged nostril show spirit, while the whole expression of the face abounds in docility, kindliness, and honesty. We candidly confess we should greatly hesitate in buying a horse with a bad doubtful-looking countenance, though many worthy men and many well-disposed horses are unfortunate in this particular. We may not value a friend the less for it; but it would certainly not induce us to form an acquaintance with the man so arranged without cogent reasons for so doing. Books tell us what a perfect horse is, but they do not quite tell us where to find him. So we have to look out. Get a bridle on the horse and test him in his stall first. Give the strap a sudden sharp jerk. When the horse throws his head up, holds his neck stiff and ears rigid, and his eye assumes a glassy look straight out from either side, he is the stamp likely to put his feet through the dashboard, or his fore feet over the other horse's neck, the first time you hitch him up. When you harness up a horse, and he turns his head round flat towards the side, and looks at you with a meek, lamb-like expression as you take your place in the seat, if you have not a temper that is "child-like and bland," you will probably put a head on that horse that will make him look differently before you get far on your journey. Balking or jibbing horses are of two kinds—those which

L

want to go too much and those which don't want to go at all. The first is the nervous, jibbing horse; the second the sulky, balky horse. A good way to manage the first is to unhitch him at the first manifestation of the evil spirit, and without any blustering or whipping, get on his back and run him about three miles at the top of his speed. Nine times in ten a horse will, after this treatment, when put in harness again, pull as steadily as the most sober-minded old horse in the world. A very usual way to manage the second kind, those experienced in horse dealing say, is to trade him off to some one in want of a good, steady, reliable, old family horse. A favorite, but not generally successful plan, pursued with horses of either of these types, is to pound them over the head with the butt of the whip or with a sapling. This is useless, but natural. There is nothing in animated nature that can develop bad bile in a man to such an extent as can an animal of this kind. There is a legend of a man who hired a horse and went out for a drive. The horse balked; the man lighted a cigar, took out a newspaper, settled himself back in the cushions, and read two hours and forty-five minutes by his watch. Then that horse got ready to go, and the man must have been pretty well prepared for a better world. This process would be tiresome, but quite likely more effective than rubbing dirt in the mouth of the sulky one or kindling a fire under him. The latter sort of inducement to "go," has, it is said, proved effective with confirmed jibbers.

Judging Age.—What experiences there are in judging the age of horses by the teeth! While all the little black cups or hollows are still in the teeth of the horse's lower jaw, the animal is not over six years; when those in the corner teeth only are left, the horse is under nine. When the cups are all gone in the under jaw, but are still left in the teeth of the upper, the horse is probably not older than ten, but this is not a certain rule. The shape of the teeth tells much to the experienced observer. In youth the cutting surface of the tooth is long from side to side; in old age long from front to rear. When the cutting surface of the teeth in the upper and lower jaws are worn smooth, and so long from front to rear as to resemble in shape the nails on your little finger, the horse is probably not less than 15, and perhaps 20 years of age.

Good Mothers, Good Stock.—"Good horses, like great men have good mothers." Reliable animals get their

goodness that way. Speaking of that most reliable of all, the Clydesdales, Topsman, Darnley, Prince of Wales, and Old Times, all of them had excellent mothers, and of the four only Prince of Wales had a sire of more than ordinary merit. The early improvers of cattle fully recognised the force of the above truism, and the pedigrees of cattle in herd books are tabulated according to the dam's side.

Judging the Horse from the Foal.—The future height to which a newly-born foal will attain, when a full-grown horse, may be approximately ascertained by doubling the length of his fore limb, measured from the fetlock to the elbow. From the knee to the ground the limb is nearly the full length of the adult animal, but it is decidedly shorter from the knee to the elbow than at maturity.

To Choose a Heavy Draught.—The characteristics of a good heavy draught horse are large deep chest, straight shoulders, a little inclined to flesh, thick body, not too much belly, straight loins, the hindquarters a little depressed, thick through the thighs, and sound, sizeable feet. The horse that has sound, well-formed legs, feet, and chest, and thick short muscles in the thigh, is strong and likely to be steady in a heavy pull. The speed is not so material; there are draught horses that are quick, and those that are slow. The steady, light horses are good for farm work when the ground is light and even; the heavy, slow horses, with firm tread are excellent for new heavy ground, or on bad, uneven roads. A horse for drawing loads, to be well formed ought to be high in front, having high and projecting withers, large chest, front legs strong and set well apart, back and loins straight, hindquarters a little depressed, muscular, short in the flank, large sinews. With such a shape a horse is solid and able to resist knocks upon uneven roads and the weight which presses when going down hill. To be fiery is a fault in a plough horse, or for drawing heavy loads on uneven roads. A strong, slower horse is better; he resists fatigue longer, and does more service.

Clydesdales and Suffolks.—The Clydesdale is well esteemed in Australia for heavy work, and for giving strength to lighter animals. But in the eyes of not a few good judges the Suffolk Punch is looked upon as the most uniform of cart horses in shape, style, action and colour. There is a theory that the generally-prevailing colour was obtained long ago from a cross with horses imported from Norway brought over by the " Hardy Norsemen." There is not much similarity now existing between the Norfolk trotter and the Suffolk Punch, but it seems to be recognised as a fact that sufficient family likeness still exists to stamp them as being of a common origin. According to Arthur Young, who wrote a century ago, there were then but two pure-bred varieties of cart horses in England, and these were the large black or old English, and the sorrel Suffolk Punch. The farmers of a portion of East Anglia have for generations stuck to this breed, and have good reasons for doing so.

Breeding Horses.—The draught horse and the roadster offer the best prospects. There are two classes of draughts, the light and heavy. The lighter and more active draught are more properly omnibus or light cart horses. Given a 1200 lb. mare, whether we get a light draught or heavy depends on two things, the selection of a sire, and the feed. The light draught or spring cart horse should weigh from 1350 to 1430lb., have good action and definite colour. He should not be a dun, a light sorrel or light grey, or have a white face or a glassy eye, and must have good clean limbs and fair style. He may be over four years old and well broken to harness. Even a heavy draught horse may be the progeny of a grade draught mare weighing 1400lb. and a pure bred-horse weighing from 1800 to 2000lb. He should not weigh less than 1500lb. in fair condition. The hack or roadster is also a paying horse, when the breeder keeps a level head on himself and breeds level-headed horses. He may not attempt to raise fast horses. But he is good for road horses that travel as fast as any Christian ought to want to go, and to do first-rate farm work, just as much, in fact, and a little more, than the draught horse, and sell at five years old for a fair price, provided that the breeder is skilled in training and driving such horses, and has a taste for it. To produce roadsters, it is not good to start with a draught nor a plug, nor with anything small. The draught may give size but no speed; the small mare may give action. Both qualities are desirable in good hacks. If we want mares well bred, with style and action, then breed to the large standard-bred trotter, and we are not likely to miss the roadster. The highest priced of all is the coach horse. Great speed is not required, but size, good high-stepping action, colour, motion, style, disposition, and, in addition, training. These are rare qualities, and like rare things, are costly. The coach horse, whether Australian, French, English, or American, is a cross between the thoroughbred or standard bred to trot, and some cross of the draught horse, possibly Clydesdale, with stylish farm mares. We have glanced over the field and indicated the various classes of horses that seem likely to pay. There is plenty of room for variety of tastes and skill. But let no one imagine that he can succeed without good judgment, skill and feed.

Mental Training for the Horse.—Whether we are interested in the midget Shetlanders or Timours, or the farm horse, hackney or the blood horse, it is now felt that animals reared without the advantages of early handling, through which they learn to look upon man as a friend rather than as an enemy, require to be put through the process called " breaking." This, as usually practised, can hardly come under the head of mental training. To get willing service from a horse, is to so manage him that he will become attached to his master. The dullest horse knows the meaning of a kick or a bite, when he deals either of these out to the person nearest him, and he is less likely to kick his friend than his enemy. One of the Arab maxims is permit your colt to live with you, having access to your tent from his tender age. When grown he will be faithful, and will take pleasure in doing your bidding, through hardship, fatigue, and privation. Without education the horse is crude in the manner of giving his work to his master, yet, after the manner of a mere brute, he may be to a degree faithful. When properly educated, he is much more than this, he is automatic, self-propelling, self-sustaining, while yet studiously holding all his powers in reserve for the word of command. As the mind of the horse gets in fuller sympathy with the mind of the man, as it should and will, provided he be properly educated, although his powers are limited, he will cheerfully go beyond this limit uncomplainingly. If he has native spirit—native as inherited from ancestry—no education properly directed will take this from him, but will rather add to it. Education, adroitly applied, shows the limit of intelligent manifestations in the average horse to be far ahead of the general belief in such matters, still there are horse owners who act as though the young horse should "rough it," both mentally and physically, until he is old enough to be put to work, without any preparation to meet those sights and sounds that cause runaways, as a rule, and from which most of the serious accidents arise. Now, it is entirely possible to educate the colt in such a manner as to take him out of fear of fright from drums, fire-arms, locomotives, paper, or other objects driven towards him by the wind while in the harness. A horse may prove to be physically fit for bodily exertion, while, from his education having been neglected, he is not fit to be trusted in any position were he is liable to be frightened. The safeguard, in his case, is to be harnessed with a mate able to hold him to his proper place. It is no uncommon sight to see country horses when put to work in cities fill this description fully. They may be startled by trifles, fear men in general, and run away on the slightest pretext, unless guarded as described.

Training Horses.—After young horses have once become sufficiently bridle wise—and an excellent system of circular machine training is now in use for that purpose—it is a good practice to teach them the meaning of words. This is not a difficult matter, provided too many words are not used at any time. The first step is to adopt some word, at the sound of which the horse is to understand that he must stop. Words that are easy to speak, and which can be made emphatic, should be chosen, such as " Ho !" " Whoa !" &c., and every time the word is used the horse to which it is spoken should be made to obey it fully. Carelessness in regard to this matter will do more to undo what has been taught than anything else. When a horse fully understands the meaning of the word used when we wish him to stop and stand still, the greater part of the work is accomplished. To make the work more effective, it is a good plan to get into the vehicle to which the horse is hitched, and having stopped after a short drive, one should get out and leave him for a short distance. Should the horse then start, the one in the vehicle can draw the lines suddenly, and thus prevent his getting away. There will be no great trouble in teaching a horse with an ordinary amount of common horse-sense to stand without being hitched, when a little judgment and patience are used in training him.

XVII.—DAIRYING INTERESTS.

DAIRYING as an export business has been of slow growth in Australia. During the long series of years since milking cattle were introduced, they were the few only, and generally classed as dreamers, who had an idea that dairy products—butter, cheese, preserved milk, bacon, hams, and lard—would become exports from this country ; yet in the very early days, Alexander Berry, located in the Illawarra district, had such an idea. He was no dreamer, but a stern, matter-of-fact man, and he put his idea to the test by exporting butter to California in the early fifties. And dairying has had lodgment in the Illawarra country ever since, and is extending there more rapidly than ever; while the business has spread north, west, and south, into Victoria, South Australia, New Zealand, and Tasmania. Even Queensland and Western Australia have hopes of

A Business-like Cow.

sharing in what is growing into one of the greatest industries of the country. The growth of export dairying has been of immense magnitude since 1882, when Mr. D. L. Dymock, of Kiama, introduced the cream separator. The exports have already reached two millions sterling for the produce of a year. The business, with tact, skill, and judgment, may be worked up to ten millions!

Materials Available for Profitable Dairying.—In Australia, climate, soil, and indigenous grass, unequalled, taken as a whole, compare favourably with any other part of the world. Possibly, the conditions are too favourable, and have led dairying into comparatively slovenly methods, from which first-class results are not likely to be obtained. Taking the climate, for instance, its very mildness has been against the business, for it has led to a want of attention to the needs of dairy stock, the results of which are seen every winter. Shelter for stock—such shelter as prevents their being pestered with insects or exhausted by heat in summer, or perished with cold during wet and raw cold weather—is as necessary here as in other lands where the temperature range from heat to cold is even less than the range in Australia. Cold tells upon the condition of stock in Australia with terrible effect. When scarcity of feed is added, the effect is destructive; and that is the case with too much of our dairying during the long winter months from May to September. Shelter and regular feeding from cultivated grasses and crops are necessities for the advancement of dairying.

DAIRY CATTLE.—The breeds are well represented. They include:

The Illawarra Strain.—Placed first by right of qualities for milk giving, hardiness, and general capacity, when they are really well bred. They are the offspring of the Shorthorns, Ayrshires, and Holsteins, sometimes named "Shipleys," first brought into the country, and good types of which have been introduced ever since. There have been careful breeders in the business all the time, and the strain has formed gradually, though with no definite basis. Shorthorn and Ayrshire blood is prominent in the best of the type; others are a good deal mixed. The reliable cows show the following points:—Long, narrow face, large eyes, small horns, large muzzle, long, fine neck and shoulders, large body, wide hips, long fine tail; teats larger than the Ayrshires, as a rule; legs rather long, but not out of proportion to the size of the animal; general colors, reds and roans. The requirements to keep up such a race are got in the grand constitution and milking qualities of the milking strain of the Shorthorns and the Ayrshires. Mixtures of Jersey and other Channel Island cattle have been tried, but tend to make the stock lighter and delicate. The Illawarra is essentially a business dairy cow; beef making is not in her line, nor, indeed, in any really high-class milking strain. Ayrshire bulls, with South Coast cattle, produce grades of beautiful animals that are a feature in so many of our dairy herds.

Shorthorns.—Really excellent milkers are got at times from the Shorthorns or Durhams; but their progeny are not reliable as milk-givers. Properly speaking, Jerseys, Ayrshires, as well as Durhams, are really Shorthorns, but the milking strain of the Durham or old Teeswater cattle are generally called "Shorthorns." Good milking qualities have a near connection with the feed, provided the cows are of a milking strain—if not the more and better fed the greater quantity of flesh they put on. This is the case with the white-faced Herefords, which should be avoided for dairy purposes. There are only few herds of the original milking strain of Shorthorns even in England.

Ayrshires.—This strain is a masterpiece of science-in-practice in cattle-breeding. The Ayrshire is the dairy cow of to-day as she was fifty years since recognised in the old world and the new. She is the product of skilful Scottish farming; improved in the face of immense difficulties which meet dairying in poor country with very changeable climate. But to continue to be the milker she is, the Ayrshire must be well kept. She is a giant to milk when the food is given her. She is not the cow for starvation and neglect; of this, those who are desirous of seeing the Ayrshire take the place in Australia to which she is entitled, may rest assured. In olden times, the native country of this breed was a poor place for dairying. Burns, in his quaint way, tells us of the hardships of those Ayrshire farmers. The climate cold and raw; the soil wet, stiff, and unproductive. The dry granite or volcanic hillsides were the only exceptions to the general bleakness of the country. There the spring grasses were early and comparatively rich, and as cattle, half-starved during winter, began to make a little flesh, the natives saw that, if the feed could be maintained, profitable dairying was within their reach. They were an observant people, those early Ayrshire dairyists, and some of them located on the hilly pastures came to see that by getting their cows on the best grass, and when the grass failed, providing for them barley, turnips, and the few other things they could grow, the cows gave milk of richer quality and greater quantity; and that it was better, more business-like, and more profitable, to feed, shelter, and milk the cows, than to let them run down during the cold, raw winter. So the best cows were gradually selected for the better treatment. The process occupied some fifty years, while the country was being drained, limed, and manured. Somewhere about the time Waterloo was fought, the Ayrshire cow had earned a leading dairy reputation. As a first-class milker, she holds it still, and she is as able to hold it in Australia as in the dairies of London, New York, or elsewhere. If she has a fault for Australian dairying, it is the size of the teats, which may be too small for men milkers.

Jerseys and Alderneys are the true Channel Island breed of dairy stock. They came originally from Normanby, are gentle, and thrive excellently in this country. For richness of milk and as butter-yielders, they are very superior; but like the Ayrshires, and, indeed, all good milkers, they must have the feed or they cannot give the milk. During late years, and both in Great Britain and America many breeders have tried to improve these cattle. So far, however, they come back to the old stock, so well defined in the native Normanbys and their descendants in the Channel Islands. The colors range from light fawn to dark brown and decided black, and the same distinctive marks are common to us in Australia, ever since the late Mr. Edward Wilson made his selection of Alderneys and sent them to Victoria. The Guernseys, for their greater weight, yield more milk and butter than the others, and carry more flesh. The Alderneys proper have or had much more black, some being nearly all black with just a steel grey patch or a few yellow hairs running through. But, as between the use the whole breed make of the feed they eat and the rich quality of their milk, the differences are not marked to any extent.

Devons.—"The pretty reds" come nearest the Channel Islanders for richness of milk; but unlike the famous breeds named they are unreliable dairy stock. Very desirable crosses, however, are got, having the Devon and also the Shorthorn strains. But all through the breeds, feed comes in as the first requirement for successful dairying, and not for milk only, or for butter or cheese.

Points of the Dairy Cow.—Of the indications of a good milker, of any of the breeds, the following is expressive:—

> She's long in her face, she's fine in her horn,
> She'll quickly make milk with grass or with corn;
> She's full in her jaws and full in her chine,
> She's heavy in flank and wide in her loin.
>
> She's broad in her ribs and long in her rump;
> A straight and flat back, with no signs of a hump
> She's wide in her hips and calm in her eyes,
> She's fine in her shoulders and thin in her thighs.
>
> She's light in her neck and thin in her tail,
> She's wide in her breast and good at the pail,
> She's fine in her bone and silky of skin,
> She's a beauty without, a milk maker within.

Milk Yielding Largely in the Breed.—The foregoing are the well-established breeds. There are risks in going to others for "improvements in breeding." Long horns on a heavy head, coarse hair, large bones, and small teats, are to be avoided in choosing cows for dairying. A long udder lengthwise of the body is best; and it should be quite elastic to the touch; that quality means capacity to make milk. A soft skin, mossy, silky hair are safe recommendations. They are evidences of healthfulness and thrift. A cow should have broad loins with long rump; a rather long, lean neck, with clean-cut face and prominent eyes These points indicate enduring power to stand the strain of a long milking season. But, even then, uncomfortable conditions of keeping, as to feed and shelter, will neutralise and ultimately destroy even these equipments. Milk-giving cows are very feminine, and the sex, as a rule, require care and attention all the time.

Milk-giving Indications.—Different breeds exhibit different characteristic shapes of both udders and teats. This is natural; udders vary in form as much as the cows themselves. A cow's udder, when the animal is sound, has four perfect teats, and in cases she may also have one to three rudimentary or very small teats. The four should give milk. Each communicates with a gland in which the milk is secreted out of the blood. This gland, in the upper portions, is solid, almost like liver, but it becomes more open in its structure below, as tubes and channels for conveying away the milk branch from it. Just above each teat the principal conduits form an irregular cavity, but of small size. The udder is the laboratory in which milk is made, so shape and size are important. Judged by anatomy, the larger the gland, the more milk should be secreted (which is not saying that the largest udders always give most milk). The teats should be of even size, and large enough to be conveniently grasped by the hand. When they are evenly and squarely placed, the form is about right. The texture of the skin of both teats and udder should be soft and mossy, covered with fine, silky hair. These general features are, as to form, indicated in the accompanying sketch. The milk comes in through arteries, which are so deeply seated as not to be observable, but the veins, which carry it towards the udder, are nearer the surface, and may be clearly seen. It is in accordance with universal observation, that the size, length, and numerous corrugations of these milk veins bear tolerably definite relation to the amount of milk which the udder is capable of secreting. But, of course, to give quality and quantity, the animal must have sufficient food to make that quality and quantity, and sufficient clean water to supply the material of which milk is made. And through the whole process it pays to keep her comfortable, warm, and quiet, without having to travel too far for her food and drink.

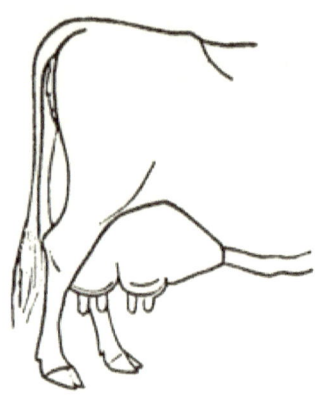

Milk-Giving Indications.

To Milk a Cow Clean.—This has always been the ambition of the careful milker, and when that end is attained, he may be generally satisfied. But to milk a cow in a cleanly way, although of equal importance, does not, in a large percentage of cases, come within the scope of consideration. Good dairy cows are often quite spoiled by bad and careless milking. It is astonishing how few milkers give attention to the delicate organism of the cow's udder, or milk system. A word or two on this point may not be out of place. The udder of the cow is divided into two chambers by an impervious membrane. This dividing substance runs in the direction of the backbone, and is so placed that the milk from one chamber cannot pass into the other. For this reason, it is advisable that we should operate, say, on a front and hind teat next the milker, and having emptied one chamber should then proceed with the other. This is not, however, the general practice. It is customary rather to operate on the teats of different chambers, taking one fore and one hind teat, instead of the two teats on one side. The idea being to preserve the natural state of the udder, and this method of milking, according to this practice, is mainly responsible for much of the malformation in the udders of so many cows. This of course is a great evil, and it detracts from the appearance of the animals, and lowers their money value when offered for sale. Milking with wet hands is a main source of sore and cracked teats, and is also a source of contagion. Again, too rapid and violent milking is to be avoided, as also conversation between milkers while milking is in progress, as both of these causes tend to make the cows uneasy, and to retain their milk.

Every Cow Should Be Tested.—This is becoming more and more a necessity in modern dairying. Efficient dairyists soon become experts at testing. Under what may be termed average conditions, an animal is of little or no value to the owner unless he is able to derive a profit by keeping it. In the dairy a good animal is the one that will profitably convert the most feed into the most and richest milk, butter, or cheese. In this, quantity is not the only consideration, neither is quality. Both are necessary. The cost of the product is more important than all else. There must be a liberal quantity, and the quality must be good. At the same time both must be secured at a cost that will leave a fair per cent. of profit when rightly managed. And there is more certainty of doing this with the dairying breeds than with others. There may be individual animals in all breeds that excel in some essentials, as there are others that fail almost as regularly. Yet, generally, there are breeds that as a class can be depended upon to convert their excess of food, the amount over and above what is necessary to sustain animal life, into milk and cream, and this characteristic is in the breed to an extent that it can be depended upon to transmit this quality from parent to offspring.

Proportions of Butter in Milk.—From the tests made, the following afford some guidance. A cow which gave 44lbs. 9oz. of milk yielded 1lb. 10½oz. butter; another gave 31lbs 14oz. of milk, and 1lb. 5¾oz. of butter; a third 46lbs. 15oz. milk, and 1lb. 3½oz. butter. These were heavy cattle, mostly of the Shorthorn type. For cows under 1000lbs. live weight, a Jersey gave 29lb. 7oz. milk, which yielded 2lbs. 4¾oz. butter; the second, 40lbs. 12oz. milk, and 2lbs. 3½oz. butter; the third, 33lbs. 11oz. milk, and 2lb. 3oz. butter—the third yielding the largest quantity of butter in proportion to her live weight. The weight of this good little cow was 834lbs., or about 7½cwt.

How Much Feed.—The experience is that a real dairy cow can make good use of from two to two and a half per cent. of her own weight as food, or say, twenty to thirty-five pounds of solid feed daily, and all the clean water she can drink, for an animal weighing a thousand pounds. While this may be approximately correct, we should remember that the richer and more concentrated the feed, the fewer pounds will be required, always provided there is coarser feed with it to ensure digestion. Thus, five pounds of pollard, or maize meal, or wheat bran may be equal to twenty pounds of bush hay; but where both are given, the value of each is increased. And while 10lbs. of oaten hay may be a full feed or ration for a small animal, it does not follow that 20lbs. of poorer hay—that would show by analysis to be half as rich—would, in practice, be of equal milk making value to that same cow. There is a limit to the ability of the animal to chew and digest both bulky and concentrated stuff; very concentrated feed may be too rich for the digestion of the cow. Portions of each—mixed feeds—are best. This is the case, frequently, with pollard, bran, and maize meal. So, when we have poor, bulky stuff, it is safer to mix with it something richer rather than to feed it alone in excessive quantity.

Conveniences for Milking.—The quantity of milk that a cow gives depends to a great extent upon how it is got, the mode, time, and regularity of milking. Cows do best that have one regular milker, and the time of milking should be carefully attended to, and not be subject to

Comfort for Milker and Cow.

variations from day to day. The udder should be rubbed clean with a dry cloth, when that is necessary. Wetting the hands or teats with milk before milking is bad practice, both for the comfort of the animal and the cleanliness of the milk. The milker should have short finger nails, for long finger nails will be sure to hurt the teats and cause inflammation.

Stalls and Bails.—Conveniences for holding the cattle in position while milking are necessary in Australian dairying, where the milking is in yards where flies and other annoyances disturb the cows. Bails designed to work easily are very helpful, to open and shut without the need of much movement, for the insertion or removal of pins, &c. When young cattle are being broken in

—the process in careful hands is really a system of teaching—for dairy purposes, it is very convenient to be able to fasten or unloosen the bail without going into the stall. The bail illustrated is convenient to work, and removable when necessary. The stanchions are 2 x 4in. hardwood put together with wooden pins or bolts. The bed piece is two two-by-four inch scantling,

A Handy Milking Stall.

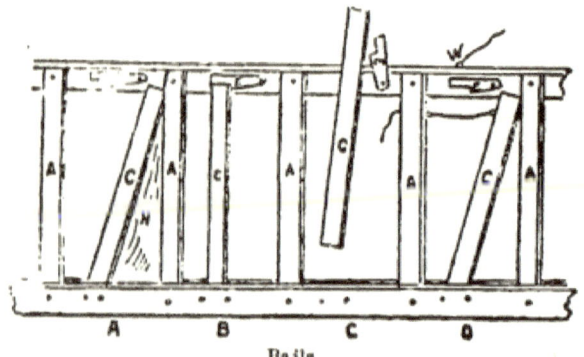

Bails.

and so is the top piece. In the illustration, one is removed to show how they are fastened; *aa* are the stationary parts, *cc* the movable slides that hold the cattle in; *ee* are automatic fasteners which hold the stanchions shut. In stall a the slide *c* is shown open. When the animal puts her head in place, a push on *c* closes the stanchion, *e* drops automatically and holds it shut, as shown in stall B. The movable part (*c*) has no pin in the lower end to hold it in place, but one on each side of it. A pin at the top keeps it down when it is shut. In stall c is shown how the movable part is moved from its place when taking the stanchions apart. Stall D shows a simple contrivance by which the cattle can be shut in as they enter their places, and let out, also, without going between them. A strong string (*s*) is tied to the staple (*n*) and passes through to any convenient place. Pulling on this will close them, and the one attached at *w* and *e* will open them and let the cattle out.

Preserving Milk by Heating.—The object of "Pasteurising" milk is to destroy "the bacterial germs" of fermentation or decay. But by "scalding" up to the boiling point, milk is injured seriously. As it becomes known that the germs can be destroyed much more effectively while the milk is at a temperature far below the boiling point, the safer and better process is followed. Germs in milk, both vegetable and animal are destroyed, and the milk effectively "Pasteurised" at a temperature of 155 degrees. The apparatus shown in our illustrations is quite effective for the purpose. The can or pail (A) is fitted up as seen in the second illustration. The bottles (B) (B) (B), as many as may be required, or the pail can hold, are filled with milk, or other fluid substance to be sterilised. The bottles stand upon a perforated grating (D), and are surrounded by water as shown. Into each bottle is inserted a plug (C)(C)(C) of cotton wool or other porous substance. Heat is then applied gradually to the vessel, and brought to about 155 degrees. Thirty minutes of that temperature is ample, as a rule, for sterilising the contents of the bottles, and milk thus treated will remain sweet during several days. The object of the porous stoppers is to allow

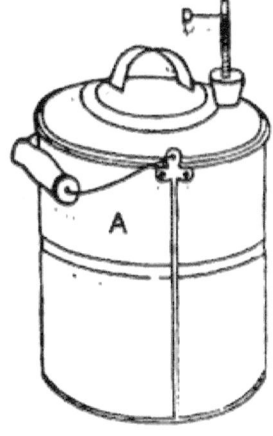

Pasteurising Pail.

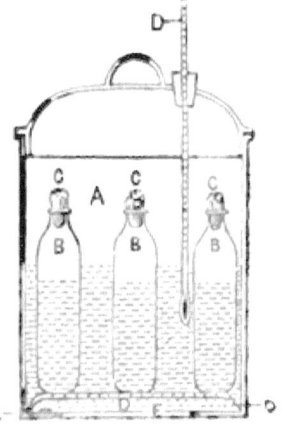

the escape of vapours from the contents of the bottles, while preventing the admission of any other vapours. To finish the process up to the point of actual sterilising, *the water* is brought up to nearly the boiling point, or 200 degrees, for three minutes or so, and the bottles are then taken out, cooled, and sealed or corked tightly, in which state, and in a temperature of 55 degrees or lower, it remains good for an indefinite time.

Butter Making.—Setting the milk for cream, and converting the cream into butter by hand labor, is still followed as a process; and for making home supplies the process answers very well. But for business purposes, and where the product has to be sold in competition with factory made and creamery butter, the hand made process suffers badly. To carry it out in a satisfactory manner, a real dairy room is necessary, with entrance and windows so arranged that flies and other winged abominations cannot enter. They are fearfully mischievous when they reach milk which is set in shallow pans. Coolness and semi-darkness aid in the rising of the cream, which is then skimmed off, and, if sufficient in quantity, may be converted into butter at once, with the aid of some one of the many churns available for this branch of work. Or the cream may be held back for one, two, or more days, to "ripen," or until there is enough for a churning.

Ripening the Cream.—To get the rich flavor which is in request to a lesser or greater extent in all butters, except the really sweet, unsalted, made direct from new milk, three agencies or generators of fermentation are brought into action. They are: Buttermilk from a previous churning, cream already ripened, or a special ferment as a starter. Before butter factories were thought of, the first two agencies were in use in extensive, well conducted dairies. And butter often went wrong then, as it does still. There is much room for improvement in order to start and complete the bacterial action or souring, possibly more so than at any previous time in all the experiences of dairying. Skill comes in at every point of the operations of fermentation, skill in selecting, regulating and working the flavor as required. In this, the effect of lower temperature is very marked; 50 degrees Fahrenheit seems the point of safety at which ferment material should be stored, whether it be butter-milk, cream, or special preparation, and then churning at something like the same temperature, after ripening, which may require from 6 to 24 hours, according to the skill and method of the operator. The time in which cream ripens in ordinary practice is influenced by the weather, and the cleanliness of the milker and appliances. The temperature at which the cream is set for ripening, and the amount of fat present, also influence the process and extent of this first fermentation. Hot or warm muggy weather has a tendency to hasten the change; while a clear, bright atmosphere, as

Factory Cream Separator.

well as cold, is slower for the growth of the bacteria, which develop the changes. It is the milk sugar and casein that are broken up when cream sours. Thus thin cream, with 10 to 15 per cent. fat, contains more milk-sugar; and acid, or tartness, is generated faster than in cream which contains more fat, and less milk-sugar and casein.

Factory System for Butter-Making.—It is to the credit of our dairymen that they were amongst the first outside of Denmark and Sweden to entertain the feasibility of the factory system. For this change New South Wales is largely indebted to the efforts of Mr. D. L. Dymock, of Kiama. The system is both co-operative and proprietary. The milk is taken over from the dairymen as quickly as possible after it is got from the cows, and is paid for, according to the contents of butter fat and the ruling price of butter; an ordinary fair calculation to all parties being that 25lb. of milk, or $2\frac{1}{2}$ gallons, should yield 1 lb. of butter. This is very close to a correct estimate, as worked out by careful analysis of milk and also by the churn tests from fairly well-fed cows.

Cream Separating Machines.—They are of different patterns, but all get at the result of separating the cream from the milk in much the same way. The cream or butter particles of new milk are the lightest part of the fluid, and rise to the surface of their own gravity when milk is set

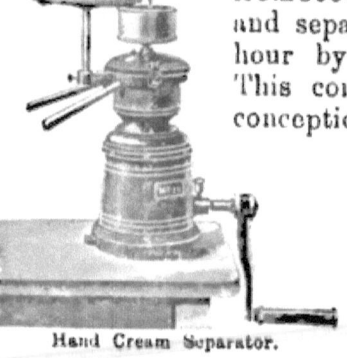

Hand Cream Separator.

in pans. And this separation of cream particles is completed, almost instantly, by the machine, the revolving separator of which is moving at the rate of from 3000 to 5000 revolutions per minute, and separating 25 to 250 gallons per hour by hand, steam, or other power. This contrivance is a really scientific conception, long in use in laboratory practice, and founded on an acquaintance with the fat globules in milk, and a knowledge of their different specific gravity from the liquid in which they float, and a further knowledge of what must be the behaviour of a mixture of such globules and such liquid when subjected to centrifugal force. In operation, the milk runs in a steady stream into the top of the separator, and the heavier portion—in reality the skimmed milk—is thrown to the outside of the machine, and is discharged in a steady stream. The cream meanwhile is gathering in an inner layer, and is discharged from another outlet. Amongst the advantages of the system, it is more cleanly, everything heavier than cream is extracted promptly, and very curious substances are thus seen to be present in milk, whether coming from the poor condition of the animals, from poverty of feed, from dirty milking, bad water, exposure to excessive cold or rain, or other causes, need not be followed at this stage. The evils of contact from flies, dust, &c., that can scarcely be avoided when milk is set out to get the cream to rise in pans, are also overcome.

From Cream to Butter.—The whole of the operations, from the time of milking to the production of cream, are accomplished in the factories, as a rule, during the cool of the morning—a change, indeed, from the time when the whole day, and often the night, had to be occupied in milking, creaming, churning, &c., by the dairyman and his family. The process allows us to see that the fatty matter in milk is not uniform. A part of the milk from cows on good grass consists of the essential oils of the grasses, and which give the nutty flavor to butter and cheese. But the milk of poorly fed cows is deficient in both the butter fat, and the flavoring oils of grasses. Thus, cows fed on artificial feed may be oily and rich enough in butter fat, but poor in the true butter flavor. Hence when butter is gathered from a number of dairies, it is liable to be defective in that uniformity of quality and appearance which have such marked effect upon this product when offered for sale.

The Creamery System.—It is to overcome the defects of butter making in small lots that the creamery system has found favor. With that end in view, the cream is cooled as much as possible, and sent off to the creamery or central factory for butter making. It is there cooled down still lower and made into butter in a temperature of from 55 to 60 degrees, and water as low as 40 degrees is used for washing and the other operations of first-class butter making. Butter made at this colder temperature can be separated more effectually from the water and casein of milk, which forms from 24 to 40 per cent. of the cream, than is possible in a higher temperature, a most important feature in butter for keeping or export.

The Water of Butter.—There must be some water in it, or the composition would not be butter. The healthy proportion is about 12 per cent., or 12lbs. of water in 100lbs. of butter. The test for the quantity of water is simple enough, and it is seldom we find less than 11 per cent. There is very often much more, over 22 per cent. sometimes, and then the water is an active agent of destruction. Possibly more butter, put up to keep, is lost from excess of water and bad salt than all other causes combined. It is the water which carries the salt, which averages between 1·20 and 2·50 per cent. No amount of working can take out all the water gathered in with the butter from the churn, but skill can work the quantity down to the point of safety, say 12 per cent.

Butter-Making Machinery.—From the earliest times churns of some sort were in use for separating the true

Churning.

butter fat from the water of the milk or cream. In Scotland, the United States, and in other countries as well, butter is made direct from the milk without creaming. But this process is suitable only for cold climates, and where the butter can be marketed at once, and the buttermilk has a value. The forms of churns are as various almost as the countries where they are used, all sort of appliances being in favor, from shaking the milk in a bottle till the butter comes, to the revolving of a disc driven by machinery. But there are safe general rules for churning, amongst them : 1. That the cream should be churned at a temperature of 55 to 60 degrees if at all practicable; though, in the colonies, butter is often made in a temperature above 70 degrees. During very hot weather it is considered better to lessen the speed of the churn when the butter begins to form. 2. When during the churning the temperature increases, the butter can be helped by adding in the churn very cold skimmed milk or water. 3. As soon as the butter "comes," that is, forms in a granulated state, and there is actual separation of the butter from the buttermilk, the churning must be stopped at once. 4. When cream has been churned at say 58 degrees, or the mass of butter has not a higher temperature than 62 degrees, it may be put into the butter-worker without any washing; this is the Danish system. 5. Should it be preferred to wash the butter, then the butter-milk should be allowed to run out by the tap or plug placed on the lower part of the churn. Fill the churn with cold water and let it run from the tap in the same manner.

Butter Workers.—In the factories, butter is not handled at any stage. It is worked over, and salt is applied, by various contrivances which press the mass so as to squeeze out the butter-milk and water, and such particles of casein as may be free, and can be floated out. Centrifugal machines are being introduced for this purpose also.

A Small Butter Worker.

The Salt.—Salting is a most important part of butter making. Very serious damage is likely to result to butter in which lime, magnesia, sulphur, and other natural compounds of salt may be present. Their detection should be part of the butter maker's art. It is not difficult. The salt left in A1 butter varies between 1 and 2 per cent.

Coloring.—Annetto, a vegetable coloring, is used for those who like something deeper than the natural straw color of butter. The caramel of sugar gives a rich wholesome color. The juice of carrot is also used.

Further Ripening and Making Up.—1lb. and ½lb. packets, put up in nicely prepared printed paper, give a further attraction to butter. Or it may be put up in enamelled boxes or kegs for transfer or export. Further "ripening" in the mass is also in order in some of the factories, much the same rules as guide the ripening of cream being followed.

Bad Flavors in Butter.—They are acquired simply enough. Should either cream or milk or butter be put along with a substance that has any other flavor, most likely the butter will absorb it. Flavors of leather, kerosene, onions, cheese, bacon, soap, turpentine, and other substances have been got in that way. Bad flavors may also be got from feed. Lucerne, sorrel, turnips, bitter weeds, and other substances affect the flavor of both milk and butter. Lucerne hay is better; turnips may be fed after milking. Scalding to 155 degrees and then suddenly cooling removes some odors, but does not drive out the flavor of others got from bad feed stuffs, or bad water.

CHEESE MAKING.—The modern cheese maker works closely upon chemical lines. All the operations from the time of cooling or heating the milk to a fixed degree of temperature; the use of coagulating materials, or rennet, all bring about chemical changes. The thermometer, use of litmus for acid and other tests, the qualities of the milk for butter fat, and the solids that form cheese, all come into the operations of cheese making.

Australian Cheese.—Cheddar, the product of the whole milk, butter included, is the favourite product for home use and for export. To make such cheese, of sufficient quality, there must be the milk from well fed cows. The product of even one cow in bad condition, or that has fed on rank stuff from swamps, upon the leaves of trees, or drank of unclean water, has spoiled many makings of cheese. But all being well, including suitable appliances for cooling, heating, curdling, extraction of the whey, salting, preserving, and curing, the product should be up to the standard of sound Cheddar cheese, and the product equal to 1lb of cheese for each gallon of milk used.

Composition of Cheddar.—The lb. of cheese thus made is composed, in the practical sense, of one-third true cheese matter, amongst the best material known for building up muscle, sinew, and flesh; one-third butter fat and warmth-making material; the remainder being salt, flavouring matter, and the water of composition.

The Process of Making.—Here the intention is to be introductory only. The many excellent works available—Oliver, Millard, Wright, Dowling, Long, Sheldon, and others—give details in fulness which is beyond the scope of an elementary work. The practice may well follow the close study of the chemistry and practice of cheese making, though the details given here may be helpful.

Cheese for Home Use.—All of us, who either make butter or send milk to the factories, have at times a few gallons of milk which can be worked up into cheese. With, say, 10 gallons of milk, or a little over 100lbs., we can make 10 to 11lbs of sound cheese, always acceptable upon the farm table. We do not use all the cheese we might with advantage to the food supply of the family. And if we don't want it, then a 10lb. cheese soon finds a customer in a neighbour, or storekeeper. The appliances necessary for making small cheese for home use are—a deep pail or milk can, a tub big enough to set the pail in surrounded by water, a hoop or hoops big enough for from 7 to 14lbs. of cheese. Suppose we take the evening and morning milk for our purpose. The former can be put to cool during the night; the morning milk can be cooled in the pail, set in cold water. Mix the two, stirring thoroughly; and, by pouring hot water round the pail, we can raise the heat of the whole mass of milk from 80 to 90 degrees; 84 degrees is a safe temperature for milk made ready for cheese. To thicken the milk into curd, use the fluid rennet, directions for which are given on the bottles; or that sold in lozenges will do. One lozenge, of the strength purchasable for a shilling a box, is reckoned as enough for 10 gallons of milk. Dissolve the lozenge in water, and stir it into the warmed milk, then cover with blanketing. The milk thickens in 12 to 15 minutes from the time of adding rennet, and should be ready to cut in from 30 to 40 minutes from the time of thickening. It is found to be workable in practice to allow double and one-half the time taken to thicken to secure curd ripe for cutting. The curd should then be tough enough to be readily lifted with the finger, and fit to be cut by a long bladed knife into squares of an inch. This liberates the whey or watery part of the milk. The whey is run off with a syphon, or dipped off by means of a shallow dish, put into a vessel, and heated to 100 degrees, and poured over the curd, which is again covered to keep in the heat. After half an hour the curd will be tough enough to lift with the hands, and can be heaped upon a table to permit the remainder of the whey to drain off. The curd is then broken as small as beans, by rubbing with the hands, the whey being so carefully pressed out, that no cream may escape with it. The broken up curd is then covered on the table, and thus left until decided acid action sets in, when salt is rubbed in at the rate of 2 to 4 ozs. of finely-ground salt to say 12 pounds of curd, which is then placed in a hoop or mould, lined with a clean cloth dipped in the whey. The curd is pressed into the mould firmly but slowly. It is then further pressed, during a night generally, then taken out and set on a board, and turned once a day until perfectly firm. Cheese is all the better in flavour, and more wholesome, by being "cured," which means keeping it in a cool, dry place for a month, six weeks or longer. This "curing," is caused by bacterial ferment which ripen the curdled milk into flavored cheese. It is a desirable process, and gives us a really welcome addition to the dairyist's table.

Rennet in the Chemical Sense.—It is of the nature of pepsin, spirit of salt, &c. These substances are in the digestive system of the calf. The purpose of it in nature is to coagulate the milk and so render it easy of digestion. In the human economy, the gastric juice is akin to rennet. The stomach of a ruminant or animal which chews the cud is arranged with four divisions, adjoining each other and leading directly from one to the other. Each of these parts of the stomach has a special function to perform. The first, when the animal is old enough to eat grass, is mainly employed to hold the food until it has time to chew and so bring it into a fine state of division; the second is employed as a compressor to force the food to the mouth to be there chewed; the third is used as a filter, to effectually divide the chewed food allowing only the sufficiently fine portions to pass onward into the fourth stomach, where it is acted upon by the gastric juices. This stomach is known as the rennet stomach, because from it the digestive substance is prepared, whether it be in a concentrated form or not. This stomach may be used fresh or preserved in a solution of salt, or rubbed with salt and dried. In either case, when soaked in warm water, it yields up its essence, a substance possessing the power of curdling milk—that is of coagulating the cheese matter and the butter. The amount of acid in rennet is seldom more than two-tenths of one per cent. The quantity of pepsin varies considerably. The risks of making rennet from the stomach are that should there be any decomposition of the membranes there will pass into solution substances generally of a disagreeable odour, and the further risk of unpleasant taint to the cheese. Pepsin is a peculiar ferment; it causes other substances to undergo changes without undergoing any material change itself so far as known. Experience and observation, however, encourage the belief that rennet continues its digestive properties when absorbed as food with the other contents of cheese.

Cheese Factory System.—Jacketed vats are used, wherein heat can be regulated by steam supply from a boiler. The milk—having been cooled the night previous and the cream prevented from rising by frequent stirring—is usually about 65deg. in the morning. Into this is run, after cooling, the morning's milk, and the temperature of the whole is raised to about 84deg. in hot weather, and up to 90deg. in cooler weather, making a mean temperature of about 85deg. for setting in mild weather. When colour is used, the colouring liquid is mixed with the milk, and then sufficient rennet added. Coagulation begins in about ten minutes. Prepared chemical rennet as fluid, powder, or in lozenge form, is now in general use in preference to the rennet made from the stomach of the calf. When colouring matter is used it is in a liquid state and prepared from the best annatto. Hansen's prepared colouring is in favour, and also the form known as annattoine. It is easy to reduce to a liquid state, and is put up in packages accompanied by a recipe for its preparation and use in cheesemaking. One tablespoonful (½oz.) is generally used for 20 gallons of milk. A slight agitation is kept up until the milk begins to roll thick and heavy, for the purpose of preventing the cream from separating, but care must be taken not to stir too long, or a smooth compact mass of curd will be impossible, a broken, spongy mass may appear in its place, from which many of the fine particles of butter will be washed off in the whey. As soon as the curd breaks smoothly across the finger, leaving the finger clean and the clear whey settles in the broken place—say in 35 minutes from time of adding the rennet—

the curd is fit to cut, which is done as quickly but as gently as possible, first with a horizontal knife lengthwise of the vat, then with a perpendicular knife until the pieces of curd are about the size of beans. If the milk is very sweet, the pieces may be left coarser; if it shows more ripeness and is souring rapidly, the curd is cut finer still, so as to secure even action of the heat in a shorter space of time, and before the acid gets too much developed. Move the curd about gently, only enough to prevent packing, while raising the temperature of the whole mass gradually and steadily, but more or less rapidly, according to the state of the milk, to 96, 98, or 100deg. as experience shall have determined to be the proper point for the district. Hold the curd steadily at the desired point of temperature until the action of the heat is nearly or quite complete, and acid, just a taste of sourness, is got. The use of litmus test paper is desirable at this stage, as it shows the first trace of acid and the extent of acid development. When a curd-mill is in use, draw off all the whey early, as soon as there are any signs of acid. To aid the flow, raise one end of the vat, draw the curd away from the lower end and pile it up along each side of the vat; leave it to drain, and when the course is desirable let the curd take on a little more acid or "ripeness," occasionally cutting it lengthwise and across into convenient pieces to handle, and turning it so as to air the bottom and inner portions, and to give the outer portions that have cooled somewhat the advantage of more warmth. When the whey that drains from it is unmistakably acid, or when an iron heated to a black heat applied to the curd will draw it out into fine threads a quarter or half an inch long, commence to break or grind the curd as soon as possible, and apply from 2 to 6oz. fine table salt to the curd per ten gallons of milk. The curd may then be filled into moulds at once, and sent to press, or allowed to stand and drain for an hour or so, according to temperature, and what experience may prove to be the best course.

Another system, and it answers well, is not to grind the curd, but allow the whey to drain off pretty well in the vat, while thoroughly stirring and separating the curd, then throw the mass out on a table, and rub it down with the hands to the size of peas or wheat grains, and then apply, as evenly as possible, from 2 to 6 oz. of fine salt per ten gallons of milk, then cover it up, if necessary, according to the state of the acid and the amount of whey left, to carry away the free salt. Air the curd well and put it to press, having regard both to the acidity of the curd and the temperature of the atmosphere: 74 deg. is a favourite temperature. If put to press too warm in hot weather, the curd may ferment in the centre of the cheese and cause it to swell and lose flavor. In cool weather the curd temperature must be worked high enough to make a smooth face to the cheese.

Pressing and Curing.—As pressing, in some form, is always resorted to for ordinary cheese, it is a matter of importance to get the best and most convenient appliances. The gang-press, with improved iron vats or hoops, is in favor in the factories. It is compact, economical, and does its work satisfactorily. Great variety of other presses are also in use, the principle of which is the lever, weighted lightly at first, and heavier as the pressing goes on. A very good press is made by fixing a notch of wood to the wall of the room in which the pressing is done; the butt of a sapling is then fixed to rest upon the cap of the cheese-vat, the end being weighed as may be desired.

Temperature, Acid, &c.—One of the most difficult points in cheese making is to determine exactly where the heat and acid development should be arrested, and the salt applied to the curd. Experience and judgment tell at this point; some acquire the skill in a few months, others scarcely ever reach it. No fixed rule can be laid down, as the milk of different cows, and of different localities, as well as of different years and different seasons of the year, work differently. Averages can only be given here. Each cheese maker must determine for himself or herself the degree of heat and acid required for the time and place. The importance of having curing rooms, in which the temperature can be controlled and kept between 70 and 80 degrees, is beginning to be more and more recognised, and more pains to secure this end are taken in putting up buildings for dairy purposes.

Points in Cheese-making.—When the salt is added and thoroughly intermixed, a clean cloth wrung out of warm water is placed inside the cheese vat to prevent the curd adhering and the almost powdered curd is pressed in by hand firmly, putting a rounded top of curd on, bringing the ends of the cloth over all, and fastening them into the edges of the vat with a block. Experience, and the size of the hoop, show how much curd is required, to make a desired weight of cheese, after it is pressed. In some dairies, before the cheese is removed from the press, it is put under pressure with a cloth wrung out of nearly boiling water, to give toughness to the skin. It is then removed to the cheese-room, and turned daily for a fortnight or three weeks, and afterwards at longer intervals.

Digestive Cheese.—There are several means of securing a soft and rapidly-curing cheese, all of which combine not only to make a cheese soon ripe, and believed to be more digestive; but then it does not keep. These conditions are less heat, less acid, less salt, and more rennet. The secrets of cheese making are in the proper use and degree of these several agents. And also to produce a firm, flaky, but not crumbly, sweet flavoured article, that will improve at least for a year, and melt in the mouth like butter, leaving a clean sweet taste on the palate. Such a cheese is not likely to be fit for use in much less than sixty days. A good deal of judgment may also be exercised in the size of cheese made. For instance, a Cheddar, or whole milk cheese for family use, weighing about 6lb., is coming into great favour in the Sydney market.

Special Cheese.—Where small quantities of specially rich cheese are made, extra cream is added to the milk before warming; coagulating is followed as in other systems of working. A favourite plan is to set the new cheese before the fire, and, by frequently turning, it sets with no other pressure than the weight of the curd. Early next morning it receives a dry cloth. At this time, should the weather be cool, the hoop containing the cheese is again warmed before the fire. Changing again takes place at ten o'clock, and also at two, and if everything has gone on well (the condition is indicated by a uniform yellow colour and an elastic feel to the touch), it should be ready to take from the hoop that afternoon. Some makers find that twelve or even twenty-four hours tend to mature this rich cheese better; and, perhaps, for larger sizes this latter course may be advisable.

Cheese by Evaporation.—This process is in favour in Canada. The water is evaporated down to the cheese standard, without adding rennet. The sugar is thus incorporated with the casein and butter. Salting, pressing, and curing are followed as for other cheese.

Cream and Skim-Milk Cheese.—For soft cream cheese mix two pints of milk and one pint of cream; raise the temperature to 86 degrees, mix three to six drops of Hansen's rennet to each pint. Stir all the time in one direction, and put the mass in a draining bag for twelve hours (or eighteen, as the case may be); after six hours, shift the outer curd inside and the inner curd outside; then hang up again for the remainder of the time, to let the whey drain off. Then put this luscious cheese into little shapes lined with paper.

For Skimmed-Milk Cheese.—A large vat is heated by steam. The milk is raised to 94 degrees. Add the colouring matter (Hansen's annatto). The colouring is dissolved in water for cheese, and in oil for butter; stir well, and then let the mass coagulate; next cut it in cube-shaped pieces with a curd knife, up and down and across; then drain off the whey, and put the curd in the mill and grind into small pieces like grain; then put it into a cheese hoop (lined with muslin) and press. This cheese ripens best in a temperature of 60 degrees. Fit to eat in about two months.

Floating Curd in Cheese-making.—This is troublesome at times, and especially when cows take to eating bush trees, rank weeds in swamps, and other rubbish. It is a result of unhealthy ferment, and to deal with it the curd is broken as finely as possible, gradually adding salt while the breaking proceeds. Raise the temperature very slowly to 104 degrees Fahr. Cook as firm as possible, draw off the whey, and wash the curd in cold water until cooled to 70 degrees Fahr., when it is piled and allowed to mellow in the usual way, and vatted at 60 Fahr. To remove the whey, cut the curd in narrow lengths, say three inches wide and nine to twelve inches long. Then pile on edge length and crosswise. Soda has good effect, at times, in checking fermentation, dissolved in the rennet—¼oz. to 100 gallons of milk is sufficient. We have found in this climate that doubtful ferments and acidity are most likely to be present in milk from cows that are on poor feed or bad water, or when the milk is retained beyond the right time for cheese-making.

XVIII.—THE PIG.—To Raise and Use Him.

The pig is a popular institution on the station and the farm, in towns where municpal laws are not enforced, and

The Pig That Pays.

in the country. Yet Australia does not export pork to any extent, and well-fed and cured ham and bacon are by no means so general as might be. This is the more singular because maize—the great pork producer of America—grows to the fullest perfection of quality and weight of crop over a large extent of country, and other foods—sugar cane, sweet and common potatoes, wheat, barley, milk, pumpkins, &c., are plentiful. Perhaps the feeling that it is of no use making more pig meat than we can consume is due to the cheapness and abundance of beef and mutton; and that when higher prices rule for the latter, pigs may be more looked after. Be that as it may, there are few more useful or more satisfactory things about a place than a good pig in the stye, when put up in a proper manner for fattening. The animal agrees well with the climate. He enjoys robust health and a lively appetite. He puts on flesh as rapidly as in any other part of the world. The smaller sizes, those ranging from 80lb. to 150lb., dead weight, are the animals most in demand by butchers, and the most suitable for home use. Larger sizes may do for curing in wholesale, always providing that the food given keeps pace in quality and quantity with the improvement. No breed has been invented yet that thrives without feed, though the better sorts make the best out of what they eat. The poor lots make bone, muscle, and trouble amongst neighbors. When stinted of their food, the best sorts become tyrants, and others become miserable spectacles. It is a good rule in pig keeping that keeps up the breed by keeping the troughs well supplied.

The Pig That Pays.—Most people have their ideas as to best breeds of pigs. Colour has much to do with the choice. While numbers, possibly the majority, prefer the Berkshire, black with white points, others give preference to whites, to the Cheshires and medium Yorkshires, and some people actually detest black pigs. And yet the Berkshire cures A1 for sides and hams, and the Essex and Tamworths are not far behind for quality. But white pigs have their points, and are not objected to any more than the well-bred black sorts. It is astonishing how quickly even coarse pigs " breed up " when due selection, care in mating, paddocking, and feeding are attended to. To breed up, or improve, a male animal of the chosen type is the main requirement. In a really good pig, we find neat neck and shoulders, round ribs, thick loins, stout thighs, small head and snout, short legs, long and silky hair. This type of animal should be aimed at, whether black or white, thorough-bred, half-bred, or common bred pigs are kept. And now that there are prospects of exporting, it is well to know that the general run of bacon and hams for London or other English market are got from animals weighing about 150lb. to 200lb. dead weight. The curing trade regard all pigs over the top weight as inferior.

What Pig Points Mean.—Neat in the head means a nose neither too long nor too short, a nice, shapely keen-looking face, with bright mild eyes, broad forehead, a good-tempered appearance. Ears, soft and pliable; when they fall a little to the front without actually being lopped, the point is good. Light neck and shoulders; for the coarser parts of a side of bacon, and those which fetch the lowest price are the neck and shoulders, and the lighter those parts the better the side, and the higher price it will make. Deep in the ribs. Looking at this from a bacon curer's point of view, a pig that is deep and round in the ribs will of necessity produce a larger proportion of first class bacon. Thick in the loin. A pig with heavy loin has capacity for food, together with good digestion and strong constitution generally. The loin is high-priced, and the weight of that should be kept up. Stout in the thighs. The hams are most important, and in the case of pigs killed for the ham and middle (flitch) trade, the most valuable of all. Long silky hair indicates strength of constitution as well as lean meat. Such are conditions which indicate a happy union between thriftiness and lean meat, a union which suits both the curer and the producer.

Judging the Age.—As a general thing, we are content to take the pig by general appearances, with respect to age. But the teeth, like those of other animals, help to tell the tale. The animal is born with eight teeth, four corner incisors and four tusks. On the eighth or tenth day second or third temporary molars appear. At four weeks old four nippers appear, two in the upper and two in the lower jaw. At the fifth or sixth week the foremost temporary molars are in the upper and lower jaws. At the age of three months, intermediary incisors appear above the gums. At the sixth month, the "wolf teeth" appear, and at the same age the third permanent molars. At the ninth month, their permanent corner incisors should be visible, permanent tusks, and second permanent molars. At the twelfth month the permanent nippers should be in view. With the twelfth and thirteenth month the three temporary molars shed, and their permanent substitutes, which at fifteen months of age will have fully appeared, are cutting through the gums. With the eighteenth month the permanent intermediary incisors and the hindmost permanent molars should make their appearance, and with the twenty-first month should be fully developed. Then we have a full mouthed pig.

Pen and Paddock Feeding.—Pen feeding until the fattening time is reached is not profitable with pigs in Australian practice. The animals require much attention when penned; they fret and suffer in flesh when they are not attended to. They do better in paddocks, on a piece of good soil, with a stretch of swamp in it, from the time of weaning until they are penned for fattening. They may be fed in paddocks, but not at regular times. A whistle or horn should call them, and they should get nothing without calling; then they do not "loaf" around waiting for the slop-pail, but occupy their time rooting and grazing as well-ordered pigs ought to do. When there are shelters in the paddock for warmth, and in case of storm, pigs are profitable stock and do not exact so much attendance.

Points in Feeding.—Pigs allowed to roam at will over good grass, lucerne or other green feed, and which got all the milk and grain they would eat, made the most rapid growth, and made the best use of what they ate. Those fed on grass, with milk and maize, on a small patch made more rapid growth than those fed on grain alone, and apparently made a slightly better use of the food eaten. Green grass appears to be of the greatest value as an appetiser. Pigs kept on grass alone made but slow growth

—so slow that it would require two seasons for maturity—making the profits very doubtful. Pigs kept in a movable pen on lucerne ate within seven pounds as much grain as did those in a paddock covered with grass, but did not make as good use of it. Exercise is necessary to increase eating capacity, and probably digestion, that growth may be both rapid and economical.

A Natty Pen Arrangement.—That some people have an idea that pigs do all the better when they have comfortable camping places, is made evident in the accompanying series of illustrations. The pen was built to accommodate two families — a mother and her young, and a group of fatteners. The size is 20 feet long by 13 feet frontage. The position of the pen being in somewhat ornamental grounds, the building is arranged in keeping with the surroundings.

The Pen Finished.

The first sketch shows the pen complete. It is of hardwood timber framing, covered with weatherboards; corrugated iron roof, nicely ornamented. The second sketch shows the framework. The floor, and two feet up the sides, is hardwood, 6 x 1 stuff.

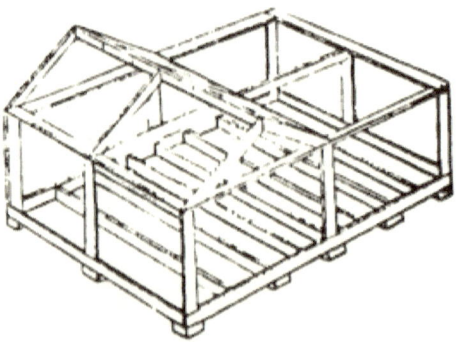

Framework of the Pen.

A main feature of the pen is the feeding arrangement shown in the third sketch. There is a trough shown by the dotted lines *a b*, over which is a heavy swing partition. The operation of this swinging arrangement is seen in the first illustration where, on the lefthand side it is shown pushed inwards, so that feed may be put into the trough (B). As the pigs get their heads into the trough they push the swing outwards, where it is stopped, so that they cannot get out. Modifications of these devices will suggest themselves to the many who like to have even their piggeries convenient and comfortable; the latter feature is all important.

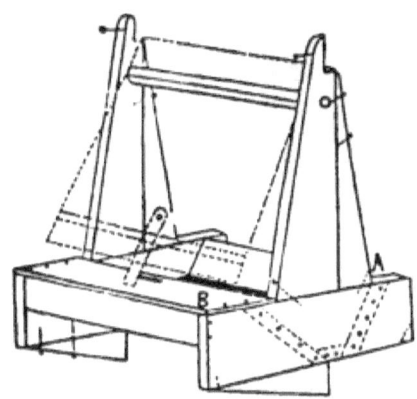
Feed Trough Arrangement.

As a Farm Helper.—There are opportunities for his capabilities in this country. He harvests corn in A1 style, and in a manner that as a rule pays as well as shelling it and sending it to the grain markets. For fertilising the land and exterminating weeds, then pigs come very near perfection. They utilise the grass and coarse feed quite as well as sheep, and perform a work in stirring the soil that sheep cannot do. The nose of the pig is made for rooting, and we follow nature's hint by giving him a job on the soil. A moveable yard, large enough to keep two or three pigs, can be made of strong hurdles or of stout inch boards, say 14 feet long and 6 inches wide Split stuff will do, though it is heavier to move. A barbed wire at the bottom prevents pigs from shifting a fence. For the corners use heavy posts. Nail the boards or palings to the posts about 6 inches apart, making four lengths or panels 4 feet high. Fasten the corners with stout hooks and staples, and we have a pen or yard 14 feet square, which is easily moved by two men. When we place two 50-pound pigs into this yard they use up all the weeds and other vegetation in it in three or four days, and thoroughly disturb the soil several inches in depth. The great agricultural enemy, sorrel, soon disappears before them; so does nut-grass, that terrible pest of the coast farmers. Corn and other feed can be given when necessary. When they have done their work satisfactorily, the pen can be moved onward and onward, as required. The advantages of this method are that it fertilises the land for grass or crops, destroys weeds and insects, and mixes and fertilises the surface of the soil about as well as it can be done. Even ferns and small brush are effectively destroyed. Worms and caterpillars are available food for the pig, and it is not the least of the benefits t at small stones, if they are in the soil, are brought to the surface, where they can be seen and removed. The keeping of pigs gives opportunity for disposal of produce in times of plenty, when it does not pay to send maize or wheat to market. It is advantageous at such times to turn the grain into pork or bacon. Many of the farm products which otherwise might not pay may be utilized by having the pig among the live-stock as part of the system of the Australian agriculturist.

The Pig a Factory.—Provide him with a good feed and he makes good bacon; but if stinted, no matter how perfect his breed, his form, and fattening qualities, he cannot make flesh. A badly-fed sow cannot have vigorous healthy pigs of good size, with a tendency to grow rapidly and mature early. Thrifty pigs should weigh at four months 70lb. to 80lb. During two months of that time the pigs get most of their living from the sow, and during the next month they eat far less food than older pigs. On most farms a suitable patch can be laid out where sorghum, pumpkins, sugar beets, chicory, carrots, or mangold-wurzel will grow. These, with a little corn, make splendid bacon-yielding material.

Pigs on Grain Stubble.—Possibly we do not in all cases utilise the pigs as much as we might do by turning them into the stubble to pick up the shelled grain, though, of course, it is not always expedient to let them roam over stubbles. In some cases want of suitable fences to restrain the pigs and other reasons may prevent this practice being followed out, but it could certainly be more generally pursued to good advantage. Especially is this the case during a dry season. In a wet time, when the stubble is lightly ploughed soon after harvesting, the shelled grain would start growing, and there would be a certain amount of green crop for feed or to turn under, and in this way there would be some return in the shape of manure, but in a dry season the grain would not start till too late in the year. When pigs are allowed to run in the stubble, there will not be much of the shelled grain wasted, nor much chance of weeds and other bad growths springing up. They hunt over the ground and root out all they can find. Even nut grass roots disappear before pigs.

Wheat and Maize as Feed.—When wheat is cheaper than maize, weight for weight, and when mixed with maize it gives a better result than maize alone. Thus—

	Flesh formers	Heat givers.	Fat.
Wheat	10 ...	65 ...	1¾
Maize	9½ ...	70 ...	5
Maize and Wheat mixed .	10 ...	67½ ...	3½

Maize is a rapid fattener of the pig, but the meat is neither so firm nor so good in flavour as where the maize is mixed with wheat, or when milk helps the maize. For fattening, therefore, it is advantageous to use one-hird wheat to two-thirds maize, while for growing pigs and stores one-third maize may be added to two-thirds wheat.

Australian Points in Pig Raising.—Gum leaves and bush scrapings generally, make excellent bedding for the farrowing sow—altogether much better than straw. The little suckers are great on burrowing, and when covered up in straw are in danger of being overlain by the mother and smothered. Then the bush stuff is dryer, warmer, and altogether more cleanly. The experience is that pigs that farrow amongst gum leaves very seldom if ever worry their young. But, perhaps, that may be because of a habit of rubbing the little ones soon as possible with a sponge and a little encalytus oil. It is an unfailing precaution against a very common mishap, especially during warm weather. The first litter here as a rule is smaller than in England. Six, seven, and eight are the numbers with us, and more often six than eight. In the old land, ten is common with both the white and black breeds. But the after litters are up to the full number, and our pigs breed longer than in England, where the long, cold winters tell upon the mothers.

To Select Breeding Stock.—In selecting for breeding purposes, whether male or female, it is important to choose from among large litters that have been well suckled. Some breeds are noted for prolificness, others could probably be made equally prolific if closer attention were paid to this well established law of nature. The milking qualities of the sow (which, by the way, are just as hereditary as in the dairy breeds of cattle), should not be overlooked; for no matter how large a litter a sow may produce, they are a drawback unless she can suckle them well. The question of whether the youngster is to be a profit or a loss is largely decided during the few weeks that he draws his mother sustenance. Many dairy cows of strong milking inheritance, and that have been brought up to the milking period, are spoiled by bungling milkers. There is no such danger for the brood sow. The youngster when hale and hearty, before he is an hour old has mastered the science of milking, and has acquired greater proficiency than the most skilful dairyist. That organised appetite, which we call the young pig, is thorough master of all the instruction ever given on the subject of milking. He milks quietly, thoroughly, and yet gently, except when his rights are disputed.

Killing and Curing.—To do up a pig promptly, a sharp knife is requiste, with a blade about eight inches long, not more than an inch wide, with a rounded point. Have it very sharp. If his pigship is about 150lbs.—a good handy size, by the way, for home use—one used to the work would bale him into a corner of the stye, grip him by a leg and an ear, tumble him with his head towards the righthand side, and with his feet towards the operator, who then places his left leg across the pig, and quickly inserts the knife at the centre of the neck and as low as the fore-leg. Or, by whipping a line round a hind leg, the pig can be raised by a sapling laid over a rail, upon a triangle (as shown in engraving), or other convenient arrangement. There is no noise from a pig raised in this way. And when the knife does its work, the animal is in the very best position for bleeding effectively. Touch the heart with the knife (easily known by a film coming over the eyes of the pig). The animal feels no pain after that. He bleeds freely, and dies in peace. The sticking is a main feature, for unless well done the animal does not bleed freely; and unless well bled, the meat does not keep well. The mistake in this matter often arises from inserting the knife too high up in the neck instead of the breast, where the heart is. As soon as the animal is dead, souce him with hot (*not scalding*) water. The usual practice is to put him into a tub or trough, deep enough to cover the whole body; but the job can be done as well by putting him in before applying the water. Tuck the head and feet under the body, then pour in the hot water, and commence scraping off the hair at once. The hair comes in flakes from a young, good-conditioned pig, but sharp knives and an approach to shaving have to be employed to get the back bristles from old and coarse stagers. By the time it is off, the feet, ears, and snout will be soaked, and the hair can be scooped off with the hands or the knife. Take off the hoofs, clean the head at once, and keep actively at the other parts, pouring on water where the hair sticks, until it is all off. Then lift him on a board, douse him with cold water, and shave off any bristles that remain.

For Hanging-up or Sousing a Pig.

Scalding and Cleaning.—A safe temperature of water for scalding pigs is 160 deg. If the heat is much greater, it sets the hair fast, and may break the skin; when much lower, the hair will not loosen at all. As low as 140 deg. may do for a fine-haired pig, provided 75 or 100 gallons of water are used; but, where a tub is employed, the heat must be at least 150 deg. In the open air, and in cold weather, this may not be high enough. 160 deg. is the point for pigs over 75lbs.

Cutting up the Pig.—The body should be allowed to cool thoroughly. When pork is tainted, after salting, it is almost invariably for want of thorough cooling before cutting up the carcass. A good way to cut up a pig, is to saw or chop down the back, and make two sides. The shoulder is then cut off as at 1, the

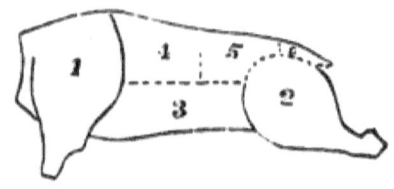

Cutting-up a Pig.

ham nicely rounded as at 2, leaving the small rump-piece with the tail. The belly (3) is cut off, and the loin (4 and 5) is cut into two more or pieces, as may be desired. The rib-bones should all be taken out and used fresh. The shoulder should be freed from the ribs, and, with the hams and the belly pieces, cured and smoked by themselves. The belly is often cut up into long, narrow pieces, weighing 5lb. to 6lb., and, after being carefully cured and smoked, is readily saleable as breakfast bacon.

Curing Hams and Bacon.—Cut out the ribs, using a sharp heavy knife for the purpose, and passing it close to the bone, the rule being to cut out the bones, and nothing more. In warm localities, where the meat is wanted for home use, it is safest to cut out the bones of the hams also; follow them out closely as in the former case, leaving only the small bones at the points of the hams and shoulders. In cooler localities the bones may be left in, in which case a sharp saw should be used to trim those on the surface quite flat. Leave neither holes nor protuberances, fill them with bran soaked in lard when necessary, and the appearance will be improved very much. Use purified saltpetre—about one ounce to 50lb. of meat. Pound it fine; run a steel or skewer close alongside the bones, pushing down the salt-petre with it, giving particular attention to the places were joints occur. Then rub in salt as much as covers the meat, say 10lb. for 100lb. meat; but double the quantity of salt should be handy. Surround the meat with salt, pack it on a table or board to drip; rub it again 10 or 12 hours afterwards. Rub it well, and again the next evening, and the next, changing the pieces from top to bottom of the heap each time, placing boards between the pieces, when it is desired to flatten them out nicely. It may then stand for 12 or 14 days being rubbed occasionally.

Smoking.—After about 14 days, wash the meat quite free from salt and hang it up until just dry, no more; then smoke it with tea-tree, wattle, stringy bark or other hardwood. Those first-named are the best. Do not allow flame, the heat of the smouldering fire, or draughts of drying air to reach the meat. To darken the colour, a little sweet oil may be rubbed on; smoking for 10 or 12 hours, either at once or during different times during a week is sufficient for ordinary tastes. The smoking is all the better done in a cool, close place To get rid of salt on the surface, and also to improve the colour, of the hams or sides, they are dipped in water of 180deg., having $\frac{1}{4}$lb. soda in, say, ten gallons of water. Let the meat drip, then hang up till dry, and smoke.

Pickling—A popular American Method.—Rub the hams and shoulders with salt, and let them lie 36 hours. Then cover with brine for from three to six weeks. When taken from the brine, insert a strong string in the large end, and hang the pieces in the smoke-house, hock-end downward. By this means tenderness and flavour are given to a portion of the ham often treated badly. When they are sufficiently smoked and dried, wrap each in brown paper, and put in a loose bag of strong calico. Tie up the mouth of the bag carefully, leaving out the string by which it was hung up, and return to the hook in the smoke-house, or any other safe convenient place. Hams thus treated keep for years.

Curing with Sugar.—The sides of hams are neatly rounded and trimmed, well sprinkled with salt, and allowed to lie twenty-four hours to let all blood escape. Then use for curing: 1$\frac{1}{2}$lb. coarse sugar, 1$\frac{1}{2}$lb. fine salt, 3oz. saltpetre pounded fine, 1lb. salt. This is enough for $\frac{1}{2}$cwt. of meat. Lay one of the flitches on a table or bench, where the brine can run off, and rub a quarter of the mixture well into it; lay the second flitch on the top, and proceed in the same way; lastly the hams, taking care in every case to have the flesh side up, with plenty of the mixture sprinkled over. It should lie thus for a month, turning it every other day, putting the top flitch to the bottom, and adding a little pickle if much brine has run off. Then wash off the salt, hang the meat in the smoke for ten days, not too near the fire.

Lard *versus* Meat.—Lard is a very good thing for making pastry and for some other purposes, but, in a warm climate, people do not appreciate lard. The pig of the future will not be a dumpy "bladder of lard," but a succession of streaks of fat and "lean pig." The sooner we realise the fact, the sooner will pig-raising become profitable. Fat pork is altogether too greasy for this climate, though it is nice and very nourishing when rounding Cape Horn, and during the bleak European winter.

XIX.—THE POULTRY YARD.

Making a Commencement.—The management for eggs and for table birds is the concern of this department. Poultry fancing, that is, the breeding and development of birds or breeds for special points or for show purposes, is a much more exacting occupation. To be successful with fancy poultry, calls out the very best qualities of the stock breeder. The chapter on the Physiology of Breeding is worth attention in that connection. Some who commence the study of poultry life in the more modest manner of this department, may follow into that of the poultry fancier. The training should be helpful in that direction, but, meanwhile our attention will be directed to poultry for their egg laying or their table qualities, for home use or as a business. We will soon see that there are very marked differences in the breeds of fowls for the purposes aimed at, and that requirements in the form of necessary accommodation, both indoor and out, care in feeding and general attention, and to the qualities of the feed for building up young stock, for egg laying, and for making high-class table birds, all come into the pursuit of poultry farming.

The Kind to Keep, and Where to Keep Them.—The latter is the more important matter of the two. Fowls, to do well, must have room; must have suitable house, roosting, and yard accommodation, the right kinds of food and clean water, the run of grass and weeds, with their belongings of insects. These living things mean that fairly good soil answers the best for a poultry run. They must also have gravel and lime in the form of a carbonate, such as bone, shells, limestone, etc., dry places to shake themselves in, and moist places to scrape in.

Fences.—The place being available, it becomes necessary to fence it in an effective manner; for unless the whole property is to be given up to fowls, indoors and out, they must be fenced in, or dissatisfaction, annoyance, and trouble follow on their trail. Seven feet is not too high for the fence of the place in which layers are to be confined, though lower fences do for the heavier breeds. Palings or wire-netting should surround the enclosure, as well as gates. To make a hen satisfied that she must stay within an enclosure, leave no room for any doubt upon her mind as to whether she can get out of it; she must not succeed, or there will be trouble in that neighbourhood. Fowls are persevering in proportion to their early successes. Contentment on their part is the result of feeling that they cannot do the other thing. Then they become satisfied with their lot, lay many eggs, or grow big, as the owner may desire. In their fenced-in enclosure should be the roosting and laying places. This is necessary, for poultry in this country have many enemies, including dogs, guanos, hawks, &c., and mean thieves of the man kind.

Wire-Netting Fences.—They answer well for poultry, are easily erected, and cost little. Hardwood posts of the desired height, say 6 feet above ground and 2 feet in the ground, are set and rammed in firmly. About 10 feet apart answers. Then stretch a wire firmly on the top, another at bottom, and where two widths of wire-netting are used, a wire where they join is desirable. Unroll the netting flat on the ground along the posts. Then carefully raise it to position on the posts, and fasten all along the top tight, exactly the height of the wire above the bottom line; go the full length of the roll fastening the top, and let the bottom hang. One man can draw it tight, while another fastens it; draw it just tight enough so that it doesn't sag between posts. After the top is fastened, draw the bottom down in place, and fasten, being careful not to draw the wire down any wider than it was made—that is, 6ft. netting should be exactly 6ft. from top to bottom, other widths the same way. If the wire is properly woven, it will remain straight and even when put up as above, and not have that unsightly warp which some fences have.

Moveable Pens.—This is amongst the handy contrivances made possible with wire-netting. Four posts are sunk in the ground. Strips of batten connect the four on the

Portable Fences of Wire-Netting.

ground line; then the wire is set up, and we have a run that keeps the birds in place, and is not unsightly in any part of the grounds. A roll of wire netting is amongst the materials of great use in working poultry. When sickness occurs, a temporary pen can be set up for the patients away from the others, and in a quiet, shady, well grassed spot, is of the greatest use for restoring birds to vigorous health again.

Buildings.—There is immense scope for the display of taste in poultry buildings. Our concern will carry us amongst

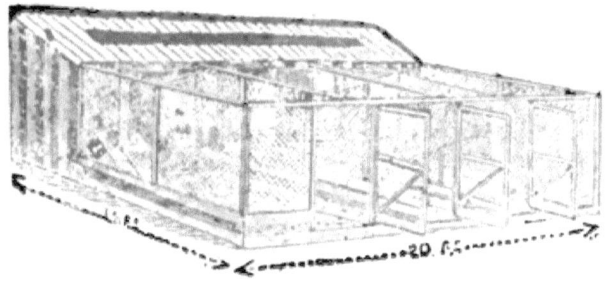

For a Small Place, as for Breeding Pens.

orections put up for use mainly; leaving decoration to the taste of the owner. The absolute requirements are tight roofs, through which water cannot enter, close walls, and floor of dry earth, raised sufficiently to prevent the inroads of dampness, even in wet weather. Ventilation is best provided for by windows or shutter openings. Wood, iron, slabs, bark, and other materials are available for buildings. When shade or shelter can be secured from trees or vines, the advantages are very decided.

For a Small Lot.

Roosts, Nests, Water, &c.—Much of their comfort and health is dependent on how fowls roost. The roosting and laying places of hens should be sufficiently tight to protect the inmates from rain, wind, and enemies. There should be no roosting on trees and fences. Place roosting sticks, at least 3 inches thick, across the building about 20 inches apart; no roost should be higher than 3 feet. A good plan is to have the roosting sticks set upon a levelled frame; in any case they should be so arranged that at any time they can be removed, cleaned, and replaced with the least trouble. Nest-boxes (barrels and kerosene cases answer well) are placed in the quiet, shady, out-of-the-way places, where birds are not likely to roost on them. They should always be supplied with dry sand or soil, gum leaves, &c., and each contain a nest-egg. Drinking vessels being provided in the yard, and supplied with clean water, we are ready for the inmates. The reason for recommending low roosts is that laying-hens are often ruined by jumping or falling from high places.

Let the Hens Roost Low Down.—A laying-hen, of genuine egg-laying breed, is a wonder—a nervous, irritable, egg-laying machine. The natural state is vigorous activity; and all the time such a hen is a delicate concern. She has immense capabilities for egg making and laying, but the organs are complicated in the extreme.

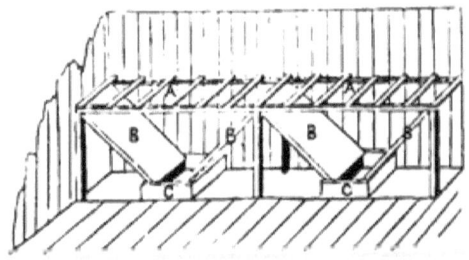

Let The Fowls Roost Low Down.

Thousands of hens are ruined every year by rupture or other injury to the egg-producing organs from falls, being chased, and other disturbances. Then this danger is aggravated when hens roost high up. The jump, flight, or fall from a high perch is always dangerous. So let us get the hens to roost low down. Three feet is quite high enough for roost sticks. Our sketch shows a very good way for arranging them, as at (A). (B) (B) are boards sloping under the roost sticks for the droppings to fall into a box (C), or there may be no box, when there is a deep layer of dry earth for a floor, which can be raked over daily.

Food, Drink and Digestion.—Fowls need good sharp grit or gravel. They have no teeth; their food must be ground up in the digestive system. Good grit keeps the birds in a healthy condition. And fowls need a constant supply of clean water. A fowl does not drink much at a time, but comes often. Water makes up the largest part of the body and the egg. Fowls need green food summer and winter. Cabbages hung up in the hen house answer excellently. Keep the place clean, be careful what you feed, and success follows. But don't forget to feed early in the morning. It does not pay to keep more hens than we have time to attend to.

Clean Water.—This is the precaution against disease. The water fountain shown in illustration has a colonial look about it. It is made from a four-gallon kerosene tin. A hole is cut as at (A), and a piece of tin, bent half-circle fashion, (B), is soldered to the bottom of the tin, so as to surround the hole. We then have a true water seal, and a continuous supply of say half an inch of water, as long as the contents of the four gallon tin hold out. The requirements are that the tin be perfectly air-tight. The outlet hole may be about half an inch high, by one inch or two inches wide. An efficient "fountain" on the same principle can be made with preserved meat, jam, and other tins. When set upon a raised board or box, in a shady place, a supply of cool, clean water is ensured to the yard.

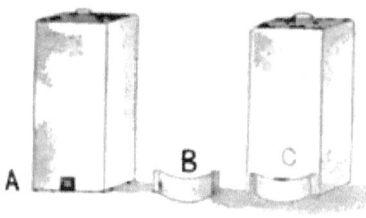

Poultry Fountain.

Feeding.—This is a leading consideration. Fowls must be fed often and every day, early and late. They require careful feeding; but attempts to provide special food leads to no end of tribulation, and little else. They will eat any good food when healthy, and are scarcely worth troubling with when unhealthy. Wheat, oats, barley, pollard, and bran are all good. Maize, whole or cracked, is too fattening, if given without other grain, bread, rice, meat, anything and everything that man uses, is readily eaten by fowls; but while the former can educate himself into using all sorts of messes and mixtures, into suffering from dyspepsia, indigestion, gout, medicine swallowing, and many other forms of stomach ruination, fowls suffer from all such attempts at "civilising" them, and wherever anything of the kind is persevered in, they become discontented, diseased, and die. A reliable system of feeding is to give soft crumbly food in the morning, which in winter should be blood warm; and grain with meat, broken bone, oyster shells, and other bone, flesh, fat, and egg-forming materials at other times. Laying fowls require all the good and suitable feed they can eat. More care has to be used with the breeding hens, than the fleshy table breeds. Comfortable quarters on good grass land, and liberal feeding with meat, are safe foundations for poultry farming for eggs.

Poultry in Confinement.—Some curious and much needed tests have been made with a view of observing

the temperaments of different breeds of fowls and their adaptability for confinement. With this end in view, a series of sheds were erected each eighteen feet by five, and in these, breeding flocks of five to nine birds, Brown Leghorns, Minorcas, Redcaps, Andalusians, Plymouth Rocks, Wyandottes, Houdans, Hamburgs, Langshans, Dorkings, and Cochins, were put up. The floors were originally covered with straw, but this was soon changed for dry earth, and the condition of the birds at once improved. The first breed to develop any vice were the Minorcas, which laid well for two months, and then commenced feather eating. The next to develop this habit were the Andalusians, which were succeeded by the Hamburgs, Wyandottes, and Redcaps. Then it was decided to change the treatment, with a view to curing them of the propensity they had acquired. The birds were allowed their freedom on grass, and they at once abandoned the habit of feather pulling, but which they recommenced when again confined in the pens. This is a nice point for considering with poultry, and shows how desirable it is to have a run for even a small flock. The Leghorns—one cockerel and seven laying hens—did by far the best, as they laid well all through the experiment, sometimes providing six eggs a day, and developed no vice or symptoms of ill-health whatsoever.

Peculiarities of Breeds.—They are so well defined now that we reckon their merits and drawbacks with something like certainty. Taking the laying breeds first, they are smaller, more wiry, are more timid, and more able to fly fences and roost upon trees than the heavier, flesh-forming, table birds. The egg-layers are not disposed to sit, or to become broody, to the same degree as the flesh formers. Their eggs are larger, from 1½oz. to 2½oz., are white as a rule, and do better in small confined places, than the heavier breeds. *Leghorns.*—Brown, white, cuckoo; combs, large, upright; all are hardy. Have laid up to 170 eggs during second year, and 700 during life; weigh up to 7lb.; capital foragers. *Hamburgs.*—The "red-caps," black pencilled, spangled; solid, red combs; second year up to 180 eggs; during life, 660, but smaller eggs than Leghorns; weigh up to 6¾lb. *Minorcas.*—Black; large upright combs; eggs large, not so numerous as foregoing; weigh up to 8lb.; fair foragers. *Houdans.*—Black with white; have top knot and fifth toe; second year, 150; total, 650 (light coloured eggs); weigh up to 8lb. *Polish.*—Black, with white top knot; much the same egg capacity as Houdans, but smaller birds; weigh up to 6¾lb. *Andalusians.*—Slatey blue; look like game; egg capacity and weight much the same as Houdans. *Wyandottes.*—Beautiful laced feathering; supposed to be from a cross of Brahma with laced Asiatic; fine, firm flesh; laying capacity 390; best year, 140; good mothers and fair foragers; weigh up to 8lb. *Spanish.*—Black, with white face and ears; second year, have laid up to 170 eggs; total, 650 (eggs extra large); breed reputed delicate; weigh up to 7½lb.

Egg-laying Type.

Pullets of the foregoing commence to lay when six to seven months old. They lay best in their second year.

Table Breeds.—Colour of eggs mostly brown; smaller in size than the egg layers; weigh from 1½ to 1⅜ozs.

Game.—British, Australian, Indian and others—Heavy, rich flesh and full breasts; capacity for egg laying, 470; best year, 100; good mothers; weigh up to 9lbs. *Dorkings.*— Silver grey, white legs and five toes; eggs white; capacity, 500; best year, 120; weigh up to 10lbs. *Rocks.*—Ash grey, towards black; supposed to be cuckoo with Asiatic, hardy and domestic; egg capacity, 400; best year, 110; weigh up to 9 lb. and are excellent foragers and good mothers. *Dominiques.* —Lighter than Rocks; flesh finer; not so hardy; egg capacity about same. *Langshans.*—Termed "black cochins," and have feathered legs; good winter layers; capacity, 380; best year up to 100; flesh firm and fair; weigh up to 10½lbs.; are poor foragers. *Orpingtons.*—Black, bronzed, supposed cross of minorca with langshans; clean legs; egg capacity about the same as langshans; hardy; excellent flesh and good mothers; weigh up to 10lbs. There are, also, buff and white orpingtons; all are fair foragers. *Brahmas.*—Light and dark; flesh, coarser; egg capacity, 350; best year, 100; weigh up to 11lbs.; poor foragers and delicate. *Cochins.* —Buff, white, dark; feathery legs; flesh poor; egg capacity, 300; best year, 60; weigh up to 12lbs.; poor foragers, great eaters, and lazy. *La Fleche.*—A noted French breed, of the Spanish type, have proved delicate and inferior in Australia.

For Export.

Crosses for Table Birds.—Game give weight and quality of flesh. Game with dorkings are hardy, have light-coloured legs and weigh up to 9lbs. Houdan-dorkings are suitable, and make good cross for eggs and table birds. Houdan-orpingtons are suitable, also Houdan-game. The houdans are, also, in favour for crosses with orpingtons, Plymouth rocks, brahmas and cochins. Heavy-breasted, firm-fleshed birds, with white legs, and weighing up to 9lbs., are desirable.

For Export.—A bird with yellow skin, clean white or yellow legs, small in bone and plump when dressed.

BREEDING.—Hens, Turkeys, or Incubators?—Much experience is available concerning the merits of hens, turkey hens, and incubators for hatching. So far as the time is concerned there is no difference; but as to the results, very marked differences occur. Briefly it may be said that it is best to gain experience with hens, or turkeys, before venturing upon an incubator. A good deal will be learned during a season or two with hens, which will simplify matters when the incubator is taken in hand.

Self-regulating Incubator.

Hatching Time.—Which ever process we follow, the cooler months—from July to September—answer best for bringing out chickens; but, with the precautions mentioned regarding nesting, hen mothers, vermin, &c., other seasons will do, though there is always the serious risks of vermin during hot weather. With the aid of incubators, chickens can be raised at any time. Hen-eggs, of all breeds, take 21 days to hatch out; ducks, 28 days, with the exception of the Muscovy, which often takes 35 days; goose, 30 to 35 days; Guinea and pea fowls, from 28 to 30 days; turkeys, 28 days.

The Breeding Stock.—Select the fowls from which the next year's stock of chickens are to be bred and place them apart from others. Even if not pure bred, a careful selection of half-a-dozen hens which are in good health and good layers, and a vigorous male of the breed considered best for the purpose in view, will give eggs more sure of hatching and more hardy and vigorous chickens than can be got from twice as many eggs taken from a larger stock without selection. In selecting fowls to breed from, it is better that the sexes should be in no way related, the hens should be over a year old, rather than younger, and the male bird is better at two or three years than at one. Never use males of one year old if older ones can be had. If there exists any imperfection which should cause a bird to be rejected as a breeder, it will usually be seen distinctly in the second year, while in the bird of less than a year it might not be noticed. But for ordinary purposes, good physique in both the male bird and the hens are the main requirements. For stud purposes, five hens and a male bird make a nice pen. For the smaller breeds, 6 to 8 hens may be allowed. Where practicable, the male bird should be smaller than the hens.

Plain Breeding Pens.

Eggs and Places for Setting.—The eggs must be quite fresh. When over eight days old, in the summer season, the progeny will be weak to a certainty. To carry eggs a long distance, pack them in bran or sawdust. They carry better by road or on horseback than by steamer. The shaking of a vessel at sea generally proves destructive to the reproductive properties of the eggs. In setting hens, nests on the ground made of dry sandy or loamy soil answer well, with a sprinkling of broken down gum leaves. The nests are healthy, and are easily kept clean and free from vermin; or the nests may be in boxes or barrels. They should be where the sitters cannot be molested. The hen should be roused from the nest every day after the second day of sitting, and induced to drink and feed freely and dust herself. These are the best precautions against vermin. A sitting hen requires steady nourishment, to keep up her courage and natural heat. When the weather is very dry, it is a good plan to sprinkle both eggs and nest with warm water every day when the hen leaves it. On the 19th or 20th day, unless the hen comes off of her own accord, lift her off and look over her eggs. But be careful not to drag the mother bird while moving her, for eggs may be broken unless great care is used. Place one hand under each wing and then quietly lift her up, taking care that she carries no eggs in her feathers. Some, if not all, of the eggs may be cracked and chipped where the young ones are struggling to get through. Take away any shells of chicks that have hatched out. On the 21st day take the sitter off her place again. By this time all the chickens should be hatched out, and if the mother has not pushed all the empty shells out of the nest, it is advisable to clear up all litter and put mother and brood on clean dry earth in a coop or otherwise.

Coop for a Sitting Hen.

Incubators.—Self-regulating machines are best, and possibly the best results are got from those in which the eggs are placed in sand. The temperature must be very steady, ranging between 101 and 105 degrees. An occasional cooling for half an hour or so does no harm, and by some experienced operators is believed to be necessary.

Eggs While Hatching.—Turn them every day after the second day. Prompted by nature, hens turn their eggs from the outside to the warmer inside of the nest. From the 7th to the 10th day use an egg-tester, and examine each egg before a bright light. If all is well, red streaks or veins will be visible in the fertile eggs on the 7th day. Others show a dark mass in the centre; they have to be rejected. Such eggs are useful when boiled, for feeding chickens. On the 19th or 20th day, some of the eggs may be cracked, but may seem no further advanced than the day before. In this case, it may be necessary to remove a small portion of the shell around that part where the beak of the confined chicken has made an opening. This requires the utmost care, and should never be done except as a last resort. Warm water, of blood heat, or, say, 100deg., is useful for freeing the chicks sometimes. It may enable a weak chick to free itself out of its shell, when it has not strength to do so by itself. Only too strong help might be given and the life destroyed.

An Effective Egg-tester.—The light (A) of a lamp or a candle answers very well. A cylinder (B) of paper is set around the light, into which a round hole is cut. This gives a streak of clear concentrated light, and by holding an egg-tester shield (C) into which the egg (D) is placed in the ray of light, remarkably clear observations can be made. With a little practice the condition of the contents of the egg become visible.

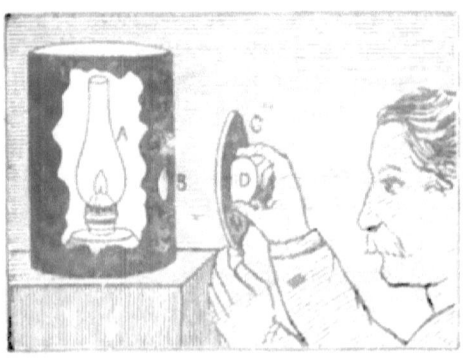
Testing Eggs.

After the seventh day of incubation, fertile eggs will be observed to have a dark patch in the centre and a number of red streaks radiating from it, giving it the appearance of a long-legged spider. An unfertile egg, sure to go bad, is distinguished by a dark spot adhering to the shell, and by a cloudy and ill-defined appearance, but no red streaks.

Moisture in Egg-Hatching.—I am afraid that mistakes are being made, and other mistakes are likely to be made, by stifling both hens and incubators for want of sufficient moisture. Serious disappointments have occurred from this cause, and from an idea which has somehow got abroad that moisture is a bad thing in incubation. No doubt too much water would be bad—it is bad in every sense, whether we have to deal with it in plant life, or in animal life. Water simply drowns life action when there is too much of it, and if incubators are allowed to sweat moisture about the eggs, they will go bad to a certainty. But the anatomy of the egg, and the process of hatching from first to last, all show that moisture—that is, healthy life moisture—is a necessity for life all through. Both hens and incubators require such a degree of moisture, or chicks cannot come forth in a strong, robust, healthy state. When eggs are hatched in leaves, as in the case of the Australian scrub turkey, in manure substances, or in the nest-like arrangements of Egyptians, Indians, or Chinese, their climate, habitations, and surroundings supply the required warmth and moisture. Our experiences are just the same. Thousands of chicks are lost during every hatching season when dry winds prevail. Life heat, from 102 to 105 degrees, just moist, is the state of things for generating life in the egg, and developing healthy chickens.

Hen Mothers.—The hen mother I refer to is a box, say 12 x 24 x 9, the 9 inches being the height in front. The top of the box slopes downwards towards the back, so that it is about 4 inches high at that side. The inside of the top and also the back is lined with woollen rag, or short wool sheepskin will do. This hen mother may either have a wooden floor, or it will do without the floor, if it is arranged on dry earth. The chicks can be taken from the hen or incubator when 24 hours old. They may then be put in families of 20 or 25 in a grassy pen, but quite dry, fenced with boards, from 2 to 10 feet square, and about 2 feet high, and so close or tight at the bottom that the smallest cannot squeeze through. Young ducks will do well treated this way; but they will try to get through any opening, no matter how small. The pen should be movable, and be

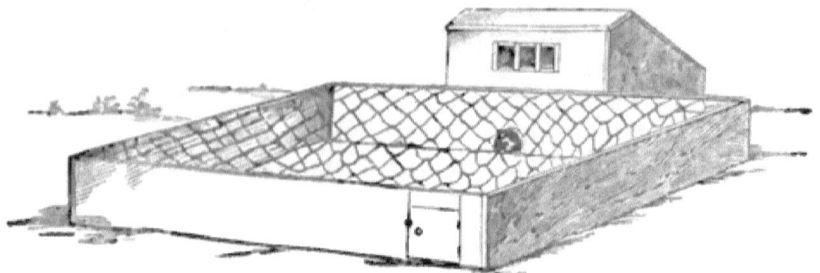

Portable Hen Mother and Yard.

frequently changed, or it will soon become foul. When they have a "hen mother," both chicks and ducks do better without a hen than with one. Young ducks are very restless; they are ever on the move, and hens become nervous at the noise and continuous motion of ducklings, and often lose their heads and trample the little restless things to death.

Hen Mother and Hen Chickens.—A first brood of chickens put into a hen mother may be a week old. They

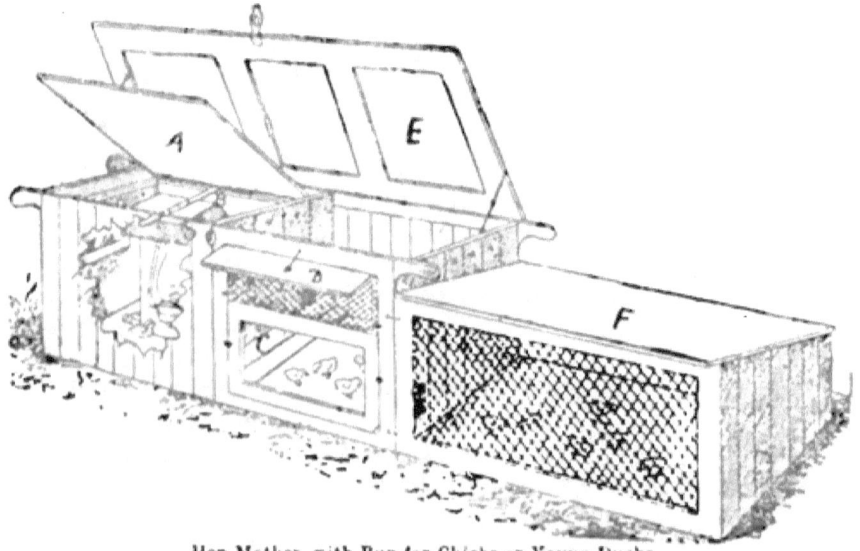

Hen Mother, with Run for Chicks or Young Ducks.

can then pick and forage, and younger chicks put with them are warmer, and soon acquire the arts of chicken life. But, when for the first six weeks chickens remain with their mother, it may be found most convenient to confine the hen in a roomy coop, and allow the chicken to run outside. It is best to place the chicken's food and water where they alone can get at it, while corn and other feed is put inside for the hen. The coop and yard should be portable, and must be kept scrupulously clean, and be frequently shifted from place to place. Adult birds may thrive in a tainted atmosphere and on impure soil, but for young chickens these conditions mean certain death. Where there is grass, the chickens should not be allowed out too early in the morning, while the dew is heavy on the ground, or cramps may be their fate.

Young Chickens and Young Ducks.—About the close of the sixth week, the hen is likely to abandon her charges. Suddenly all her former tenderness and devotion are then turned to harshness. She will drive the chickens from her, and if any of the wee things creep to her for warmth and shelter, she will often peck at them unmercifully. She knows that they will then thrive better by themselves and hence she refuses them care any longer. So after all she is "cruel only to be kind." Here again the advantages of the hen mother all favour the chickens. For a week or two the youngsters, when suddenly abandoned, need extra care and attention. They must be fed well and warmly housed. If a spell of cold weather comes on, a sprinkling of pepper may be added to their morning meal. Their best camp will be a warm box with dry leaves or leaf mould, where they can cuddle together, or warmth can be supplied by a lamp, hot water, a hot stone on top, or other means. Early roosting is not good for fleshy, well-nourished chicks. Should they roost on sharp, narrow sticks, they are likely to be deformed.

Ducks.—The established varieties are well represented in this country, and they all do well. In addition, we have Australian ducks, native to the soil or water. They are small, but make up for it in quality, being more of the type of game birds than any of the imported breeds. The weights (standard) of domestic ducks are: Pekin drake, eight pounds; Aylesbury drake, nine pounds; Rouen drake, nine pounds; Cayuga drake, eight pounds; Muscovy drake, ten pounds. The duck of each breed averages about 1lb. less in weight than the drake. Pekins and Aylesbury breeds are white, Cayugas black, and Rouens of varied colour. The Muscovy does not really belong to the duck family. The eggs require the same period for hatching as those of the goose, while the produce of a mating of the Muscovy with other breeds causes a sterile hybrid.

Rouen Ducks.

Breeding, Rearing and Marketing.—They do better on good grass without water than when they have water without the grass. Board floors are best for the camping places of grown ducks, with bush scrapings or litter on the floor. When in confined yards it costs about 3d. per lb. to produce ducks. They eat twice as much as chicks, but they make up by growing twice as fast. Feed ducklings on soft stuffs, and have shallow pans of drinking water near, as a duckling may choke to death if deprived of water while eating. Very cold water for drinking causes cramps in ducklings. So, also, does water on their backs. The Pekin and Muscovy are considered the most rapidly-growing breeds. When crowded in yards, ducklings often die suddenly, due to eating the filth in the yards. Dampness is fatal to ducks, both adults and ducklings, hence they must have *dry* sleeping places.

Geese.—All the varieties are common—the handsome white, the Toulouse, the China, and improved Irish. They are healthy, and a desirable addition to the poultry-yard wherever there is plenty of good, rich grass, or soft, green feed and a liberal supply of water. They are really grazing birds. Those who breed generally assign one gander to four or five females. In mild seasons the goose lays early; she sits with exemplary patience, but ought, during incubation, to be well supplied with food and water placed in a convenient and undisturbed situation, to which she may have free access. The gander is very attentive to his favourite, sits by her, and is vigilant and daring in her defence. The goslings, or gulls as they are termed in some parts, require the same treatment as ducklings; it is advisable to pen the mother for a few days upon a dry grass plot or green sward, supplying her with water and grain, of which the young will partake; green food, as chopped cabbage or beet-leaves, crushed maize, and the like, may be given. One thing is imperative: let not the young be starved upon poor grass, for poor pasturage occasions disease and mortality; a few handsful of corn, given morning and afternoon, are turned to good account in the goose economy.

The Turkey.—The young are more difficult to raise than fowls or ducks, but are quite healthy in after-life. Full-grown and well-bred birds bring splendid prices, and are much in demand. The mothers are excellent sitters. The young suffer from exposure, and attacks of hen-lice or other vermin are fatal to them. Dry, sandy situations, on limestone or volcanic country, answer best for turkeys, and when extra care is taken with them at the early stages they do very well. It is desirable to keep only young male birds, say those between two and three years old, and they should be apart from other fowls.

Guinea Fowls and Pigeons.—All the varieties are healthy, and do well with the care found to fit them best in other countries.

Diseases of Fowls.—They are not numerous in this country. The exciting causes are damp, developing cramp from exposure, want of proper shelter, exposure to draughts, indigestion from feeble life action, defective feeding and accidents, mostly from roosting too high. Young birds and laying hens suffer most from these causes. The most serious disease amongst older birds is roup, due to much the same causes as those from which young birds suffer—cold, damp, and exposure. Nearly all digestive ailments are aggravated by want of grinding material in the crop. Pounded gravel, limestone, crockery, or glass should always be within the reach of fowls. Cold draughts of air blowing across them while roosting or down on them, will cause swelled heads and eyes, and, very likely, lead to roup. It is often the case that rupture, weak legs, and other complaints are caused by high roosts, the birds being injured by jumping or falling therefrom to the ground. The roosts should be low.

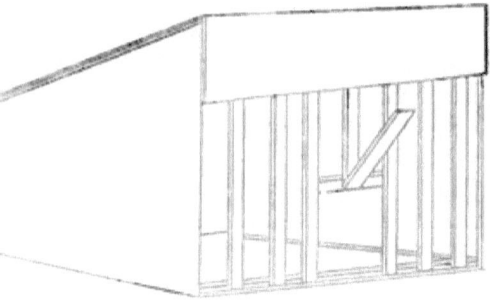

A Portable Hospital Coop.

The Safeguards.—When poultry have plenty of space to roam in, if only for a few hours each day, and they are not molested with dogs or by quarrelling with neighbours' fowls, they have more certain prospects of continuing in health. They require very little doctoring. When much of that sort of thing becomes necessary it is evident there is something wrong in the breed, in the feeding or the location. By far the greater proportion of diseases arise either from exposure or overcrowding, or neglect in preserving cleanliness—often all combined. The first requirement in case of sickness is to put the patient in a separate pen.

Symptoms of Disease.—The first symptoms of nearly all fowl diseases are moping and diarrhœa At this stage much evil may be warded off. When a fowl hangs its wings and looks drooping it should be caught and put in the hospital pen. See at once whether it appears purged, and, if so, give immediately in a tablespoonful of warm water, a tablespoonful of the purgative mixture, and when purging ceases, give a few drops of spirit of camphor. Repeat this next morning, and, in most cases, the disease will be checked, care being taken, of course, to give the invalid warmth and shelter. Oil, as a medicine, is not so certain in this climate; salts made by dissolving an oz. in half a pint of water is more effective.

Roup.—This is the most serious of fowl diseases here as in Europe. The early symptoms are loss of appetite and drooping, then weak eyes and appearances of cold, gatherings of matter about the nostrils and eyes. The disease is highly contagious, being communicated through disease germs issuing from the sickly beak contaminating the drinking water; therefore let all fowls affected by it be at once put by themselves. Keep them warm, squeeze out the matter from the nostrils, wash the beak with Condy's fluid, add peppers or other spice to the feed, with green stuff unlimited, and put in the water a little sulphate of iron. Roup runs its course rapidly, and in a week the bird will be either almost well or so nearly dead that it had better be killed.

"Fowl Cholera" comes on like a feverish cold, and, like roup, quickly develops disease germs. Other symptoms are thirst, debility, anxious nervous movements and greenish droppings. The treatment is to isolate the patient at once, giving a purgative dose, and adding spirit of camphor to the food or drinking water. Should the patient become worse, a few drops of camphor mixture, from 3 to 10, may be given twice daily with warm food.

Cramp, Sore Eyes, Sore Heads.—These are symptoms mostly of the more serious diseases described. Isolate the birds in warm pens, and try to bring up their vitality by warmth, tonic drinks, and stimulating feed. Sores on the head may develop from attacks by vermin. Washing with Condy's fluid in warm water, carbolic or eucalyptus soap, or the soda-resin-petroleum mixture—the latter for extreme cases only—seldom fail as remedies.

Crop Bound.—A serious, but easily detected ailment of fowls. It is caused by some stoppage in the digestive process carried on in the crop. The passage between that part of the digestive apparatus and the gizzard, or grinding stomach, is small, and may be choked by something the bird may have swallowed, an onion skin, a bit of rag, or other material. A more common cause is feeding with wet cold, soggy, semi-cooked bran or pollard, or other stuff, during cold mornings. The birds being hungry bolt a lot of this, and are unable to warm it up sufficiently for digestive purposes. The crop is swelled up, the bird droops, and may perish, as numbers do every winter—starved to death while the crop is full to gorging. As soon as a case is seen, catch the bird, and pour water, as warm as can be borne, down the throat, till the crop is full; then work it to loosen the food, and dissolve it in the water; some may be got out of the mouth. Try and relieve the mass by dissolving it; then give a purgative dose; and put the patient in a quiet, warm pen. In more serious cases, the crop may have to be cut open, the contents removed, the crop washed and stitched by two or three loops or surgical stitches.

Apoplexy.—Very prevalent at times, and as it carries off its victims suddenly, and, generally during the night, it causes great alarm amongst poultry owners. Apoplexy is most prevalent in alluvial districts, where grit or gravel is scarce. Old and young fall victims; no particular breed are exempted. The first stages are staggering gait in the birds affected for one or more days before death; or the head is slightly twisted back on the neck, or to one side. The patient is soon afterwards found in a sitting posture, or half turned on its back. If disturbed, its gait is staggering, and it seems involuntarily compelled to go to one side; attacks of convulsions occur at intervals, in one of which the poor bird expires. Cause: The appearances after death are effusion of blood on the brain, or otherwise a turgid and congested state of its blood-vessels. Here, it is usually supposed that this disease is the effect of high and unsuitable feeding, especially with maize. The birds in best condition, and those of the flesh-forming type, usually suffer first. Various remedies have been suggested, such as bleeding by cutting the comb, giving purgatives, drenching with cold water, reducing the supply of food, &c. In practice, it is best to always see that the birds have plenty of grit material. Reduce the feed, and change the whole stock when this complaint becomes serious.

Gapes.—Choking and suffocating symptoms indicate this disease. The cause is found in numbers of small worms which infest the windpipe and throat, causing the patient to gasp for breath. When taken early, it may be sufficient to give, for two or three days, a morsel of camphor the size of a grain of wheat, and to put camphor in the drinking water, or a little turpentine or sulphuric acid may be given daily in meal, taking care, of course, that deficiencies in diet and shelter be improved. In fully-developed cases, the worms must be removed by introducing a feather or a loop of horsehair, saturated with kerosene, into the throat, and turning it round during withdrawal, the operation to be repeated several times, till the worms are extracted.

Loss of Feathers and Feather-Eating.—This trouble is supposed to be caused by want of green food or having no dust bath, but it is often a symptom of depraved, morbid apetite, not easily cured. Additions of meat to the feed, sulphate of iron in the drinking water, and a run on fresh grass, aid in curing.

Vermin.—They used to be, and may be still, in neglected cases, the most serious drawback to poultry-keeping in warm climates. During dry summer weather the little pests, peculiar to fowls, attack human beings, or horses, and may become fearful scourges. To keep them in check, sitting and broody hens should be put apart from others, then rubbed on the head and under the wings with sulphur ointment, and dusted with flour of sulphur and lime daily. The fowls should also have shady, damp places in which to roll and clean themselves. The vermin, be it well understood, cannot travel or live in damp places, nor do they like dry dust. Soda-resin-petroleum spray mixture and hot lime-water are most effectual for clearing them off.

Scaly Legs.—Caused by small parasites. Usually a dressing with kerosene is effective ; rub it in freely, and after an hour or so, wash off with Condy's fluid or carbolic soap. In very bad cases use soda-resin-petroleum mixture, washing afterwards.

Soft-Shell Eggs.—Lime material, or crushed bone, oyster shells, lime-stone (not lime) wanted in feed.

Egg Bound.—This may be caused by want of vitality in the hen. See to the feeding; give purgative, oil applied with a feather, or a syringe, or more mechanical means may be necessary to give relief. Be careful not to break the egg while operating.

Rupture, Abortion.—Passing of discolored matter indicates rupture, often caused to laying hens by their falling from high roosts. Isolate the patient, and use remedies same as for egg bound.

Oil is destructive to insect life generally, and in the form of kerosene, or some of the vegetable or animal oils, is effective against them.

The Moulting Time.—A time of trial and risk to fowls. It extends through March to July, and has much to do with winter laying. When a hen begins to moult in March, she is not likely to be in full plumage again until May or June, and she cannot lay again till the moulting has been completed. When the weather is mild, however, during April, and the winter does not set in before May or June, she has a longer rest, and may begin laying, and then continue through the winter. Hence, this rule must not be overlooked, that if the hens begin to lay before cold weather they are likely to lay during the winter; but if cold days overtake them before they begin to moult, they will probably not begin again before spring.

Broody Hens.—When not wanted for hatching, they are looked on and treated as nuisances sometimes. Yet it is a natural condition of hen life, and may be indulged to give the birds a rest, by setting them on two or three dummy eggs. Kindly skill and attention are requisite to do the right thing by them. Cruelty is stupid, and has the desired effect less frequently than injury or death to the clucker. The

Coop for Curing Cluckers.

coop shown effects the object more readily and easily. The clucker or cluckers are put in, and then the coop is tilted up as shown. Biddy becomes very much disgusted when she has to occupy an angular floor like this, and is so glad to escape after a day or two of discomfort, that she forgets to cluck, eats heartily, and gets to laying again.

XX.—CROPS FOR FEED, SILOING, &c.

That cultivation must be increased to provide feed for such times as the early months of 1895, which racked the energies of the most skilful in the dairying business, was made painfully apparent. Never before were such quantities of feed stuff purchased. Hay, maize meal, pollard, bran, and molasses, were amongst the feed stuffs in demand. But the best of them are poor and unsatisfactory in comparison with the maize, sorghum, oats, rye, barley, and the grasses we can store up in ordinary seasons for feed in times of scarcity. That green feed, as well as grain, and other substances could be preserved in pits, or silos, is no new discovery. In Biblical times they were used for storing grain. There are several silos for grain storage near Sydney, built in early colonial days.

Dairy Silo.

The Silo.—As brought into use in recent times for storing soft feed for stock in Europe and America, the silo is an excavation or pit in the ground, built of brick, as a rule, laid in cement; stone has also been used. In New South Wales, silos of this elaborate sort have also been put down; but, since it became evident how suitable is the climate for preserving feed, with as much moisture as possible in it, silos have been simplified very much. For instance, excavations are made in granitic and other porous soils, and in these places (without artificial walls) feed has been stored upon the siloing principle, with results as good as the best. In other places, silos have been made partly in the ground, and partly above the surface. The part above ground is lined with timber, and that below is sometimes lined; in other cases, the soil forms the sides. Barns,

Ensilage Stack Above Ground

sheds, and other erections have been used; and stacks above ground, of much the same form as haystacks, are in favour. The object in view, in all cases, is to compress the stuff sufficiently close to allow mild fermentation to set in, but to prevent overheating, and the active fermentation and the destruction sure to follow overheating.

Requirements for Siloing.—The success of the operation depends very much upon the conditions of thorough drainage of the sides and bottom of the silo, expulsion of air from the mass of forage ensiled, and upon keeping air out with its ever-active germs of fermentation after the ensilage is covered in. Whatever may be put into a silo should be thoroughly well trodden in, and rammed down at the sides into a compact mass. The same rule applies to ensilage above ground. This packing of ensilage is greatly facilitated by passing the material through a chaff-cutter, as the long stalks of uncut stuff occupy greater space and offer more opportunity for stagnating air and unhealthy fermentations. To secure the exclusion of air, it has been found useful to cover the mass with close-fitting boards, or shutters, in one or more divisions. Where a silo can be all filled at one time, and where there is no intention of re-opening it to put in more stuff, dead weights to press down the mass appear to be the most economical. But where the coverings have to be removed to add more to make up for shrinkage, the value of mechanical appliances of the clutch or screw kind, becomes evident. To avoid the necessity of refilling, a super-silo, or over silo, removable at will, has been usefully employed. By filling to the top of this addition, sufficient material is provided so that the silo itself may be full to the top after shrinkage, which should not amount to more than one-third of the bulk, when the material is cut and well trodden when first put in.

The Crops Available.—Corn, giving as it does so very much more feed than any other crop, is ranked first; then come oats, wheat, rye, sorghum, rye or barley with vetches, lucerne, rape, chicory, native grasses, cornstalks, variegated thistles, &c.; in fact, anything that affords food for stock can be preserved in this way. Oats, because of their qualities in milk-giving material, form the richest feed of all. When corn stuff was put in green, the ensilage was so juicy as to soak and soften the more woody parts, so that the stuff came out more evenly.

Enjoying a Look at his Ensilage Crop.

Taking Out the Feed.—When put in whole, the ensilage has to be cut out with a hay-knife or broad axe in strips a foot wide, when it is easily pitched out and put into feed troughs. But the better course is to cut the stuff before it is put into the silo or stack, from which it can then be taken and fed like chaff.

Form and Capacity of Silos.—Experience in ensilage making favours round silos, next square, so as to have the least possible outside space. It is there where air or damp are most in contact, and where ensilage becomes colored or goes bad. Depth is a recommendation. Twelve feet is a good depth, 20 feet better, the pressure being more effective at the greater depth. Where the arrangement is such that great depth is secured, and yet the stuff can be taken out as near to the level where it is fed to stock, the less labour is necessary. The weight of ensilage varies according to

CROPS FOR FEED, SILOING, ETC.

the crop, whether it has been cut short, and the depth of the silo. Thus ensilage may weigh from 20 to 25lb. per cubic foot near the surface; at 12 feet deep may weigh between 40 and 50lb. So the greater the depth the greater the capacity per foot. To store 50 tons, say 12 feet in depth and 12 feet diameter is necessary. The further calculation is that silos of 20 feet diameter hold 109 tons, 122 tons, 135 tons, 149 tons, 163 tons, 179 tons, and 194 tons, when 17, 18, 19, 20, 21, 22, 23 and 24 feet deep respectively. A silo 30 feet deep and 15, 16, 17, 18, 19, 20, 21, 22, 23, or 24 feet in diameter, will hold, approximately, 105, 119, 134, 157, 168, 187, 205, 225, 246, or 268 tons of ensilage when well made and pressed.

Ensilage from Native Herbage.—During spring and summer, grass and herbage grow more rapidly after rain than stock can consume it, and in many cases the greater quantity is lost or becomes food for bush fires. The making of bush hay is expensive, is attended with risks, and only in special cases is the dried bush hay of any great value. On Liverpool Plains some 1500 tons of bush grass were converted into excellent ensilage. In appearance the stuff when opened up seemed rather wet, but it did not smell unpleasantly, and stock took to it quickly. The work of getting and stacking it employed 26 men, three mowing machines and an acme hay-raker during two weeks.

Cutting Down for Ensilage.

Cost of Ensilage.—In the case stated, the cost of making the ensilage was 4s. per ton, but with the appliances now available, and the experience gained, possibly 2s. 6d. may cover the cost. Maize ensilage costs about 6s. per ton.

Ensilage as Feed.—Although disappointments have occurred, because of the extravagant claims made

To See the Silo Opened.

regarding the superiority of ensilage in comparison with other kinds of feed, the material still advances in the estimation of those who have made it carefully. The advantages of the system are beyond a doubt, for any available fodder stuff can be stored away in any weather, and at the least cost for making feed; and that coarse, woody matter is made more digestible is reasonable. The quantities of corn and sorghum ensilage given to cows in milk may range between 30 and 60lb. daily. When given with 4 to 7lb. of scalded maize meal, pollard, or bran, or better still, a mixture of all, milking cows have done extra well upon such feed.

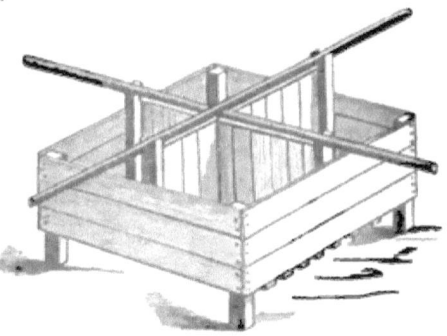

Handy Feed Arrangement.

For Moving Ensilage Stuff, Hay, &c.—The accompanying sketches, represent a simple contrivance for moving green corn, &c. It consists of a pole ten or twelve feet long, tapering to a point at one end. Near the large end is a ¾-inch hole, to which a clevis is attached. A stout rope, 15 to 18 feet long, is fastened by one end to a whiffletree, and at the other end is a ring four inches in diameter. When in use, the pole is thrust through the shock or cock to be removed, or the load may be built upon the pole, the rope is run through the clevis, and over the top of the pile of stuff, the ring being slipped over the small end of the pole. Then a horse is attached to the whiffletree and started. The draught tightens the rope, and binds all compactly together while it is moving. When the clevis is provided with a small pulley wheel or loose sleeve of iron, it saves friction and wear and tear of the rope.

For Moving Ensilage Stuff, Hay, &c.

Loaded up for the Silo.

Chemistry of the Operations—Any changes made in the silo are of a chemical character, due to fermentation, and require close attention. Fermentation can be regulated in two ways— by drying or wilting out less or more of the natural sap of the cut stuff before it is put in the silo or stack; or by shutting out the air by means of pressure, got either by tramping in the stuff, loading it above, or by rope pressure, as in the Johnson stack apparatus. The more natural moisture there is in the stuff when put up the less it heats, and the temperature can be regulated between 120 and 140 degrees—the limits of safety in green ferments. A very effective apparatus is being introduced to aid in regulating the temperature. It is an auger, with a handle so long that it can be sent six feet into a mass of stuff. The handle is hollow right down to the boring point, and into the handle a thermometer can be inserted as required, and the temperature tested. With this aid, good stuff to operate on, and the knowledge that fermentation cannot go on without air, the chemistry of ensilage-making becomes simple enough. There is one other point worthy of attention: Milking stock like a little sourness in their feed; it promotes the secretions of milk. The stuff full of sap when put in is the most likely to sour. To make the sweeter ensilage, it may be the better practice to let the stuff lie a little after it is cut, in order to get rid of some of the sap. That the fermentation of ensilage between 120 and 140 degrees makes dry stuff more digestible is a main feature of the change. Then, in a dry season, it is a great advantage to have the sap in the feed. Experiments and experiences are confirmatory that while filling in the stuff, or immediately thereafter, a heat equal to about 130 degrees can be induced which shall pervade the mass in the silo, and when, after that stage, the silo or stack is tightly closed, fermentation ceases, the ensilage remains sweet until re-opened. These results are attained by not too rapid filling, the temperature being watched; and as soon as that of one layer or portion reaches, say 130 degrees, another layer of three or four feet in thickness may be added, levelled off, packed closely around the sides, and left for a day or two to heat in turn. Pits filled in this way turned out beautifully, and the cattle, especially milch cows, have had healthful excellent feed. Chemical change and heating of plant material is developed by cutting, by which the juices are exposed to the action of ferments, the germs of which are almost universally distributed. The very fine cutting which used to be recommended is probably unnecessary, but lengths of from four to six inches answer well. Neither corn nor grass, when packed whole, come so certainly into a uniform heat, and there is the greater risk of over-heating, mould, &c. This applies equally to ensilage stacked above ground as to that stored in pits.

Other Feeds Available, Cob Meal included.—Pollard and bran make excellent feed; but, to get all the benefit to enable the stomach of the cow to digest it, the feed does best when c o o k e d , or scalded, otherw is e there is loss. Maize-meal with the same treatment enriches and increases the flow of milk. About 6 lbs.

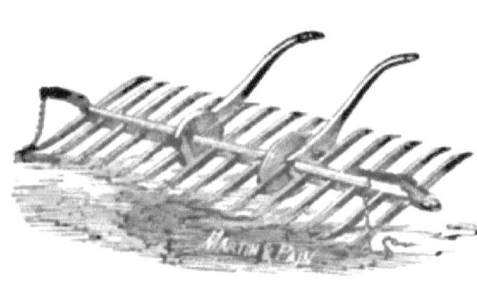

Revolving Hay Rake.

of either, with ensilage or other feed, as much as the animal can eat, make ample feed for a cow giving milk equal to 1 lb. of butter daily. Then meal made by grinding the corn, cob and all, has long been in use, and is known to be economical feed. This has been proved by those who have used both, and now we have the results of recent experiments at the Kansas Agricultural College, where ten beasts have been fed, five on corn-meal and five on cob-meal, under exact conditions, each tied in a stall four feet wide.

Warmth, Shelter and Feeding. — This is a most important point, and to dairymen in particular. The first call upon food is to maintain the animal heat, and even in our favoured climate cows exposed to the cold of winter fall off in their milk, in its quality and quantity, to a far greater extent than dry weather accounts for. The loss may be even one-third of the milk supply. To prevent such loss, sheds, stables, or such shelter as saves the stock from suffering cold and wet are the most certain safeguards.

Warmth in Winter and Shade in Summer.

Haymaking.—The value of hay, as feed, need not be underrated, in order to see the advantages of ensilage. Haymaking requires skill, and machinery specially suitable. Then it suffers from the risks of wet as well as excessively dry weather, neither of which affect so much the cutting and storing of ensilage, in either pits or stacks. Webster defines hay as dry grass, cured for future use as food for animals. But it is as well to know, that to preserve the valuable qualities of herbs or grasses, they must first be wilted in the sun, and then dried in the shade, and in the operation there is loss of flavour and of valuable juices. "Make hay when the sun shines" does not mean too much sun, as we have it at

Rake for Hay, Ensilage Stuff, &c.

times; it means that the grass should be stirred and wilted as evenly as possible after being cut. It does not mean that it should be left bleaching in the sun and dews two or three days after cutting, until it has lost nearly all that is attractive for food, and has become much as flax should be for the brake. The revolving rake seen in the illustration, does good work in gathering up stuff either for hay or ensilage.

Measuring Hay in the Stack.—For calculation purposes it is usual to estimate a cwt. of hay to the cubic yard. For instance, in an oblong stack: Suppose it to measure 20 feet × 10 feet × 15 feet, the cubic contents are 20 × 10 × 15 = 3000 cubic feet. This divided by 27, the number of cubic feet in a yard, will give the weight in cwts., say 111 1-9 cwts., or 5 tons 11 cwts.

This feed cover is useful where open-air feeding is followed. It is made of weatherboards held in position by wire stapled to the boards. The arrangement makes an excellent cover, from which the cows can eat at the ends and calves at the sides with the least risk of waste..

A Handy Feed-Cover.

XXI.—GARDEN AND ORCHARD.

Vegetables—Fruits—Flowers.

The Home Garden.—Supplies for home use are a first requirement, whichever branch of agriculture we enter. Fresh vegetables are at once the most healthful and nourishing of food supplies, and nowhere can we get them so sound and fresh as from the home garden, which at once reduces the expenses of housekeeping, and supplies the table with just what the agriculturist deserves to have, the very best vegetables, and fruits; and flowers to make a real home.

Arranging the Work.

Extent of the Home Garden.—For a family of eight persons, and to have supplies for the poultry yard and the pig, and an occasional sweet mouthful for the cow, from half to an acre is ample.

What an Acre Holds.—43,560 plants, 1 foot apart; 10,890 at 2 feet; 4,840 at 3 feet; 537 at 9 feet; 193 at 15 feet; 134 at 18 feet; 108 at 20 feet.

But an Acre?—43,560 square feet; or 10 square chains; or one chain wide by 10 chains long; 66 feet is 1 chain; 60 feet by 726 feet make an acre; or 220 feet by 198 feet; 640 acres make one square mile.

Plants per Acre.—The following shows the number of plants required per acre.

Feet apart	No. of Plants	Feet apart	No. of Plants	Feet apart	No. of Plants
2	10,890	9	537	20	108
3	4,840	10	435	21	98
4	2,722	12	302	25	69
5	1,742	15	193	30	48
8	680	18	134	35	35

Rule.—Multiply the distances into each other, and with the product divide 43,560 (the number of square feet in an acre), and the quotient is the number of plants.

Starting with Vegetables.—Where there is choice of soil, then a decidedly sandy loam is the best for a kitchen garden. It is easiest to work, and we cannot get vegetables without manure. The seed-sowing time for the cabbage, turnip, pea, and onion tribes extends through February, March, April, and May, and can be carried on still longer where the soil has been made very rich, and an occasional soaking with water can be administered. In preparing land for vegetables, two things are essential: that it be rich in plant food and closely fenced. The reason for the former will be obvious—the climate we have to deal with is changeable and occasionally dry. Vegetables to be first-class—and we trust the operator aims at nothing short of the best—must go on growing continuously. A check to their growth from poverty, drought or disease, invariably affects the quality. And fencing is necessary to keep off the domestic and the wild pests that never fail to harass an exposed garden.

Cold Weather Crops.—Cabbage, lettuce, cauliflower, brocoli, sprouts, peas, carrots, turnips, onions, leeks, parsley, herbs, &c., are sown from February to August, when possible in sheltered seed beds or after rain. Richness of soil, fair cultivation, and the use of water enable the grower to extend the cultivation of these crops, it may be over the entire year.

The Warm Weather Crops.—Beans, sugar, corn, cucumbers, melons, marrows, tomatoes, capsicums, &c., are sown from July right through the warm weather, their success, as in the case of the other classes, depending upon the richness of the soil.

Radishes, beets, shalots, mustard and cress, rhubarb, celery, asparagus, are more general crops, that are worked at any time of the year the weather and convenience will allow.

Experience Helps.—In no department of agriculture does the experience of the old world come more to our aid than in the kitchen garden. The same system of shallow covering in clean, well-raked ground applies admirably here; as does transplanting into rich, clean ground, frequent hoeing, care in staking and tying up climbers, &c. Some of our very best vegetable gardeners are men who were trained in the old land. Depth of soil and drainage are essential requisites. In this fast-growing climate plants root deep when they have the opportunity. The quick growers are also heavy feeders, and will stand as much manure as can be conveniently given them.

Mulching.—Mulch covering is a decided aid to our kitchen garden. Almost anything that is not too solid, that is light and of a vegetable nature, answers for this purpose. Straw, old hay, dried cow manure, leaf mould, leaves, small branches, burnt and scrub soil; all these things and many others aid us in having fine vegetables during the summer season and do no harm in winter. Scatter the mulch an inch or two in depth around the crops. It keeps in the moisture, keeps the surface from packing, and keeps the land clean and cool. Water-sprinkling without mulching is like labour in vain; but the effects of water upon mulch are decidedly beneficial.

Sowing Garden Seeds.—Whether for vegetables or flowers, the old rule, to cover the seed with its own thickness of soil, is still about the best guide to anyone in doubt as to the depth of covering material for seeds. Loose vegetable stuff makes the best covering. Onions for instance do best if sown on the surface, or on a shallow ridge slightly higher than the ground level, and then to sow on the ridge, by making a slight mark if in drills, or if in beds by sowing on the surface, raking gently and regularly in and covering with short manure stuff. Most seeds do better when the ground is made firm by rolling or treading before sowing. Generally sowing in drills is the most satisfactory and economical, being much easier kept free from weeds and stirred between the rows. The usual plan is to mark out with a drill marker several at a time; or, on a small scale by cutting a notch in middle of the end of the rake and stretching a line, and then pressing the rake handle along the line. Turnips and onions only require slight pressure, carrots and parsnips a little heavier. Very neat work can be done in this manner. Larger seeds, as peas and beans, &c., can be sown in drills opened by a spade or hoe. On sandy soil, treading the seed in firmly is generally beneficial. The distance the drills should be apart, is a matter to be decided by the condition of the soil as to richness and the height the crop will grow to, about the same distance apart as the height of the plant is usually right. We can have the drills well apart and the plants closer in the row where space is valuable; but if plenty of room is available, it is best to err on the side of abundance

Making the Rows Firm for Sowing

of space both for the rows and between the plants, that is in all sorts of vegetables that ripen their seed, or those used in the pod or fruit. Beets, carrots, turnips, parsnips, all that class may be sown pretty thickly together, so as to send them to the kitchen in a young state, by just thinning out as required, and leaving enough in the rows for a full crop. Whilst still very small, beets, carrots, &c., are much more succulent and tender, and are well worth the extra trouble in preparing for the table. Cabbage and cauliflower and lettuce are sown in seed beds for transplanting, and may be used from the home garden before they are too big. French beans and peas should be pulled whilst quite brittle and tender.

The Shade or Bush Frame.—These are the handiest and certainly amongst most effective contrivances in Australian

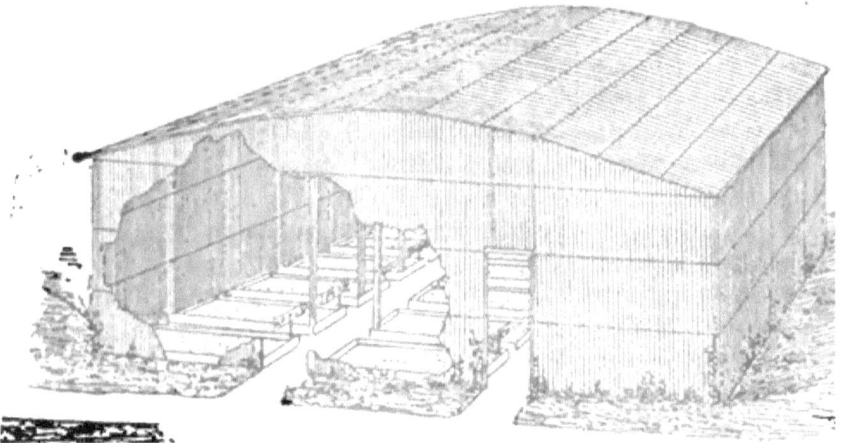

Bush House, with Propagating Beds for Seeds, &c.

practice. What we require is protection from drying winds and heavy rains, and this we get by making up a seed-bed in the ordinary way, such as that recommended for tobacco, for instance. Then to furnish shade and shelter, stakes are fitted at the corners, and a cover of bushes, old bamboo shade stuff, calico, or sacking, is made to fit over the bed in such a manner as allows of its being fitted close to the soil, or say six inches above it, or it can be fixed two or three feet above. This gives shade, and admits unlimited air. It is a real climate improver. With its aid we can raise vegetables, flowers, or other seedlings, as required, and an occasional spring of lettuce, mustard and cress, or other salad, during hot, dry weather. And thus from four to six weeks can be gained in growing early vegetables. Lettuce, radishes, early cabbage, tomatoes, celery, egg-plants, mustard, &c., may be sown in the frame by the first of February, and amply repay the little extra trouble it will be to care for them.

The Bush House.—This is becoming and deservedly so, a special feature of the Australian garden. It may be a very simple affair, or it can be as elaborate and fanciful as taste and outlay allow of. The principle is the same, and that is to get shade, and shelter, without shutting out the air. To effect this, any framework can be set up, of any desired form or size. The roof should be high, to make it convenient, say eight feet at least. Then the sides and roof are covered with bush material, laid as evenly and neatly as possible. The brushwood of young tee-tree answers admirably; laths and 2 x 1 hardwood are also used; also bamboo blind stuff, and close mesh wire netting.

Securing Bottom Heat.

All that is required is to divert the direct rays of the sun, and to break the force of heavy rain. In very exposed places, it is desirable to make the sides from which drying winds come as close as convenient. In a house, or shelter arranged in this way, the growth is immense. Where water can be spared, the place becomes delightful. It is evergreen, literally, and in addition to the plants, ferns, &c., that do so well when thus protected, seeds, can be raised for the flower garden, and where there is space, for the vegetable garden as well. Nurserymen and gardeners are taking more advantage of the opportunities the bush house offers for raising seedlings of all kinds. Some have over an acre of bush house accommodation. It may well become a feature of every garden, whether for private or business purposes; for, with a little taste, and no great outlay, the bush house may be ornamental as well as useful, and many things can be brought to perfection which would be impossible in the open air.

Where we have the help of a little artificial heat, a propagating pot and a bell glass (as *f* in the illustration), plants are raised in this way with certainty. Prepare the propagating pot by putting bits of charcoal to a depth of two or three inches, as in *a b*. Then fine loamy earth (*c*), and finally the cuttings (*d*). The younger shoots, from the extremities of branches, make roots most readily. The needful bottom heat is got by packing in a less or greater quantity of fresh stable stuff. As it decays, moist warmth is given off to the surrounding soil.

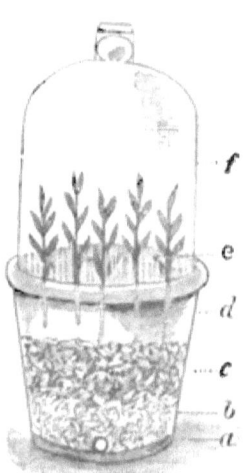

A Propagating Pot.

For Raising Little Things.

Warmth. — Temperature between 70 and 80 degrees — and moisture are of immense help in carrying on propagating work of all kinds.

Dig Deep and Plant in Long Rows.—Let us have the use and benefit of at least 2ft. of soil. So much for preparing, and let us sow in long rows; they make a big difference in gardening. The cost of working is lessened so much that once adopted no one is likely to again drop the system. It has advantages in both old

Digging Two Spades Deep.

and new places. The soil of the former is sure to be full of the seeds of weeds. These are kept in check more easily and with less labour in long rather than short rows. Then on new places, manure is generally scarce, so we can use it in the rows, either under or over the seed, or between the rows of plants as the case may be.

Long Rows in the Vegetable Garden.

Transplanting.—Fig. 1 shows a plant nicely set out, the roots are spread all round; No. 2 has been pushed into

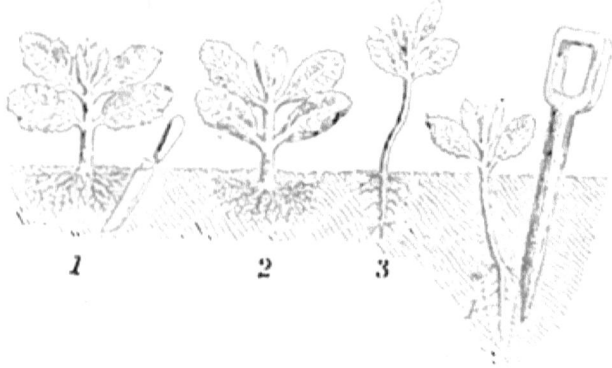

Transplating Cabbage, Tomatoes, Tobacco, &c.

the ground, the roots being left up too high instead of spreading downwards, as in No. 1; No. 3 is planted too shallow, and No. 4 is too deep. The planting trowel shown near No. 1 is better for this work than the dibble shown at No. 4.

Thinning Out.—Our active growing seasons force vegetables into becoming half-starved weeds unless thinning out is attended to very closely. Take carrots, for instance, which are grown in rows and also sown broadcast. When thinning is neglected they will be the sort of things seen in the first sketch sent (A), mere twisted fibrous roots. But when thinned, so as to have two or more inches space either in the rows or sown broadcast, we get good sized, well-grown vegetables. As a whole, and when they are for home use mostly, I now prefer to grow carrots sown broadcast. When the beds are kept clean, thinned out, and watered during dry weather, very heavy yields are got, and the quality is equal to carrots grown in rows. Radish and parsnips may be worked in the same way, and can be sown together and at the same time. The radish are so much quicker than the parsnips, that with care to prevent absolute over-crowding, they can be off the ground before the spade is required for the parsnips. The quality of both, as grown in this country, can be very fine.

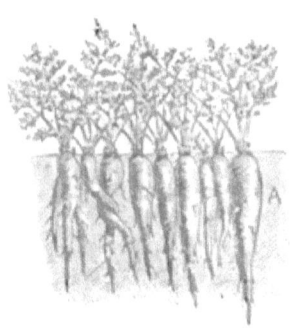

Carrots Crowded.

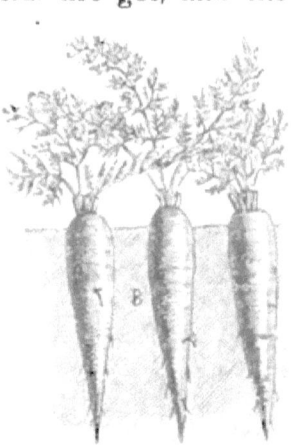

Little Gardeners.—And the children naturally take great pleasure and interest in plant growth. Parents should encourage them in this taste, and ever be ready to give them a few hints upon the subject of plants and flowers. A little seasonable advice, and a few pence to purchase seeds, and by helping in the work occasionally the young lives are filled with happiness. There is not only considerable healthy interest manifested, but they could not possibly be better or

Admiring Her own Work.

more innocently employed. A portion of the home garden might be given up to each child, and some very creditable results ensue. These little gardeners take quite a pride in pointing out the results of their skill to friends and relatives. They are so fond of anything grown by themselves and watch so anxiously a flower on the point of blooming.

Give the Boys a Bit of Land—To work as they think fit and to dispose of the produce on the same terms. Both boys and girls are all the more healthy, independent, and industrious when they earn something, and feel that they have a perfect right to their earnings.

Market Gardening on a Big Scale.—Chinamen do not control the market garden business in other lands. Their skill is not of the kind which surpasses that of the European systems of vegetable gardening. Their efforts with fruit are very defective. The occupation of market gardening offers decided inducements in Australia for skill and capital. To keep up the immense supplies required by London and the great cities of Britain generally, and also Paris, New York, and elsewhere, as well as our own profitable market gardens, they are the work of skilful white men, who succeed by the unstinted use of manures. Large capital is employed. A case may be cited of a garden of 85 acres. The soil is sandy. Everything on the place is conducted in a strictly business manner; accurate accounts are kept, so that the exact cost of rent, labor, interest on capital, manures, seeds, labor and marketing and returns for each crop may be ascertained. Only such kinds as prove most marketable are grown. The yield of a year was 5425 barrels early cabbage, 3150 bushels early potatoes, 3000 bushels onions, 4650 bushels late potatoes, 12,000 bushels carrots, 3000 bushels onions grown for seed, 20 bushels white beans, 175 barrels squash, 3 tons Hungarian hay, 100 bushels onion sets, 150 bushels Brussels sprouts, 40lb. carrot seed, 150lb. beet seed, 1500 bushels sweet corn, and 275,000 cabbage plants to carry over. The horses and other live stock, poultry, &c., get a large proportion of their living from the farm. The land is allowed no rest, a rotation of cropping is kept up; the land is cropped twice a year; for some crops three times.

LAND FOR FRUIT CULTURE.—If it is for home use

The Tree We Aim at Making.

only, then the nearer the garden is to the house the better; when surrounding the house it is all the better. But if we require a larger area, and there is a choice, then the best soil for the majority of fruits is a good stiffer loam, such as would yield good consecutive crops of grain. A lighter soil, while working more freely, does not give such stamina to the trees as to ensure long life, nor is the fruit so long keeping. These remarks are especially true of the apple tribe, and apply to fruits generally. Under-drainage is an absolute necessity; where it does not exist naturally (which is rarely the case) it must be provided by the careful, forecasting orchardist, as described in the chapter on draining. The exposure of land intended for fruit is worthy of consideration, experience pointing to the eastern and north-eastern slopes as being especially favorable. Accessibility to market speaks for itself, and needs no comment. The cultivator who resolves to either wholly or in part prosecute fruit-growing as a business will spare no trouble in order to obtain a suitable piece of land for his orchard; fertile soil, not too steep, good exposure, sufficient under-drainage, and an accessible market, are absolutely necessary in order to ensure success. Skilful manuring tells effectively in the orchard.

Fruits Available.—The experimenting stage has long been worked out in Australia. In the elevated districts, immediately west of the great Dividing Ranges, the apple, pear, plum, peach, nectarine, cherry, apricot, grape vines, &c., the fruits of the temperate zone are thoroughly at home. In the coastal districts, the orange, lemon, lime, date plum, loquat, mango, olive, banana, &c., find a congenial climate, and flourish abundantly; while in both sections of the country the grape thrives well, but does best where the rainfall is between twenty and thirty inches. Some of the plums, Japan plums, apples, pears, &c., thrive also on the coastal lands, as do peaches of the Chinese races; and the orange succeeds in favourable situations further inland, as well almost as in the coast country.

Experiences With Varieties of Fruits.—Every district in the country has its experiences of varieties that do well, and of others, found excellent in some parts, which prove unsuitable in others. Suggestions from neighbours, from the catalogues of nurserymen, and from the experiences of those who have knowledge of the country generally, are of much usefulness. The foregoing applies to fruit trees especially, and the merits and defects of each family of which, for marketing in the fresh state or for preserving, are generally well known.

Seedling Trees.—Seeds sown in boxes are more easily seen to, and can be watered and shaded more effectively, and then when a suitable day can be chosen for transplanting, few losses need occur. Seeds of trees that make a tap root that is not wanted are very often best sown in seed boxes, and then transplanted in nursery rows when fit. The question of leaving the tap root on trees depends a good deal on the soil and how they are worked. Trees the roots of which feed near the surface, such as oranges, may be better without the tap, but trees of the citrus family on deep, well-drained soil, with the tap root are longer lived and make more upright growth. Where unhealthy and wet subsoil underlies the ground where trees are growing, the taproot may get down into such soil, and when wet spells occur, suffer badly, and the trees look unhealthy and die off but too frequently. Where the under-drainage is good and the subsoil porous and healthy, a taproot should be an advantage to a tree, especially in the dry seasons. Oranges, and lemons, last longer and give better results, provided the drainage is right, when the seed is planted where the tree is to be grown. Indeed, in suitable soil, deep and well drained, experience says that many trees would do much better if sown where they are to remain, either to bear fruit or to be grafted or budded. They would take longer to bear, but live longer; still, we must be guided by circumstances to make the best use of the soil and the position we work in.

Measuring Off for Trees.—The implements required for laying out land for orchard trees are a surveyor chain—or a length of fencing wire about $7\frac{1}{2}$ chains long with an iron ring at each end does very well; half a dozen hardwood stakes well pointed; a batten of the length the trees are to be apart, with a notch for the side distances when used for triangle planting; and a few hundred pegs about six inches long. We will presume that the land is not fenced all round, and that it will be necessary to mark and peg out correct top and side lines. To commence operations, drive one of the stakes firmly into the ground at one of the projected corners. Now place one of the rings of the wire over the stake and stretch it along the line of the proposed boundary, and drive in short stakes till the line is marked off straight. Another corner is then marked. The next line is to be at right angles. To find a right angle, mark off exactly 60 feet along the first line, and put in a temporary peg, and from the corner stake stretch a line as nearly at a right angle as you can guess, and put in another temporary peg, at 80 feet. When the two pegs are proved to be 100 feet apart the angle is a right angle. When there is any difference the second line and peg must be shifted inwards or outward until the required 100ft. is attained. Having found the right angle, stretch the chain down the proved line to the end, and put in a stake, this being the third corner. Now find the other right angle, proceeding exactly the same as before, and a stake will stand in each of the four corners, with the sides and ends for guidance. We can then measure off the top and side lines for triangular or square planting, as may be desired. Putting in a peg where each tree is to stand.

Selecting the Trees.— Maiden plants, that is plants that have made one year's growth from the buds or graft, are best for planting in this country. Older and larger trees carry more risks. They do not transplant so well, and may lead to gumming and other annoyances of the orchardist. The roots should be kept moist. A dip in liquid soak, made up with cow manure is helpful for that purpose.

Putting in the Trees.—They are to be put in exactly where the pegs are placed, the accompanying sketch shows an ingenious contrivance for ensuring this. The "planting board" (*a*) is a piece of deal about 6 feet long, with a hole near each end; a notch is cut in the middle. To use this planter, place the middle notch against the first peg, and then place a peg into each of the end holes as in (*a*). The centre peg may then be lifted, and the board moved round on one of the end pegs as seen at (*b*). The hole is then dug between the pair of pegs, and large enough to spread out the roots nicely. When planting the tree, the board is again fitted on to the two pegs, the tree is rested in the notch in the board and it is then where the planting peg was placed. When necessary, stakes are driven in after the holes are dug, but, as a rule, trees are more hardy and vigorous when they grow without the aid of stakes.

Watering Newly-Planted Trees.—In very dry weather, it may be necessary, where possible, to damp the soil in order to get it to lie close to the roots, but care has to be used here also, for until the roots start into growth, water may do more harm than good, by inducing fungus growths to fix themselves upon the newly planted wood.

Tree Planting.—This work calls for all the care and skill we can devote to it. Distance apart, method in  planting, and preparation of the land all have their effect. Two well-defined methods of arranging trees for orcharding are followed—planting in squares or in triangle. The triangle system offers many advantages, as set off against the somewhat greater difficulty of laying out land for this kind of planting. Amongst the advantages are the greater number of trees per acre, and the increased facilities for working the land with horse labour, the land between the rows of trees being workable in three or four directions. The system also allows of planting on irregularly-shaped pieces of land, such as that shown in the third illustration. In arranging land for triangular planting, say the trees are to be 20ft. apart, the spaces in the first row (A to F), the 3rd, 5th, 7th, and so on, will be 20ft. apart. The 2nd (B to C), 4th, and other rows, where the trees come between two trees in the 1st and 3rd, will, by measurement on the side lines, be 17ft. 4in. The triangular slope (as between A and B) makes up the difference, so that when the trees are planted they will be 20ft. apart from each other, in which-

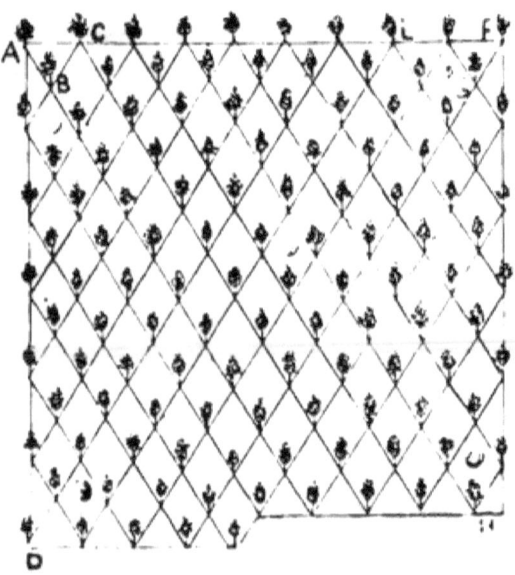

ever way they may be measured. The side-line measurements, for various distances apart, from 10 to 20ft. are:

Top line.		Side line.
20ft.	—	17ft. 4in.
18ft.	—	15ft. 7in.
16ft.	—	13ft. 10½in.
14ft.	—	12ft. 1in.
12ft.	—	10ft. 4½in.
10ft.	—	8ft. 8in.

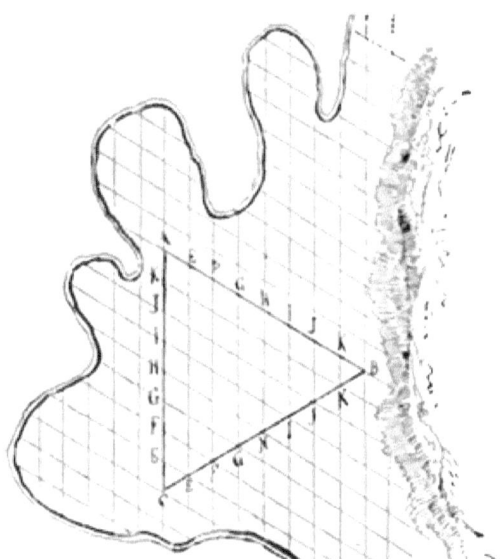

To plant in squares, the land is measured off in equal distances, top, bottom, and sides, pegs inserted, and trees planted as in the square method.

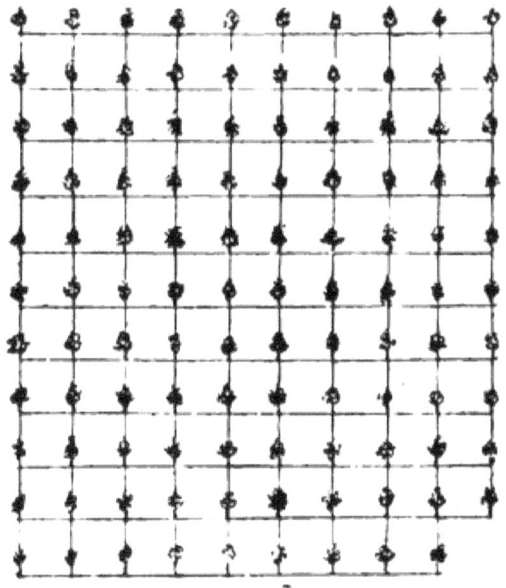

Planted in Squares.

GARDEN AND ORCHARD.

The number of trees at different distances in square and triangular planting are:—

In squares.		In triangle.
20ft., 108 per acre	—	125 per acre.
18ft., 134 ,,	—	154 ,,
16ft., 170 ,,	—	195 ,,
14ft., 222 ,,	—	255 ,,
12ft., 302 ,,	—	347 ,,
10ft., 435 ,,	—	500 ,,

Pruning the Newly-planted Trees.—The end bud where the cut is made may be about 30 inches from the ground, which answers for most orchard trees in order to secure strong, healthy side growth from the buds along the trunk.

Large or Smaller Orchard Trees?—This is a very important question at the season when we are arranging either to plant new trees, or to regulate those we have, by pruning. The old idea was to have trees as large as possible; the tendency now is to keep down the size. Both methods are within control by closer planting and regulating the pruning, until we work on to a system in which trees that can be pruned from the ground without ladders, and the fruit gathered under similar conditions. The type of trees we aim at making is shown at the beginning of this chapter. It does not pay to climb high ladders to prune, regulate, or gather fruit in orchard work.

Doesn't Pay to Work Trees Like This.

Cultivation and Manuring in Fruit Growing.—The requirements for quality of soil, draining to make sure of depth, and manuring are dealt with in preceding chapters. Cultivation, that is the maintenance of a loose, clean surface, is as necessary here as in the field or vegetable garden. The selection and application of manure requires very close attention in order to supply what the different fruits require in the form of vegetable matter, ammonia, potash, phosphates, lime, and the other ingredients.

Pruning Reminders.—Taking oranges and lemons first —they may be thinned out at any time and the points of too vigorous growth pinched, but the stems and lower branches must not be exposed to the sun. When one branch commences to run away or grow faster than the others, it has acquired rank or sucker habits, and should be pinched or cut to check such growths. If any branch or shoot starts to crowd to grow under another, rub it out. Apple and pear trees require shortening and bending of the branches to develope fruit spurs, but when they begin to bear require very little pruning. Cherries much the same. One-third to one-half of the latest growth should be pruned off peach and nectarine trees, and they are the better for it. When the growth is thin and weakly, cut back the top growth of plums, but do not prune off short spurs on plums or apricots. It is on them we get the fruit. Raspberries, blackberries, currants, and gooseberries need a great deal of pruning out and thinning. The canes of raspberries which bore last season should be cut out and fresh canes bent over for bearing. Grape vines should be pruned according to age and variety; but generally three buds may be left on the young bearing wood or spurs of old trellised vines. Weak shoots and those on the lower sides of bearing wood should be rubbed out. The number of

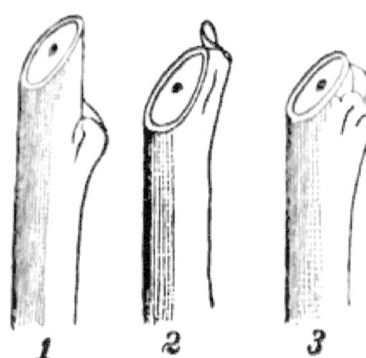

The cut in Fig. 1 is too far from the bud. No. 2 is too close to the bud. No. 3 is the right distance from the bud

branches to a bush or stake vine may be three to five and each of these, as the vine grows older, may support two spurs, of one season's growth, with two or three buds each, from which the fruit is obtained.

Pruning for Form.—There is every inducement for the exercise of skill at this work. Pruning commences with the planting. All branches should spring from buds that form at the same time as the roots that grow after

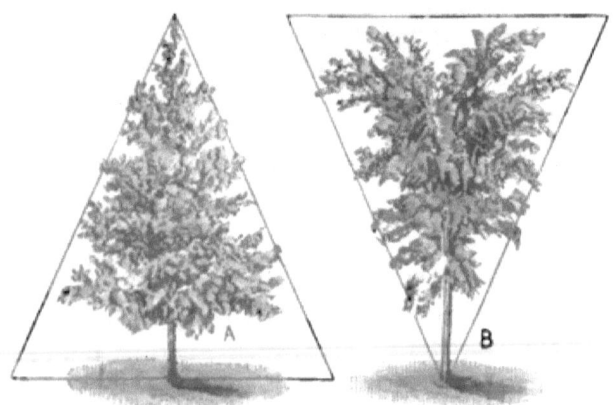

Pruning for Form.

planting out. This means close cutting back. Then we train the trees to be broad at the base or at the top. The former is preferable for orchard purposes. The general tendency is to keep fruit trees under 12 feet in height.

Pruning for Fruit—Leaf and Fruit Buds.—Young fruitgrowers are often at a loss to distinguish between these two kinds of buds. A young tree, for instance, to which it is desired to impart more vigour is checked by cutting away leaf-shoots and leaving fruit spurs. Fruit buds of apples, pears, cherries, &c., are generally distinguished by their rounded and obtuse form; while leaf buds are more slender and sharper. Many fruit spurs are really stunted shoots, originally produced from leaf buds, but which, making but little growth, become fruit-bearers. In the pear, and some other trees, they are never less than two years old, and they often continue to bear for many years. Whatever tends to a free circulation of the sap, and consequently to a rapid growth, causes the formation of leaf buds rather than fruit buds. And whatever tends to retard the motion and increase the accumulation of sap in any part (roots or branches) induces the production of fruit buds. The vigorous one-year shoot of the cherry is mostly supplied with leaf buds; but the short spurs on the second year's wood, which are but shortened branches, may be covered with fruit buds, with usually a leaf bud in the centre. This also explains the chief reason why young and vigorous trees of the apple kind, the wood and bark of which are comparatively soft and yielding, and through the large and unobstructed vessels of which the sap flows without restraint, do not bear so freely as the older and more rigid wood, in which the circulation is slower. A young tree growing in very vigorous condition may not produce fruit buds for many years; while, if checked by skilful pruning, it bears at the right age. The varieties of fruit available for planting are very numerous—perhaps too numerous.

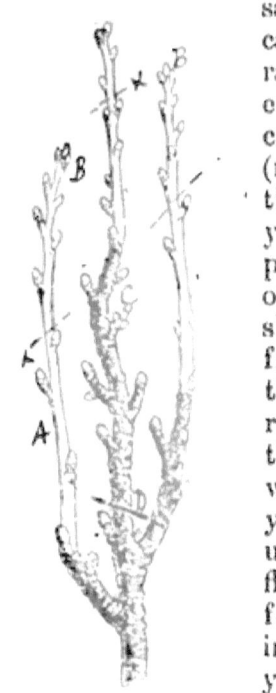

Pruning for Fruit.

BUDDING and GRAFTING.—Both operations are followed with the same object in view—to secure desirable sorts of fruits, flower or foliage plants, upon roots suitable for their most vigorous growth. Grafting is done in the early spring season, from July onwards, according to the variety of plant and the location. Budding, or grafting with a single bud, is an autumn operation,

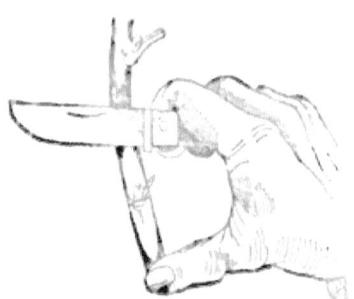

How the Bud Is Taken Off.

by which a single bud is worked upon a desirable stock, usually a seedling.

Peaches and roses are amongst the first plants amongst us ready for budding. The operation as worked out here is much the same as budding in other countries, with, of course, the difference of the seasons, and that here less care is supposed to be necessary in preparing the buds and in attention to the details of tying upon the stock and after treatment. All the same, it will be found that the more carefully the work is done, the more success follows the operations of budding. The buds used should be taken from the bearing wood of fertile trees—that is, trees that have flowered and fruited. Trees younger than three years are not sufficiently matured for propagating purposes. The young bearing wood, the growth of one season, contains the buds suitable for propagating. The wood should be fully ripe and well matured; the buds plump and firm. The illustrations accompanying this article show how the work is done. With care in selecting the right materials for working and practice, the rest comes easy for effective budding. Practice and attention to details are the chief points.

Cutting a Bud for Insertion.

The Stocks.—Healthy plants grown from seed are best for fruit trees, and rooted cuttings in the case of roses. About half an inch in thickness is a good size for a stock to bud on.

Cutting Off, Inserting and Tying the Bud.—The illustrations show clearly how this work is done. The bud is cut off from the chosen wood, about half an inch of bark being left above and below the bud. When taken off, a small portion of wood may be found attached to the bud. It is best to remove this. To make the opening on the stock, make a cut across, then another downwards—the first being about an inch across the downwards cut about three

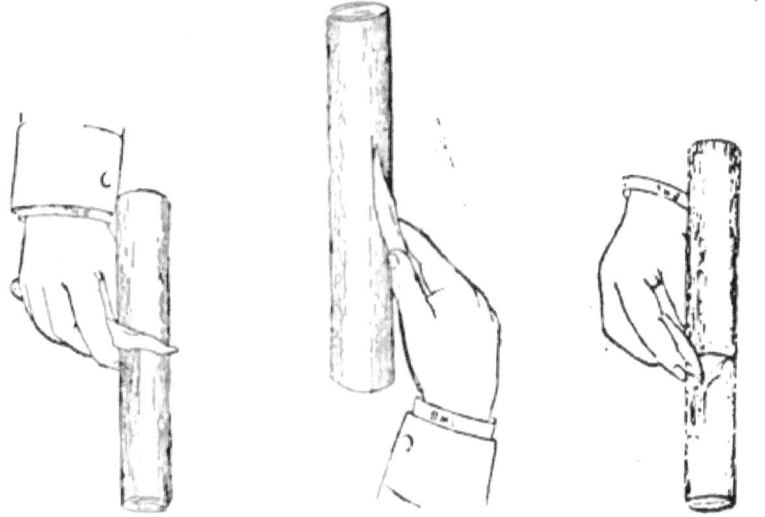

The Cross Cut.　　　Cut Downwards.　　　Opening Cuts for Bud.

inches in length. Then open the cuts thus made by folding them over slightly, as shown in the engraving. This work has to be done quickly, to avoid the sap of the bud, or the sap of the stock, or both, from drying. The bud (which is usually in the lips of the operator while he is making the cuts) is then inserted. In order to make an effective

-ted.

junction between the sap flow in the stock and the sap of the bud, which we desire to unite, the upper part of the bark is cut across, and the bud is then pressed upwards, so as to join the parts. The parts are then tied, thin strips of calico being in general use for the purpose. Worsted thread is also used, and answers well for small plants, also "raffia," a fibrous material. Veneer budding and ring budding, the latter for soft bark plants as a rule, are also practised; and some operators prefer to insert the bud from below the T cut, in But in all cases, the leaf growth on the

GARDEN AND ORCHARD.

stock above where the bud is inserted is left on until the bud starts into active growth, so that it may be supplied with sap material. Orange and peach buds, and some roses, may start growing at once, and the growth on the stock above them may then be cut off before the season closes; others are slower, as apples and pears, and may remain dormant till spring.

Budding is found most suitable for fruit trees generally, and for roses, in this country, and is gradually taking the place of grafting for orchard purposes.

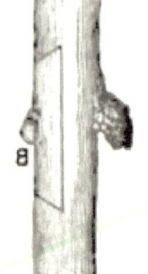
Veneer Budding

The Principles of Budding and Grafting.—Grafting, like budding, is that operation in gardening which unites a plant—or a portion of a plant taken from a tested variety, fixing it upon a plant of same order which has roots, and which will support and furnish the graft with a part of the nutriment necessary for growth. The graft then supplies that portion of plant food got from the air. As the poet says:—

"Which does mend nature,
or change it rather;
But the art itself is nature."

Tongue or Splice Grafts.

The plant that receives the graft then is usually furnished with roots. It has to draw its nutriment from the soil and transmit it to the part grafted. It is called the stock. In some cases, as grape vines, apples, and a few others, the

stock is a simple cutting—or bit of root; but it is planted
in such a manner as to be soon furnished with roots.
That portion of the other plant which is to be grafted on
to the stock should have at least one eye or bud,
it is, however, better to have two or three buds
if possible. It is called the graft, or scion, and it is
analagous to a cutting put to root in soil. The scion
continues its growth through the stock; but notwithstanding the intimate union of the stock and the graft,
they really preserve their individual characters and
constitutions distinctively, their layers of bark and wood
continue to be developed without the wood vessels or
fibres converging with each other; it is, as it were, a
federative union which leaves to both their own characteristics. The objects of grafting are to change the
character of a plant by modify-
ing the wood, the foliage, or the
fruit which it is required to
produce; to excite the development of branches, flowers, or
fruit on the parts of a plant
where they are deficient; and
to restore a defective or exhausted tree by transfusion of the
fresh sap of a vigorous kind.
Thus a variety naturally delicate
becomes robust when "worked"

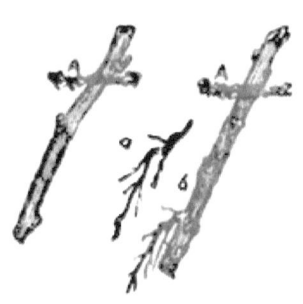

Root Graft—Apple.

on a more robust stock, and the consequence is a
more abundant production of flowers and fruit.
Thus it is that fine and delicate kinds of grapes
that do not thrive on their own roots are
made to produce large and fine bunches when
grafted on some vigorous stock such as the
Isabella, Syrian, or Gross Colman. The
peculiar qualities of some plants can only be
preserved by "working." This is especially
the case with variegated or striped roses.
These retain their gay markings when budded
or grafted; but become plain when grown on
their own roots. So in grafting a great

Insertion.

deal of the success depends on the skill of the operator. The other essential conditions are affinity between the species. We cannot be too careful in seeing that the two portions are of such character to be thoroughly suitable for the union we desire to perfect. Vigour of the stock and graft, the condition of their sap, their intimate union, the season, and the temperature are other essential conditions for success in this operation.

Grafting Clay and Wax.—Clay for grafting is prepared by mixing one-third cow droppings, free from straw, and two-thirds clay or clayey-loam, where possible adding a little hair, like that used in plaster, to prevent its cracking. Beat and temper it for two or three days until it is thoroughly incorporated. When used, the clay should be of such consistency as to be easily put on and shaped as may be desired. Grafting wax of excellent quality is made by melting together three parts of beeswax, three parts of rosin, and two parts tallow. While yet warm, it may be worked with the aid of a little water like shoemaker's wax, by the hand. Wax to be laid on with a brush in a fluid state is made of half a pound of pitch, half a pound of beeswax, and a portion of cow droppings, boiled together. Another mixture, which is spread while warm on strips of coarse cotton or strong paper, and wrapped directly about the graft, answering at once to tie and protect it, is composed of equal parts of beeswax, turpentine, and rosin. And another grafting wax and suitable for laying on strips of calico or paper is made of tallow, beeswax and rosin in equal parts, or as many prefer, with a little more tallow to render it pliable. Grafting wax is a much neater and perfect protection than grafting clay, but the trifling cost of the latter, where a great deal of work is to be done, accounts for its greater use by nurserymen and gardeners generally. The purpose of both is similar. It is to prevent drying of the parts we have joined, and to aid in keeping them in position, and the more carefully these points are attended to, the more are we likely to be successful in perfecting the work we are at.

A Handy Fruit Gatherer.—This is a useful contrivance for bringing down oranges and other fruits from trees where they are difficult to reach by means of a ladder. It is made of iron wire bent as shown, and fastened to a bent piece, which in turn is fastened to a pole of any desired length. A clip piece of wire or wood projects from the top, and with it the fruit is disengaged from its stem, and drops into the gatherer.

Cutting v. Pulling Fruit.—Where possible, fruit should be cut from the tree. It keeps better. Very handy cutters for the purpose are being introduced, and do excellent work.

Neatness in Marketing.—It pays to size or grade fruits, to wrap lemons, apples, &c., paper, and to use the

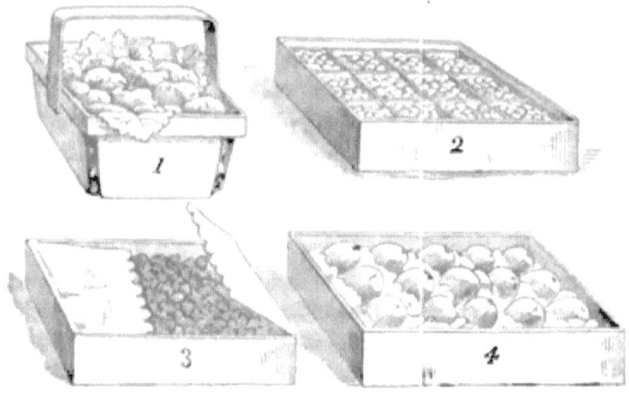

Put up Fruit Nicely.

neatest cases and packages available. A half-case of strawberries, cherries or other fruits, put up in packets, made of thin wood chip is very attractive to buyers of these fine fruits. The illustrations show cases arranged for carrying plums, apricots, peaches, &c., neatly edged in with blue or other colored paper, or for apples, pears, or other marketable commodity.

Grapes and Wine.—This is a special branch of Australian agriculture. The grape in some of its varieties grows in all parts of Australia, even in the colder districts where frost holds the land in its firm embrace during several months of each year; and in the drier interior, where the rainfall is uncertain, and too limited for the production of other fruit, if we except the fig and the almond, which both delight in dry country, when they get an occasional soaking. The grape, some of its many varieties at any rate, does better than other fruits in dry country, without the soaking. It is a deep-rooting plant in every case, and is at its best when the roots have opportunity to get away down into the fissures of rocks or amongst boulders where they gather in the mineral food of plants—from which the richest flavoring of the grape is evolved. That is the character and the habits of the grape-vine in other lands, and the family show much the same characteristics here. All of them require five months of real hot weather to develop their fruit to its rich maturity, and three or four months of milder spring or autumn. Where freezing frosts occur, vines require winter shelter. It is under such conditions that the great vine at Hampton Court grows so vigorously.

Soil for Grapes.—Possibly the greatest mistakes have arisen from planting in soil that is too poor in plant food. Volcanic and carboniferous country answers best. Not one of the family like rich, rank, or flat land; but all require lime, potash, and the material for making flavourings.

Varieties.—Next to soil and climate, come the sorts of grapes suitable for different locations. Immense experience has been gained on this point. In almost every part of the country sorts have been proven, which answer better than any others, so far as known. Thus, in the districts where the rainfall averages between 15 and 25 inches, the finer flavoured grapes, the muscatels and muscats, do excellently well. In coastal and warmer country the more robust growers find what they require. In the tropical parts, American sorts of the Isabella type, come to absolute maturity. In some locations the acid secretions, so prominent in this family of grapes in less favourable quarters, are checked at the sugar stage, and the fruit ripens sweet and extraordinarily rich in spirit matter. That is, when they have room and are cultivated. All grapes starve when crowded; 6 x 6 is close enough for the more feeble sorts, 8 x 8 is a standard distance for wine grapes, and some are grown 20 or more feet apart, and yield heavier crops than if three were grown in that space. They are grand rooters, and find their own way downwards where there is the material of life, and the natural drainage is good enough; so that deep preparation of soil is not so necessary for this fruit. Cuttings of matured wood are used for plants; they are put in where they are to grow, the soil being opened by plough, spade, bar, or fork.

Grafting Grape Vines.—A good deal of this kind of work, in order to secure blight proof roots, and also for renewing old stocks, and displacing sorts that are not so good for wine making, is going on. The scion, for insertion, is cut wedge shape, as is the stock when a blight proof cutting is used for rooting purposes. When old vines are worked over, the stock is cut off about three inches under the ground, as shown, and then opened by the grafting tool, or a knife or chisel answer the purpose. The scions—two generally in each stock—are inserted in the cut, and tied in position. The soil is then heaped firmly round the graft. With these conditions failures seldom occur.

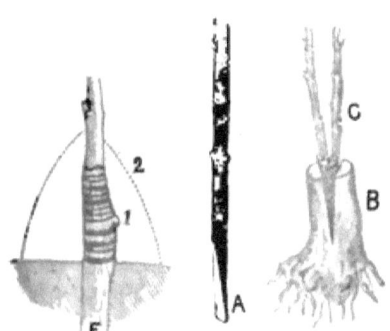

Splice Graft.   Grafting Old Vines.

Grafting Tool for Vines.

Spring Treatment of Vines.—The sketch below illustrates a first step in the way of regulating growth, as the

vines break into leaf for the season. The plant shown has been pruned effectively. The new wood on each arm from *b*, and the short spurs on the upper side all along both arms, being the wood of last season's growth, from which the coming crop is expected. To aid the development of strong buds on the upper side, those that break on the lower side (*a, a*) of the bearing wood have to be rubbed out as they appear. This rubbing out of buds does not check the vigour of the vines, but it directs the sap to the upper buds, where it is required to give them strength for bearing.

FLOWERS AND SHRUBS.—There is no limit to the beauties available for adorning the Australian home, and

making home life attractive. In all seasons of the year we can have flowers, from some of the myriads of annuals, shrubs, or flowering trees that grow so well. Roses, bulbs, climbers, creepers, and the many varieties of ferns available, all come into the possibilities of flower gardening in Australia for adding to the home attractions and for decoration. (See calendar of seasonable work for directions).

The Soil Necessary.—The directions given for soil selection and treatment for farming and gardening apply equally here, as does cultivation. The same means for improving a bad or poor bit of land may be employed for deepening the flower patch, draining, manuring, &c.

Flowers in a Business Sense.—The skilful application of opportunity amongst flowers may be as effective here as in other lands. Plants in pots, cut flowers, new or improved specimens got by selection, hybridising, and other processes of gardening, are as enticing here as in Europe and America. The Isle of Wight is famous for seedling raising. The numbers of ladies engaged there in raising plants, flowers, bulbs, and fruits, are immense; and London and other seedsmen pay good prices to known people for good things. New and improved bulbs, cosmos, and many other novelties are got from them. The chrysanthemum has been treated ever since it was introduced into this country as a hardy herbacious perennial, but it may be raised from seed yearly and be treated as an annual with the greatest facility and success; and, doubtless, lovers of this autumnal favourite may be induced to give attention to the raising of seedlings, inasmuch as this practice, apart from the prospect of obtaining something new and distinct, is accompanied by immense interest and pleasure from the time the seed is sown to the production of the flowers. In raising seedlings, it is good practice, as soon as the young plants have grown sufficiently, to take off cuttings and root them. It affords better and quicker opportunity for testing the merits of any seedlings of promise.

Seed Sowing and Propagating.—The rules and practices laid down in the chapters on vegetable gardening, tobacco culture, and other branches, are suitable for flower growing.

Bush and Glass Houses.—The former is helpful in every branch of gardening in Australia—for seed raising, propagating, and shelter for plants that suffer in the open ground.

Summer-flowering Plants.— Annuals, of the many varieties available, may be sown in spring to be ready for planting out as required for flowering. Plant out cuttings of penstemons, phloxes, fuchsias, &c., that may have been struck earlier in the season. Cuttings of chrysanthemums may be put in to make strong plants for flowering next season. Amongst other shrubs and plants available are: —Acacias, yellow, from 2ft. to 30ft. high; ageratum, blue, 1ft.; agonis (billotia) marginata, white, 5ft.; aloes, orange, red, &c., 2ft. to 6ft.; alyssum, various, rock plants; amaranthus (late, annuals); antirrhinums, all colours, 18 inches; armeria formosa (sea-pink or thrift), 18 inches; banksias; bouvardias, several colours; brugmansias;

budleas, varieties; calendula, marigolds, yellow, white, double, &c.; callas (so-called pitcher lily); canarina campanula, orange, 3ft.; cassia, yellow, 5ft.; chrysanthemums; clematis; coreopsis (annual), yellow, 2ft.; daphne odora, red, white, 3ft.; dianthus, various, 1ft.; euphorbias, red, scarlet, 1ft. to 3ft.; fuchsias, 1ft. to 6ft.; gaillardias, reddish, yellow, 2ft.; grevilles, brown, greenish-yellow, 6ft. to 40ft.; pampas grass; hibiscus; heliotrope, blue, 18 inches; ipomœas, climbers, blue, red and white; jasmines, white, yellow; lasiandria, purple, 7ft.; honey-suckles, scarlet, 10ft.; mesembryanthemums, red, yellow, orange, &c., 1ft.; oleander, pink, red, yellow, white, 10ft.; passion flowers; pelargoniums, various; penstemons, various; petunias; phlox drummondii, colours, 18 inches; plumbago capensis, blue, 2ft.; roses; salvias, scarlet, red, blue, 2ft. to 3ft.; tecomas, yellow, 6ft. to 10ft; tritonia, yellow, orange, 1ft.; veronicas, blue, red; violets; pansies; and hosts of others, described in the nurserymen's catalogues.

Bulbs.—Some of the many varieties can be in flower all the year, as described in the chapter on seasonable work. The requirements for bulbs are loose, rather sandy soil, made rich where the roots are to form.

Specialities in Roses.—The number of kinds catalogued is unlimited. The great desideratum is, of course, to secure those which are of vigorous growth, good, healthy, and pleasing foliage, good-shaped flowers, and free-blooming disposition. Those qualities are found largely among the tea-scented and Noisette kinds, the following amongst them: Marechal Neil, golden yellow; Reine Marie Henriette, deep pink; Madame Mathilde Lenaerts, deep rose; Francisca Kruger, coppery yellow; Madame Lambard, salmon pink; Niphetos, pure white; Rubens, rosy white; Safrano, buff; Souvenir d'un Ami, rosy pink; The Bride, pure white; Jean Ducher, salmon yellow; Homer, rosy pink, very free; Catherine Mermet, rose; Alphonso Karr, bright crimson; Devoniensis, pale yellow; Lore Tarquin, rosy pink; Madame de Watteville, rosy white; The Queen, white; the Meteor, dark crimson; Madame C. Kuster, pale yellow. For climbing or pillar roses: William Allen Richardson, orange yellow; Lamarque, sulphur yellow.

These and many others are reliable for garden decoration and for cut flowers.

Climbers.—They will, as a rule, require deep, moderately good soil, and sufficient trellis, frame, wall, stake, or other support. That shown in the illustration may be brought into use for many purposes. It is simply a row of posts, say 10 feet apart, the end posts being stayed firmly. Over the top a stout wire is fastened, and two other stout wires are stretched along the ground from two to three feet from the posts as shown. Strings or wires are then arranged between the ground and the wire on top, and to these latter the plants are trained. Concerning varieties, the seedsmen catalogues offer much information.

A Simple Pretty Trellis.

Saving Seed.—To secure strong, full-grown vigorous seeds too many should not be allowed to mature on any plant, and then every flower can be saved for seed bearing. To leave a few pods along the bottom of the stem for maturing seed after picking off the best flowers is bad practice. When several pods are left to ripen, the strength of the plant is absorbed by them, and the growth is consequently checked. This is as correct of flower seeds as vegetables, beans, peas, &c.

Plants from Cuttings.—One of the most satisfactory methods of propagation. We can depend upon plants from cuttings being identical with the parent plants from which they were taken, whether they are for foliage, flower, or fruit bearing. A cutting from young wood is the most likely to grow. It should have from four to six buds. Sandy soils answer best for this kind of propagating, and shade and shelter from drying winds with moderate watering help them to root. Roots are also got by suspending the cuttings in water in bottles. It is an old-fashioned method, but as effective as ever. The process of root forming is shown in the second illustration. The sap travelling downwards, as it does, gathers at the bottom, where a "callus" forms. From this the first root germs are sent out, and when they get into open free soil, with sufficient nourishment, roots are formed as shown in the third illustration. Some plants make second and third tiers of roots, which spring from the buds higher up and it may be necessary to cut them off.

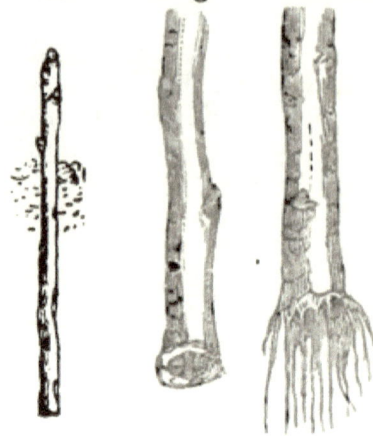

The Cutting. How Roots Form.

Propagating by Layers.—Many kinds of trees and shrubs can be increased by layers in a temperature equivalent to that of which they are natives. Springtime—July to September—is a good time of the year for this kind of propagation. A layer is a branch bent into the earth, and three parts of the layered wood are cut through at the bend by a long sloping cut; it is, in fact, a cutting only partially separated from its parent. The layer will emit roots into the soil at the cut or tongue. The sap forms cellular tissue on the tongue at the cut part, which ultimately throws out roots. When rooted, the new plant may be severed from the parent and set out where required. Should the cut show a tendency to close, it may be kept open by inserting a grain of wheat or maize, a piece of gravel or charcoal; when the soil is heavy or stiff, the cut part should be covered with light sandy soil. Oranges, lemons, figs and other fruits can be successfully propagated by layers.

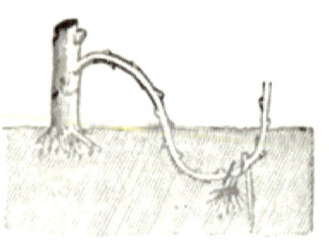

Layering.

Plants from the Leaf.—Gloxinias, foliage begonias, some of the gesneras, and other plants can be propagated from their leaves. The gloxinia leaf makes buds freely, which develop flowers next season. It is from the ribs of

Leaf Throwing out Roots.

the leaf taken from the plant when in the full vigor of growth that roots develop. If several plants are required from one leaf, the mid rib on the under surface of the leaf should be notched in several places. This under surface is then placed on the soil, the mid-rib slightly pressed in and pegged down to keep it firm without any soil over it. At each fracture of the rib a little callus develops and quickly throws out roots.

Leaves and Buds.—Leaves of the rose, camelia, the orange family, and others strike when treated as for leaf growth in moisture and warmth, but although they make roots under such favourable conditions they do not seem to have the power to form buds. Few plants can form another of its species without first organising a bud—the necessary step in the process of multiplication. Buds spring exclusively from the soft pulpy or cellular matter that constitutes the flesh of plants, and not from their solid woody parts. This cellular matter is formed by nature out of organisable fluids largely formed in the leaves, hence it follows that leaves are really the great agencies of propogation in any case, whether cuttings, layers, or other methods of multiplication are followed.

How We Improved the Place.—It was rather nice when we got it; that is, there were nice trees and shrubs about it, but not so healthy as could be, and the arrangement in planting was too formal—looked too stiff; not enough homelike. So we went to work upon it, and with such will that there was all the enjoyment experienced which can be got out of work which improves and adorns the home. The first improvement was made by draining the land. There are about two acres in all, and upon this three tons of quicklime were spread. It was thought by some who were observing the operations that the lime would kill every plant it touched. But not it! What a change that liming and draining has made on the place! Truly enough, lime is food for plants. During May, June, July, we commenced changing the position of the trees and shrubs, and adding others. We commenced early, you will see, which is a good plan where you can, before the season is over, and prune back closely. All of which we did; and how the plants have flourished! After an absence of a year, I scarcely knew the place—it is a veritable Australian home!

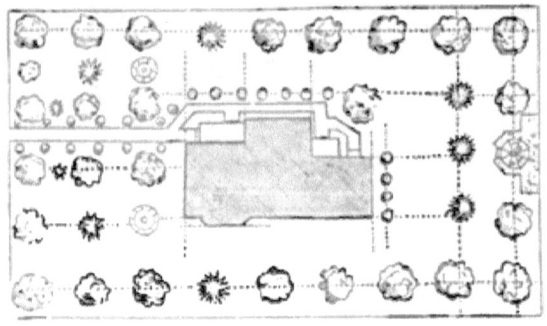

The Arrangement as We Got It.

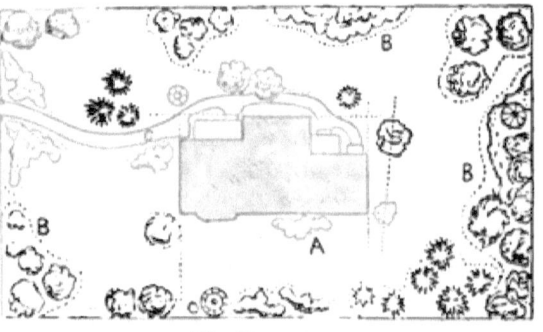

The Place Now.

Packing Cut Flowers.—In the first place, gather the

flowers either very early in the morning, or the last thing at night. Then put them away in water till wanted, in order that they may absorb all the moisture to keep them fresh through their travels. Wooden boxes are more suitable than those of cardboard for packing flowers. They may cost a trifle more, but the extra outlay will be well worth the better condition in which the flowers are preserved. When possible place at the bottom of the box a sheet of dry, not damp, cotton wool, and over this lay a sheet of soft tissue paper, on which to arrange the flowers in rows, taking care that the head of each rests immediately over the stem of the preceding one. Avoid the mistake of overcrowding. The box ought to be about ten inches in depth, and should not contain more than one layer of flowers, or the results may be disappointing. When sending ferns, put them at the bottom of the box, placing soft paper between them and the flowers. Maidenhair should be kept very moist when packed. A "refresher" in common use for keeping up the freshness of cut flowers is nitrate of potash, or sweet nitre ; $\frac{1}{4}$oz. per pint of water is about right. The same "refresher" is good for growing plants as well, but it is then applied to the soil of course.

XXII.—FRUIT AND VEGETABLE PRESERVING.

THE PROSPECT.—This branch of agriculture offers many inducements for the most careful application of skill that can be brought to bear upon it. The demand for fruits preserved by bottling, canning, drying, candying or crystallising ; and as jams, jellies, and other preserves, is unlimited. The right materials are here to supply the demand. With the facilities available for carriage, the market for Australian fruit preserves is unlimited.

Requirements for Success.—Properly matured first class fruits of the kinds in demand ; pure, white Australian cane sugar ; the necessary appliances for preserving ; attractive methods of marketing are all necessary for the full development of this trade.

The Fruits.—Nearly all the varieties held in favour in Europe and America are already grown in Australia, and several others that offer sufficient attractions. New varieties—possibly too many—are coming continuously into notice, and amongst them, occasionally, are sorts which prove more suitable than what had been grown previously. Cane sugar of the very best quality is also available.

Contents of Fruits and Vegetables.—When ripe, water has the lead in all varieties, the proportions ranging from 60 to 90lb. of water in 100lb. of fruit; carbon and sugar come next in most fruits, then minerals, acids, and the various flavourings peculiar to each. The latter are all important, and it is the aim of the fruit preserver to secure all of the flavouring, and lose as little as possible of the sugar. The water is the substance he deals with most decisively. It is the part of fruit which carries with it the greatest risks. By controlling the water contents, fruits can be preserved for lengthy periods. But before the stage of ripeness is reached, fruits undergo various chemical changes, in which the mineral contents got from the soil, and starches in various forms, play important parts. The result in the processes of maturing being the peculiar flavour of each fruit.

Stages of Fruit Growth.—There are three well defined stages in fruit growth. At first the fruit embryo is much like the leaf in its tree life, taking up carbon from the air, and giving out oxygen; but the fruit is all the time helped by the leaves. In the ripening stage, the fruit reverses its action; takes up oxygen and gives off carbonic acid, after storing its quantity of carbon. The fruit flavourings are developed during the ripening; also the sugar, acids, and alkaloids. The full sugar change occurs mostly after growth ceases. In some fruit considerable change arises at the time the size is increasing. In grapes the acid becomes alkaloid, and decreases in proportion to the development of sugar. Some fruits ripen to perfection on the plant, as grapes, bananas, &c.; others mature better after picking. Raspberries, strawberries, blackberries, and pears gain in this way. The grape does not ripen after being taken from the vine, but evaporation may remove a considerable portion of the water and thus improve the flavour. Most apples follow a middle course—partly ripening in the fruit house—as do oranges and lemons generally. After fruit is matured, we may wish to keep it for use, either fresh, dried, or preserved. But the natural fruit ferments become active in ripening, and continue their work afterward. Then there are minute fungus growths, always ready to operate upon ripe fruit, and especially while all the natural moisture is present.

Fallen and Bruised Fruits.—When fruits drop from the tree they quickly begin to decay. Fungus and other growths attack and destroy them. When bruised, the decay is still more rapid, and no process of preserving can rectify the damage or improve the quality. Damaged fruits that have been preserved decay rapidly when opened. The question of when to gather fruits, and how to preserve them, are closely related. The success of the latter depends on the former.

Preservative Agencies.—The aids available are *heat* to destroy fungus growths, or by evaporating such portion of the water as may be necessary; *cold* to check bacterial or ferment action; or *drying* to reduce moisture and consequent risks in that direction. Further, there is the process of excluding the air, and its spore contents by bottling or tinning, and so shut out the cause of decay.

Supplies for Home Use First.—In warm climates we should have fruit, fresh or preserved, on the table with every meal. It is more wholesome than meat, and we can use it more often. Fruits and vegetables contain all the requirements of healthy life, in their best forms. To eat fruit half-a-dozen times a day is not too often, during hot spells. Nature suggests at such times to eat little but often, and in fruit we have both meat and drink. Stewing is the foundation process for the home table. Use plenty of sugar, and then see how old and young revel in the wholesome seasonable change. Fruit on the tables of the growers is a most effective way of convincing other people of how good fruit diet is.

Bottling may be our first step in preserving. Apricots, peaches, plums, pears, quinces, cumquats, cherries, marmalade, jams, &c., are possible, and without stint for use when fruit is scarce. There is no unapproachable secret and but small expense in bottling. The process is simple, and depends on the fruit being sound to start with; then sorted properly, and, either in the bottles or in the preserving pan, heated to the boiling point until cooked, according to the nature of the fruit. All germs which cause decay are thus destroyed. The bottle is sealed while hot and the contents may then keep for years. Apricots should be split in halves, peaches stripped of their skins by dipping them in a boiling bath of water, with 2 to 6 ozs. caustic soda per gallon of water; or a sufficient quantity of stronger or weaker soda to make an effective skin stripping bath. Then dip the fruit in cold water, and the skins slip off, leaving the fruit beautifully smooth.

Time for Cooking.—Judgment and practice soon give the necessary experience. The following will be found helpful, the variation depending on ripeness, appliances, &c. Apricots, take from three to ten minutes; peaches, six to twelve minutes; cumquats and pears, from ten to fifteen minutes; quinces, twenty minutes; plums, from ten to twenty minutes; cherries, from five to twelve minutes. The covers or tops are put on while the contents are boiling hot, in order to secure a vacuum, by the condensing of the steam. In bottles closed up when in this condition there will be no mould or other sign of decay after long keeping. Soft tough parchment paper or paper dipped in spirits, quickly applied, and tightly bound on while hot, and a coat of some waxy material put on afterwards, answers well; but bottles with spring or screw tops are handy, reliable, and not costly.

Sugar or Syrup.—So far as acting as a preservative, sugar or syrup has but little effect. The quantity used is matter of taste. From 6 to 20 oz. sugar per pound of fruit is used, but the flavour is injured and the sugar as well by cooking fruit and sugar together. This part of the subject will be dealt with separately in syrup making for preserving, candying, &c.

Without Syrup.—Quince, pear, clingstone peach, currants, gooseberries, and other fruits that have distinctive flavourings and sufficient body, may be bottled or canned without syrup, the space being filled with boiling water, and the contents closed to secure a vacuum, as in other cases.

Heating Bottles.—This is usually done by placing them in cold water, which is brought gradually to the boil; but, with practice, bottles can be heated while held in the hand, ready for receiving cooked, boiling hot fruit, by gradually heating them with warm and then with hot water.

Heated Air Process.—Fruits are cooked by heated air and then bottled or canned.

Canning.—Bottling was the predecessor of canning. Cans of tin were first used by fish curers in the north of Scotland; by them brought into use in Nova Scotia, and other of the British-American settlements. The process has been improved and extended enormously in America. In Australia it is used largely for meat preserving, and is equally adapted for fruits, vegetables, white sugar corn, peas, and other products.

Grading and Stoning Fruit.—In the factories, fruit is graded, or sorted, into sizes, and for appearance. It is then pitted, pared, or skinned, as may be required, dipped in clean, cold water, drained, and packed neatly into the cans by women mostly. The cans are then filled to the very top with syrup of strength according to the grade or quality of the fruit. The top is soldered on, a very small hole in the centre of the cover being left

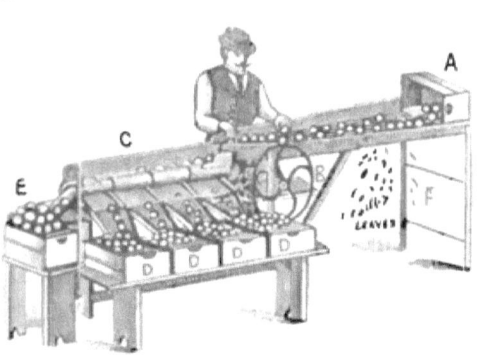

Grading Fruit into Sizes.

open. The cans are then lowered into a cooking bath, which may be water only, or some substance as lime or salt, to give more heat, when tough fruits are being handled. As in bottling, the time allowed for cooking varies from five to twenty minutes. The cans are then raised, steam issuing from the top. The hole is then soldered close, and the cans are dipped in cold water, to secure a vacuum. They are then put in a hot testing room, and should no change occur they are scoured, labelled, and painted, and sent out the handsome tinned goods in such general use. Machines are used for stoning and pitting fruit in the factories.

Stoning or Pitting Fruit.

FRUIT DRYING.—This process is peculiarly adapted for Australian fruits. The requirements are not expensive. From £5 to £10 covers the cost of such a dryer as shown in the illustration. It is made of iron or timber. It may be of any desired size, say from 6ft. high by 4ft. in front, and 4ft. deep, or any larger size required. The open door shows arrangement of trays on which the fruit is spread. Below is a stove, or fire, which may be arranged on the ground, the smoke passing away in a chimney behind. The fruit is either pared (as apples), cut (as apricots, pears, &c.), or dried whole. Many other forms of dryers are in use. In

A Simple Fruit Dryer.

California, where fruit drying is an enormous business, scores of designs are seen. In Victoria and South Australia, drying houses of sun-dried clay, stone, brick, iron, and timber are in use.

American Dryer.—Mr. Frank Coffee, of the Universal Nursery, Wahroonga, has introduced a rapid working and effective dryer of the American type. The fruit is inserted at the front (A) and can be returned from the back (E D). G are the frames used. They are made of wood, as a rule, iron being likely to color the fruit. Sizes to fit openings of 4 feet are found to be handy and workable.

American Dryer.

The Shelton Dryer.—Professor Shelton, of Queensland, has arranged a dryer in which the fruit trays are placed upon racks on endless chains, so that any desired degree of temperature can be regulated. The trays are moved by the lever, seen in the front view of the machine. Their

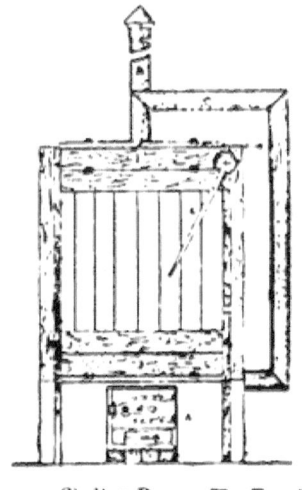

Shelton Dryer—The Front.

Shelton Dryer—Inside.

position is shown in the second illustration. The ground plan shows the furnace, or fire box, and arrangements for heating and passing off the smoke.

Home Dryers.—Machines have been arranged for drying with the aid of the heat of a kitchen stove or fire place. But they proved too slow in operation for profitable use. Sufficient size is required in all cases to secure a rapid current of heated air.

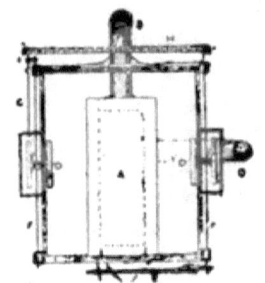

Shelton Dryer—Ground Plan.

A Portable Dryer.—The size is 7ft. long, and the same in height to the eaves, and 4ft. wide. The frame is made in three sections of 2in. by 4in. scantling, one for each end, and one for the centre. The whole of the further end and the back of the dryer are enclosed with tongued and grooved stuff, allowing the centre board to extend a foot above the peak to help to form the upper ventilation. The other end is covered in the same manner to within 2½ft. from the ground, which is closed with sheet iron. On each side at the bottom a 4in. space is left to admit air. If the draught is at any time too strong, a piece of iron or board can be set against the opening on the windward side. The front side has an 8in. strip along the eaves to allow the roof boards to extend over without interfering with the trays, or the door (E);

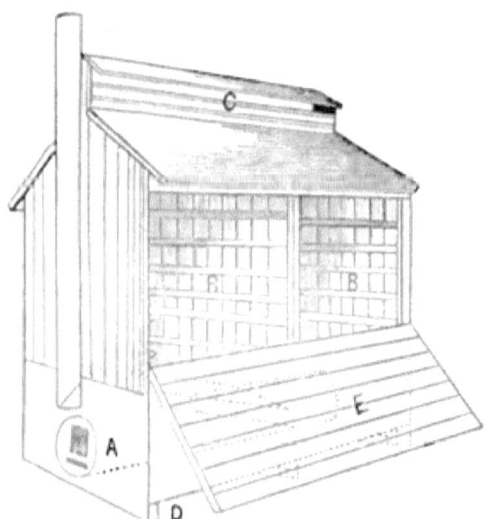

Simplicity Fruit and Vegetable Dryer.

this latter being hinged at the lower edge; the upper edge being held in place when closed by buttons on the eave strip. Into this open space, the fruit trays are slipped on pieces nailed to the sides, care being taken to fill up the spaces behind the slats, so that the hot air cannot pass without going through the fruit.

Drying Trays.—They are made of timber; or strong wire netting for the bottoms. Three feet eight inches square is a good workable size, leaving a space for the heat to pass around the ends and a 4in. space in front; the second tray is kept forward so as to leave the same space at the back, and is on the top. This arrangement gives a strong current of hot air between the trays. For the stove or heater, two cast-iron heads, 15in. diameter, form the ends, having flanges for sheet iron; one head, as in illustration, (page 287), has a door for wood, and below a draught hole. The sheet iron cylinder for the fire is made with a stove-pipe hole on each side near the back end. This machine dries 500lbs. in apples or peaches a day. Where an 18in. or 26in. cylinder is used, spaces for three sets of trays are placed, thus allowing of longer return pipes, saving more of the heat, and allowing more work to be done.

Circular Dryer.

The Drying Medium.—It is the same, heated air, in all cases. Sun drying is risky and uncertain. Currents of heated dry air are arranged to pass under, through, and over the fruit in the dryers, extracting the moisture, until just sufficient is left to have the fruit flexible. The more water that can be left in with safety, the better the quality of the fruit. But that point of safety may mean that from two-thirds to nine-tenths of the whole weight has to be extracted. Thus from 7 to 10lb. of apples, make 1lb. dried; from 2½ to 5lb. plums make 1lb. dried prunes, and others proportionately. Ripe well grown fruit giving the highest returns.

Time and Heat in Drying.—From four to ten hours, according to the fruit contents of water, and the capacity of the machine to send through heated air, from 120deg. to 220deg. The greatest heat is applied to the fresh fruit, until signs of wilting are seen, in say, fifteen to thirty minutes.

Advantages of Drying. — Less cost for appliances; suitability for small as well as large quantities; convenience and lower cost of carriage. As a rule the weight is reduced 75 per cent.; or 100lb. is converted into 25lb., which retain nearly all the properties of the fruit, except the water. The water is restored for use as required by soaking the dried fruit over night.

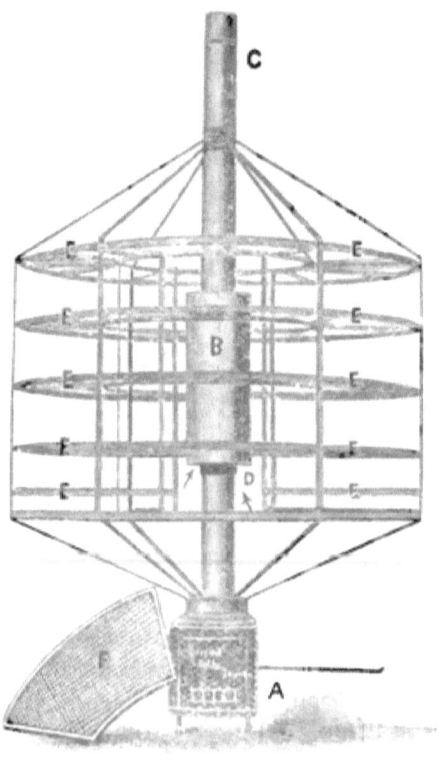

Circular Dryer—Inside Arrangement.

Drying in the Sun.—There are always risks from change of weather, flies, &c., and sun drying may occupy from five to twenty days, involving much labour. In some cases a combination of sun and dryer is carried out. And rough drying is done in big bush chimneys in cases.

Open Air Drying.—This is possible in very dry parts. The process of drying illustrated shows how trays

Drying on Lucerne, in the Open Air.

of fruit are so arranged, on mown lucerne or grass, that dust is warded off, and covers can be dropped over a number of cases, from a central point, by connecting the covers with wire or rope. But open air drying is always risky, as even a shower or heavy dew discolours the fruit.

Drying Potatoes, Tomatoes, Herbs.—Potatoes dry nicely, and are in active demand on stations, at the goldfields, and other places. The potatoes are washed, and peeled by means of a machine similar to an apple parer. They are then boiled, then broken up, not too fine, spread evenly on trays, and placed in a dryer. The drying process takes about ten hours, at temperature of about 140 deg. When the contents of the trays are thoroughly dry, they are exposed to the air in a cooling chamber, then ground to about the consistency of bonemeal, and packed in tins for export. The great advantage in boiling the potatoes previous to evaporating, is that they are much more easily prepared for table afterwards, and very much less water is required, the latter being a very important consideration in places where water is scarce. The potato meal does not require soaking before being used. Four cupfuls of water are added to one cupful of potato, boil for ten minutes, and the product is ready for use. It cannot then be distinguished from potatoes cooked in the ordinary way.

Tomatoes are dried at a lower temperature, as are vegetables, herbs, &c. The process here for tomatoes is to cut the fruit into sections, which are placed, cut side up, on the ordinary drying trays, and put out in the sun, then finished in the dryer. In Italy, where large quantities of tomatoes are dried, they are put into coarse cloth bags through which the pulp is squeezed, leaving the skins and seeds in the bag. The pulp is spread on boards and dried in the sun. When dried, it is packed in boxes for export. It is largely used in soups.

Prunes, Raisins, Figs, &c.—The plum (the prune d'agen is considered the best) when ripe, is shaken off the trees (p. 292). The prunes are then dipped in a hot lye made of potash ¼lb. to gallon. The illustration shows a contrivance for dipping on a large scale. The tank (A) contains the lye; by means of tackling the dipper (B) is lowered into the tank, and, when sufficiently treated, is raised as at (C), and discharged upon tables. The fruit is then sorted and dried. Prunes are among the very nicest of dessert relishes and food.

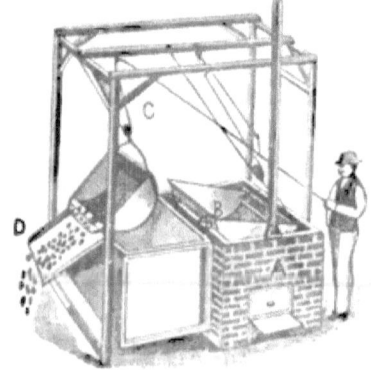

Dipping Prunes.

To prepare the fruit for the table, it is soaked in cold water over night. It swells to the size of the original plums, and is then stewed. Raisins are dried partly in the sun; then finished in the dryer. In the French method of curing prunes, each grower, as a rule, dries his produce in an oven sufficiently to keep for about two weeks. The prunes are then sold to factories, where they are fully cured. After being graded by use of wire screens they are packed in long hollow metal tubes; after being filled, a cap is screwed on to make them airtight. The tubes are put in an air drum, low temperature steam is turned on, and the prunes are thus "cooked" for a longer or shorter time, according to the size of the fruit, at a temperature of about 210 deg. When cold, they are ready to pack for market.

The Californian sun-dried prune is delicious when stewed, while the French being already cooked in the

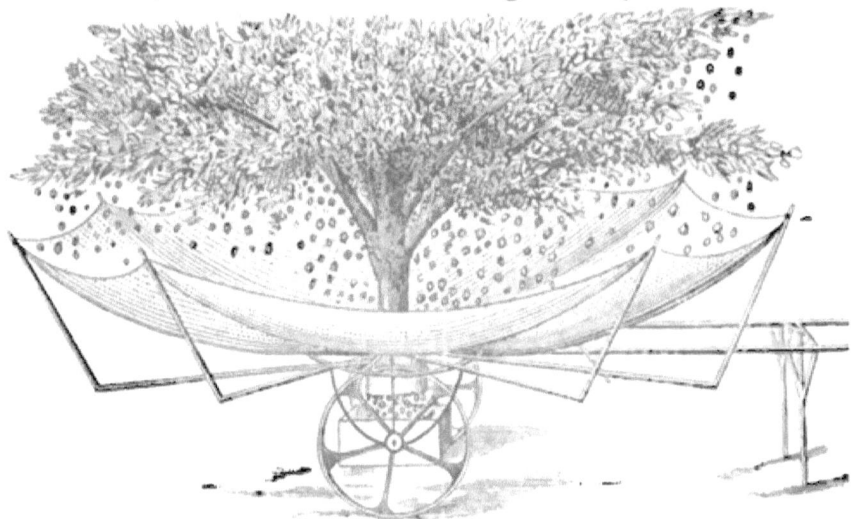

Harvesting Prunes for Drying.

process of curing, tastes well before stewing, but becomes rather bitter afterwards. But French operators can be profitably followed in their method of grading.

Sulphuring.—When fruit is cut it loses colour. This is the effect of oxidation or contact with the air upon the exposed parts. To check this action, sulphur fumes are brought to bear as in a bleaching process. The effect is very decided upon cut fruits that have to be dried. In operation, the fruit trays are put in such numbers as may be required in a close box. Sulphur fumes are got either by burning sulphur in the box or in an outside burner, the fumes or smoke being brought into the box through a tube. The colder the fumes are the better. Half a pound of sulphur is enough for 50lb. of fruit, and 10 to 30 minutes completes the operation. The fruit is then dried as desired. During the drying, the sulphur disappears.

Candying or Crystalising.—This process is amongst the most attractive and elegant for fruits, lemon, orange, and other peels, ginger, &c. Only thoroughly matured and undamaged fruits are suitable. The fruits are, in the cooking stages, treated as for bottling or canning. Then saturated in cold syrup and dried to crystalisation stage, as with peels. Peels, gingers, &c., that contain oils, earthy, or other flavourings that have to be got rid of, are first soaked in salt and water from 10 to 30 hours to get rid of the undesirable flavour. The fruit is then washed to clear off as much as possible of the salt. Then "cooked" in fresh water, strained, and dried. It may be necesssary to change the water in cooking several times to extract all the salt. Then drain the fruit and put it into a first syrup. The action of this syrup is to displace the water in the fruit The time for first saturation depends upon the nature of the fruit, from two hours to six days. But in any case the syrup has to be changed as soon as signs of fermentation appear. A second syrup is then substituted for the first, and after another saturation, a third syrup displaces the second, and a fourth or fifth when neccessary, by which time the fruit, peel, cumquats, ginger, or other material should be saturated with sugar. The finishing syrup, No. 5, is boiling hot when the fruit is put into it, the time for amalgamating the two depending again upon the nature of the fruit. When saturated, the fruit is taken out and dried, rapidly or slowly according to whether it is to be glazed or crystallised. For the latter purpose sugar may be sifted upon the fruit as much as will stick. For peels, cumquats, figs, ginger, &c., the finishing syrup is allowed to crystalise.

Syrup.—A key to success for most of the canned and crystalised fruits, indeed for fruit preserving generally, and jam-making as well, is got in the treatment of the sugar or syrup. Only the whitest cane sugar is suitable. Beet sugar is risky. No. 1 syrup is made by dissolving in boiling water 1 part of sugar in 3 parts of water—3lb. of sugar in 1 gallon of water is a standard syrup for canned fruits. No. 2, 1 to 2; No. 3, 1 to 1; No. 4, 2 of sugar to 1 of water; No. 5, the strongest syrup made, is 3 of sugar to 1 of water. The sugar is heated before amalgamating, where practicable. The nearer it is to the temperature of boiling water the better. As soon as the sugar is absorbed, the syrup is ready. It is then quite clear, there is no loss of flavour or colour by carmalising or burning. Syrups of any required strength are added to the fruit in the various stages of cooking and preserving as described.

Temperature in Syrup Making.—The thermometer is useful in manipulating sugar. When reduced to syrup in the boiling state there is a marked increase of heat. At 215 to 218 degrees fruit with sugar is in the most effective jellying stage; it is smooth, slippery, and does not candy or granulate. This is the "small thread" stage in sugar making. At 220 to 228 degrees granulation sets in—the "large thread" stage. At 231 degrees we have crystalisation—"small pearl"; at 232-3 "large pearl"—candying.

Pop Corn.—Great fun and a wholesome edible is got by roasting or "popping" the kernels of the pretty little pop corn which grows well wherever other corn grows. Put the dry kernels in a deep fry pan; a "popper," or a covered pan is better. A slow heat is best at first, then increase it, and the kernels burst out into great balls of flour like substance. They are nice that way, and better when dropped into No. 5 syrup boiling hot. As coated, they are taken out and allowed to candy. Dry sugar may be shaken over them to make crystalised pop corn.

Marmalade.—Seville oranges, lemons, and citrons are used. Wipe the fruit, slice thinly, picking out the seeds. Use all the juice, and one third or more of the skin. Water is then added, the quantity being dependent upon the fruit and season, the proportions varying from 30ozs. (1½-pint) water to 3¾lbs. water to each lb. fruit, which is allowed to soak in the water for 12 hours, or longer in cold weather. Then boil; by steam heat in jacketed pans is best. When the fruit is nearly cooked, add sugar, heated, as in syrup making, say 1½ to 3½lbs. for each lb. of fruit. Then boil until the marmalade sets as a jelly when cooled, a trial portion being dropped on a plate for test purposes.

Shaddocks make extra fine, clear marmalade, but the pith has to be removed with the seeds. Quince, and tart apple are also used, the skins being cooked with the fruit.

Jams and Jellies.—Use ripe sound fruit only. For jelly use drip or jelly bags saturated first in hot water. Cook in jacketed pans, without which there is not sufficient control of the temperature. Cook at first in the juice, or by adding water where necessary, as quinces. Add the sugar from ¾ to 1½lb. for each lb. of the fruit, without checking the boiling, and cook till the jam or jelly sets when tested. The thermometer, as in marmalade making, is useful in boiling.

Straining for Jelly.

Flavorings and Colorings.—Much can be done by skilful blending of fruit juices; as a flavoring of lemon, grape, &c., in apple jelly; or the stones of peach, apricot, plum, &c., for flavoring those fruits. Brown and reddish colorings are got from caramel and cochineal; golden from annetto, saffron, and tumeric; blue, green, and other colors are also got, but not from safe materials, and none of them are natural. Different colors are also got by inserting glazed paper in the centre of the jars, filling each side with the jelly, and withdrawing the paper, soon as the contents are set sufficiently.

"Curing" Fruits.—Lemons, pears. etc., are improved by being stored in dry, airy places, where a portion of their natural moisture is evaporated.

XXIII.—ATTRACTIONS OF PLANT LIFE.

RUDIMENTARY BOTANY.—All mankind, or nearly all, and all womankind at some stage of existence, have taken such interest in plant life as might have induced them to master the rudiments of botany. And many follow up the pursuit sufficiently to make it a source of life-long enjoyment. As a step towards the desire to know more of plant growth, a book or books on botany may have been purchased —most works of that kind are valuable; but not one can give all the information required by reading only—not for a first, second, or even a third reading. That is got by close study of the principles laid down, and by cultivating acquaintance with the subjects—the orders of plants described. When investigation is added to reading, the knowledge is got as we proceed, and plant life opens out into paths even as attractive as animal life.

Commencing Early.

Botanical Classification.—To the specialist, minute classification upon the lines followed by botanists in all lands is necessary. Many of the terms and names employed —difficult though they may seem—are really more closely descriptive of the plants in view than even the "plain English" common names and terms which it will be our effort to use at this stage. Botanical science terms may follow after. Thus *annual plants*, or annuals, are those that grow from seed and flower, and mature seed again in one season, or during one year. We may at once recognise many plants of that nature, such as poppies, cosmos, corn, and scores of others. *Bi-annuals* are plants that live over one year, but not over two; and *perennials* include the great mass of shrubs climbers, and trees which live longer than two years. This arrangement seems so simple that the question is quite natural, " Then why use Latin terms in any form when common terms are so effective ? Why not call corn, just corn, and be done with it ?" And that may answer by-and-bye, when all the world speaks the same language, and all are equally agreed as to the common name, and which plant is described when we say "corn." But the corn of Australia may be so very different from the corn of other lands. And the Australian ash tree is different from the ash of Great Britain ; ours is a gum, and our apple tree is closely allied to the eucalyptus, and wholly distinct in every way from the apple tree that bears apples, the only apple tree known to myriads of people. Numberless other instances tell us that if every country were to name its plants in " plain language " in the way that seemed best to them, hopeless confusion would ensue, and botanical identification would be impossible.

Classification by Methods of Growth.—Another easily understood arrangement is that which separates plants which increase in size from the inside (botanically termed *endogens*). This includes the great families of grasses, grain yielders, and others. Then another great family, the *exogens*, grow from the outside, and include shrubs, trees, and plants with bark generally. The third great family are *acrogens*, which include ferns, the fungus tribe, lichens, and others that do not flower, and many of which live on other plants.

Life Development of Plants.— The illustration explains the process of plant life generally. In the first stage of development from the perfect seed (*a*), warmth, moisture, and air are all necessary for the changes that follow (*b c*). Then the seed leaf (the *plumule* of

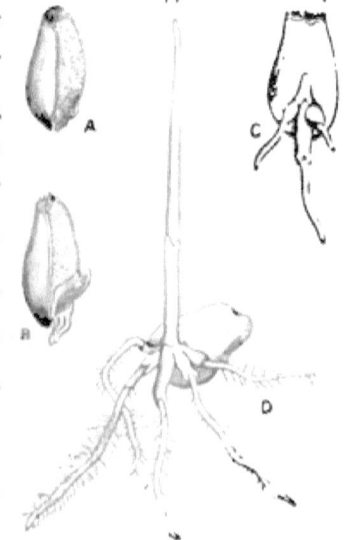

First Stages of Plant Life.

botanists) comes up out of the soil. At the same time rootlets, the *radicles (d)* are developing underground. All new plants spring from seed, and the seed must be sufficiently sound and matured to nourish the young plant to the stage described, whether it be the seed of a tiny daisy or the beginning of a huge gum tree.

Leaf Growth.—When the seed is right and its surroundings healthy for plant life, leaf growth follows the appearance of the *plumule (a)* above ground. Leaves *(b d)* are of many kinds, some long, some short, some oval, some round, some with saw-like edges, some are quite smooth and plain, and each form has its name in botany, and can be identified anywhere. But all leaves have the same work to do—there is work for all useful life. The leaves are the lungs of plants. It may seem strange, but the bulk of the solid

Development of Leaf Growth.

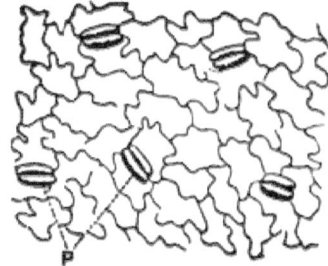

Breathing Pores of Leaf.

Leaf Breathing.

matter of plants, the stems, timber, and bark, from wheat to oak trees, is supplied through the leaves. For the air supplies most of the solid food material of plants. What a great garden ground is thus opened up for the inquirer!

Flowers Tell Something.—What hosts of flowering plants we can see! Annuals, bulbs, climbers, roses, fruit trees, grasses. Those that flower are by far the most numerous. And the colours tell a good deal concerning odours and scents. The pinks, red and white, smell most sweetly, the darker colours less so. And there are great families of plants that do not flower; the *acrogens*, which include with others the ferns, mushrooms, lichens, mosses, and many more, are a most interesting host.

Flower Development.—Flowers mean much to the botanist the gardener, the florist, the bee keeper, the

In Flower.

farmer, and all who take a real interest in plant growth. That is, who look upon them as things of life interest as well as things of beauty or of profit. The colour of flowers that open at night is generally white, that night flying moths see and come for the sweets in them. Pale red flowers are liked by bees, and flies and beetles also search them for sweet sap; brown flowers are attractive to wasps; and pink, red, yellow and white flowers, by pollen storing and pollen eating insects. Bees gather the floury substance actively, and carry it home as food material for their young. And while doing this, they also fertilize the plants they are collecting from, and so aid in giving us flowers and fruit. The pollen is the active fertilizing material of plant life, but it must come in contact with the pistil, the central organ seen in the accompanying illustration, and bees and other insects, the winds and other agencies, help in the process. Thus the

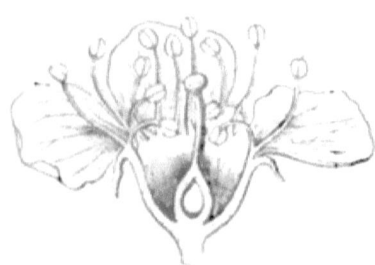

Development of Seed

"fruit" of botanists, that is the seed, is formed below the pistil. But some plants—notably some varieties of strawberries—have not got both of these organs. Some have the pollen, others have none. The former are termed staminate, (with stamens), or pollen bearers. Those without pollen, are termed pistillate. While referring to the strawberry, and the rule applies to other plants as well, it becomes useful in the practical sense to know that both kinds of flowers are necessary in order to get crops of fruit; and that very serious losses and disappointment have occurred through weeding out the pistillate, the seemingly more delicate plants. Careful Mother Nature! How well she knows the importance of each part of the most marvellously complicated of plant life. Thus the pollen of grasses growing in or near water is arranged to resist the dissolving effects of water, which, as a rule, melts pollen generally. Then the many means which flowers possess, for the protection of this so valuable pollen from rain and dew, are never ending sources of delight and wonderment to the keen observer. The closing of flowers at night, the drooping or nodding of flowers, the possession of sheathing sheltering apparatus for the arching of portions of the flower leaf over the stamens, are all instances of nature's care for plant life. In some poppies, the flowers roll up at night over the pollen which has been shed upon them during the day. In others there are parts that act like a brush, sweeping the pollen out of its case towards the pistil, so that the winds may carry it to its destination. In the camphor laurel, the pollen cases close in wet weather, and so shield the grains from injury. Flowers fertilized by the agency of the wind are generally thin and narrow in form and leaf, and quiet in color. Some are borne on trees which flower before the formation of the leaves, others are on lowly plants with long narrow leaves, so that there may be few obstacles to the pollen laden breezes. The fertilization of corn and fruit trees is mostly managed by bees, which also fertilize clover and lucerne; arums by flies and bees, and hibiscus by ants and flies. This latter family include the apparently distant relatives, the jam yielding rosella, and the somewhat underrated *sida retusa*, or "Paddy's lucerne," of which several varieties are of Australian origin.

Hybridisation.—That intensely interesting and practical branch of botanical usefulness, by which such wonderful results are got in flowers and fruits, is dependent upon the transfer of pollen grains by artificial means from plant to plant. The process offers such attractions!

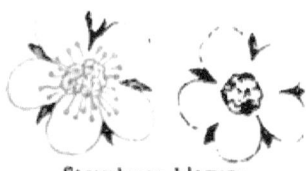
Strawberry Flowers
(staminate and pistillate).

Orchid Life.—This curious family of plants (for which Australia is specially notable) offers most interesting

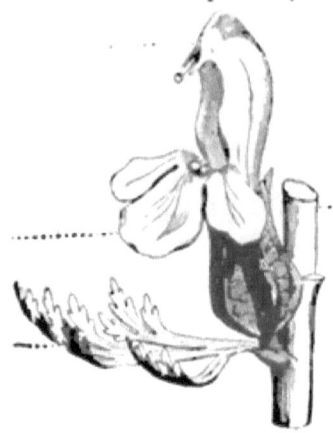

botanical study. There are two distinctive branches of orchids, one of which grows from the ground like other plants, and has lily, or iris-like leaves, as a rule. The others are epiphytes, which means those plants that lodge upon or grow upon others by a system of hair-like grippers, having bulb-like terminations. The pollen and pistillate arrangements of the family, as a rule, are such as make insect action for their development a necessity. Without this insect help, orchids would have passed out of existence, as many other families of plants have done, and we would have none of the butterfly, bee, beetle, spider, boot, slipper, or other curious forms taken by those wonderfully attractive flowers.

The Pea Family.—The "legumes" of botanists are classified by bearing the seeds in pods. It is a family of immense extent, forming a thirtieth part of the known plant life of the world. The welcome pea of our gardens, the lucerne and the mighty Moreton Bay chestnut, the wattles and myals of the Australian bush come into this order.

Australian Gums.—The eucalyptus—another great family—are classified in a general way by their bark. The gums usually are the smooth-bark trees. The leaves and timbers aid in the classification and are peculiar. The oily sacs of the leaves, which contain the essential odors of the family, are visible when held to a bright light. Some of the leaves are richly scented, and all are healthful.

Figs.—This is another curious family, especially in the formation of the seeds and fruit. Australian plants of this order have been termed vegetable snakes or pythons, by reason of the enormous strength of some of the family, which crush and absorb the largest gum trees within their snake-like limbs. The origin of these trees may arise from the deposit of a single seed, small as that of a mustard seed, in the fork of a gigantic gum, far up. The fig seed germinates there, sends out thread like feelers or root fibres, which thicken and grow strong from what they gather in from the host plant and the air. In a brief time the tiny fibre becomes a strong rope-like substance, which reaches the earth, roots there, and swells and grows strong until, with the aid of other limbs, formed in the same manner, the great gum tree is surrounded, and is absorbed by the fig.

Why Should Plants Live on Animal Matter ?—In some cases the reason is very evident: There is not enough vegetable food in the soil where they are to support them. This is the case with a very curious family common enough in Australia, the *Drosera* of botanists, the sundews of gardeners. What a tale they tell the observing—that the soil is too poor, for some reason or other, to support vegetable life sufficiently for useful purposes. The definition, that "plants are organisms that remain stationary in and live upon the soil," is disturbed by microscopic and everyday observations. [*See illustration Page* 303.]

Jumping Seed of Grass.

Seeds Travel.— In Autumn, the air is thick at times with seeds, some borne on their own feathery wings, often from very distant places. And other seeds are sent in such masses along the ground by winds that they make immense banks along fences in the pastoral districts, and it is said that railway cuttings have been so filled with these masses, that the trains had to stop till they were cleared out. Many liguminous plants, and balsams, castor oil, and others, send their seeds to long distances, as the seed vessels come to maturity and spring open. The seed in the illustration is a type of several of our Western grasses which spring from place to place, until a nice moist, rich spot is reached, and there the seed locates and grows. But, all the time,

Animal Absorbing Plants.—[See Page 302].

it is telling a wonderful tale of the climate and rainfall of the location it belongs to. Some seeds are so coated with hard glass-like material that they may lie for months on the surface of the ground exposed to fierce sun heat and drying winds, and then, when rain comes, they spring from place to place, till the required spot is reached for their development into nourishing feed for stock.

How New Sorts of Plants Are Got.—Seed is the source. While heredity is a well-marked principle in vegetable life, there is a constant tendency to depart from the higher forms got by skilful treatment, sometimes for the better, oftener for the worse. The reversion may be in the form of a wildsport, or a distinct reproduction from a late or remote ancestor. The cabbage grower of to-day might scarcely recognise in the coarse wild collard of the sea-shores of northern Europe the parent of our improved varieties; nor the celery lover see his favourite in the bitter weed, as found in its native habitat; nor the epicure in water melons, the bitter indigenous fibry things found covering whole districts in Africa. The present development in plants is the result of selecting specimens. The wild carrot of the field was experimented with not long since, and after seven years of selection, high culture and skilful treatment, it developed into a root quite soft, juicy and palatable. Good sized and fairly edible tubers, after five years of cultivation, have been produced from the wild potato of Mexico. The originals of garden vegetables and garden flowers were caught, tamed and improved through cultivation and selection, covering longer or shorter periods of time. The same work of selection and improvement of good qualities in vegetables is yet going on, and more earnestly than ever before. We may, possibly, be going too fast, introducing many new things of little merit, rather than attending to the selection and perpetuation of reliable varieties that have proved suitable for this country. Seed growers know that the purest crops will sometimes develop very queer "sports." For instance, cabbage of apparently absolute purity may produce some plants like the wild collards of Denmark, which is a result of reversion alone. The grower is powerless to prevent this natural physiological freak.

Changing the Nature of Plants.—The fruiting season of plants has been changed by systematically picking off the flowers which appeared before or after the time required. Annual plants may be made perennial by persistently destroying the flower buds as they appear. This has been done with the cotton plant in Australia. Few plants except those which are distinctly woody, have perennial parts; in tubers, rhizomes, and bulbs, the older portions die after new portions have been formed. The power to produce offshoots or stolons is the real difference between annual and perennial herbaceous plants. Even in the case of those annuals which throw up only a single flower stalk, if the flower buds are removed before they expand, and the flower-stem cut up into sections, plants may be raised which will live for many years if annually treated in the same way.

Pleasures of Thought and Work.—And yet even the few changes of plant life, thus briefly outlined, may seem difficult at first. But let us consider the great difference, visible all through nature and the world we live in, even between one man and another—that one is poor and another rich, that one is strong and another weak, that one is sick and another well, that one knows a great many things and another very few; that one thinks much and another very little, if any. In all our plans for what we hope to do another day, in all our reading, all our learning, in our amusements, let us try and *think* about what we are doing. Get into the way of asking the meaning of what we see or do. All have not the same power of thought, but all can think, and can cultivate that amount of thought which is natural to each for study and work. It is true of every one of us, that to do anything for good, or what is more important, for the good of fellow men, we must use the mind and not the hands only, in what we are doing. The study of plant life then comes, with many other pleasures, into the enjoyments of existence.

XXIV.—ENEMIES OF THE AGRICULTURIST.

THE more serious sources of annoyance and loss to the cultivator arise from fungi and insects. In the dairy, and in wine making, we have to gain the acquaintance of bacterial visitors and their effects upon both vegetable and animal substances; but so many of them have beneficial tendencies, when they are developed aright, that agriculturists, as a body, are coming to look upon such changes as they make with kindly eyes. There is no such feeling towards the larger fungus growths, a few only of which have a direct value for man, necessary though they are in the plan of nature. And insects are only so much less objectionable because the bad ones are more easily reached, and there are many

Sections of Sugar Cane.

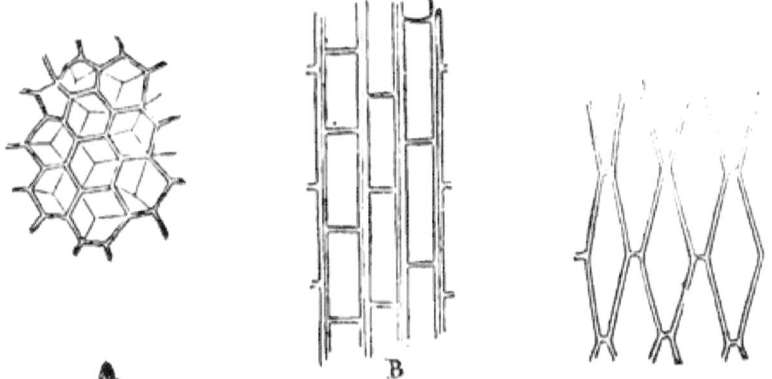
Healthy Sap Vessels of Potato, Sugar Cane, &c.

friends of the agriculturist amongst them, in the form of ladybirds, ichneumons and others. A, shows sap cells of a plant in which the starchy matter is secreted in the case of the potato, and saccharine, or sugar matter, in the sugar cane. It is here that fungus growths make serious attacks. B, illustrates cells near the skin or rind, where gummy matter is formed. C, ordinary form of intermediate cells between the two. The A and C cells are influenced very much by wet and dry weather—the C cells especially. At one time they may be almost dry, while when growth is active, and after rain, they may become gorged with sap. And that is the most dangerous time for the spreading of fungus attacks, as a rule. The enemy, at such times, increases enormously by absorbing the sap and destroying the cells and tissues of the host plant.

Fungoid Enemies are true parasites—things that live upon other things. Some of them attack animal life in their operations; and to such an extent is this visible through the microscope that it has become questionable whether animals feed more upon vegetables than vegetable life upon animals. Our concern, at the present stage, is with vegetable parasites. Domestic animals in this country, so far, have been wondrously exempt from ailments of epidemic kind—a fact due, in great measure, to the very excellent system of stock inspection common to all the colonies, and the departments of which work well to each other, and to the benefit of the whole community.

Fungi, Growing from Section of Leaf of a Host Plant.

A, upper side of leaf; *B*, lower side; *C*, developing seed heads of fungus; *D*, spore or seed cups; *E*, seed cup springing from breathing pore of plant; *F*, developed seed head; *G*, spores or seeds of fungi located in breathing pore.

Fungus growths may be divided into two easily observed divisions: They are those which appear generally as blackish, smut-like dust upon the leaves of lemons, oranges, and various flowering shrubs, as mildew on grapes, &c.; and the much more numerous and destructive fungi growths penetrate the leaf, twigs, or fruit of the host plant, destroying leaves, twigs, fruit, and the whole plant as they increase. The former are termed *epiphytes*, or things that live outside. The more dangerous fungi are *endophytes*, that live inside the host. The *epiphytes* may indicate other diseases in the plant, as do all fungus growths, and the drainage and manuring should be seen to, while the fungus is destroyed by spraying—Bordeaux mixture being effective for the purpose. When *endophyte* fungi are present the leaves may appear spotted with whitish, yellowish, or brownish blotches which spread more or less rapidly. The leaves and leaf stalks become affected, and the disease then saps the strength of the crop. Such, for illustration, are the visible symptoms of strawberry fungus or "brand," passion fruit and melon "scald," potato blight, &c. Occasionally—all at once as it may seem—the leaves perish, it may be in masses, and the whole plant wilts as though it were scalded. The term "scald" has long been applied to attacks of this kind, and the idea is still prevalent, even amongst skilled men, that the check to growth has been caused by such a change of weather that the leaves, or it may be the whole range of plants, are scorched by the sun, by sun-heated air, or by hosts of minute insects too small to be visible. Foliage plants are often attacked in this way. But in reality, the disease may have been present and spreading long before it was observed. That terrible enemy of wheat, the rust, is of this very dangerous kind. It may be upon the crop for weeks, even months, in spots, visible under a good glass; then should moist weather occur while the wheat is ripening, the rust becomes epidemic.

Specific Names.—The names given to these fungi growths are numberless—they are bewildering in some cases. But they are useful for scientific classification, while the foregoing classification may be ample for the ordinary purposes of those whose main objects are to identify the enemy promptly, in order to check or destroy the invader as soon as possible, and before serious mischief is done.

Means of Checking Fungus Growths.—Sulphur, in its many forms, is found effective against fungus growths in the early stages, and in the form of copper sulphate (bluestone), iron sulphate, sulphuric acid, flour of sulphur, &c., is a necessary part of the equipment of the agriculturist.

INSECT ENEMIES and FRIENDS. — Fortunately the agriculturist is helped by the latter, or the insect enemies, which are everywhere, in all lands, would be too many for all his efforts to check or destroy. For identification purposes, names are given to the myriads of these things, but as a classification for everyday use it may be sufficient, as a first step, to identify them as insects living by sucking the juices of plants; others that eat plants; and those that live upon the vegetable destroyers. Foremost as plant enemies are the *aphides*, or plant lice. The name means exhaust. They are fearfully numerous and destructive during dry summer seasons. They are everywhere —on the roots, limbs, branches, and leaves of plants, and continuous war should be waged against the whole tribe, for they are destructive in the field, in the vegetable garden, and in the orchard. They are terribly annoying in the flower garden and summer house. The *peach aphis*, *rose aphis*, and *cabbage aphis* afford easily observed specimens of the family generally, their mode of life and method of destruction. They appear for the season in numbers during August, and unless checked continue to increase and destroy all through the spring, summer and autumn, in proportion to the means taken to keep them in check from the time of their first appearance. The ants, as seen in the illustration, follow aphis on fruit trees, that they may gather a sweet sap ejected by the smaller insects. The rose

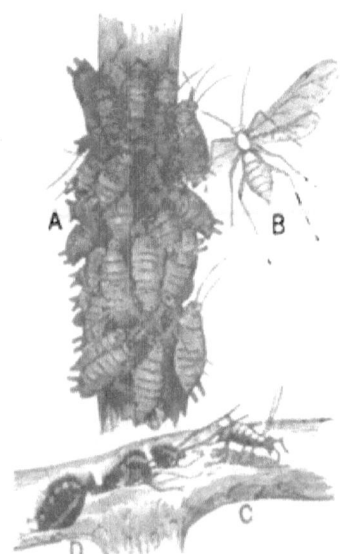

Aphis and Ants

aphis, in the form of a light green fly or insect, congregate in sleepy-looking masses, near the points of the younger shoots and the buds, and upon other parts of the plants as well. The grape vine aphis, termed phylloxera, live on the roots and also on the leaves at times, as do similar insects on other plants. When examined under a powerful glass, they seem to be crawling about listlessly, as it appears, or are fastened by their snouts or proboscis to the plant, the juices of which they are sucking. Cabbage aphis are found in similar masses under the younger leaves of the plants. Almost every tree and other plant in the garden has visitors of the aphis kind, and their mode of life is much the same.

"American Blight."—The woolly apple tree louse (misnamed "American blight") has long been known in Europe, and is proving very destructive in parts of Australia. The insect is a plant louse of the aphis kind, is quite small, and fastens itself in crevices of the bark, where it deposits masses of minute eggs, so small that a very powerful observing glass is necessary to see them. The effect upon trees is to literally exhaust the part they settle on of all sap. The wood seems honeycombed, swells into knobs, and soon becomes prey to disease. Many remedies have been tried to cure trees infested with this scourge, amongst the most effective being clay-lime-sulphur paint for winter dressing, and

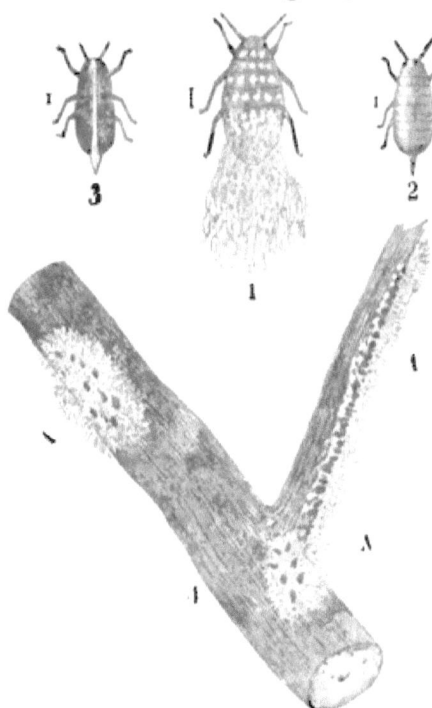

Woolly Aphis—"American Blight."

soda-resin-petroleum paint or spray for other times. When taken early, they may be eradicated; but when the disease has got into the roots and limbs, the better course is to cut down and burn the tree root and branch, and plant sorts of apples which resist the attacks of the louse.

Scale or Cocus Insects.—Scale insects are at times, when they are allowed to increase, very destructive upon

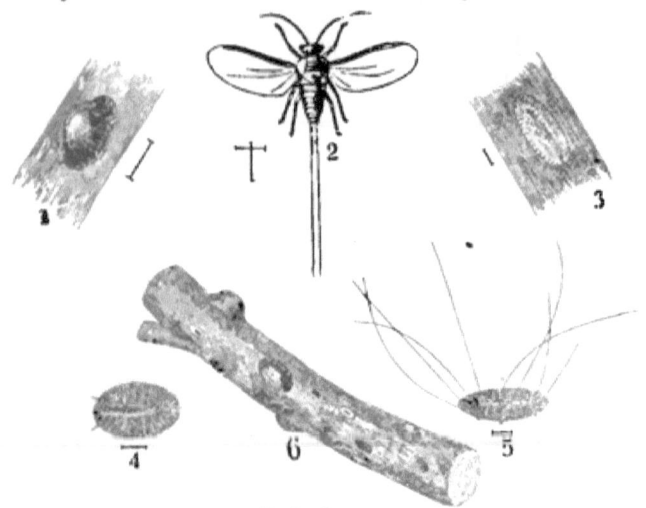

Scale Insects.

pear, apricot, peach, orange and other trees. They are covered by a horny scale or shell when grown, but are more easily kept in check than woolly aphis, unless they have been allowed to become too numerous. They cling to the bark singly and in masses, sucking the juices, portions of which they eject, until black, sticky patches are seen on the wood. The females are stationary, and they cover their eggs with their horny shell until the young hatch out, when the mother insect shrinks and dries up. The eggs and the young scales are carried about on the feet of birds and insects from plant to plant, and also by the wind at times. The males have wings during the autumn season, and are much smaller than the females. Rather appropriate "common" names are given to scale insects—thus 1 in the illustration is the oyster scale, that mite which damages oranges and lemons; 3, muscle scale;

4 and 5, scale larvæ, much magnified; 6, black scale; 2, insect in the winged state. Their methods of life make scale insects more difficult of eradication than the ordinary aphides. But by the use of clay paint and alkaline oil mixtures they also can be kept in check.

Codlin Moth Grub.—This, the *carpocapsa pomonella*, "the fruit devourer" of science, is one of the worst of fruit eaters. The mother insect, *A* in illustration, appears as a moth during August and September, and lays eggs

Codlin Moths on Apple Blossoms.

in the flower cups of apples (*B*), pears, and other fruits at times. The eggs (*C*) hatch in from 10 to 20 days, and the grubs eat into the young apples.

Risks from Introducing Plants and Animals.—That many of the worst parasites from which both plants and animals suffer have been introduced is only too true. The greatest care is necessary in introducing new things, for parasites, both fungoid and insect, exist in other countries much more destructive than any we have yet had to encounter.

The "*Buffalo gnat*" of America is a fearful pest, and would be a bad visitor here. It propagates in water, the

Mississippi watershed being specially subject to ravages of this mosquito-like pest, the attacks of which are so awful that cattle become terrified at the sounds made by these gnats, and to flee from the pests are often drowned.

To Check Fungi and Insects.—In the application of means for checking destructive insect pests, it is well to note that they all obtain their food by sucking or biting; sucking insects are provided with tube-like sucking mouths, by which they penetrate the tissues and pump out the juicy contents. Biting insects have jaws, with which they bite and destroy the entire substance. It is evident then that an insect subsisting upon the liquids inside of a fruit, leaf, or twig is not likely to be killed by a poison applied to the outside of a leaf which might kill an insect eating the leaf; but there is another way of reaching them. Insects do not breathe as we do. They have, instead of noses and lungs, rows of very small breathing openings along the sides of their bodies, with air tubes which branch and spread out through all the tissues of the body, carrying air to them. It is a fortunate circumstance that

Hand Sprayer at Work.

Spraying in the Orchard.

a very little of any oily substance will close these small openings, and smother the insect as effectually as clasping the wind-pipe will smother a man. But oil is injurious to plants. Hence oily substances, dissolved with alkalis to prevent the oil injuring the plants, are used for checking and killing insects. Fumigation, from sulphur and carbon compounds mostly, has long been in use, and is still effective where plants can be covered.

Friendly Insects.—Were it not for the natural enemies which plant lice, scales, &c., have, like all animals, they would soon become destructive beyond the powers of man to keep them in check. The best known destroyers of plant lice are ladybirds (*Coccinella*) and their grub-like larvæ. Well-known ladybirds are about the size and form of split peas. The perfect insect is of dull orange colour, and usually has nine small black dots on the wing shells. These insects lay their tiny eggs near the plant lice, and as soon as the grub hatches out it proceeds to devour its natural food. They may be often seen upon potato plants, upon melon vines, and on other plants. The grubs vary in colour on different coloured plants. They do not look nice, but it is safe to conclude that when they are about more disagreeable visitors are disappearing. The young of various flies are also destructive to plant lice, upon which the mother flies deposit their eggs. The young maggots devour great numbers of aphides.

Knowledge of Fungus and Insect Life.—That some acquaintance with the methods of insect life, even the very rudiments of entomology, are useful to the agriculturist is evident. It is during the early stages of insect attacks, the same as those of fungus attacks, that the most effective efforts to check or destroy them are made. An hour spent then may prevent heavy losses more certainly than weeks of toil, expenditure, and lamentation after the pests have got a start. The skill is in being able to identify and check the enemy at the beginning, and is a sort of skill which young folks acquire rapidly and eagerly. They are soon able to identify the enemy and their works, and the presence of friendly beetles, ichneumons, and others, which may be clearing off the pests by eating them or their eggs, or depositing eggs on the bodies of their enemies, which are from that stage doomed to destruction.

XXV.—HOME HELPS.

Good Bread and How to Make It.—Good bread is the rule in Australia, bad bread the exception. This is the case in the bush as well as the towns, and is attributable in the first place, to the excellent quality of the wheat and flour; and in the next to the skill in bread-making that pervades the community. It is an accomplishment of which Australian women may well feel proud. Good bread means good digestion, contentment, health; for all of which the country is somewhat famous. The first requisite for good bread is good flour—not necessarily the whitest or finest flour, but sweet, dry, wholesome flour, made from sound grain, without mixture of any kind. Whatever the price, this is the cheapest, the most healthful flour. Even in public establishments it has been proved by actual tests, extending over months and years, that the best flour is the cheapest in the end. Flour can be tested for its "strength" or bread-making qualities, in the manner described in the author's "Helpful Chemistry for Agriculturists."

Yeast.—This is another important ingredient in bread-making. A simple and thoroughly good way of making it is to put 1oz. of hops into 2 quarts of water; boil until the water is reduced by one-third; strain this, and add to the water two tablespoonsful of sugar; when the mixture is cool add two tablespoonsful of flour, and bottle the mixture. This should make about 3 pints, and what is wanted first for use should be put into a bottle that contained yeast before. If no such bottle is handy, a few drops of vinegar or a bit of dough will cause it to ferment. It is ready for use as soon as fermentation sets in, or in moderately warm weather about twenty-four hours after the fresh yeast is made. It keeps for weeks when corked tight and put away in a cool place. One pint of this yeast is sufficient for 12lbs. of bread.

Making the Bread.—To make, say 15lbs. of bread, use water slightly warm, say of 80 degrees in cool weather, and colder water in warm weather. Put 2 quarts water, or skimmed milk if it can be got from a butter factory, and 1 pint yeast and sufficient salt into a dish. Add flour sufficient to make a thin batter; beat it up until thoroughly mixed; do not spare the beating at this stage. This is the "sponge," and when it is tough and elastic, and fine with beating and working, tuck it in nicely with flour from the sides of the dish, and cover it over with a cloth and place it in a warm or cool place (according to the weather). A good "sponge" will spring or rise three or four inches during the night; in cool weather it takes longer. When ripe, turn the sponge out upon a table, into the flour necessary to make bread—say 8lbs. flour if we are making 15lbs. of bread. It may be home-made flour, or pollard, or bran, or coarser flour, or maize meal may be added at this stage. Mix it until the dough is just stiff enough not to stick; work it well; don't spare elbow-exercise—that is one of the secrets of bread-making. Form the well worked dough into any desired shape or size for loaves—pans are the best for baking—and let them stand until it rises an inch or so; then put into the oven and bake.

Camp Bread.—A bit of dough the size of the fist, put away in a cool place, in flour, will keep for three or four days, and make good bread. To use it, mix up the dough in about 3 pints warm water; mix them thoroughly; then add a tablespoonful of sugar, with salt and flour, and mix up the sponge as in the former case, and make it into bread in the same way. This can be repeated in warm weather until the bread begins to have a sourish taste; and this again can be corrected by adding a little baking-soda, until compelled again to make yeast.

The Oven.—In the bush, this is an important part of successful home life. "Is marriage a failure?" has a serious look in the face of a bad oven. The so-called "camp-oven" is simply a flat-bottomed iron pot, with a lid less or more hollowed to hold fire or ashes. The dough, when ready for baking, is put into this pot, which is set into a mass of hot ashes, covered over, or a fire is kindled around it, bottom, sides and top. It is a hasty process, entailing close watchfulness, and risks of burnt fingers and clothes, and swearwords at times, when the man is called on to come and help over a difficulty. It is altogether a barbarous arrangement, and should be beneath the notice of a man who can use brains and hands. An oven is easily made. An iron nail or oil-can makes a good one. Set it lengthways upon stones or bricks, sufficiently high to save the wife from stooping any more than is necessary to get fire under it. Then cover the oven body round with a sheet of iron or anything that will stand fire, leaving about an inch of clear space between the iron drum or oven and the cover. Over the latter put a layer of clay, working it well to make it stick and prevent cracking; the thicker the clay the longer it will hold heat; the more it is worked the less it cracks. Leave an outlet for smoke at the top or back of the oven. Fit a lid of wood or iron to the mouth of it. Put in a shelf to form a sole. Use iron-bark or dry gum-bark for the fire, and there you have an oven, not much to look at, perhaps, but it is all there for baking—anything from a biscuit to a roast—fit for a man that is able and willing to work for the best food in the land. He deserves it. But he who allows his wife to destroy temper and fingers over an iron pot deserves the burnt offerings that are often found in such barbarisms. Colonial ovens, on the above correct principle, that is, with a confined space for fire or hot air round the sides and top, are made of iron and sold in the towns. Ovens are also made of brick and stone, or by scooping out a white-ant nest, and are heated by kindling a fire inside until sufficient heat is gained; then put in the article to be baked, and close up the front tight to keep in the heat until the cooking is completed. On a pinch, bread can be baked in red-hot ashes; ashes from bark are the best; or by heating stones, as is done in the South Sea Islands, putting the bread or meat amongst them, and covering up the whole until the baking is completed.

Baking Powder.—A good article is made by mixing 3 oz. tartaric acid, 5 oz. bi-carbonate of soda, and ¼lb. of arrowroot. These proportions can be carried out to any extent. Dry each of the articles separately in the sun or oven, and when perfectly dry mix them thoroughly, and put the mixture in a bottle, corked tight to keep off the air. Two teaspoonsful of the powder makes 2lb. of bread, or nearly as much biscuit. Mix the powder with the flour and salt, then add cold water or milk to make dough. Do the mixing and kneading quickly, and bake in a quick oven.

Self-Raising Flour.—There are several processes for making "self-raising flour," among which the following are fairly good :—100lbs. well-dried flour, 10¼oz. tartaric acid, 12oz. bi-carbonate of soda, 8oz. white sugar, 1½lbs. salt. The ingredients must be perfectly dry, and reduced to fine powder before mixing.

"Machine Milk" for Bread-Making.—Those who are near enough to a cream-separating machine might try the effect of using the skimmed or "machine milk" instead of water, or as part of the water, for bread-making. It is extra excellent.

Maize as Food.—In maize we have an every-day instance of the peculiarities which regulate what we eat and drink. In speaking to a dozen persons upon the healthfulness of maize as food, eleven would readily admit that, in one form or other, it is pleasant, easily digested, and strengthening, but it is doubtful whether one of the twelve uses the article—not because of its scarcity, for maize is amongst the things seen everywhere, but from little difficulties in the way of preparing it for food. Difficulties also arise from not finding freshly-prepared maize-meal or flour in the stores, and thus it does not find its way to the table to anything like the extent merit and real value should secure for it.

Green Corn.—When the grain of maize is just full upon the cob, and when, upon pressure with the thumb, the sweet juice can be squeezed from it, pull off the ears, strip the wrappers from them, and boil the cobs with meat, or in water, or roast them. When cooked, the grain comes off freely. Cooked cobs can be sent to table in various neat ways that will readily suggest themselves. The grain tastes like green peas, and may be either eaten from the cob without further preparation, or after being pared off with a knife, can be served up as peas. There is a peculiar flavour in this green corn, not unlike cooked oysters, to enjoy which is an acquired taste; but it is very easily acquired, and few things are more nourishing. In America vast quantities of the grain are put up in cans in the same way as preserved meat and fruit, and it comes into use while the corn is out of season. In Australia we have had fresh green corn on the table during seven months of the year. The white varieties are most in favour for cooking: but all are good.

Maize-Meal.—To make the best meal or flour, the grain must be dried in an oven until quite crisp, then, if there is no grinding-mill handy, a hand-mill (sold by the ironmongers at from £2 to £4) answers very well. These hand-mills make excellent meal; they grind a bushel in an hour, and last for years. Grind the corn coarsely at first—the work is too hard when the meal is ground fine at one operation; then screw up the mill as fine as may be desired, and grind what will be necessary for not longer than a week. It should always be fresh.

Porridge.—There are few things better than maize-meal porridge for persons of weak digestion. It is also good food for strong men. Boil the water, and pour in the meal gradually through the fingers of one hand while stirring with the other. It requires at least half-an-hour's boiling, and is all the better of being boiled still longer. Eat with milk, molasses, or butter. When cold, it forms into a stiff mass that is excellent when fried.

Puddings.—They require four or five hours' cooking. The meal makes up well with suet, eggs, milk, molasses, currants, spices, or other pudding fixings. Stir the ingredients into as much meal as may be desired, making the whole into a stiff batter. Let it stand a bit, and prepare a pudding-cloth by first dipping in boiling water; then dredge flour over it and put in the pudding, tying it so that water will not get in and make the pudding heavy. Leave plenty of room for swelling—maize-meal swells more then flour. Put the bag into boiling water, and do not let it go off the boil until cooked.

Baked Puddings.—A quart of meal, half-pint of milk, 1lb. molasses, and eggs and other fixings to fit, make excellent puddings. Scald the milk and mix it with the molasses and meal, stirring the whole thoroughly together. Add eggs and any desired spice, with salt, &c. Pour the whole into a well-buttered pudding-dish. Bake it well, and use while hot. It is good. Various other puddings, boiled and baked, and known by various names, are made by modifying the foregoing, and using more or less molasses, eggs, essence, or juice of lemon—one of the best seasonings for maize-meal puddings, &c. They must all be well cooked, and special care taken that water does not get inside the cloth while boiling. To turn them out nicely, dip the cloth in cold water as soon as taken out of the pot.

Bread.—To make bread from maize-meal, it must be worked up in the first place with boiling water, and then the meal and water must be allowed to incorporate and "leaven." Put the meal into a dish, add the salt, then stir in the water boiling hot, until there is a stiff, well-mixed batter. Let this stand covered with a cloth until it is blood-warm, then mix yeast with the dough (a little more than is allowed for wheat-bread); knead the whole thoroughly; don't spare the elbows. If the dough should get sour, mix a little soda in warm water and stir it into the dough; mould the loaves as desired, and bake. Maize requires longer baking than wheaten bread; and to prevent a hard crust forming, each loaf should be wrapped up in a damp towel until required for use. The foregoing is a most wholesome bread. A finer bread is made by mixing one-half or less wheat-flour with the meal, and using warm instead of hot water in making the dough. The other process described answers for the remainder of the work.

Home-made Soap and Candles.—The cold weather season is the time for using up the spare tallow and fat, and making supplies of soap and candles. To make good, hard, white soap, we must have clean tallow or fat, lime, and soda. If a yellowish tinge is considered desirable, resin is used. The following proportions may be doubled to any extent for making larger quantities; though the experience of makers differs a good deal about the relative proportions of tallow, lime, soda, and water used; but this will be found to depend a good deal upon the heat of the fire, hardness or softness of the water, all of which differ in nearly every case, and can only be settled by experience:—

1.—7lbs. soda and 7lbs. lime, to be boiled in five gallons of water for half an hour; when cold, pour off the clean water or lye; add 6lbs. fat and ¼lb. resin, and boil about 4 hours; test the soap by pouring a little upon an earthenware vessel; as soon as it acquires the right feel of soap, pour the whole mass into a tight box of a good shape for cutting the mass into bars when it cools. Cut it with a thin wire, or string will do.

2.—A new branch of the soda trade now supplies caustic soda, which for years has been used in soap-making. Melt your fat in plenty of water, and keep putting in small quantities of caustic soda, until saponification takes place. It is well to test all your soap just as jam is tested. When you think it looks soapy enough take out a spoonful and put it in a mould, and if it becomes solid be satisfied. Next apply it practically to your arms and neck, and if you feel no smarting or irritation then your soap is right; but, if in washing, the skin smarts, then there is too much caustic soda in it, and the boiling must be continued, while fat or tallow is added in sufficient quantity to absorb the caustic property of the soap. Lately there has been introduced a special lye for soap-making, and by following the directions upon the tin, a good household soap can be made. In making soap, boil it well, and towards the end "give it a galop," as soap-makers say, and remember that soap, like candles, improves by keeping.

Soft-Soap.—The difference between hard and soft soap is that soda is the alkali used for the former, and potash for making soft-soap. It is safest to purchase the potash, as it is not plentiful in our native timbers, but fresh ashes from mangrove and oak may do; swamp oak is amongst the best for the purpose. Any sort of tallow or fat will do if reasonably clean. When the potash is to be got from wood-ashes, make a hole at the bottom of a tub or barrel; plug up the hole, and nearly fill the barrel with wood-ashes; pour in as much water as the ashes will hold, and let it stand for three days ; run off the liquor, now called lye, and pour in more water, until three degrees of lye are taken from the ashes. Put the first lye into a pot with as much tallow as it can saponify or make soapy, and boil about three hours ; then add the second lye, and boil about two hours more ; draw off the water as it separates from the soap, and add the third lye and boil for an hour or so, making three boilings of about six hours in all. Allow the mass to settle, and as it cools, draw off all water that remains under the soap, which is then ready for use. In first experimenting in soap-making, as in cookery and fruit-preserving, disappointment may be a first result. It may happen that the saponification is faulty, and if so, add a little lye, and boil the whole over again, stirring it well in the meantime. Many a boiling of soap is spoiled for want of a log of wood. In making starch the laundress knows by the appearance when the proper quantity of boiling water has been poured in, and in the same way practice will soon enable anyone to tell by sight when saponification takes place. As soon as soap appears in the centre of the boiling mass withdraw the fire, and leave the boiling mass covered up till it partially cools before pouring it into the moulds.

CANDLES.—They can be made from any tallow, but the cleaner and firmer it is the better the candles. Equal portions of beef and mutton tallow answer very well. When beeswax is added, in the proportion of about 3 oz. to a pound of tallow, we have an improved candle. Should the fat be old, discoloured, or offensive, it can be purified by the following simple process: Put a bucket of water into a copper, and the fat with it. When well boiled withdraw the fire, and sprinkle in a handful of powdered alum, and repeat the sprinkling now and then as the tallow cools, when it will be sweet, clean and white ; and if a piece of rough string has been laid in the bottom of the boiler, the alum will be found crystallized on the string, and can be pounded up and used again. Moulds to make half-a-dozen at a time are sold by the tinmen. They are rounded to a point at one end ; through this end twisted candle wick is passed, and fastened in the centre of the other end to a pin or skewer. The wicks should first be dipped in alum or lime water, and dried before they are put into the moulds, to prevent their burning too rapidly. When the wicks are all placed, pour in the melted tallow.

If the tallow when run into the mould be too hot it will stick to the tin, and then the application of hot water is necessary, which spoils the look of the candles. To obviate this, let the tallow cool until a scum forms on the surface. This scum begins at the edge, and moves towards the centre, and it is just when the last clear spot vanishes, that the temperature is perfect for moulding purposes. It is better that the temperature be under than over this degree, but if it be too cool the candles will have a honey-combed appearance. When the candles have thoroughly cooled, press them downwards with the thumb, when they will give way with a click, and can be easily drawn out with an awl.

PAINT FOR OUTSIDE PLACES.—Few things please better than a coat of paint, and the winter season is the time to do it. Be the object a slab wall, or any rough outside place, it is not only preserved, but the surroundings are much improved. Amongst other compositions found useful for this purpose, the following are favorites :—

1.—Unslacked lime 20 lbs., slake it with water, covering during the process to keep out carbonic acid; strain the liquid through a fine sieve or bag, and add to it 5lbs. or more salt, previously dissolved in water; rice, 3lbs., boiled to a thin paste and stirred in boiling hot; Spanish whitening, ½lb.; clean glue, 1lb., previously dissolved. Add hot water to the mixture, enough to make a nice thick paint, stir it well, and let it stand a few days covered from dust; then put it on hot, if possible. This will last on wood, stone, or brick for years, and is suitable for coating iron roofs.

2.—" Machine," or skimmed milk, 2 quarts; fresh slacked lime, 8 ozs.; linseed oil, 4 ozs.; common whitening, 3 lbs. Put the lime in a stoneware vessel; put upon it sufficient milk to make it like thick cream; add the oil a little at a time; mix thoroughly; add remainder of milk, then the whitening made fine; strain the paint, and keep the whole well stirred while using.

SHEEP SKINS FOR HOME USE.—Make strong soapsuds with warm water; when cold, wash the skins in it, carefully squeezing them between the hands to get the dirt out of the wool; then wash the soap out with clean cold water. Dissolve alum and salt, each half-a-pound, in hot water, which put in a tub of cold water sufficient to cover the skins, and let them soak in it over night, or say for twelve hours; then hang over a pail to drain. When they are well drained, spread or stretch carefully over a board to dry. While they are still a little damp, have 1 oz. each of saltpetre and alum pulverised, and sprinkle the flesh side of each skin, rubbing in well; then place two flesh sides together and hang in the shade for two or three days, turning the under skin uppermost every day until perfectly dry. Then scrape the flesh side with a blunt knife to remove any remaining scraps of flesh; trim off projecting points, and rub with pumice stone and with the hands; they should be very white and beautiful.

Kangaroo, Wallaby, 'Possum, and Smaller Skins.—These are cured singly. Tack each skin—using galvanised tacks—to a board, wall or fence, spreading them fully, flesh side out. Dissolve alum—about two ounces for a large wallaby skin—in a pint of warm water, and with a sponge or flannel rag dipped in this solution moisten the surface all over; repeat this every now and then for three or four days. When the skin is quite dry take out the tacks, and rolling it up loosely the long way, flesh side out, draw it quickly backwards and forwards through a large smooth ring, or anything of a similar kind, until it is quite soft; then roll it the contrary way of the skin and repeat the operation. A very good and simple process in use in the bush is to sprinkle the flesh side, after scraping it well, with equal parts of pulverised salt and alum; then fold the flesh sides together and roll the skin compactly, in which state it should remain ten or twelve days. Then it is opened, and sprinkled with bran or sawdust to absorb the moisture, and rolled up again for twenty-four hours; the process is completed by thorough rubbing and manipulation, as above, on which the pliability depends. Skins, when taken off, should be freed from grease or flesh by thorough scraping, when they may be dried, and left to wait the leisure of the owner.

Indian Soft Skins.—Trappers wash animal skins with soap and soda to free them from grease, then rinse them in clean water to cleanse them from the suds, then rub as dry as possible; after which the skins are put into a mixture of two ounces of salt to a quart of water containing one ounce of sulphuric acid added to three quarts of milk or bran-water, and stirred briskly for forty or fifty minutes; from this the skins are put into a solution of soda, and stirred till they will no longer foam; then they are hung up to dry.

Medical Help in Emergencies.—To the timid mind there is something dreadful in the idea of meeting an accident, or being taken sick in places beyond the reach of medical aid, and the feeling is natural. Visitations of the kind are amongst the distressing features of life in the bush, when those concerned have not the skill or the courage necessary to help themselves, or to help another in a case of emergency. But, fortunately, colonists are seldom so placed. The amount of downright medical skill afloat in the bush might seem surprising. It is seldom that one comes to a station, a plantation, a large work in progress, or other place where bodies of men are collected, without hearing of one or more who can treat an accident or ordinary ailment in case of emergency. It is an admirable peculiarity of bush life, and one that will be still more extensively cultivated as the medical school becomes a more general colonial institution.

The following notes—always keeping in mind the remedies likely to be available in the bush—have been put together with the view of aiding those in a pinch while beyond medical aid. It is in every case the desirable and safest course to call in a medical man, if one can be reached; but in the meantime it is simply the duty of those around the sufferer to help—to do whatever can be done.

Flesh Wounds.—These are of various kinds—punctured, a tear, a bruise, a shot, &c. The first, in a warm climate, is dangerous. It may lead to lock-jaw and other serious consequences. The first care is to extract any substance that is left in the wound, and if this can be done without exhausting the patient it should never be omitted, although the pain may be severe. If this cannot be acccomplished, wash the wound and apply poultices to encourage the injured part to suppurate or throw out the foreign substance. In other cases the parts of the wound should be brought together as naturally as possible, and either held in place by means of a stitch or two brought through the skin with an ordinary needle and thread, or by strips of adhesive plaster or bandages. Nature is very kind in such cases, and if the patient is kept clean and quiet, and the bowels are kept regular, the cure may prove rapid. Where the wound is on the face, or other part where a mark tends to disfigure, the bandages should be covered with oiled silk, or cotton, or rubber, to exclude the air. At times a poultice of gum-leaves (boiled if possible) is tied around the wound. To relieve pain, an effective plan is to burn sugar in a pan, and hold the wounded part in the smoke that arises.

The Head—Broken Bones.—The colonial "buster," or fall from horseback, very often results in a damaged head, or in dislocation of an arm or leg, or both. Falling timber gives very bad wounds, and the sufferer has to be treated with every consideration and care. In such cases no time should be lost in securing the best medical aid available. But at once lay out the patient where he will be easy and quiet; cut the hair from the wounded part; wash it clean, and bring the parts together with a plaster or with bandages. Stitches are not desirable in wounds of the head, as anything irritating is liable to bring on erysipelas. When the scalp has been injured by severe bruises, warm-water dressings will in general be found the best application, unless there be considerable heat and inflammation, when, if procurable, a lotion of sugar of lead, in the proportion of 2 drachms of the sugar of lead to a pint of water and 2 ounces of vinegar, is to be applied slightly warmed, on pieces of lint or linen. Owing to the number of pieces of bone composing the skull, a simple fracture seldom extends far, as it is usually confined to one bone; in such cases the fracture may be a mere crack, as in a pane of glass, and perfect quietude with the necessary precautionary measures in keeping down inflammation, and keeping off flies, may be sufficient.

General Treatment.—The object is not to cure broken bones, but to get the broken ends into their proper places, and keep them there. A door, a flour-sack cut open, a sheet of bark, or a blanket fastened at the four corners to two saplings, makes a hammock, on which an injured person can be placed. In case of injury to the arm or hand, a splint is helpful, but whatever is used let it be long enough to reach from the elbow to a little beyond the ends of the fingers. Cover this with anything soft, then not only the arm but the hand will rest comfortably. The hand must not hang lower than the elbow. In cases where the patient is insensible, lay him gently in a dry, quiet place, and in the most natural position possible. Keep the mouth and nose clean, keep off flies or insects, and keep up the heat of the body with warm clothes, tins of hot water, stones, or anything handy. Stimulants should be used with the greatest caution, as tending to excite and bring on inflammation.

Burns and Scalds.—Keep the air from the injured parts. Cover the injured parts; cloth, cotton, if possible (but anything in an emergency), white of an egg, flour, oil, or starch, are useful agents for that purpose. When a person is discovered on fire, he or she should be brought to the ground as speedily as possible, with the double object of smothering the fire and covering the injured parts. A coat, a blanket, a sack, anything that will keep away the air and smother the fire should be wrapped around the sufferer. Do not attempt to tear off the clothes; *smother out the fire;* that is the best thing that can be done. Do not take off anything that adheres to the flesh. Cover all sores with flour, white of egg, molasses, or soap, or starch, or oil, and put poultices of bread or bran over any burnt pieces of cloth that may cling to the wound. They will come off freely in five or six days, when a new skin has formed. Do not puncture or peel off any of the skin;

it is the best possible covering. In cases of prostration or great shock to the system, stimulants may be given, such as brandy, and warm-water bottles, bricks, stones, or anything that will keep up the natural body heat should be applied to the feet, under the arms, &c.

Gum Leaves and Banana Leaves for Wounds, Sore Eyes, &c.—The leaves of the gums generally, and of the plantain or banana, form useful applications, thus:—As a dressing for blistered surfaces, for which purpose they are admirably adapted in hot climates. After the removal of a blister, gum leaves, or a piece of plantain leaf smeared or coated with oil, should be applied to the denuded surface, and kept in its place by means of a bandage. The first sensation it occasions is peculiarly cooling and soothing, and the blistered surface generally heals satisfactorily. For the first two days the upper smooth surface is placed next to the skin, and subsequently the under side, until the healing process is complete. It should be changed twice daily, or oftener if required. As a substitute for indiarubber or guttapercha coverings in the water dressing of wounds and ulcers, banana leaf is decidedly good; the younger the leaf the better it is suited for this purpose. Two points require attention—(1) the piece used should be sufficiently large to cover or envelope the whole part; and (2) it should be carefully kept in its place by bandages, &c. If properly applied, evaporation of the natural fluids is effectually prevented. As a shade for the eyes, in ophthalmia and other diseases of the eye, no manufactured shade is superior to banana leaf. The older and greener leaves answer best for this purpose.

ACCIDENTAL POISONING.—Some one has said that there is poison in everything, and, in fact, we do find ourselves surrounded with, and daily using, articles that in unskilful, careless, or thoughtless hands are dangerous to human life.

Poisonous Plants.—No better general rule can be laid down for the detection of poisonous plants than that nature has made them nauseous to the palate of both man and beast. There are exceptions to this rule, as for instance, the "poison plant" of Northern Queensland, the lantana seeds, the "native currant," and a few others that are rather pleasant than otherwise to the palate; but the poisonous qualities of these things operate by preventing digestion, and they are removed with comparative ease from the human stomach by the aid of warm water, mustard, salt and water, or other emetic. The real poison plants have generally a milky, bitter juice, disagreeable to both taste and smell, and without exception it is very painful should a drop get into a sore or the eye. Treat them as acids.

Prompt action is everything in cases of accidental poisoning. Seconds, not hours, are at our disposal to apply a remedy, and in places where medical aid is not at once obtainable, and where no other guide is handy, the following may prove useful in case of emergency :—

Arsenic—Paris green, green colourings, ague drops, rat and dog poison, &c.—Symptoms: Pain and burning heat of stomach, dryness of throat, cramps, purging, and vomiting. Treatment: Give large quantities of milk and raw eggs, lime-water, or flour and water; then castor-oil.

Strychnine—Dog and rat poison, &c., nux vomica.—Symptoms: Twitching of the muscles, convulsions, lockjaw, or the body is bent backwards. Treatment: Try to empty the stomach by an emetic, then give linseed-tea or barley-water, and to an adult thirty drops of laudanum occasionally to relieve the spasms. Hurry for a medical man.

Acids—Oxalic, sulphuric (vitriol), nitric (aqua fortis), muriatic (spirit of salt), carbolic.—Symptoms: Horrible burning sour pain from the mouth downwards. The skin of the lips, mouth and throat may be dissolved. Treatment: Water or milk in quantity, carbonate of soda, magnesia, whiting, chalk, or lime-water; or knock a piece of plaster off the wall, pound it small, and give it in milk or water. While one person attends to this, let another cut some common soap into small bits, and give a teaspoonful with water, or a tablespoonful of soft soap.

Laudanum.—Opium, paregoric, soothing syrup, syrup of poppies, &c.—Symptoms: Giddiness, stupour, the pupil of the eye very small, lips blue, skin cold, heavy, slow breathing. Treatment: Empty the stomach as quickly as possible by vomiting; hot water, mustard and water, salt, or soap, or tickle the throat with anything that is handiest. Then for an adult, if it can be got, give fifteen grains of sulphate of zinc in a little water; to a young person half the quantity; to an infant a teaspoonful of ipecacuanha wine. After vomiting, give plenty of very strong coffee, put a mustard plaster round the calf of each leg, and if cold and sinking give spirits and water. Get medical help. Keep the patient roused till the effect has passed off by beating the soles of the feet, walking, or dashing cold water on the face. Remember that if the patient goes to sleep at this stage it is the sleep of death.

SUNSTROKE.—When the temperature rises over 100 degrees, and the weather is moist, care is necessary to prevent the exhausting effects of so great a heat. Temperance in living is of the first importance in this respect—not temperance in eating and drinking only, but in the clothing worn, in government of the temper, &c. As means of prevention, it is advisable to wear head-coverings that, while light, give shade and air to the head and neck. For these purposes the colonial shell-hat, and calico or other pugaree attachments, are good. Loose clothing should be worn, and of the lightest possible colour. The symptoms of an attack are sharp pains in the head and giddiness, and unless the patient is of very strong nerve, and can get under shade at once, he falls to the ground insensible—the victim of over-heated blood. To cool the temperature of the body, by applying water all over, and by exposing as much of the body to the coolest possible currents of air, are means of the first consideration. Bleeding is often effective, and the application of mustard poultice to the back of the neck, rubbing the spine with spirits, ammonia, or turpentine, are all aids towards recovering the patient. Sometimes a man exposed to the direct rays of the sun is struck down without any warning; and sometimes the high temperature of the atmosphere under cover, or at night, especially if the air be fouled by defective ventilation, may induce symptoms of sunstroke. Whatever checks perspiration, whatever induces nerve-weariness, or embarrasses the normal working of the organic system, powerfully predisposes to heat fever, or apoplexy.

Snake Bites.—Australian snakes, with few exceptions, are timid, and get out of the way. But at the season of the year when snakes are pairing (during January and February) they are less timid and more dangerous than usual. In the event of being bitten, the following may be of value :—In former times everything in the shape of a snake was considered poisonous; but of late years colonists know that many of the more common snakes, notably the carpet species, are not poisonous. The death adder is the really dangerous reptile of the snake tribe, because it is sluggish, at all times, and retains its position until touched, when it bites instantly. None of the snakes are known to attack; they bite only when disturbed in logs or elsewhere, or when trodden upon by men or animals. They are easily disabled, and seldom escape when attacked with a whip, stick, or other weapon. Most snakes move about at night, and lie in a semi-dormant state during the winter months, in logs, hollow trees, amongst stones, heaps of bark, &c. It is in all cases advisable to have a stick handy, and to look cautiously about when working near places that give cover to snakes. In the event of a bite, the flesh around the wound, to the size of a sixpence, should be cut away to the depth of about an eighth of an inch, or scarified at once to cause a free flow of blood, and warm water applied to induce bleeding. The late Dr. Bancroft, of Brisbane, recommended the immediate application of leeches to the wound to be effective, and leeches are plentiful enough in scrubs, swamps, &c. A bandage or piece of cord should, if practicable, be tied tightly between the wound and the heart, and the blood and poison sucked out with vigour. If the patient cannot do this himself, there is no great risk to another person doing so, as snake poison is dangerous only when it comes in contact with a wound. Drowsiness is the first symptom of snake poison; and as soon as it appears every effort should be employed to keep the patient awake by moving him about, rubbing, &c.; medical aid should be called in as rapidly as possible. Stimulants are valuable in such cases. If bleeding the wound has been neglected, then much depends on giving large doses of stimulants, whisky, brandy, rum, weak ammonia, &c.

APPARENT DEATH FROM DROWNING.—The following instructions for restoring persons apparently drowned are issued by the Royal National Life-boat Institution. Send immediately for medical aid, blankets and dry clothing, but proceed to treat the patient *instantly*, on the spot, in the open air, with the face downward whether on shore or afloat; exposing the face, neck, and chest to the air, except in severe weather, and removing all tight clothing from the neck and chest, especially the braces. The points to be aimed at are—first and immediately, the restoration of breathing; and secondly, after breathing is restored, the promotion of warmth and circulation. The efforts to restore breathing must be commenced immediately and energetically, and persevered in for one or two hours, or until a medical man has pronounced that life is extinct. Efforts to promote warmth and circulation, beyond removing the wet clothes and drying the skin must not be made until the first appearance of natural breathing. For if circulation of the blood is induced before breathing has recommenced, the restoration of life will be endangered.

To Imitate the Movement of Breathing.—Standing at the patient's head, grasp the arms just above the elbows, and draw the arms gently and steadily upwards above the head and keep them stretched upwards for two seconds. (By this means air is drawn into the lungs.) Then turn down the patient's arms and press them gently and firmly against the sides of the chest. (By this means air is pressed out of the lungs.) Repeat the movements alternately and perseveringly about fifteen times in a minute, until a spontaneous effort to breathe is perceived, immediately upon which cease to imitate the movements of breathing and proceed to induce circulation and warmth.

Treatment After Natural Breathing has been Restored. —Rub the limbs upwards, with firm, grasping pressure and energy, using handkerchiefs, flannels, &c. (by this measure the blood is propelled along the veins towards the heart). Promote the warmth of the body by the application of hot flannels, bottles of hot water, heated stones, bricks, &c., to the pit of the stomach, the armpits, between the thighs, and the soles of the feet. If the patient has been carried to a house after respiration has been restored, be careful to let the air play freely within the room. On the restoration of life, a teaspoonful of warm water should be given; and then, if the power of swallowing has returned, small quantities of wine, brandy-and-water, or coffee, should be administered. The patient should be kept in bed, and a disposition to sleep encouraged.

EXPOSURE AND STARVATION.—The time during which a human being can exist without food depends upon his mode of life, his temperament, and his bodily condition. Well authenticated cases have come to notice of persons being in the bush without food for ten or twelve days, and still alive. In these cases the mind has been affected before the person had disappeared, and the body did not crave that regular solid nutriment demanded by a healthy organization. In such cases it is almost certain also that the sufferers had obtained water, with the aid of which human nature holds out much longer. In ordinary cases the bodily powers are exhausted in four days; delirium sets in and completes the destruction. With water, a cool, collected man has held out for seven days and nights, and still retained his faculties. Children have been known to live five days without food. It is curious that children discover food material in the native plants and grasses much more readily than adults. The chapter on "Attractions of Plant Life" is well worthy of study in this connection. Even a slight acquaintance with the indigenous vegetation discloses many sources for the support of life. On reaching a person exhausted by hunger, great caution is necessary. Milk is the best of all nourishment in such cases; next to it is bread and water, reduced to the consistency of milk. Whatever is given must be in small quantities—the eagerness of the starving person to have nourishment must be restrained. Stimulants are worse than dangerous, and should on no account be given to a person exhausted by hunger. Put warm clothing around the sufferer, lay him in bed, if possible, but not so near a fire as to get direct heat, and so gently nurse the nearly exhausted spark of life into fresh vigour.

XXVI.—REMINDERS FOR SEASONABLE WORK.

As explained in the opening chapter (page 14) the seasons in Australia may be classed as *Spring*, commencing in August; *Summer*, in November; *Autumn*, in February; and *Winter*, in May. With such modifications as may arise from the location in which we may be operating, this classification answers very well in order to form a fair idea of the usual weather of the season in view, and the crops and crop treatment most suitable

For detailed information concerning the seasons, the rainfall, prevailing winds, &c., perusal and study of Chapter I., and the records and reports of the Meteorological Observer, are recommended.

FIELD WORK FOR THE SPRING SEASON.
August, September, October.

Usual Weather.—The temperature of both air and soil, and the sun heat rises sensibly during August. The native grasses, shrubs and trees, and many spring herbs, show evidences of warmer weather. As do stone fruits in the earlier sections of the country. Wheat, oats, barley, and other cold season field crops, make active growth. Rain usually comes in light showers. Heavy dews have a stimulating effect upon vegetation. Dry weather is indicated by westerly winds, and shelter from them is a decided advantage.

Planting.—Where early ploughing has been followed, we can, with but a light fall of rain, get in corn, sorghum, millet, chicory, artichokes, and summer crops generally. For all these crops well prepared manure is advantageous. It is at this stage where real skill comes into Australian farming. (Read up the chapters on " Cultivation, Manuring, and Irrigation" carefully.) Add mineral fertilisers, such as sulphate of ammonia, potash, and phosphates, to the manure heap, where one or more are necessary for the crop in hand, composting them with coarser stuff in accordance with the wants of the crop.

Maize.—May be planted from August onwards. Where a start has been got, and the crop is showing up, the safe prospect for bringing maize on to maturity is in keeping the surface soil loose. This prevents rapid evaporation of the moisture in the soil, of which growing corn takes the full benefit, and the land is in the best condition for absorbing any showers that may fall.

Wheat.—Usually sown during May, earlier or later, according to location. The crop is well grown by August. The risky time for rust comes towards the end of October and November. Harvesting appliances may be got in order, so that should the enemy appear during muggy warm weather, the rusted pieces can be cut out at once. Stuff thus cut may be useful for hay. If rusted patches are allowed to stand the disease spreads quickly, and may ruin the whole crop.

Selecting Wheat for Seed.—As wheat approaches ripeness, real good work can be done by selecting wheat ears that ripen early and clean. Dry seasons may develop very superior varieties of wheat. It is by such means that the very finest sorts have been got.

Potatoes, Swedes and Mangolds.—Usually planted earlier in the season, but with rain in the late districts these root crops may be got in still. In the warmer districts they should be so well forward that hilling up and thinning comes into the seasonable work.

Beets.—For either sugar or feed, beet seed may be sown now. From ten to fifteen pounds of seed per acre.

Onions.—Thinning is especially necessary during dry spells. For this crop, the soil must be kept clean and open, and the plants so thinned out that heavy, solid bulbs are got. Where sowing has still to be done, the seed should be drilled into the rows so that transplanting will be unnecessary.

Pumpkins and Melons.—Every available spare piece of land may be got to yield these crops during summer; plant now. They keep weeds in check, and mellow down new rough land for future cropping.

Buckwheat.—Where wheat, oats, barley, or other cold weather crops have missed, this is an excellent catch crop, and is well worth being tried on land that is not required for other purposes.

Rye.—This is a rapid-growing crop, and does well during spring weather. When vetches are put in with rye the combination makes excellent feed for cutting green or for ensilage.

Grass Land.—When dry spells occur during spring, there is opportunity for freeing the land from sorrel, docks, thistles, and other weeds. They all suffer with the spring grasses. The latter grow quickest when rain falls on soil that is warm, and weeds can be still further checked by pulling them out as they appear. Top-dressing with manure, and harrowing the dry soil, helps the grasses to get ahead of their weed enemies, amongst which "tussock grass" is becoming very serious.

VEGETABLE GARDEN.

Crops Available.—The variety for spring cropping is enormous, and a good deal can be done to help them on during dry spells with but a little water. Beans, both dwarf and climbers, tomatoes, peas, cucumbers, marrows, and melons being in the list of crops for sowing and planting at this time. Cabbage, lettuce, and salads, also beets, for home use can be kept going all through the season.

The Cabbage Tribe.—Good sorts for planting for spring and summer growth are Colonial King and St. John's Day. They stand hot weather better than the earlier kinds.

Mulching.—As warm weather advances, and especially during dry times we find the benefit of having plenty of short stuff for mulching. With its aid seedlings can be kept going, and great growth can be got with very little water.

Beans.—Dwarf beans are always in favour. Canadian Wonder and Negro Eye still hold leading place, and many other sorts also deserve attention. They all require fairly rich soil, and planting in rows from two feet to thirty inches apart. The seed is dropped into the furrows about three inches apart, and thinned out to about six.

Climber Beans.—The Lima and others are held in high esteem for quality. They do best on poles about six feet high, or on such trellis as are illustrated in the chapter on "Home Gardening." The rows may be four feet apart, and the plants from eighteen inches to three feet apart.

Depth for Planting Beans.—Not deeper than two inches. There are disappointments every season from planting too deep.

White Corn.—This delicious vegetable, which might be an item in every garden, may be planted now. It is an agreeable, healthy product, and as suitable for small as larger places. Plant in rows from three and a-half to four feet apart. The plants to stand about one foot apart.

Water Cress.—Set out sods of roots, or single plants. Running water is an advantage, but not absolutely necessary. An occasional soaking, just to keep the soil moist, is sufficient.

Salads being in great demand as hot weather advances, frequent sowings of lettuce, cress, &c., may be made. The best summer sorts of lettuce are those of the drumhead class, which comprises many good varieties. The chief properties of good lettuce are crispness and sweetness. To develop these qualities, rapid growth and very rich soil are necessary. For lettuce, indeed, as for celery, the soil cannot be too rich.

Celery—Plant out, and earth up earlier lots to secure tender, crisp stems.

Radish and Parsnips.—They may be sown together, and fair crops of radish may be got by thinning before the parsnips require the land.

Asparagus.—Where water can be given, cutting may go on till Christmas; although, November very generally sees the end of this delicious vegetable.

Tomatoes, Cucumbers, Melons.—They may be planted. Creeping and climbing plants all require watering. Where plants are not making strong growth, fewer shoots should be allowed and fewer fruits produced. Water melons should not have as many shoots as rock melons. A water-melon plant with eight shoots, each carrying one fruit in the first instance, is about a useful arrangement. Where cucumbers can be trained upon banks of loose stuff they fruit their very best.

FRUIT GARDEN

Summer Pruning.—Careful thinning of fruit trees is labour well bestowed. We can get quite as much weight of crop in smaller numbers of larger size, and much finer quality than when trees are crowded with small, woody specimens. We can also save the trees from a heavy strain of seed bearing, and much heavy pruning in winter by thinning out badly-placed and over-bearing shoots at this time.

Grafting.—In the late districts, orange grafting is in season. Both buds and grafts that have taken require attention, by loosening the bandages and making grafts secure against heavy winds.

How Much Fruit on a Tree?—There is an ordinary calculation by fruit-growers who aim at making produce of the highest quality. It is to thin out until about six inches of space is allowed to each fruit on the tree. This rule applies with good effect to apples, apricots, peaches and oranges. Of course, observation, experience, and practice are all required to be able to work out the system effectively.

Spraying.—Aphis may become bad as warm weather is felt on the early peaches and plums. They must be checked at once, or there will be serious trouble. Soda, resin, petroleum, kerosene, soft soap, and other sprays, are effective preventatives against the increase of these destructive pests.

Grape Vines.—They are shooting out new growth freely now. Thin out all undergrowth and such shoots as may not be required, tying up the growing limbs snugly. Use the sprayers with soluble sulphur compounds freely to keep fungus in check.

Grubs and Caterpillars.—Moths—codlin moth amongst them—and butterflies may be around, and the eggs they lay hatch out into the grubs and caterpillars which eat off leaves and plants as the warm weather advances. Bordeaux mixture, with a little Paris green in it, settles them.

Strawberries.—They should be fruiting freely, but require stimulating by liquid manure and cultivation to keep up the growth with effect. Roots intended to produce plants for setting out should not be allowed to fruit. To check leaf blight, spray with Bordeaux mixture.

Gooseberries, Raspberries, &c.—Keep the young growth well off the ground by pinching off badly-placed shoots, and so secure fine fruit and prevent mildew. During dry weather, weak liquid manure helps the crops on very much.

Stocks for Fruit Trees.—Sow now the seeds of peach, almond, plum, orange, lemon, loquat, and other fruit trees saved when the fruit was ripe. It is from seedlings got in this way that the best stocks for budding and grafting are got.

SHRUBS AND FLOWERS.

Native Plants.—They are amongst the attractive things in the garden during springtime, especially the heaths. They resist the dry weather so well. And on their merits of beauty many native plants deserve attention and a place in both outdoor and indoor gardening.

Sowing.—The seeds that can be put in to secure plants and flowers for the warm weather season include amaranthus, candytuft, dianthus, gaillardia, larkspurs, lobelia, pansy, petunia, stocks, and hosts of others.

Annuals.—Planting out may be carried on as actively as may be necessary to fill in all the space available. The selection of seeds for annuals is enormous.

The Daffodil Family.—Jonquils, polyanthus, in addition to the always favourite daffodils, should be plentiful, where the directions given for planting and for the cultivation of bulbs have been followed.

Other Bulbs.—We can now get in the first of the double-flowering dahlias, making the soil rich and loose for their rooting in full strength.

Roses.—They require extra care at this time, now that the growth of the season is fairly commenced. Look out for aphis. Pinch out all badly-placed buds; keep mildew in check, and encourage firm, healthy growth, which is the really natural state of the Teas, Hybrids, and Noisettes in this country. Neglect is fatal to the whole rose family.

Climbers.—They require close attention where the buds are breaking into flower and leaf. Tie them up snugly and to such supports as will prevent their being knocked about by heavy winds.

Hollyhocks and Carnations.—Both of these families are the better of applications of bone manure where it can be applied without making the surface unsightly, or liquid manure in other situations.

Thinning—Summer Pruning.—There should be heavy growths of buds now, and thinning out is highly beneficial to prevent overcrowding, and to give us vigorous, healthy, fine flowers.

Violets and Pansies.—They are just coming to perfection. The flowering is helped by the process recommended for hollyhocks, &c.

Grass.—Now is the time to make a firm foundation for grass, whether edgings, plots, or the larger pieces for lawns or playgrounds. See that every weed is got out, mow closely, and add to the surface a light or a heavier coating as may be required of rich soil. Roll firmly where the soil is dry, and the results include firm soles of rich grass that delight the eye all through the summer.

BUSH-HOUSE AND CONSERVATORY.

More Bush-house Shelter.—Look up the chapter on flower gardening. The bush house is in reality the very backbone of flower successes during spring as well as summer weather.

Ferns.—They hold out better than most things during dry spells. Cut off all decayed fronds to give strength to others. Most ferns do best with shade, but there are exceptions. Cheilanthes, Woodsias, Pellæas, Northoclænas, &c., are better without it, and thrive in the full light and with abundance of air. Gold and silver ferns, too, in a modified degree, do admirably under very similar treatment. The Filmy ferns, Todeas, Trichomanes, &c., which in nature are found growing under dense shade or overhanging rocks, and in many cases under a constant drip of water, must have special shelter.

Fuchsias.—They start off into summer growth, but suffer badly without water. Liquid manure helps to keep up the vitality, as it does all soft-wooded plants breaking into flower and leaf.

Propagating.—By division of the roots, and by cuttings, many soft-wooded plants just starting into growth can be increased at this time. For making cuttings root freely, sandy soil is best.

The Newly Potted.—If at all possible, let the roots have the moisture they require direct, by setting the pots in water. Water that has come through pipes, carrying, as most of it does, iron in a bad form, should be avoided. Rain water is best, and, where possible, a tank should be reserved for sprinkling.

Renewing.—Pots that have to be used again, and woodwork that shows signs of decay, will be all the better of renewing now to prevent spread of fungus growths, which are always active at this time.

SEMI-TROPICAL CULTIVATION.

In the Paddock and Field.—The true spring of Australia is felt with full force in the warmer sections of country. Grass begins to make active growth. Sugar-cane can be planted; also maize, sorghum, sweet potatoes, yams, arrowroot, tobacco, and crops for feed. Look up the chapter on Semi-Tropical Cultivation.

In the Garden.—Bananas, pineapples, mangoes, and tropical fruits generally of the evergreen type, can be set out.

Shrubs and Flowers.—Our dependence during the next six months will be for floral beauties upon the thousand and one shrubs that can be grown in the open air. Annuals are not so satisfactory for summer flowering.

The bush-house is our mainstay for ferns, fuchsias, gloxinias, primulas, mimulas, azaleas, rhododendrons, and other beauties, which require artificial warmth in the colder south. Water and shade, with shelter from winds, are our requirements to have a steady blaze of flowers and foliage all through the summer season.

SUMMER FIELD AND GARDEN OPERATIONS.
November, December, January.

Summer Weather.—We can be certain of having heat enough during this and the two months following. Rain is more uncertain. Heavy thunderstorms have been common in November in former years; so have dry spells.

Summer Farming.—Our most certain course of action now, seeing that we are fairly in for summer heat, is to get all the work we can done by the cultivators; to have the surface loose and open, so as to keep the crops growing by taking in all the rain that falls, and so resist the effects of dry spells.

Feed for Winter.—Now is the time to get in winter feed for making ensilage or hay. In no part of the world are more suitable or heavier yielding crops available. (See chapter xvii.—Dairying.)

Wheat.—Harvesting commences in the early districts northwards in November, and reapers and binders require to be got into thorough working order for the crop.

Select Seed Wheat—Harvest is the time to do it. By marking off the pieces that are most thrifty and suitable for the district. Such wheat, when allowed to ripen thoroughly, and then threshed out by hand, gives the best promise we know of for seed wheat.

Maize.—Go on planting, giving the crop all the manure that can be spared. Maize will take any quantity of it, and any sort available, though manures rich in ammonia and phosphates are the best. Manure means big cobs and plenty of them.

Harvesting for Hay.—Oats, barley, rye, and vetches are all ripening for the harvest, whether for hay or ensilage.

Catch Crops.—Cape barley is very quick, so is buckwheat, and either or both of them may be sown at this time where there is land available that is not wanted for other crops

Potatoes.—Care is required now. Where they have been hilled up, and all weeds killed, very little need be done until they are fit for digging, but when ripe, dig at once, or they may start growing again. Stirring of the soil is as likely to injure as benefit potatoes in growth during the warm season. In the warmer sections potatoes are planted in January and February.

Tobacco.—This crop requires constant attention from seeding to harvesting. It should now be showing for the full crop of leaf, and in addition to such cultivation as keeps the land clean and open, flowering buds have to be pinched off, and the leaf thinned until eight, ten, or twelve leaves are left upon a stem, according to its strength. This treatment tends to mature and ripen the crop for harvesting.

Chicory.—Seed may be sown for chicory as a fodder crop and for ensilage. February sowing answers better for the roots used with coffee.

Oil and Fibre Crops.—Linseed, hemp, castor oil, and oil and fibre seeds generally may be sown.

Harvesting Seeds.—Lucerne and clover seed may be left as long as possible—that is, until they commence to shell out naturally — before reaping. The more matured the seed the better it is.

VEGETABLE GARDENING.

For Christmas.—It is looking forward certainly, but it is worth while sowing what lettuce, mustard, and cress, and such other salad comforts as may be all the more welcome at Christmas. Sow now in rows, and thus avoid transplanting.

Beans.—They are the basis of our summer supplies. Dwarfs and climbing beans do well all over the country, and may be planted to any extent required for home use or marketing.

Saving Seed.—The better course is to allow all the fruit on a few rows of peas and beans to go to seed. When some are picked and others allowed to ripen on the same plant the seed is weak, and fails to give satisfactory results.

Asparagus and Rhubarb.—Both should be coming on to ripeness for summer supplies. They require about the same treatment—nice, clean, open cultivation, with liquid manure, where vigour is necessary to keep a strong growth going.

Onions.—The early plantings should be coming on nicely, nd are all the better of the treatment recommended for asparagus. Later sorts may still be sown, but in the rows where they are to grow when thinned out.

Cucumbers and Melons.—For fruiting, let the vines, if at all possible, raise themselves off the ground. They fruit better when there is plenty of air about them, and are more free from attacks of grubs.

Tomatoes.—They also are all the better of being raised off the ground, and both are the better of liquid manure, which shows immediate effects when applied to the soil direct during dry weather.

For Winter Crops.—We have to commence now for winter cropping. Lettuce for summer and autumn may be sown at any time, and, provided the seed is good, always yield to some extent. Sow the seed now in the rows, so that there need be no transplanting. Towards the end of November, and during December and January, seed-beds of cabbage and cauliflower may be started to supply early plants.

FRUIT GARDEN.

To Bring On Heavy Crops.—Active work is necessary, whether the season be dropping and vigorous for growth, or dry and backward. During the former, surface culture keeps rampant growth in check; in backward weather it stimulates the crops.

Thinning.—Unless this is attended to, poor fruits are sure to follow. Peaches, apricots, plums, and grapes all suffer from this cause. In a few hours spent now in careful thinning, rubbing or breaking out buds and shoots, more effective work can be done than during hours spent in winter pruning.

Spraying.—A necessary part of orchard work here as elsewhere. Fungus growths and insects multiply immensely unless checked. With the use of sprays good service is done at the right time.

Cultivation.—Keep the surface soil loose. That is the key to success during the summer season. It may be done by coating the surface soil with a few inches of bush scrapings, leaves, &c., where such effective helps to orcharding can be obtained.

Citrus Fruits.—Lemon or orange trees suffer badly when dead or decaying wood is allowed to increase on the branches. The presence of even a few dried-up shoots is indication that there is more on the tree than it can support. Use the pruners freely, and clear out all such drawbacks to orange and lemon culture. Mulching and the use of bush scrapings, as recommended in the preceding paragraph, is more suitable than surface cultivation for this family.

Stocks for Citrus Fruits.—As the season of growth proceeds, observation is helpful in guidance as to whether seedling oranges, or lemon or orange stocks, are best for budding or grafting. The belief that the lemon is the stock for lemons and the orange for orange is coming more generally into favour.

Olives.—The time is suitable for planting cuttings or truncheons of suitable sorts to make trees. From the older plants, and, indeed, from all orchard trees, all suckers, and bad and rampant-growing shoots, should be removed as soon as they appear.

Trees Fruiting.—Figs, guavas, loquats, mulberries, cherries, plums, peaches, and others now developing fruit, are aided during dry spells by even moderate soakings of water. See chapter on "Irrigation" for methods of application.

Budding.—As the buds for next season's growth mature, after the fruit is off, budding commences. (See page 265.)

Strawberries.—Where strong plants were set out on richly-manured land, and the enemy of the strawberry (the leaf fungus) has been kept in check, this fruit should be showing up well. Strawberries are helped in fruiting by mulching and watering.

Tomatoes.—Give liquid manure, and keep the vines well off the ground on trellis or other supports, in order to get heavy, clean crops.

Grape Vines.—They should be in full growth now. Use sulphur freely; thin out badly-placed shoots, and tie up the stragglers.

FLOWERS AND SHRUBS.

Roses—The "queen of flowers" has the lead at this time, and when carefully attended to the response is very handsome. Seldom have there been finer flowers than during October, but as soon as they have passed their prime, pinch them off, in order to give the swelling buds the sap they require. All approach towards seed-forming is fatal to flowering. The very early roses may be budded.

Propagating.—Roses that were shy of making roots from cuttings earlier in the season may be induced to root now. Shade and shelter from winds help rooting. Petunias respond to the same treatment. Herbaceous plants generally may also be induced to root from cuttings at this time.

Layering.—Choice **roses** and flowering shrubs may be layered, and a little mulch, and **an** occasional watering will prompt them to make roots the sooner.

Bulbs.—Set out gladioli, dahlias, tube-roses, and trigardias for successional blooming. The earlier dahlias and gladioli require staking, and liquid manure is helpful where the growth is not vigorous enough.

Ferns.—Cut out all the rusty fronds; give shade, part of the day at least, and water freely where there is vigorous growth.

Annuals.—They are getting **out of season**, although developed seedlings may be set out. Balsams, zinnias, portulacas, amaranths, and sunflowers are safe and hardy enough. To raise others, they must be sown in pots either in the bush-house or in some shady, sheltered corner.

Edgings of **alternanthera** may be planted in moist weather. Hedges may be clipped and kept trim as required.

BUSH-HOUSE.

How Helpful It Is!—When dry spells occur at this season, the bush house is an effective help and a safe attraction in the garden. With shade and protection from winds, and just a little water, so much can be done.

Shade.—But we must avoid overdoing the shade, and particularly avoid any living shade over the growing plants. It is death to all flowering and ornamental favourites except ferns.

Things Coming On.—Cinerarias, fuchsias, primulas, gloxinias, achimenes, and tydeas may require regular looking to, or they will be quickly overrun and destroyed by vermin.

Water Treatment.—As orchids cease blooming, they need less water. All flowering plants may be the better of weak liquid manure applied to them at intervals of three or four days. Choice ferns may still be transplanted and put into suitable places, always seeing that the soil is light, open, and well drained where they are to grow. Stag horn, bird's nest, and elk horn ferns should be freely supplied with water to keep them luxuriant.

Coleuses should be amongst the attractions, and need attention to keep the bush-house gay. They can be either raised from seed or propagated from cuttings **all** through the season. Well trained balsams in pots, pelargoniums, &c., will help to make this retreat attractive; also good cockscombs.

Propagating from Leaf.—Foliage begonias strike readily from leaves during this time. Lay them flat on a damp, loose surface, just pressing them into the soil; then shade, and the leaves may send down roots in a few days. It is late enough to pot ferns, but if this has not already been done do it at once.

Enemies.—Fumigation with sulphur or tobacco smoke is effective if they can be shut in with it closely under a frame; but not without. Some spray or wash is the next best treatment.

IN THE WARM SECTIONS.

Field Work.—Cane harvesting and sugar making are in full blast now, and while the work is on they act wisely who each season root out all diseased or feeble **stools of cane, and plant strong, vigorous sets of reliable sorts, using** body cane where possible.

Maize—Sow to any extent. Arrowroot.—Plant medium-sized bulbs. Potatoes.—Dig as soon as ripe. Should they show for a second growth, the crop will be spoiled. Sweet Potatoes and Yams.—They are starting into growth now, and tilling and clean cultivation help to make crops. Cotton.—Thin out the plants to prevent overcrowding. Misses may be made up by planting seed in well-manured hills. Tobacco.—Prepare for harvesting. Pinch out all flower stems, and take off all leaves that are defective. Close, well-roofed barns are necessary for curing. Peanut and Oil Seed Crops.—Plant out as may be desired, and keep the earlier plantings clean and the crops growing.

Garden Operations.—The work in this department, for both fruits and vegetables, is much the same as in the south. The exceptions are such as coffee, tea, bananas, pine-apples, rosellas, and a few other purely semi-tropical products, which can be transplanted at this time. In the flower garden, annuals do not answer so well, but substitutes are got to any extent desired in the great choice of shrubs available for flowers and foliage.

AUTUMN FIELD AND GARDEN OPERATIONS.
February, March, April.

Autumn Weather.—The change from summer heat to the cooler autumn time is gradual as a rule. In the colder districts, the night temperature is noticeable first, and is usually felt early in February; but in the warmer districts of the coastal country, February is, at times, the hottest month of the year, and semi-tropical crops, sugar cane, corn, sorghum, sweet potatoes, ginger, &c., make enormous growth at such times, as do the summer grasses and indigenous pastures generally.

Rainfall.—Heavy and general rains are common in February. March and April are drier as a rule, though heavy floods have occurred during these months.

Maize.—This is still the leading crop, and it is helped on to maturity by surface cultivation, which is advantageous in building up big cobs, as long as there is any growth in the crop. Harvesting of maize becomes general as cold weather is experienced.

Maize for Winter Feed and Green Manuring.—In the warmer sections, excellent results are got by sowing maize broadcast at this time, either for feed purposes or for green manuring.

Winter Feed Generally.—Oats, barley, rye, vetches, rape, and other seed crops may be sown in order to come in for use as the indigenous pastures dry off for the season.

Wheat.—Sowing commences in March and goes on in the different districts till May. Early ploughing is an advantage for making a wheat crop. When the land is made ready, as described in page 76, the seed can be sown in dry soil should the season be dry, and an excellent spring may be got by rolling the land firmly.

Root Crops.—The stubble of land that was under wheat last season makes an excellent foundation for potatoes, which may be planted now; also swedes, and field carrots. See chapter viii.

Cultivated Grasses.—This is a good time for growing pasture grasses, which may either be put in with or without a grain crop. Rye grasses hold a leading place in cultivated pastures, but cocksfoot, the clovers, prairie, and other strong growers all deserve a place. Fair results are got at times by chipping the surface soil only, and sowing as the chipping goes on, but the true cultivation is the preferable **process to** get strong growth of **pasture.**

VEGETABLE SUPPLIES FOR WINTER AED SPRING.

The Home Garden.—This may be made a profitable and attractive feature of the homestead in all the departments of agriculture, and in all parts of the country (see pages 244 to 280). The choice is immense.

Some Good Things Available.—We are just entering upon the season to have vegetables in abundance. Where the summer series are backward, including melons, cucumbers, tomatoes, &c., they should be pushed on to maturity as rapidly as possible. We cannot make them grow much after February, so that manuring, either liquid or solid, is not helpful in that direction. But, by using the hoe as freely as circumstances may allow, we can help them along towards ripeness. When the weather is dry, and all the better for our purpose, we stir the surface soil somewhat deeper, to check the surface root action, and so force on as perfect maturity as we are likely to get after this month. Celery claims attention. Advantage should be taken of the first dry days to earth it up; the soil should not be so moist as to adhere together when earthing, but should be in nice friable condition. Sow peas in any quantity required. Turnip and radish may be sown at intervals, and parsnips sown with the radish, when required; monthly sowings may be made of spinach and carrots. Small sowings of onions may be made. A few growers also make a sowing about the middle of March for transplanting and growing into full-sized bulbs for early spring, when dry bulbs begin to get scarce and dear. Sow for parsley. Slips of marjoram, winter-savoury, tansy, tarragon, and thyme may be planted. Shallots, garlic, potatoe and tree-onions may be planted, and fresh sowings made of cabbage, cauliflower, and lettuce : while transplanting is being carried on until the full crops are in the ground.

Vegetables for Autumn Cropping —Artichoke, green globe; asparagus, giant Dutch, Connover's colossal; broad beans, broad Windsor, green Windsor, green gem, long pod; beet, blood-red, silver and spinach for the green tops, which are an excellent substitute for spinach; borecole, dwarf green; brocoli, early white, white mammoth—very hardy, grows to greater perfection in cold localities than the cauliflower; Brussels sprouts, hardy; cabbage (early), St. John's Day, early York, sugarloaf, ox heart; medium early, marble head, east Ham, London market, Enfield market, king, Winningstadt; late, large, drumhead, flat Dutch, Schweinfurt, red drumhead (for pickling), Savoy, large drumhead, green curled; carrot, shorthorn, intermediate; cauliflower, early London, large Asiatic, Stadtholder; celery, white solid, turnip-rooted, or celeriac; chervil, curled; shallots, garlic : kohl rabi or turnip-rooted cabbage; leek, London flag; lettuce, drumhead. Neapolitan—in cold districts, white cos; mustard, white; onion, brown Spanish, brown globe, silverskin; parsley, triple-curled; parsnip, hollow crown; peas, Yorkshire hero, Veitch's perfection, McLean's little gem—in cold districts, rising sun, Bedman's imperial, blue Peter, Laxton's supreme radish, long scarlet, red and white turnip, French breakfast, black Spanish; salsify; scorzonera; sea kale; spinach, prickly, New Zealand, crach; turnip, white stone, white nepaul, snowball, red American stone, orange jelly, Laing's garden Swede; potatoes, Brownell's, early rose, white rough, snowflake, &c., are desirable sorts; rhubarb, Myatt's Victoria. Also, herbs, sage, thyme. Tomato plants are to be found in most gardens at this time, and, where good sorts only are grown, these self-sown plants can be set out, but will require shelter during the cold weather.

THE FRUIT GARDEN.

Seasonable work.—Budding is still in order. [See page 265]. The stone fruits operated on may have the bandages loosened and regulated, to prevent them cutting into the wood. Go on budding the yellow mundy and other late sorts; as the fruit ripens and the buds swell, they are ready for operating. Grape harvesting for wine is in season.

Fungus and Insect Enemies.—They include codlin grub, "blight," and other pests. [See Chap. XXIV.] The time is on for making war against them, and it should not be neglected. Use lime sulphur clay paint freely upon the trees after the leaves fall, and so clear out hosts of enemies.

Transplanting.—Towards the end of February, in the cooler districts, transplanting of the orange tribe, loquats, guavas, cherimoyers, &c., may be carried on, so as to allow the trees to settle and make some new roots ere the cold weather sets in.

Draining.—This work can be carried out during cooler weather, and wherever trees have been suffering, or have shown signs of root weakness or disease, it is worth while examining into the state of the drainage.

FLOWERS AND SHRUBS.

Beauties in Season.—Where the attention necessary to ensure success has been given them, dahlias, amaranthus, cockscombs, &c., should offer sights worth all the labour given previously. The dahlias still require attention; pinch or cut back, where necessary, and give liquid fertilizer liberally; the response will prove how good is the treatment. Thin out the weakly growths, and keep the shoots securely tied to stakes.

Enemies.—Set 3-inch pots, with a little soft hay, in an inverted position on the stakes, as traps for snails and ear-wigs; they are troublesome at this season, and do great damage to flowers. The same treatment applies to autumn-flowering chrysanthemums; caterpillars are the troublesome pests to contend against with this class of plants. The surest remedy is handpicking. As the stems of gladioli die down, lift and store the bulbs in a cool place; see that they are properly named.

The Bulb Season.—For the approaching bulb season, prepare beds with well-rotted manure and leaf mould, and plant the following, not too deep: Anemones, Ranunculus, Narcissi, Scillas, and a few hyacinths for winter flowering; all these are more effective at the flowering season when planted in groups in separate beds. See that the sites are well drained, for if heavy rains should set in, and the soil becomes soddened with water, then bulbs and tubers rot off.

Propagating.—Finish putting in soft-wooded cuttings as the weather gets cooler; when rooted early, the plants are better able to stand through the winter without extra protection. Carnations, pelargoniums, zonale geraniums, penstemons, iresines, ageratums, verbenas, cineraria maritima, good varieties of snapdragons, lobelias, &c., are amongst the desirable things. Fine types of lobelia can usually be got by striking cuttings from seedlings; for they are very variable. Take up the layers of flowering shrubs propagated last spring and establish them in pots; they are transplanted to their permanent quarters more readily that way. Look over the shrubberies and any plants that are overcrowding their neighbours, mark for transplanting, which operation can be done as soon as the ground has had a thorough soaking. Early autumn is the best for setting out, as the plants get established before the succeeding summer.

Seasonable Seeds.—Sow seeds of pansies, candytuft, campanula, Virginian stocks, helichrysum, calendulas, silene, alyssum, nemophyla, German stocks, ageratum, Phlox drummondii, gillias, double flowering pyrethrums, dianthus, wallflowers, &c.

BUSH-HOUSE AND GREENHOUSE.

An Active Time.—Rampant growth is the rule in the bush-house during early autumn; a chief trouble is to keep plants from rooting into the soil; as a preventive, place under each a saucer or a piece of slate. Pot-grown pelargoniums should now be breaking finely; it will be necessary to shake them out, and after pruning back the roots, re-pot in good, fresh soil. Fuchsias may be in their second flowering, and have some liquid manure given them. In the frames, cinerarias, primulas, and calcolaria should be ready for first potting. Cuttings may be made and treated in the manner recommended for garden. Caladiums, very early started, may show signs of rust, which should be cut out at once. Preparations for ensuring a stock of coleus of the best descriptions by the cutting process should not be delayed.

In the greenhouse, orchids may be liable to scale insects at this time, which must be attended to, as they will cause disease and death if allowed to remain. (See Chap. XXIII.) Ferns and climbing plants should be carefully attended to, as mealy bug may be prevalent. Gloxinias may go to rest as they progress towards that period; but some may be coming into flower, and, therefore, should have stimulating treatment. On favourable opportunities, whitewash walls with quicklime, keep stages clean, and have the temperature so regulated, as far as practicable, according to the weather, a little warmer or cooler, that visits may be a pleasure.

SEMI-TROPICAL OPERATIONS.

Field Work.—Cane has to be kept clean, and trashed in the early districts, preparatory to crushing. Plant potatoes; early rose, Brownell's beauty, ruby, snowflake, and hundredfold are good sorts. Harvest corn as soon as it is fit, and house it in dry barns. Sweet potatoes require a final hoeing up. Some may be ready for lifting. (See Chap. IX.) Sow for lucerne, clover, prairie, rye, and cultivated grasses generally; the practice recommended for the cooler districts being suitable here also. This is a good time for setting out buffalo grass, which is propagated from clumps of the roots. Sow for wheat, the recommendations for the cooler districts being suitable. Sorghum may be sown, and maize and millet to cut green for feed. Sow for mangels. Tobacco should be ripening, and preparations are necessary for housing and curing the crop. Sow oats, barley, tares, vetches, &c.

Garden Work.—The sun heat is likely to be sufficiently powerful to make the setting out of cabbage, cauliflower, &c,, a ticklish operation, but it should be done at every opportunity, giving sufficient water to the young plants to start them strong; fresh sowing of seeds are necessary to keep up the supply of plants. Onions, beet, parsnips, and carrots are safe crops, and can be got in at once. Sow for turnips, lettuce, Brussels sprouts, savoys, &c., and make the land as rich as possible for setting out plants. Beans can be planted still; also peas. Earth up the celery, and prepare land for mustard, cress, and other salads, which may be grown in abundance all through the winter, if water can be spared for them.

Fruit Garden.—Attention has to be paid to the peach and other trees budded during January. Where the stocks are sluggish in sap flow, let the roots have some fertilizer with water to stimulate them. Where bananas and pines are backward, liquid manure is absolutely necessary to bring on the fruit before winter comes, with frost, perhaps.

Pruning—Planting.—It is considered good practice to prune peaches and stone fruits generally, as soon as the fruit is off, by cutting out freely such limbs and branches as are not necessary. The time will soon be on for transplanting, and the variety of fruits available for the warm districts is really endless. Trench and drain the land thoroughly, in order to be ready for them.

Fruits Available.—The peaches include flat China, which come amongst the first of the early sorts; then the large family of peaches, apricots, and nectarines, oranges, lemon, limes, citrons, guavas, of which there are now several very excellent sorts, the purple and yellow being suited especially for the northern districts, loquats, date plums, Brazil cherries, mangoes, &c. Plant out strawberries as soon as the shoots are rooted sufficiently for removal.

Flower Garden.—The bulb-planting season is now on. Sow for annuals. Prune roses. Carnations, pinks, geraniums, &c , can be set out. In other respects, the reminders for southern districts are suitable.

Flower Seeds Available.—Abronia, ageratum, sweet alyssum, antirrhinum (snapdragon), aquilegia (columbine), bartonia, double daisy, calliopsis, Canterbury bells, candytuft, carnation, chrysanthemums, clarkia, collinsia, cowslip, cornflower, dahlia, dianthus, digitalis (foxglove), exhscholtzia, forget-me-not, fuchsias, gaillardia, geranium, hollyhock, larkspur, lavender, lobelias, lupins, marigold, mignonette, nemophila, pansy, pelargonium, pentstemon, phlox, pinks, picotee, polyanthus, poppy, pyrethrum (golden feather), scabiosa, stocks, sweet William, verbena, sweet violet, wallflower, zinnia, &c., &c.

For Greenhouse and Bush-house Culture.—Auricula, begonia, calceolaria, cineraria, cyclamen, gloxinia, mimulus, primula. Sow in well-drained pots or boxes, and transplant during showery or cloudy weather.

WINTER FIELD AND GARDEN OPERATIONS.
May, June, July.

Usual Weather.—Warm days, cold nights, and stoppage in growth of all crops of the warm season are in order. When rains fall at this time, they are heavy as a rule, and precautions are necessary to ward off visitations of the flood kind. It is the season for cold weather crops.

Wheat.—May is a favorite month for sowing, and where early ploughing is attended to, the seed can be got in, even during dry weather. Many new sorts of wheat are being tested, and quite a good number give promise of being valuable; but wheat growers have to experiment carefully, and possibly, the better course for growers to follow for the main crop is to take the advice of the miller or agents who are buyers in their districts as to which would be the best sorts to sow—sorts already grown in the district. The steeping of seeds cannot be neglected without risk. Bluestone makes the most effective steep. Four gallons of water, containing half a pound of bluestone, into which the grain is put for five minutes or so, is about right.

Other Grain Crops.—Barley, for grain, malting, and green feed can be sown at any suitable time during these months. Rye can be sown, and if for feed, vetches, with the rye do well, and are excellent either for cutting green or for the silo.

Peas, Roots, &c.—Peas may be sown as a field crop, where there is no risk of frost; in colder districts, it will be as well to wait until the end of the season. Bone dust or superphosphate is the manure for peas and beans, and a capital machine is being introduced for sowing the seed and manure in one operation. Sow onions for a field crop, or plant out where sets are available, they do capitally on rich, well-farmed ground. Swede turnips, field carrots, beets, and cabbage can be got in. Potatoes planted in February-March should be coming on promisingly. They do not require much hilling up at this time of year, but the rows have to be gone over in order to destroy weeds, and secure a loose bed for the crop. The summer-grown potatoes should be dug as soon as the tops wither. Harvest mangolds, pumpkins and swedes as they ripen. It is the better course to market them as soon as they are fit; or where required for winter feed, to pit them, as soon as possible, covering the pits sufficiently to throw off rain.

Grass for Pasture.—Look up the notes for the autumn season as to the sowing of grass seeds. The work can be carried on during May, except in the colder districts, where frost may injure the young growth. In such places, better wait till August.

VEGETABLE SUPPLIES.

The Work in Season.—To keep the cabbage, cauliflower, and lettuce tribes going is a first requirement. Sow more seed; when for home use only, those which turn into hearts quickest are safest. Carrots: Sow and thin out those already making roots. The narrow-bed system is most easily managed to keep the crops growing and free from weeds. This includes carrots, parsnips, salsify, and similar root crops. Onions: Continue to sow in good, rich land, and if the soil be sandy make it as firm as possible, both before and after the seed is sown. The modern giant varieties are worth giving a trial, and, providing they have good soil and are well thinned out, the results are usually satisfactory. Turnips may be sown at any time; thin out if the crops are too thick; the tops of young turnips may be utilised for cooking purposes. The narrow-bed system will be found advantageous for this crop also, as the ground about the plants remains more open from the absence of feet-treading. Asparagus should be in growing condition, and therefore must be left alone until the stalks become yellow. Where our practice has been followed respecting planting tomatoes, well trellised and facing the sun, a supply of this wholesome fruit should be abundant. To save seed of tomatoes, select the best shaped fruit, and if any peculiar feature is seen in samples save them for seed. Peas may still be planted, and the ground well forked up amongst crops that are growing. Sow broad beans as required in moderately rich land. Beds of spinach of both the round and prickly-leaved can be got in every month to keep up a regular supply. Globe artichokes may be harvested, divided, and transplanted. Continue to earth up celery; with growing crops, liquid manure will be of great service. To raise herbs from seed, sow now; the seed germinates quickly, and gives good plants for putting out during the winter months. Take up old stocks of herbs, divide, and after well heading back, replant. Rhubarb can be transplanted; good, well-trenched land, low-lying if possible, is suitable. The ordinary tuber artichoke should be ready for digging; a good plan is to take up each day what is sufficient. Sow for radishes; the olive-shaped are perhaps the prettiest for the table, and equal to the best in flavour and crispness. Mustard and cress can be easily made a feature in the garden for salading purposes, and plots should be allowed for the very excellent land cress, perennial cress, and the New Zealand spinach, all of which are health-giving for salads, &c. Clear away dead leaves of all kinds of vegetables from growing crops, and manure as freely as circumstances allow.

WINTER IN THE FRUIT GARDEN.

Planting.—Where fruit culture is attempted on shallow, thin, or wet, badly-drained soil, the risks of disappointment are largely increased. But where the land is right, planting out of oranges and lemons may be carried on now, so as to get some root growth before really cold weather sets in. In arranging for apple trees for planting, see that they have been worked on blight proof stocks. As a guide for planting deciduous trees, the leaf-shedding may be considered a fair criterion that the tree is at rest, and therefore ready for the change. Plant cherimoyers, guavas, leeches, Chinese raisins, and one or more of Japanese plums in fair, rich land, in order to test them.

Pruning.—(See Chap XXI.) Where pears and apples are shy bearers, it is a good plan, at the pruning season, to shorten the root growth, and cut or pinch back the young, rampant shoots, to develop fruit buds. The apricot, at times, also seems a shy bearer, and root pruning and spring pinching are generally effective in bringing the tree into bearing form. Grape vine pruning is on; in all cases where fungus is observable on the vines, it is the safe plan to burn the prunings and leaves, which may be raked up for the purpose. As raspberries have now made their shoots for next season's fruiting, they may be pruned without delay, leaving to each stool a few stout canes, and then remove all others.

General Work.—Continue to transplant strawberries; keep runners away from those planted; well loosen up the ground. The eradication of weeds has to be attended to, as when allowed to grow they form shelter places for snails, slugs, and other pests.

FLOWERS AND SHRUBS.

Seasonable Operations.—Dahlias, where cut and manured in the autumn treatment, seldom fail to give vigorous growth. But the elegance of cosmos and chrysanthemums are pressing those beauties closely to occupy the place held so long by the dahlias. The chrysanthemum tribe, of late years, has been brought to great perfection by hybridisation. The colours are exquisite, as are the forms of flowers classed as incurved, anemone-flowered, Japanese and pompones. The lists of varieties offered by nurserymen are ample for those who love either form or colour, or blendings of both.

Things Worth Looking Up.—Amongst other beautiful things flowering at this time may be dahlia imperialis, which has a majestic appearance; its single pinkish hued flowers hanging in graceful clusters; it requires liberal treatment, and a good sheltered position. Dombeya Natalensis loaded with beautiful white flowers. Cuttings of this plant may be struck, any fairly good garden soil suits. The composite Veronia Arborea has clusters of pale lavender flowers, very striking. Cyclobothra fusca is a remarkable flowering bulbous plant from Mexico, flowering at this time; it requires a rich, sandy loam.

Propagating.—May is a busy month for transplanting shrubs and making fresh flower beds. Next month we may commence pruning, manuring and digging shrubberies and flower borders, and as the work is proceeding divide herbaceous plants, taking care to leave the youngest portions of the plants in the ground; also plant out spring flowering seedlings, of which there ought to be plenty. When planting pansies and violets, give them sufficient well-rotted manure, or disappointment in the shape of small flowers will ensue.

Sowing and Saving Seeds.—Sow for Virginian stocks, alyssum for rockeries or rough places, pansies, German stocks, and double French and German carnation-striped poppies in small pots, are very attractive. Poppies make a grand display in October and November. Save seeds of amaranthus, cockscomb, balsam, gaillardia, zinnia, and the French and African marigolds. Put decaying plants into the compost heap; the decaying vegetable matter makes excellent manure for pot plants.

Roses.—Put in cuttings (but do not prune the plants back yet); select well-ripened wood and cut with a sharp knife into lengths with seven eyes attached; cut out the four lower eyes, to prevent the plant from suckering. Insert this portion in the ground, the three eyes above ground to form the future branches. Take up and pot or plant in their permanent quarters any layers that have made roots of choice varieties of roses.

Bulbs.—As anemones, ranunculuses, and hyacinths get above ground, give them a good top dressing of well-rotted manure.

Grass.—Lawns that are poor induce a great many weeds to root upon the surface, now is a good time to get them out; in the spring a light top dressing of good, rich sifted soil can be applied to help on the grass vigorously.

BUSH AND GLASS HOUSES.

Seasonable.—The tubers of caladiums, gloxinias, tydœas, and achimanes, after the foliage has died down, should be carefully stowed away. An excellent way to preserve bulbs from decay in winter is to place them in powdered charcoal in a rather warm and dry position. Encourage the growth of primula and calceolaria; give them occasional waterings of weak saltpetre water or manure liquid. Put into single pots the fuchsias that have rooted, attend to watering and giving air where the glass house structure is not artificially heated, close early in the afternoon to save the sun heat. Artificial heat must be used with discretion, as it is a very undesirable plan to keep plants growing too fast in winter when they ought to be at rest, thereby lessening the chances of healthy growth and flowers during th ensuing season.

Bush House.—Epiphyllums showing flowers should be transferred to the glass house, also the earliest batch of cinerarias, which may now be showing their flowers. Pelargoniums have to be kept well nipped back, and as soon as possible attended to in the way of repotting. This treatment is suitable also for fuchsia cultivation; both must be kept as hardy as possible. Cyclamens may require liquid manure, and caladiums and tuber-rooted begonias put into their resting place for the winter. With clerodendrons and other favourite plants, they have to go through a partial season of rest. In warm seasons, ferns may require shading and water while growing, and as mealy bug may be prevalent, a syringing with insecticide will be very beneficial. The same treatment applies to exotic palms, marantas, dracænas, and crotons, which must be kept free from all kinds of insects. Gloxinias showing signs of new growth may be brought forward and pushed on into activity. Where camellias are grown in the bushhouse, it is well to give them manure water. Seedlings of mimulas and other fancy plants should be potted off as soon as they are strong enough. Plenty of air must be given to both description of houses in fine weather, so as to secure satisfactory growth.

And Through all the Seasons.—Good soil, manure, care, attention, and cultivation are necessary in all departments, to ensure success.

WORKS ON AUSTRALIAN AGRICULTURE,

BY

ANGUS MACKAY.

PUBLISHER'S NOTICE.—The Agricultural Works of Mr. Mackay are in more general use in Eastern Australia than all others combined.

INTRODUCTION TO AUSTRALIAN AGRICULTURE.—Class-book of the Education Department of N.S. Wales. Science combined with Australian practice. 1s.

ELEMENTS OF AUSTRALIAN AGRICULTURE.—Steps leading to further acquaintance with the theory and practice of agriculture. Contains a thoroughly practical treatise upon Bee-keeping in Australia. 3s. 6d.

HELPFUL CHEMISTRY FOR AGRICULTURISTS.—Gives working details for testing and analysing soils; making and using manures; testing milk, water, flour, tobacco, &c., &c. Arranged for the use of agriculturists who desire to test for themselves. "A work of most satisfying character for progressive agriculturists."—*Examiner*. 4s.; by Post, 4s. 2d.

THE AUSTRALIAN AGRICULTURIST.—"One of the most useful and practical works ever issued."—*Leader*. The contents include Australian farming and gardening in all branches, cattle, sheep, horse, pig, and poultry keeping; dairying, ensilage-making, seed-farming, &c., &c. Special chapters on the "Indigenous Grasses and Fodder Plants," and for "Medical Help in cases of Emergency," how to treat wounds, snake-bite, drowning cases, &c., &c. A calendar of field and garden work for the whole year completes a most useful work for suburban and country residents. Third edition. 10s. 6d.

THE SUGAR-CANE IN AUSTRALIA.—The standard work upon cane-growing and sugar-making. The contents include details for field-work of all kinds, the cultivation of sorghum, Planter's Friend, beets, &c., for sugar-making, &c. Second edition, 10s. 6d.

GRAZING, FARM, & GARDEN SOILS OF NEW SOUTH WALES.—"The most complete and exhaustive series of scientific investigations yet made into the soils of Australia."—*Northern Star*. The practical chemical analysis made of a large number of Australian soils explain what is necessary to secure crops and maintain the fertility. 1s. 6d.

THE HONEY-BEE IN AUSTRALIA.—Contains brief accounts of the native Australian Bee, the black or English Bee, Ligurian or Italian Bees; modern bee-keeping and honey-making, how to make and use bar-frame hives, &c. "Just the work for Bee-keepers."—*Capricornian*. 2s.

BATSON & CO., Ltd., 146 CLARENCE STREET, SYDNEY, N.S. WALES,
AND ALL BOOKSELLERS.

Good Land and Good Manure

MEAN

GOOD CROPS AND GOOD BANK BALANCES.

If your Land does not produce Good Payable Crops, bring up its value by MANURING, and use the very Best Fertilizer you can get, for

The BEST is THE CHEAPEST in the LONG RUN.

"GEE'S"

Complete = Fertilizers

... AND ...

Natural Manures.

These Manures, made by the Sydney Meat Preserving Company, are the most valuable, because they are made from the blood and bones of the animals which formed their bodies out of our rich pastures. **The Special Addition of SULPHATE OF POTASH makes these Manures complete.**

Send for a New and Original **Treatise on Manures** and their Economical use, with numerous valuable illustrations; also Price List. Free on Application to

THE SYDNEY MEAT PRESERVING CO., Rookwood,

OR TO

THORPE & CO., Macquarie Street, Parramatta,

BROKERS TO THE COMPANY.

☞ Feed Your Dogs on THORPE'S PATENT DOG BISCUITS. ALL LEADING STOREKEEPERS SELL THEM.